PERSONALITY IN YOUNG CHILDREN

PERSONALITY IN YOUNG CHILDREN

By Lois Barclay Murphy

B
―
B

NEW YORK, BASIC BOOKS, INC., PUBLISHERS

VOLUME I

METHODS FOR THE STUDY OF
PERSONALITY IN YOUNG CHILDREN

WITH THE COLLABORATION OF

EVELYN BEYER

ANNA HARTOCH

EUGENE LERNER

L. JOSEPH STONE

TRUDE SCHMIDL-WAEHNER

First printing, June, 1956

Second printing, June, 1957

COPYRIGHT, © 1956, BY BASIC BOOKS, INC.

ALL RIGHTS RESERVED

MANUFACTURED IN THE UNITED STATES OF AMERICA

DESIGNED BY SIDNEY SOLOMON

LIBRARY OF CONGRESS CATALOG CARD NUMBER: 56-10630

Foreword

THOSE PROFESSIONALLY CONCERNED with young children—early childhood educators, pediatricians, nurses, social workers, psychiatrists, and psychologists—are continually perplexed, often baffled by the inability or frequently the unwillingness of a child to tell what he thinks or believes and how he feels. Early in life children realize that it is not wise or safe to reveal what they think, how they feel, their wishes and daydreams, their sometimes disturbing fantasies. Moreover, with his limited experience and small command of language a child may be unable to put into words what has happened to him or what these events mean to him.

Recognizing these obstacles to communication and also the idiosyncratic experience of every child, students of personality development and child therapists have increasingly looked to a variety of procedures which will evoke naïve, spontaneous activities in which they may discover, with more or less clarity, these otherwise inaccessible relations of the child to the world and to himself.

The underlying assumption of these procedures is that while the child is learning to act in our public world he continues to live in his "private world"; he develops what Kurt Lewin called his "life space" which we may, from the outside, describe in terms of a selective awareness, a patterned perception, an idiomatic way of feeling toward and of dealing with objects and situations, an idiosyncratic way of relating himself to the world, especially to other persons and to himself. We may say that in this private world he develops an image of the self, largely in terms of how he has been treated by his family or other adults.

Approaching the child in this way it becomes clear that we cannot assume, as in customary psychological procedures, that the stimulus-situation will mean to the child what the experimenter wants or expects it to mean. Rather, we must assume that each child will invest the experimental situation—the toys, the materials, the persons—with the meaning, the significance and especially the affective coloring or distortion which they may have for him. Thus his naïve, spontaneous manipulation of materials and his responses to persons may help us to understand him as a unique personality—how he perceives the world, how he feels about it, and how he sees and feels about himself in that world.

These procedures, largely of a projective nature, offer many opportunities for gaining insight into the often perplexing activities and play of children, enabling teachers and other professional workers to establish communication with a child. Obviously this communication admits of many interpretations, the more subtle and penetrating of which demand long training and clinical experience. But children's play is never wholly occult to those who will patiently and carefully observe.

In these volumes a detailed statement is presented of a number of procedures and methods which have been developed by Dr. Lois Murphy and her associates over the years. These presentations give not only a statement of the materials and methods to be employed, but in addition a statement of the rationale for each method, plus citations of how individual children used or responded to them. These are supplemented by discussion of possible interpretations of the child's performance, and principles of interpretation—an admirable precaution against the too facile conclusions of these whose enthusiasms may outrun their clinical experience.

The second volume gives a detailed account of one child through three years in nursery school, presenting his performance with different materials and methods, plus many observations on that child's behavior and relations. Rarely do we find so full and multi-dimensional a presentation of a case nor one that gives so many illuminating insights into the way a child strives to live in his world, to master the acceptable methods of our cultural traditions, while continually relating himself to his parents and other children and adults.

These volumes may be commended to a wide audience of professional workers with children as a basic contribution to their several professional techniques. Since these records deal with normal children they will be valued not only by clinical workers but by teachers of child growth and development and child psychology.

LAWRENCE K. FRANK

Belmont,
Massachusetts

Preface

MENTAL HYGIENE LEADERS, educators, and other workers with children have become increasingly interested in how to keep children normal—how to liquidate early tensions and conflicts so as to prevent long-time repercussions, how to strengthen the child's sense of self so that he can bear the frustrations and anxieties that are an inevitable part of childhood in our complex urban life, if not in every setting.

Although we have long recognized the fact that the basic trends in character have been formed by the age of six or seven, we have tended to postpone our efforts to help children, the repair work, and even the work of understanding them, to a later age. Our generation, however, has been increasingly interested both in understanding the beginnings of personality and in learning ways of helping children at the point where troubles begin, and before their consequences have begun to distort the child's personality. We now know that many severe disturbances of childhood can be recognized very early and helped more effectively before the age of six or seven than later, when the experiences which contributed to these difficulties are so much more likely to be repressed.

In order to learn how to keep children normal we need to learn more about the deepest layers of experience in the normal child—the feelings that arise from the unplanned disappointments, longings, bewilderments, and confusions that can occur in even the most devoted family; and about the ways in which the child expresses, fights, or in some other way deals with these feelings.

If we are to understand children at these deepest levels we need methods which will take us directly to the feelings of the young child with as little artificiality or indirection as possible. But there are obstacles in communication between children and adults. Children under five may not be able to express their feelings in words; their language may be full of phrases expressing their wants and descriptions like "Garage man fixes broken bumper," which may reflect some concern about body damage, but such directly expressed remarks as "I was very angry at my mother for not giving me two ice creams" are not within the range of many preschool children. At best a grumbling "Stinky old mommie" attempts to convey the feeling.

Similarly, limitations of language prevent the rich indirect communication possible for older children through spontaneous storytelling or storytelling elicited by pictures, inkblots, etc. The Thematic Apperception Test has limited value for children below the age of seven or eight, and even the Children's Apperception Test is productive only with children whose language is mature enough to tell a story—for children of average intelligence, good material often does not come before the age of five.

Below the age of five the child's hand-eye coordination has not yet caught up to his perceptions sufficiently for him to express himself adequately in Figure-Drawing or other drawing tests, which emphasize content, although structural aspects of painting and drawing are very illuminating.

It is to this important problem—the formulation of applicable methods for the assessment of personality in the young child—that this volume is dedicated.

We have long recognized the fact that what the preschool child lacks in verbal and manual skills is more than compensated for by the richness of his spontaneous full-bodied play with structured and unstructured materials. His language is action, and what he does with a wide variety of materials can communicate even more richly and directly to us than he could communicate through words. The contributors to this volume have, therefore, experimented with a variety of play methods which do not rely exclusively on verbal expression, but which, in addition, utilize the motor, interpersonal, and other expressive responses of the child. Volume I—*Methods For The Study of Personality in Young Children*—describes the use of free or unstructured techniques both with concrete structured materials (Miniature Life Toys, Sensory Toys, Rorschach) and with the most plastic materials (dough, cold cream, and easel painting); and structured methods such as ego-blocking techniques, games with balloons, and leadership games. Volume II—*Colin: A Normal Child*—presents a detailed report of the application of these methods to an individual child. Records of behavior and emotional expression were implicit in the free methods and are also included in the records of experiments with structured techniques. As in all other situations, the behavior of young children could be counted on to be more spontaneous than that of older children and adults. In our application of these methods, we concentrated on understanding the individual child—both his ways of experiencing and his ways of dealing with his experience.

The volumes are based on records of normal children who attended the Sarah Lawrence Nursery School; they do not deal with problems of pathology or differential diagnosis. In cases of severe threat to development, such as is evident in anatomical and brain-damage factors in speech and coordination problems, or severe schizophrenic reactions in early childhood, differential diagnosis in the sense of clear discrimination among diagnostic syndromes may be necessary. For the vast majority of preschool children, however, including those with normal developmental problems, anxieties, phobias, behavior difficulties, etc., we need to know what is going on, what the child is reacting to, how he is trying to manage his situation, and what his own resources are for working through his difficulties—in other words, what kind of child he is, and how he experiences his life.

Even a sick child is first of all a child, changing and growing in whatever ways still remain open to him; this change and growth give us our best hope for helping him—as long as there is movement, as long as his ideas and feelings and behavior are not deeply frozen, there is a possibility of helping this movement to go in a better direction. Thus, methods of the sort presented here and the orientations which emerge from them can also be useful in understanding and in helping sick children— with the added provision that, in order to help, we need to be receptive to the precise, unique meaning of his thoughts, the nuances of his feelings, the balance of areas of conflict or anxiety and areas of freedom, and the developing ego, as well as the needs and drives which shape his personality.

Background for the Study

A word about the formation of the concepts upon which these volumes are based might be useful here. In the summer of 1934, I had several conversations with Dr. John Levy, a child psychiatrist, who had been doing some work on children's drawings and children's dreams, and with Lawrence K. Frank. I discussed with them some of the reactions of a group of three- and four-year-old children to a series of pictures, each of which showed a child in some dilemma or a situation which might be interpreted as such. I was interested in the fact that some children did not interpret the picture objectively at all, but *projected* anxieties of their own into the situation, and in fact that this method provided an avenue to the understanding of the children's inner feelings, which complemented the study of their overt behavior on which I had extensive data. Lawrence Frank then suggested, referring to the use of pictures, drawings, and dreams for the understanding of the child's inner life, that we could call these "projective methods."

When our research group at Sarah Lawrence started work, we discussed the possibilities in "projective methods," and their relation to other ways of studying children. Although today the term is often used loosely with no attempt to distinguish "projective" from expressive or reactive behavior, we believed that this designation should be reserved for methods which definitely produced projections of a child's preoccupations and his personal view of his world. Throughout our research, these methods were used qualitatively as a means toward more discriminating and thorough personality description and analysis,[1] and not as as way of obtaining data for the scoring of responses without regard to their context.

Three major lines of thought contributed to the early development of projective techniques—Rorschach's concepts of personality structure; psychoanalytic concepts of needs and drives, and the transfer of modes of experience from their first zones; and Gestalt concepts of the field, or life space, of the individual. The process of integrating these has been slow. For years the chief focus was on anxieties, conflicts, hostilities, and love needs, along with an emphasis on the child's image of himself. The hints offered by Rorschach regarding the importance of evaluating the way in which the individual experiences his world and the flexibility or rigidity with which he expresses his responses to stimuli from without and to his own ideas and impulses have been slow to receive extension or application in the development of other methods. The field situation with the supports and stress to which the child reacts is often underestimated.

This book on methods does not attempt to offer a synthesis of these lines of analysis. However, it does attempt to implicitly and explicitly point out several directions in which further thought is needed.

1. To stimulate, through the introduction of Sensory Toys,

---

1. Volume I is based on studies originally recorded in the monograph, *Methods for the Study of Personality in Young Children,* published in 1941. Since then, adaptations of the Miniature Life Toy approach have been made by others, notably Ruth Hartley, L. K. Frank, and their associates in *Understanding Children's Play* (New York: Columbia University Press, 1952), and by Witkin, Meissner, *et al.* in their *Personality Through Perception* (New York: Harper & Brothers, 1954). L. J. Stone's Balloon technique for studying aggression and destruction, along with Lerner's Ego-Blocking techniques, have been discussed in Stolz's *Father Relations of War-Born Children* (Stanford: Stanford University Press, 1954).

In the present volume my chapter on Miniature Life Toys has been reworked in line with additional experimentation and thinking on my part. L. J. Stone's chapters have also been revised in part. I have left Eugene Lerner's chapters virtually untouched, however, because they remain an outstanding contribution to the analysis and evaluation of social aspects of the ego in early childhood.

ways of studying the ease, range, intensity, and affect of children's responses in different modalities, which must provide the foundation for the dimensions and quality of experience; both resources for satisfaction and range of sensitivities are involved here.

2. To integrate (cf. Miniature Life Toys) the analysis of structure or form qualities, content of fantasy and expressive patterns in an over-all picture of the child's way of experiencing which would include an appraisal of his ability to conceptualize, express, and deal with his problems.

3. To evaluate not only the strength of impulses (as with aggression) but the way in which they are handled (cf. L. J. Stone's Aggression-Destruction techniques).

4. To evaluate ego-functioning in interpersonal situations (Eugene Lerner's Ego-Blocking techniques, Stone's Leadership games, etc.).

5. To show the "projective" aspects of nonprojective tests and situations (intelligence test, medical examination), as well as the formal and ego aspects of projective situations.[2]

A picture of a child's personality needs a delineation of the total picture of gratifications and needs, as well as areas of stress and conflict and ways of dealing with them. No one test, of course, is adequate. We need a battery of tests, aimed to elicit basic sensory, cognitive, emotional, and interpersonal areas of response, which will also give enough range to permit each child to be seen in both satisfying and frustrating situations.

The Children

As might be expected, the group of alert mothers who entrusted their children to the brand new nursery school at a new college, not yet ten years old at the time, were intelligent and, more than average, aware of child development needs, and their children were a superior group. Some of these mothers had professional connections either through teacher or social-work training or through close relatives who were child devel-

---

2. These are illustrated in Volume II.

opment minded. In other respects they shared the culture of the period, though with variations. Their children were born during the depression, and for the most part were born when their parents were considerably older than parents of young children today. Grandparents and other relatives played an active role in several of the families. Almost every family had a maid, generally full time. But it was usually the mother who brought the child to nursery school, and so the mothers came to be our friends.

These mothers had in common their deep concern with the welfare of their children. Compared to the American family on the sociologists' chart, they were more stable than average: divorces have been very rare in these families, and permanent residence in the Westchester area has been more frequent than is usual in these days of mobility.

As a group, the children we studied were children whose frustrations—whether of rigidly scheduled, programmed days, or overly strict feeding and toilet training—were amply balanced by many basic gratifications. They were cared-for children; even when their parents made "mistakes," as seen from our current awareness of the need for tolerance of children's trial-and-error ways of learning and growing, these parents were concerned, attentive, responsible, to the point of making personal sacrifices for the sake of their children. Many of them made a daily trip of twenty minutes to a half hour each way from home to nursery school to give their children the opportunities of nursery school experience.

At one point we attempted a study of the first 135 children in the nursery school, looking for correlations between early feeding experiences (only one-sixth of the children were nursed beyond the age of two months), toilet training experiences (many of the children were started very early), and later behavior in nursery school. We did not find any clear-cut relationships among groups, although there were isolated instances of outstanding connections between extremely rigid early handling and extreme inhibition later. What we did find was that in instances in which mothers expressed happiness and joy in having a baby, and reported that the baby was more fun than they had imagined possible, the preschool child was free and open in his emotional responses, able to express his problems in one way or another and to handle his tensions. This does not mean that basic mother-baby satisfaction prevented "problems" from arising, but it did mean that the normal developmental problems of the preschool years did not interfere with growth: the children were able to work things through with the help of their parents and teachers. We can infer that the deep satisfaction of being loved and cared for provided a basis of gratification against which the frustrations of life with busy mothers and commuting fathers did not weigh too heavily.

Since leaving nursery school the children we studied have grown up; those who are still known to us are just as normal as we believed them to be when we studied them, although some of them have met and worked through serious developmental hazards such as the death of a parent, physical trauma, divorce, or challenges to adjustment in moving from a familiar neighborhood or school to a new one; these sometimes involved intervention by parents who had to give special support to help the child through a trying period. But the good development of the children as a group means that we can now publish our material with the confidence that our work has passed a test of time and carries an additional validation offered by the present maturity of our subjects.

Observing the Children

The excerpts, examples, and summaries quoted in these Volumes were taken from actual play records. Marian Weber and Elinor Brown were expert stenographers and, in addition, excellent observers of children.[3] We found that the type of record they made, by which we could keep track of facial expression and body behavior as well as get the essential verbalizations in the child's own words, was more satisfactory than electrical recording, which still requires an observer's records of expression

3. Records quoted were made by either Marion Weber or Eleanor Brown unless otherwise indicated.

and motor behavior and the changing situation the child creates. Electrical recording has limitations in work with very young children; murmuring, whispering, sing-song voices do not always come through clearly enough for transcription, and infantile speech is harder to understand from the record than from the immediate experience with the child. Preschool children, unlike older children, are quite indifferent to and unbothered by the presence of the observer.

At the same time, electrical recording, when it is intelligible, makes it possible for an expert stenographer to transcribe infantile speech more precisely than can be done by the stenographer who spells out the words the child says instead of recording the child's language phonetically. The latter can be done after special training. Our own records include some of the common and most characteristic infantilisms, but are variable in this regard; where infantilisms were recorded, they are not eliminated from the records quoted in this book; but what is reflected here is actually an understatement of the slurred consonants and confusions that an ideal record would have shown.

Our recording goals matured during the period of working with the children; they varied with different purposes in different methods. The child's actions, and his words were recorded first, then as much report of facial expression, attitudes, changes of color or other autonomic indicators, and relation with the experimenter as could be managed.

At certain times cinema records were made, and a large part of the time photographs of the end-product of Miniature Life Toys sessions were taken. Such records permit post-session analysis of details of behavior which may not have been recorded fully by the stenographer; however, rigidities of the camera angle and location mean that the hidden camera misses much as well, by comparison with the more flexible range of vision of the human recorder. A mobile camera often interferes with the child's intimate experience in the situation with one adult. Ideally, a cinema record, photographing from two angles, plus a voice record would come closest to a complete record with children whose voices can be picked up adequately, but the expense of making and of analyzing such records is prohibitive without enormous research budgets, and such a procedure also requires an elaborate one-way vision room if the child is not to be distracted by the apparatus.

When completeness of observation of all aspects of the child's emotional, interpersonal, and body behavior is desired, a combination of two observers, one at each end of the room, produces a good result; observers who are unobtrusive and quiet distract the child less than fancy machinery does. Roles of the two observers need to be clarified, and one should have the responsibility of maintaining contact with the child, interrupting note-taking in order to give support when it is needed. Combining the two records gives a rich picture of the play session and a check on the accuracy of each observer as well.

Acknowledgments

During this period of experimentation, Evelyn Beyer was the director of the Sarah Lawrence Nursery School, and taught the older group of children; Marian Gay taught the younger group. Mary Fisher Langmuir was the first parent consultant, and was supplanted after her departure by Jane Judge. Benjamin Spock was pediatrician; Eugene Lerner and I, assisted by L. Joseph Stone, were advisors and research staff. Elinor Brown was secretary of the school and did the intelligence testing; as recorder, she was joined first by Dorothy Call, then by Marian Weber. This group worked together, with the outside help of Anna Hartoch, who made a most extensive study of the children's Rorschachs; Bruno Klopfer, who also commented on them; and Trude Schmidl-Waehner, who analyzed the children's paintings.

The thinking of all of us was stimulated by Lawrence K. Frank and Frank Fremont-Smith of the Josiah Macy Jr. Foundation, which provided funds for the first five years of work.

Contents

PART I

Experiments in Free Methods

by LOIS B. MURPHY

With Chapters by Trude Schmidl-Waehner
and Anna Hartoch

CHAPTER 1

Introduction

IN THIS GROUP of "free methods," I am including methods which give maximum opportunity for free play or free association. The medium or stimulus material may be structured, as with Miniature Life Toys, or semi-structured as with the Rorschach, but the child is free to respond as he wishes. In the case of Dough and Cold Cream, and Painting, and much of the Sensory Toy material, the medium is also unstructured. The purpose of freedom is to permit the child to relax into his most spontaneous mood so that he responds with minimal pressure: his response may then have much of the free flowing quality of play, fantasy, or dream under his own natural conditions for these—the difference is that now the child finds an adult willing to accept whatever he wishes him to share of this mood. It is not expected that the child's spontaneity will be expressed in the same ways in all these media. Different children will have different associations to the materials, so that while one child may handle toys as freely as dough, another may associate toys to the organized aspects of home life, while dough or cold cream may suggest the carefree messing delights of playing with mud or sand. Using a free approach with materials of varying degrees of structure will elicit a wide range of the uses of freedom in different children.

My approach does not represent the application of "a system," but reflects successively a response to Bergson's "elan vital," the Freudian "unconscious" and concept of conflict, Rorschach's "experience-balance," Gardner Murphy's bio-social view of the organism in society, Lewin's notion of "life space" or the subjective world of the child, L. K. Frank's emphasis on the idiosyncratic patterning of development, and Anna Freud's sensitivity to childhood feelings and experience—which I have tried to fuse into a positive approach to normal personality development.

I tried to implement this way of looking at *processes of change in the organism in its field* at an early meeting with representatives of the Macy Foundation.[1] At that time I stated that it is fundamental to observe the child when he is most free and at ease, as well as when he is frustrated or worried, as he often is when confronted by the demands of structured tests. The widest possible range of behavior is needed as a basis for evaluating the potentialities of his development. This range should include a time range—different times of the day, and sequences through the years; and the child's areas of satisfaction should be studied along with his areas of difficulty.

It was clear from our studies of children in nursery school that normal children have problems, and that sometimes they overcome them as they grow and as the situation changes; Jean Macfarlane's studies in California documented this extensively. My question was: what helps them to keep going? I assumed that we might find out something about this by studying "areas of anxiety" and "areas of security" in the same children—that energy from gratification in the latter would help the children to handle their anxiety, and that this balance of stress by comfort or satisfaction would help to explain how normal children stay normal through the ups and downs of development.

I suggested that the child's response to a wide range of materials and equipment should be observed in order to elicit an adequate sample of his motor, sensory, perceptual, affective responses, and the areas of spontaneity and inhibition in his ability to use different stimuli. "The more sharply defined the demands of the situation, the less range of response will appear: e.g., certain sorts of behavior and projections appear in a group under

---

1. March 8, 1939.

the direction of teacher . . . certain other kinds in a group when teacher is absent; a different range will be stimulated when the child is alone with an adult, and by the differences in approach of different adults (warmth-indifference, domination-submission, activity-passivity). A given situation may offer a great range of possible responses or it may be limited. . . . Each problem will suggest projective procedures appropriate to its analysis; methods will vary also with the material, particularly the familiarity, emotional value, perceptual clarity for the child." Observation of these responses should include "posture, facial expressions, verbal patterns, patterns of manipulating things. . . ." These should be analyzed for evidences regarding "conceptual clarity," and the tendencies of the child with regard to form, color, texture, and action as well as his mechanical and dramatic interests should be related to the adjustment pattern of the child.

Relationships between affective and cognitive responses might be found in evidence regarding cognitive changes paralleling emotional shifts—freedom or rigidity of fantasy, and of attitudes toward external stimuli. The "organization of affectivity" is a major problem underlying personality organizations; here I was interested in both "general affectivity," and "specific affectivity" or affective response appearing only in certain situations or in relation to certain stimuli. Patterns of variability in response to different stimuli or different situations gave basic clues to personality organization. The importance of watching for variations in different situations was also related to problems of interpretation at different levels. In the very young child much of what appears to be "repressed" or "deeper" comes out in different settings; so-called "depth" is partly a matter of time and place, not just of degree of awareness to the subject. The difference between private and public thoughts versus deep-level (unconscious) and deck-level ones must be recognized. Up to the age of five, less is repressed than is usual with older children; we must be aware of ideas withheld out of mere privacy, as contrasted with the ideas repressed by the individual and not accessible to himself. At the same time there are wide differences between individual children in this respect. In the group of children we studied, Karin showed almost no ambivalence, very little was hidden (little distinction between public and private); Camille hid certain attitudes. Disapproval may simply make opinions private; repression is a further step reflecting disapproval by the super-ego. The content of a child's problems tells us little about his adjustment: the way he handles them is the crucial factor.[2]

The free methods which are discussed in the following chapters were used precisely in order to see the child under optimally gratifying conditions: the child is alone with one adult who permissively accepts everything he does or says short of actual threat to himself, the room or the experimenter. For many children this in itself is very satisfying. The materials—whether toys, dough or cold cream, or sensory materials—are chosen because children like to play with these things.

These methods as a group provide data on spontaneity, how the child uses a gratifying situation, what preoccupations and concerns are expressed even in a non-threatening atmosphere. They are to be used along with the more provocative and challenging methods described in the succeeding parts of this volume.

We have said that up to the age of four, children are often not able to express feelings directly in words; in fact one important contribution of nursery school teachers is to help them find words for feelings instead of having to act out their rage and disappointment.

We have also said that their natural language is behavior, without amplifying the many forms this language may take. "Behavior" may include manipulation of objects, gross bodily activity, formation of structures, dramatic acting out with materials or children among other forms. Not all children use all forms of expression. But any form of expression is active, releasing, and helpful to the child's integration of his experience and resolution of his problems, provided it does not create new conflicts. The common observation that infants give up crying to a large degree after they acquire locomotion and speech and a wider range of expression is relevant here. As long as the child

---

2. In current research at the Department of Child Psychiatry of the Menninger Foundation, Dr. Nelly Tibout and I with our co-workers are trying to bring this viewpoint into focus in a study of relationships between temperament and how children cope with their problems.

cannot *do* anything or *say* anything, he must feel at the mercy of his frustrations. The potentiality of being active opens new avenues of integration. Many of the activities which result are called play by the adult; to the child they are life.

Different children use a given form of expression in different ways, for different purposes. One child may use abstract structures and form to express an idea which another child expressed through realistic toy arrangements, for instance the idea that mommie has a baby inside of her. Another child uses structures to express relationships between himself and the environment—wanting to be safe inside an enclosure. Another may use a structure to express what one can hardly call anything more than a mood or feeling: "I feel all tight and afraid to move." Forms and structures then are important for what they tell us about how the child conceptualizes his observations, his needs, his feelings as well as for what they tell us about his ways of controlling impulses, or freedom in space.

Children also differ in the range of areas and levels of play which they find satisfying. Some children find the microcosmic level of play with miniature toys more fun, more exciting, than any other type of play; but other children prefer the macrocosmic level of play with peers, and only occasionally leave it for the miniature world. Autocosmic play, with his own body as the medium instead of toys, is resorted to by the normal child at times of fatigue, or frustration in other spheres, or disappointment. For this reason experimental play sessions should not be used instead of observations in the nursery school group, or in other natural settings, but to supplement them.

Some children more than others find the quiet time with one adult especially satisfying to meet what Erikson has called the "ego's need to master the various areas of life, and especially those in which the individual finds his self, his body, and his social role wanting and trailing. The microsphere—i.e., the small world of manageable toys—is a harbor which the child establishes, to return to when he needs to overhaul his ego." This is true of play with materials other than toys. Even the experience with Rorschach may represent this "harbor."

In chapters 2, 3, and 4 I shall describe the procedures followed with materials for free play, and illustrate ways in which different children used them. "Standardization" is not our aim; nuances of cultural differences, even of different periods and areas within one culture, produce different meanings for similar forms of behavior. The response of each child has to be seen in relation to the milieu in which he is growing up and his experience in it. In chapters 5 and 6 illustrations are presented of the painting and Rorschach analyses of preschool children, as used by Trude Schmidl-Waehner and Anna Hartoch; because of their essential freedom of method they belong here rather than with the more directed procedures described in Parts II and III of this volume.

CHAPTER 2

Miniature Life Toys

Play as an Approach
to Understanding the Child

THERE IS OFTEN an almost moral tone in the voices of those who proclaim that children "grow through play," and equal solemnity in the tones of others who believe the central function of play is to alleviate anxiety.[1] Children need play, we are told, they cannot be healthy without it, it stimulates resourcefulness, independence, ability to solve problems, to get along with others. Play, like food and discipline, is a necessity for childhood.

It seems odd that play should need such a solemn defense. Kittens play and so do puppies without any stimulus from their mothers, without any meeting of the Parent-Teachers Association or the Board of Education to legislate more and better play, without special places, times, or materials.

Perhaps we can get some perspective on this if we look at children in other cultures. How do they play? How do their parents provide for play? What do they do when they play? Does this help us to understand the basic role of play?

1. See Dr. Lili Peller's excellent discussion in "Libidinal Phases, Ego Development and Play," *Psychoanalytic Study of the Child*, Vol. IX (New York: International Universities Press, 1954).

We take for granted that the adult should provide for the child's play. But in India I was amazed at the lack of toys, of pets, of paraphernalia of any sort such as we are accustomed to see children using for "play." Children wandered about, a baby on their hip, watching visitors, taking in what the grownups did, helping with preparation of food and household chores. At certain schools, to be sure, boys played vigorous games after their schoolwork was over, much like some of ours. But generally, play did not seem to be an issue, and it appeared to shade imperceptibly into work, without the sharp black-white contrast characteristic with us.

Here we project our adult polarities of work and play onto children. We know when we are playing and when we are not. But with children this is not necessarily true. Moreover, we adults are likely to resent the amount of time we give to the hours that are not play. For Western civilization feels quite ambivalent about work. Work has to be done. It is noble to work hard. We feel very good about ourselves when we do work hard, when we "accomplish something," but we resent it too. We often play compulsively to make up for the self-punishment of compulsive work habits. After a dutiful day's work we feel we have earned the right to play, and we spend this credit with an intense desire to get the utmost possible for our time and money. Even our Western children do not play this way. They play as they breathe; play is a spontaneous expression, and when a child cannot play we have an important symptom, if symptoms are what we are looking for.

This adult rejection and loss of capacity to play has made a mystery of play, while Western civilization seems to find no mystery in work; its meaning is self-evident. Play is important to the child in our culture in contrast to the Indian child partly because he is so cut off from adult activities and life; in city and suburban areas most of the important grownup things go on out of reach or sight, and this means that adult reality is not something which the child participates in, but something he gets ready for. Thus his play may be work and his work may be play; skills and feelings are integrated in play.

Getting ready for adult life involves some years of imaginative fantasy life in which the child partly rehearses for the future, partly develops his wishes, partly crystallizes and expresses his view of whatever segments of the adult reality world are open to his observation, or respond to, interact with, and stimulate him.

Partly because responsibilities and real jobs do not absorb much of his time, more energy is absorbed in personal relationships with grownups and with his peers. Play of certain kinds gives him an opportunity for elaborating and developing these relationships, and partly provides an opportunity to let off the steam, release the tensions generated by them.

Claudia Lewis was surprised at the relative "lack of creativity" of rural children in the Tennessee hills.[2] Yet as we observe other rural children who participate intimately in the life of adults whether in India or our Middle West, we see the same thing: children who share the life of the community, who experience reality with adults, may not need to spend as much time in an imaginary life, or to rehearse so elaborately to get ready for it. The fantasy-reality balance is weighted more heavily toward reality. Thus the range, intensity, and content of play and other expressions of fantasy varies greatly with the experience of children in different settings.

The following discussion is based on studies of urban and suburban children for whom play as fantasy is intensely important.

Cultural Variations in Play

Since 1937 I have made records of Miniature Life Toy sessions with children from a variety of groups: working-class and upper-middle-class children in Westchester and New York, Puerto Rican children from Harlem, children in a Kansas town, deaf children, children in India. In these we find certain differences:

1. The same theme may be expressed through very different symbols in different subcultures (e.g., the fire engine chasing a locomotive off the track in New York is paralleled by a bull killing a snake in Kansas).

---

2. *Children of the Cumberland* (New York: Columbia University Press, 1946).

2. Firmly organized structures may have different implications for children living in settings of different degrees of structuredness (e.g., children in nursery school as compared with children at home).

3. Fluid formless sequences that would be characteristic only of very infantile children in Westchester middle-class groups may be typical of Puerto Rican children in a New York slum—or other children in disorganized environments.

4. Bodily ease, autonomy, and freedom in use of space varies markedly when comparing semirural children with urban children or children in India with American children.

The quality of movement in space, muscular relaxation, flexibility of postures which the child displays may be a function of the muscular adjustments he has had to make to his life space. Children in India, and doubtless other spacious areas, show a catlike ease which I have rarely seen in children in a metropolitan area; some of this may be due to the fact that rural children can go in and out of their homes casually, while middle-class children in large cities may be required to stay indoors (until the age of seven or eight) all the time except when an adult is available to supervise outdoor explorations.

The *time-space dimensions of freedom* for the young child may thus shape his neuromuscular patterns. They can also contribute to his inner image of the world. Each subculture provides its own patterns of greater or less rigidity—the child's visual experience of streets, trees and flowers, yards, and houses; his day's design of more, or less, systematically scheduled routines; the rich or meager, pleasant or unpleasant sounds, smells, looks of the people around him all fuse into personal concepts of what the world looks like. But the visual image is not all. Everyone who has a chance to watch little children has an opportunity to learn the scope of what children absorb from the culture in which they are growing up; parents, teachers, the furniture in their homes provide not only the spaces and colors but tones of voice and feelings which make up the atmosphere of their developmental climate. Not only the texture and the pattern of the culture, but the child's sense of his place in it, can emerge if we watch closely to see just what is going on. Play tells us then about the child's own feelings about his perception of his culture, and his inner feeling of relationship to it, in other words his "idiosyncratic life space."[3]

THE EMOTIONAL CONTENT OF PLAY

We are most familiar with the things play tells us about the child's own feelings, wishes, conflicts, and problems; his hopes from Santa Claus, his fears of bogey men, or of cross mother or teacher, his more vague feelings of big threatening people in general; and we accept the fact that when—in Miniature Life Toy play—he drowns the baby in the bathtub, or rolls it in mud, or throws it far into the corner, he is expressing feelings of desire to get rid of the intruder, feelings very common in our culture with its small families and tremendous emphasis upon and excitement about each child. We are acquainted as well with the little child's annoyance with the grownups who are constantly pushing him around with do's and don'ts, high demands and pressures; spanking the grownups, or making them sleep alone, are some ways of getting back at the troublesome authorities. We can also see plenty of evidence of the child's desire for love, companionship, togetherness, in the trips he acts out with the whole family together, in child dolls sleeping with parent dolls, or in the simple hugging and kissing of child dolls by parent dolls. Wanting to be a baby again and receive a baby's love are favorite activities in the nursery-school doll corner as well as in play sessions alone with one grownup.

When children are playing with blocks or with Miniature Life Toys they are not by any means concerned only with these familiar feelings. They tell us what people, objects, and places mean, what kind of house is a house to them, what kind of mother is a mother; what bed means, how important the bathroom or the kitchen or the living-room armchair is, whether each object is associated with satisfaction, or strain, or joy, or curiosity. If the child dramatizes routines at nursery school, it is also fair to assume that these routines bear some relation to

---

3. These matters will need to be discussed in further detail and from different points of view in the sections which deal with the analysis and problems of interpretation of the record.

those with which he is familiar, and with the overtones, tensions, gaiety, or matter-of-factness with which they are carried out. If he dramatizes special events, since few children have had much opportunity to witness events outside the home, such events are likely to have some relation to those which he has experienced. They may tell us whether a policeman means limits to behavior, or punishment, or protection. They may also show us whether the world of town or village means activity of a hurly-burly sort, or the place where fathers do their work, or where people argue and fight and make trouble for each other; whether tracks mean opportunity to go ahead, or limits to the path you can take if you go; whether bodies are surrounded with a feeling of mystery and curiosity, just the vehicles for getting you where you want to go, or the instruments by which you do what you want to do; whether war means shooting and fun, or threat of being bombed; whether being active means getting approval or getting into trouble, and only passivity is safe.

We have suggested that the child's view of himself in relation to his world is also written in the language of play. Joan, redheaded, makes a bench *"for redheads only"* at the circus (of course in the front row with the best view, thus implying how special redheads are); Dorothy, depressed and isolated while her mother is ill with a second pregnancy, puts a fence between herself and the people dolls, who are all facing away from her, and faces away from the tester, expressing her feeling of isolation in her world in three different ways; Joyce starts everything from a base or area close to herself, working outward as she goes, just as she actually went through processes of increased blossoming and outgoingness as she grew more at home, in nursery school, and in life; Lucy surrounds herself with a protective blockhouse, where she sit inviolable, in the middle. Thus through their choice of toys, fantasies about them, structures made with them, and relation of their bodies to these structures, children show us their sense of freedom in a big world, or need for protection in it, their need to structure and set limits, or to break limits, their sense of adequacy or smallness, of being on the road to bigger and more expansive things, or their need to postpone exploring.

CONTENT IN RELATION TO STRUCTURE

Students in training often expect that the *content* or themes of play will provide a "diagnosis." This is not true in play analysis any more than it is in Rorschach analysis. The healthiest, best-adjusted children I have seen over the years have destroyed babies, mothers, all female authorities, wrenched the sides of cribs off, torn off tigers' tails or other appendages, and otherwise acted out strong feelings of jealousy, hostility, or fear. Such incidents tell us that the child is coming to terms with what are the basic problems of the young child in our culture: his resentment of adult pressures and of competition from babies and the opposite sex. They do *not* tell us whether the child needs help. If the child is not able to cope with his situation, if he is disorganized or disturbed, such content does give us clues as to *what* he is disturbed about, while the character of his cognitive, motor, and emotional processess, their variation and appropriateness, tells us *how* disturbed he is.

Rather than sheer content, then, the *structural* aspects of the child's play and fantasy—its clarity or confusion, order or disorganization—are more diagnostic of patterns or problems to be taken seriously. They may offer different sorts of evidence of disturbing effects of anxiety or conflict. We see some of the indications of rigidity as against functional adaptation in observing the child's block structures and painting forms, and also evidences of body image projected into the block structures and drawings or paintings of the child. But other structural qualities of coherence or incoherence, stereotypy or originality, autistic idiosyncrasy versus conventionality, tell us about the quality of internal organization, the degree of accommodation or conformity to the culture pattern, the extent to which and flexibility with which the child shapes his own design or accepts imposed patterns and, in either case, at what price.

Trude Schmidl-Waehner and others have helped us define some of the categories for formal or structural analysis of painting.[4] At the preschool level the *motor impulses* recorded in paint-

---

4. See Chapter 5.

ings are organically related to the patterns of rhythm, balance, freedom, and tightness expressed also in other kinds of motor behavior (as described by Werner Wolff)[5] and in the structures and sequences produced in play as well. Betsy, in painting, Miniature Life Toys, and in over-all activity in the nursery school, had to establish a frame or setting first, and within this she could be free. Such patterns are often a reflection of the structure of life at home and in the child's larger geographical space. From city to rural life, basic aspects of children's experience affecting character also vary enormously: a rural or small-town child may not only enjoy more motor exercise, as we mentioned above, but may practice *autonomy* from the time he can walk, free to go out of the house as he pleases, go to kindergarten alone, etc., and have no independence in school; whereas a middle-class city child who is hovered over and taken out of doors by the hand up to the age of seven or eight may lose this experience of autonomy. The culture may then correct itself; in many a modern school a child has much more autonomy during school hours than the small-town child, whose school is often more authoritarian, and can be so without destroying the inner core of autonomy grown from early years of freedom. *Balancing patterns of authority and freedom* such as these have yet to be studied in their effects on the *areas of rigidity and spontaneity* in the character of children from these different settings.

Similarly, different subcultures, and different families, give children conceptual patterns—ideas to live by—of greater or less rigidity, or rigidity in certain areas, confusion in others, and flexibility in still others; and the conceptual patterns in a rapidly transformed environment often conflict with the child's personal experience of life as he lives it.

Different children react to different aspects of these physical and conceptual realities, and reflect to different degrees, even at an early age, the rigidities, confusion, or conflicts in the life they see and feel, and the struggle they are making to formulate concepts which can encompass or clarify their experience. Disorganization in play may reflect confusion either in the child's geographical space or in the child's efforts to absorb his world.

---

5. *Personality of the Preschool Child: The Child's Search for His Self* (New York: Grune and Stratton, 1946).

WHAT OBJECTS MEAN TO THE CHILD

There is probably no culture, other than ours, in which objects are such an important part of the child's experience from birth. While a baby in a village in India is carried on his mother's hip for the first year or two of his life and experiences a world centered from her body, an American urban middle-class baby is in a crib, carriage, playpen, high-chair, each with its equipment of toys—rattles, dolls, cradle-gym rings to grasp and swing, colored things, soft things, toy animal shapes to squeak. And in a large number of instances his milk comes solely from a bottle at the start, or from a supplementary bottle at times. Our babies and children thus become attached to objects, one or more of which frequently become indispensable—"he's lost without his doggy," or his blanket, or some other object of especially vivid emotional meaning.

The roles of objects in the child's life space are consequently of almost as great importance as the roles of people, and these roles are different for different children. How the child handles individual toys, what he does with them and says about them, tell us these roles and meanings. Depending on the balance of emotional attachment to people as compared to things, and upon the activity or passivity of the child, the overtness or covertness of his problem-solving efforts, objects will be used realistically to provide a stage setting for fantasy, or in a highly personal way heavily loaded with positive or negative affect, as instruments for solving problems, or as casual tools with little or no emotional investment.

We shall discuss later in some detail the problems of interpretation and evaluation which arise in the attempt to use these data; at the moment we wish to point out that what we are getting at is a picture of those aspects of the child's experience that have so impressed him as to be brought out projectively when he is given relevant materials to use in the process of projection. The concept of life space introduced by Kurt Lewin is relevant here.[6]

---

6. *A Dynamic Theory of Personality* (New York: McGraw-Hill, 1935).

THE CHILD'S LIFE SPACE

We have already referred to the life space of the child as the world he has unconsciously selected as significant, awareness of which he carries about with him; the objects, space-relations, relations with people, of his objective world as experienced, interpreted, assimilated by him. His life space has its own dimensions, its own geometry, created by the child's perceptions of his own size, strength, and what he counts for in his world. It may have sharp boundaries created by consistent taboos, or fuzzy boundaries created by inconsistent taboos, or no perceptible boundaries, as in the case of children who move freely through space without limits of which they are constantly conscious.

This "life space," that is the composite images and feelings that have been absorbed in the process of responding to his geographical milieu, may be assumed to develop from the various visual, auditory, olfactory, tactual, kinaesthetic, and oral impressions he receives in his day-by-day living and exploring, as well as the impressions retained from motor activities and nuances of interpersonal contact, described by James S. Plant[7] and Harry Stack Sullivan,[8] which psychological science has not yet been able to define clearly. When we put it this way it sounds as if these impressions were accumulated one by one, now a sound, now a color. Actually, living does not always go on in such piecemeal fashion; the signals and stimuli from the environment to which the infant responds are sometimes unisensory, at other times dual or multisensory in their origin. Furthermore, as stimuli assume the character of signs they may become dual-sensory, and as later surrogates develop in the form of symbols, their multisensory character becomes more characteristic. Thus the immediate oral stimulus of milk is associated with satisfaction, the tactual-olfactory stimulus of breast is a sign of the imminent availability of milk, and subsequently there emerges the multi-

7. *Personality and the Cultural Pattern* (New York: Oxford University Press, 1937).
8. *The Interpersonal Theory of Psychiatry* (New York: W. W. Norton, 1953).

sensory perception of mother, whose image, rich and complex, ultimately becomes a symbol of all nurturance.

Clinical and analytic literature has emphasized conflicts connected with sex, identification with parents or competition with one parent for the love of another, and sibling competition among the chief determiners of personality development. The concept of the life space stimulates the observer to still broader awareness. We find that the child's relation to physical space, and his spatial relations to people, may be important: the isolation of a child removed from his parents, sleeping in his own room alone from earliest months, or left alone for the greater part of the time; the sense of imprisonment of the child "caged" in play-pens or cribs, attached by straps and harnesses, so that he cannot move freely; the taboos on tactual contacts with objects experienced by the child who has never had a room of his own and who grows up in an adult-oriented home with breakable decorative objects everywhere, may be more laden with feeling than his relations to his siblings. Time relations may also be an important feature of the child's life space: father going to work in the morning, returning after supper, or available to the child only on Sundays. Mother may be an always-available person, or an in-and-out person, going to work, to cocktail parties, or to meetings.

TEMPERAMENT AND DEVELOPMENTAL ATTITUDES

The child "projects" in a sense, that is, he communicates, not simply with the toys and his handling of them but with himself. What he is, his tones of voice, manner of doing things, attitudes, areas of tension, areas of freedom and spontaneity, suggest hypotheses regarding the relations between constitutional predispositions and family experience. I shall discuss temperament in greater detail at a later point; here I shall simply call the reader's attention, first to the fact that the *kind of child he is dealing with* must be foremost in the observer's mind at every point, and then offer the simplest orientation to ways of thinking about this.

By the age of two the child's "temperament" as we see it is

a product of the interaction between needs, drives, and sensitivities originating within himself (genetic or constitutional factors) and the responses to him of the people in his milieu—stimulating, supporting, interrupting, confining, punishing, or whatever combination of these and other responses he experiences. Not only the attitude of acceptance or rejection, but the tempo, activity or passivity, loudness or softness, gentleness or roughness, gloom or gaiety, empathy or obtuseness, and other *qualities of these people around him* are important in this interplay. What we see by the age of two or three is not just a constitutionally "active" child, but a child with a certain potential range of activeness who has been interrupted, stimulated, appreciated, frustrated or blocked, or any one of various combinations of these, either for his activity in general or specific expressions of it, and at this time presents certain areas of free movement and certain areas of control or even inhibition and anxiety.

Similarly a child who had strong visual or tactual or manipulative interest at the age of three months will show tendencies embedded in a complicated pattern of elaboration, constriction, exaggeration, or repression of the original responses.

To start with, it is important to watch activity-passivity patterns, energy, tempo; modalities or areas of response (visual, auditory, tactual, kinaesthetic, rhythmic), level of perception, sharpness, clarity, and their patterns of range and variation. These and other aspects of temperament will be discussed more fully in a later section.

PERSONALITY STRUCTURE

Personality structure may be seen from many different angles; those discussed by the contributors to this volume represent a few which are more or less related. We are interested, as we have said, in the dynamic relationships between spontaneity and control or inhibition; or stated differently, areas of security and freedom versus areas of anxiety or conflict, which point respectively to strengths and to difficulties of the child, and I shall discuss these more fully later on. Here we need to remind ourselves that the role and *modus operandi* of control is the important issue. Control which consists in direction rooted in the freely expressed purpose of the child who feels related to his environment is to be distinguished from control rooted in anxiety to please, to do things right, to complete a task. These patterns of spontaneity and control are usually assumed to grow from the interaction between parent and child, but are also influenced by the constitutional thresholds of the individual child. We see children who are easily restricted—one reproof is enough—in contrast to others with strong drives and less response to adult pressure.

As we see the child at play, we see a variety of possible patterns of interaction between child and adult. Aping the adult in specific, rather external items of behavior is something quite different from a generalized identification with adult posture, tones of voice, and language patterns at an unconscious level. The one may be planned or experimental, the other is unselfconscious. Both are products of positive valence toward adults, in contrast with suspicious, resistant, hostile, or other defense attitudes. All of these may be relatively open and undefensive or unsubtle attitudes, in contrast with the subtle masks that even at the age of three may disguise a child's feelings.

What is the child identifying with, aping, fearing, resisting? Mothers are sometimes seen by clinicians in terms of certain attitudes toward children: overprotective, rejecting, accepting, identifying, dominating. Again this is not a complete list of possibilities, nor is it our purpose now to give one. We have already suggested that other aspects of maternal personality and behavior are important: the parents' own temperaments, care of aesthetic detail, directness of social response, grace of movement, sharp or muted tones of voice, rapid or slow tempo, smooth or jerky co-ordinations, interest in mechanics or fixing things, or in food, color, music, furniture, travel, people—in other words, the intrinsic stimulus-value of the parent as the child experiences it. So also the parents' relation to space: dominant, vigorous, space-filling people make a different contribution from that given by retiring, quiet, unassertive parents. Some parents are habitually perpendicular, others relax into a thousand different relations to space at different times—in athletic, rough-house, or dramatic play with children or other adults. Parental style: the smart woman, the maternal sort, the feminine coy wife, the efficient competent mother, all have their meanings for children; these things are aspects of what the parents are themselves, as people, and would be whether there were children or not.

What parents bring to parenthood, the satisfaction and disappointments of their own childhood, the projected ambitions for their children, the potential ego-values children must satisfy, the assumptions regarding what a charming, or bright, or satisfying child must be, the assumptions regarding what their own heredity will give the child, the blind and alert spots in understanding this heredity, physical and social—these things too have meaning for the child's patterns of spontaneity and anxiety. What parents "know about bringing up children," what mistakes of a former generation they want to correct, what expert advice they try to follow, and with what flexibility or rigidity, what conscious adjustments to neighbors' or relatives' demands they attempt to make—these things make the "figure" of parental behavior against the "ground" of parental personality, some of whose aspects we have just suggested.

The child's personality structure as a whole, then, is the result of his response to all the conscious and unconscious expressions of his parents' personality, as well as their conscious and unconscious attitudes toward the child and his bringing-up. We shall not expect to find a child of a peasant-like mother who grew up on a farm among seven brothers and sisters projecting in her play at the age of two or three the patterns of a child whose mother goes to cocktail parties regularly.

The naïve two- or even three-year-old may not have developed great differentiation in relations with adults. All adults may be treated to the cuddling, mauling, intrusive questioning, compliance, teasing, ordering about, which we assume has developed in the interaction of adult and child at home. Objects are handled with the regard for order or casualness or blustering defiance which also reflect in some fashion the result of child impulse-interaction with parental patterns. Thus the child acts out in the play situation attitudes and behavior-patterns which sometimes duplicate, sometimes supplement behavior at home.

In using the Miniature Life Toys and Plastics, we try to build up the picture of *the personality structure of the child in his life space: what he has conceptualized from his experiences in the physical-social world in which he is growing up; the behavior, attitudes, interests, patterns of response or resistance which have developed; the individual temperament which underlies the specific patterns of response and selection; the areas of free or spontaneous response, the areas of anxiety or tension, and his methods of handling tension, which structure his world for him.* Stated differently, we wish to see the child's *needs, drives, problems, and ego-structure in relation to his temperament and his perception of his life space.*

Miniature Life Toys are especially adapted to this purpose of getting the child to show us himself in his life space because the material is adapted to his manipulation; a great many objects may be arranged within a small area in reach of the child when they are tiny and easily handled. Since the toys are directly representative of the familiar objects of the culture, we need not regard them as tools for a language of symbolization unless the child so uses them. They permit him to offer us a microcosm of the larger life space in which he moves, or of the experiences which are significant to him.

Data from Miniature Life Toy sessions are always used along with data from other test methods and observations on the child's behavior, place in the family, relation to his parents. As a result of the comparison of observations, we learn more about the meaning of the child's behavior and fantasy in the play session than we could dependably infer from play-session records alone.

This method is primarily qualitative and dynamic, not psychometric. It provides data which extend the observer's picture of the child. It is too sensitive to recent events in the child's life, the child's feeling about the experimental situation and the tester, to be used (especially on the basis of one hour) for standardized quantitative measures. Young children, especially, may use the Miniature Life Toys for exploration in one hour, organization another hour, and only later come to express fantasies.

Differences between "less and more structured materials"

and "less and more structured methods" of handling the child in the experimental situation can elicit different responses from the child. Clay from this point of view is regarded as less structured, since you can "make" everything you like out of it within limits—that is, you can impose your own forms upon it; the material is malleable, adaptable, and does not come to the child in a rigid form with limited, culturally imposed, or accepted functions. A doll bed is structured, containing its own form; it may, to be sure, be adapted by the child to other purposes, but this happens rarely, and when it does it implies more freedom in the child for "restructuring" materials given to him; or indifference to form or defiance of convention; or symbolic distancing, distortion, or perceptual confusion. A "more structured method" is used when the experimenter wishes to focus observations upon a specific point and exclude irrelevant associations as much as possible. Eugene Lerner's procedures will illustrate this.[9] For the purpose of getting a picture of the child's life space and his approach to experience, I decided to use these "more structured" materials, selected with the usual range of experience of preschool children in our culture in mind, and a "less structured" method, which I felt would reveal the child's capacity for spontaneous response to a new situation. This led to the Miniature Life Toy approach. Just as no responsible person will seriously offer to "interpret a child's personality" on the basis of one painting, no one should use one Miniature Life Toy record as evidence of the range, depth, flexibility or creativity of a child. One session, however, in combination with other evidence—biographical notes, observations, other tests—will provide important perspectives. It may indicate how a child is handling life experiences, such as the arrival of a baby or the departure of a father. As we shall see in the study of Colin (Volume II), a series of records, with their continuities and variations, will give a picture of the child's capacity for organization, for expression of his ideas through structures, themes, and fantasy play, the directness with which he can express feelings, the ways in which he can deal with them, and the shape and content of his currently salient

9. See Chapters 11, 12, 13.

experience—including those past experiences which are part of his current fantasy.

After describing the materials and procedure used, we shall discuss aspects of the data one by one, breaking down the types of information and sequences in which they appear, from which we can build up such a picture of a child. This will be a process, not of checking rating scales or experimental categories, but of moment-by-moment recording of a complex experience which the Miniature Life Toys situations and other play situations provide, then analyzing and organizing the data from this situation to build a picture of the child in his life space.

Materials and Procedure

Miniature Life Toys are a portable collection of small toys which may be used in an experimental or testing room, in a living room, or out-of-doors on a porch or terrace, or taken to a child's home. A room, at least 10′ x 12′, and preferably not larger than 12′ x 16′, is needed. It must be quiet and free from interruptions or disturbing external noises. I have usually worked in a room with a smooth-surface rug 6′ x 9′ in the center of the floor, a couple of chairs at opposite ends of the room, a desk or table and cot or sofa, and windows away from the street. Such a room seems sufficiently homelike to a small child, yet is free from distracting or competing objects which would interfere with his freedom to become deeply absorbed in the toys.

The toys are presented to the child in open boxes or piles (each of which has one group of the toys). These piles are never arranged in an organized fashion, but invite exploration and choice by their random arrangement. They are placed in a broad semicircle about five feet in diameter so that the child may, if he wishes, reach toys from any pile without running around the room to do so. This produces the sharpest contrast between children who confine themselves to minimal movement necessary to obtain the toys, versus those who leap around the room, using every opportunity to move as much as possible.

The materials include dolls, which might be representative of family members, furniture for the main areas of home activity; planes, trains, cars, boats, animals, and soldiers for activity outside of home; farm animals and a fence; wild animals; cowboys, Indians, soldiers; and Lincoln blocks and larger blocks, which can be adapted for any purpose. The material is of different colors; there are some broken pieces, some obviously old, some new in each box. In order to hold the children's interest in certain cases where repeated visits are desired, a few new items may be added at each session. Because of frequent breakage, major items have to be replaced three or four times a year. We used over three dozen cribs, almost as many celluloid babies, and a large number of toilets in the first seven years—these being the most rapidly expended toys for the generation of preschool children I saw between 1937 and 1944: middle- and upper-middle-class children whose mothers were much influenced by the prescriptions for rigid feeding, toilet training, and sleeping schedules common in the thirties. There should always be extra dolls over and above the minimum of father, mother, maid, baby, brother, and sister, but the number varies. (Some miniature pottery bowls, fuzzy dogs, and so on, which were broken, could not be exactly duplicated and substitutes were arranged as adequately as possible. The toy business, unfortunately for experimenters, is not run on an open-stock basis!) The list in Appendix I gives in detail a characteristic picture of the materials used; for the most part they are common sturdy miniature toys, of the sort available at dime stores, or stationery and hardware stores. The materials should always represent the range of experience accessible to the child in his subculture, and preferably be assembled from toys familiar in the subculture.

Children in rural areas who rarely if ever see a "policeman" or a "fireman" do not use these toys as much as city children do or in the same ways; children in cities who see no animals except those in the zoo do not as frequently use the farm animals. Children of deprived environments who live in homes which do not contain the usual middle-class equipment will not use the miniature equipment in the same way middle-class children do.

As the child comes into the room he is told simply, "Here are lots of toys for you to play with. You may do anything you like with them."

The experimenter records the child's behavior, talk, and expressive patterns. He makes the minimal response to the child's questions, only enough to maintain rapport with the child. For example, if the child asks, "What are you writing?" the experimenter responds, "I'm writing about what children like to do." If the child asks, "Was Mary here?" the experimenter says, simply, "Yes." If the child says, "What did she do?" the experimenter need merely answer, "She had fun with the toys."

When a child gives a major "lead," the experimenter should pursue it, but again with the minimal response to maintain rapport (or the release atmosphere). For instance, if the child says, "Nannie is mean," the experimenter should merely repeat, "Nannie is mean?" encouragingly, or quietly ask, "When is she mean?" The chief point is to avoid either specific suggestions or negative attitudes which would interrupt the spontaneous associations of the child.

However, if the child has been silent the experimenter may say, "Tell me about it," in this way encouraging association. Or specific questions may be asked, for example, "Why did the mother spank the baby?" "Children feel like beating up grownups sometimes, don't they?" "What do mothers say when children don't eat?" Ideally, such questions should grow out of the specific experiment and be designed to clarify further attitudes expressed or suggested by the child during the experiment. If the child is questioned it is important to note whether the questions stimulate more fantasy or lead to inhibition.

The experimenter must determine ahead of time how he will meet emergencies: for example, in the event that the child should break the furniture or attack the experimenter. In general, a casual flat "I can't let you break the furniture" is probably all that is necessary to set limits which the child will respect. In any instance where aggression or other activity produces marked anxiety (as reflected in widened pupils, glazed eyes, or tremors) the experimenter should set limits and shift the activity to a neutral area unless he is an experienced therapist who is prepared to use the anxiety therapeutically.

After the child has explored the toys, if he initiates a dramatic play, the experimenter should accept the cues given by the child and play his role as the child dictates (e.g., sleep, spank at the child's direction). The experimenter may, on a subsequent occasion, plan a more specific game or dramatic procedure designed to elaborate further a fantasy or idea the child has presented. If possible, the child should be allowed to terminate the experiment, that is, achieve closure spontaneously.

This procedure differs from therapeutic procedure. At the Sarah Lawrence Nursery School, I made a practice of taking children on a thoroughly casual basis, saying yes whenever possible when they ran up asking, "Can I go play with the toys?" and never taking a child who was unwilling to go. This, of course, creates an entirely different atmosphere from that to which children are subjected when they are taken for an appointment at a stated hour which may interrupt their play and does not necessarily catch a mood of communicativeness.

It is helpful to consult a child's teachers with reference to his behavior in the group as compared with his behavior with the experimenter. It is also important to get the teacher's report as to whether the child seemed relaxed or tense when he returned from the experiment.

On the way over to the experimental room, the children were apt to take the experimenter's hand, talk about flowers or other things seen on the way; when it was cold or wet some children were glad to be carried, while others always preferred to be independent. (These attitudes were noted as part of the record, of course.)

The termination of the play session was just as casual. If the child said, "I'm through now," the experimenter said, "All right," and offered help with clothes, if it was desired. The intention was to keep the atmosphere relaxed.

It is difficult to evaluate the presence of a one-way screen with a secretary inside, in comparison with the experimenter's pad and pencil in plain sight, as in our procedure. Many children accepted the idea that the pad and pencil were busy-work and felt actually less under surveillance when they were present than when they were not. Dr. Ruth Munroe, after reading some of these records, suggested that "The elements of the situation are familiar, unthreatening, not different enough to require a new total stance from the child." These elements may actually contribute to the child's freedom to express fantasy.

Against the background of a generally noncoercive, casual procedure, individual personalities revealed themselves in different ways. Some children were released by the experimenter's relatively quiet, accepting manner, while others appeared to want more content in their relationships. Some were freed by the absence of directions, whereas others seemed to want to know what they were "supposed to do." Some were completely absorbed in the toys, while for others the toys were chiefly useful as a point of contact with a grownup.

Between November, 1937, and May, 1941, records of 326 play sessions were made. These form the chief basis for the observations in this chapter.[10] Since then several hundred additional records of play of children from different socio-economic, racial, and geographic backgrounds have been collected; these have formed the basis for a few comparisons between widely different groups.

There is no copyright on the selection of toys and other materials, on the methods or the ideas discussed here, and I hope other investigators will continue to make their own selection of toy materials, reporting informally on the results from different setups. It is not desirable to crystallize this type of procedure into a rigid form; insofar as projective methods succeed in developing into a technique for recording the life space of children, some of them will probably have to retain a large margin of flexibility, and freedom to adapt to the needs of different children in different settings.

THE RECORD

I discussed the general problems of recording above[11] and everything that was said there is relevant to the recording problems of the Miniature Life Toys session, with certain additional

---

10. The children referred to in this study have, of course, been given pseudonyms.
11. These are discussed briefly in the Introduction.

cautions. In the more structured games such as Lerner's Ego-Blocking games, the recording problem is clear and concise: the recorder must report on what the child said and did and what expressive patterns appeared in response to each more or less standard stimulus from the experimenter.

With Miniature Life Toys the problem is more complex and more subtle; since the situation is unstructured and the child is free to do as he likes, the total situation is the stimulus—the room, the furniture, the toys, the experimenter himself, the freedom of the situation. To be invited to do "anything you like" is an amazing experience to some children who have been brought up within rigid limits. The strangeness of the situation and its multiplicity, its demand for action completely initiated by the child, for guideposts found within, may be surprising and, to a few children, overwhelming.

The record should include a picture of this response to the initial impact of the new experience; and verbalizations, both purposeful and involuntary actions, and expressive patterns should be reported as fully as possible throughout. It is especially important to note the objects and activities associated with delight, warmth, or gratification along with those freighted with anxiety, frustration, aggressive or hostile feelings, or a sense of conflict. In many instances it will be possible to provide a tentative map of the topography of satisfying, conflict-free areas versus tense, "conflicted" areas of functioning after the first session—a map to be refined as successive observations extend the picture of the child's emotional world. In the following pages, excerpts will illustrate some of the important typical aspects of the child's response that should be noted.

Analysis and Interpretation

The materials of a richly recorded play session lend themselves to analysis from many different points of view, or within the concepts of different frameworks. Actually, we found that different sets of concepts illuminated the material from different children, as if some children had established allegiance to

Freud in their infancy while others proposed to demonstrate the tenets of Fromm. Rather than look for evidence relevant to one or another school of dynamic thinking, I found that it contributed to precision to inspect carefully each play record from the point of view of what it contained: behavior, structures produced, expressive patterns, fantasy content, over-all design or pattern through the sequence of play. The implications of each aspect of the play session could then be related to the others and integrated into a synthesis of the communication of each child as a unique person. General concepts of areas of sensitivity and experience, needs, drives, character of control, ways of dealing with problems, and with anxiety, strengths and sources of gratification, cognitive and other ego functions which the child used with greatest satisfaction and/or efficiency, were adaptable to the material of different records. In Appendix I a suggested outline for training in analysis and breakdown of a record in systematic fashion is presented; this should never be used rigidly, but adapted to the questions to be answered and purposes of the play sessions with a given child in a given subculture at a given time.

There are several reasons why we have refused to develop a rigid scoring system for Miniature Life Toys. The preschool child has absorbed fewer of the ready-made clichés and concepts of the culture than has the older child with his wider vocabulary; his concepts are more idiosyncratic, closer to his own unique experiences, than are those of older children. If we force his meanings into ready-made categories we risk failing to grasp the new insight about himself and children generally, which any child may give us.

In addition, the same concepts and the same structures can have very different meanings for different children, or children growing up in different settings; the relation of the child's feeling and behavior to his fantasy and structures, all seen in relation to the actual realities of his experiences, are required for an adequate evaluation. The tester shares with the therapist the responsibility to make himself as *precise an instrument* as possible, sensitively alert to the least nuances of each child's way of dealing with his experiences.

INITIAL APPROACH

Of course the response of a child to any or all experimental or special situations will reflect not only his feelings about the particular situation but also his feeling in the nursery school situation as a whole.[12] During her first few months in nursery school, for instance, Jill did not come spontaneously to play with the toys although she would come when Camille, whom she admired and enjoyed playing with, came along. The next year, however, she was eager to come as the following typical record shows.

Jill came up to the experimenter repeatedly, wanting to come; when it was Alec's turn she ran along, then faster down the hill so that she fell down and skinned a knee and an elbow. After a big group went off to hike, the experimenter brought her up to play with the toys. Jill seemed contented in a matter-of-course way.

In Jill's case, this change seemed to be a reflection of her complete security in nursery school the second year, and her eagerness to try out any new situation that might be fun.

Cecily was also diffident when she first came to nursery school, in a way that carried over to other situations. But the second year she responded with surprising ease.

Jay kept at a distance for many months even after he had grown happily rooted in nursery school as a whole. One day at school, the experimenter played with him and with her son who was visiting and whom Jay enjoyed enormously. After this incident Jay was eager to go and play with the toys and the experimenter felt a particular intimate shared quality in laughter, spoofing, whistling, etc.—almost as if Jay and a grownup met on some mid-ground between three plus and forty minus; in a definite contrast to the two-generation relation with Karin, Betsy, etc.

Stanley kept his distance nearly all year but in the spring volunteered spontaneously one day, "I'd like to come and play

---

12. Cf. Eugene Lerner's "Active Play Techniques" (Part III) in which a more complete analysis of the child's attitude toward the experimenter is recorded. For the purposes of the present method, the main characteristics of the initial attitude are noted for their value in relation to the remaining data of the experiment.

with your toys. I haven't been for quite some time." Actually he had resisted politely all year and his phrase was startlingly like the evasions of adults in similar social situations.

These instances illustrate factors of familiarity, transference, and social context which underlay or were necessary conditions for spontaneity with some children.

Even after considerable time in the nursery school, some children are quite ambivalent about leaving the group to go off and play with toys. The following excerpts illustrate varieties of adjustment by the experimenter to the uncertainty of these children.[13]

[Carla was playing in the big room pounding the peg-board. Betsy and Patsy were playing in the same room. Carla, not much absorbed, looked up at the experimenter. The experimenter watched her pound, then said:] Carla, I have some dollies and toys over in my room, you can come over and play with them. *No.* [Experimenter, looking at Betsy:] Betsy knows my playthings. She came over to see me. [Betsy leaving her toys:] *I want to come.* Experimenter: Maybe Betsy and Carla could come together. Would you like to come, Carla? *Yes.* Experimenter: Maybe Carla could come now and Betsy could come later. Carla: *Uh.* [assent] [Experimenter took her hand, helped her get coat; picked her up when they got outdoors.] Experimenter: I'll hold you so you won't get cold. [Carla made no response; no effort to support weight, or hold on to experimenter— a little stiff. Seemed resistant in a slightly rigid way, not just indifferent like Adele.] Experimenter: I'll hold you tight and you hold me tight. [Carla leaned a shade closer.]

[Cappy was very ambivalent. Three times this morning started to come then changed her mind. Experimenter finally sat down on stone step on the edge of the courtyard playground with box of toys, let her explore them. She was actively interested, settled down contentedly.

[Claudia wanted to come when the experimenter brought Karin. When experimenter took Karin back piggyback, Claudia refused to come. Experimenter took Joyce and Joel, then brought Joel back and asked Claudia again:] When you're through with your house, would you like to come and play with me? *I'm through now.* [She left cake, climbed out of sandbox, came along with the experimenter.] Experimenter: Let's go up and see the bunnies for just a minute and then we'll go and play with your toys. [On the way back from bunnies

---

13. In the transcripts of experimental sessions presented in this volume, all remarks made by the children have been italicized.

Claudia exclaimed over the pansies too. The experimenter offered piggyback ride.] *No, I want to go the way I am.*

Camille's uncertainty seemed somewhat deeper, although she came with real responsiveness.

[When the experimenter approached Camille she looked at her with quiet poise and a reserved, hesitating smile.] Experimenter: When you're through with that you could come and play with my dolls and toys. *Mmmmm.* [Smiling, waiting, still hesitating; not withdrawing, yet not continuing with her play.] Experimenter: You can tell me when you're ready. *Mmmmm.* [She came over to the experimenter smiling, still approaching-withdrawing.] Experimenter: Shall we get your things? Where are your things? [Camille follows with the same inquiring, hesitant smile. Makes no move to find clothes. The experimenter looks for Camille's cubby with no assistance from Camille, and takes out snowsuit. Camille makes no move to put it on.] Experimenter: Shall I help? *Mmmmm.* [Lets the experimenter put snowsuit on.] Experimenter: Can you zip it? *Mmmmm.* [She zips it.] *Now my hat and my mittens.* [She goes to cubby.] Experimenter: Here's your hat. [Camille pulls it down.] Experimenter: I guess you won't need your gloves . . . shall I pick you up? *Mmmmm.* [The experimenter picks her up. She holds on moderately, apparently hesitant yet responsive. When the experimenter brought her in she again looked at L. J. Stone with the same smiling appraisal.]

Definitely positive responses to the experimenter's invitation ranged from the quiet compliance of Karin, or the laconic definiteness of Jeremy, to the active demands of Betsy.

[The experimenter came directly to Jeremy as he played with blocks and said:] Would you like to come and play with me sometime today? *Mmmm.* [laconically] Experimenter: Would you like to come right now? *Mmmmm.* [In same positive tone, with minimal elaboration. He ran ahead to get his coat, but stopped at the desk, passive, apparently expecting the experimenter to get his things and put them on. His hands and arms and shoulders had a curious soft flexibility as the experimenter dressed him. His fingers spread and curled in little unconscious irrelevant movements at every adjustment. He was passive as the experimenter wrapped him in her coat and carried him to experiment room.]

Karin always comes with the same wide-eyed compliance, putting her hand to mine with matter-of-fact trust. There is no playing up, no self-consciousness, neither dependence or independence, but a calm, trusting acquiescence and assurance that an adult is friendly, meanwhile going ahead to participate or discover, as the case may be.

Betsy bounces coyly up to the experimenter and announces the intention of playing. When the experimenter first came in, at 9:00 A.M., Betsy jumped up eagerly, demanding to go. Alec, perhaps not seeing the experimenter, did not react until after Betsy did, but appeared enthusiastic. The experimenter explained to Betsy that she had had the most turns, so that this was really Alec's. When the experimenter returned after Alec, Betsy jumped up determinedly.

In general it was Alec, Camille, Betsy and other children who *demanded* to come who produced the fullest and most dynamic fantasy. This may mean that the experiences of playing with toys alone with one adult, or in a situation where they feel free from external pressure or stimulus of a group situation, is an experience which some children definitely want or need, or are able to use, more than other children.

BEHAVIOR WITH TOYS

The initial action of the children with the toys varied quite as strikingly as their attitudes when approached in order to come to play with the toys. Alec and Claudia dumped all the toys out of the boxes at once with loose sweeping gestures, while other children pawed through them, looking at one thing after another, and still others took out one at a time, setting up each toy vertically. Since the boxes were on the floor where the child was invited to sit, picking them up and dumping out the toys was actually a rather definite aggressive gesture.

Some children at this age level, like seven-year-old children, seem to feel under compulsion to react to or make some use of every single article in the box, while at the other extreme of selectiveness, Patsy would hunt throughout the box for a specific toy that was wanted, or asked the experimenter for whatever was desired. This pattern of selectivity in contrast to being dominated by the stimulus is an important one to relate to other aspects of personality, such as the tendency to impose patterns, to carry out one's own purposes in whatever setting one finds oneself, in contrast to the pattern of submitting to real or supposed environmental demands. In cases where a definite preoccupation with a specific object such as bed or toilet occurs, it is essential to check the question of a momentary versus a more deep-laid fixation by repeated experiments over a period of time.

At the same time, the degree of *selectivity* undoubtedly was related to the child's feeling about the toys. It is true that this kind of material is, by and large, of dependable interest to nearly all children this age, but some children are definitely not interested in it. Dick, a bouncing, perhaps hyperactive, vigorous boy, who enjoyed big, sparking cars (cars with guns that shoot automatically as the car goes) and other aggressive toys enormously, who always covered big areas whether painting or at play, expressed his own feelings of the inappropriateness of this material to his "areal" pattern when he said: "They're too little to play with, I don't like these things."

It is not sound, however, to jump to the conclusion that boys in general at this age are not interested in toys like this, since Alec, Jay, Kene and others played with them with complete absorption comparable to the degree of absorption shown by Camille, Betsy, Dusty and other girls. There is some indication that boys, particularly conscious of their five-year-old transition to a more clear-cut masculine role, are apt to reject toys like these between the ages of five and seven, or until they are able to distinguish between the reality role of playing with toys and the more structured pattern of "making a play." As Erikson has shown, students of college age find it easy to "make a play" with materials like these.[14] This, of course, is largely a matter of cultural sanctions. When a wide range of objects, sampling the range offered by the culture, is presented to a child, his patterns of selection are in themselves a first important clue to the content of his life space as structured by his temperament, his interests, and anxieties.

In addition to differences in *degree of interest or absorption*, other important qualitative differences in attitude appeared. An extreme stereotyped pattern is illustrated in the following record of Adele.

---

14. Erik Homburger Erikson, "Studies in the Interpretation of Play: I. Clinical Observation of Play Disruption in Young Children," *Genet. Psychol. Monog.*, XXII (1940), 557-671; "Configurations in Play: Clinical Notes," *Psychoanalytic Quarterly*, VI (1937), 138-214.

[Adele looks around, steps on toys. Moves over, embarrassed.]*Oh pretty little things.* [Picks up kitchen cupboard.] *Cute little thing.* [Picks up lamp.] *Cute.* [Inspects icebox; looks at the experimenter.] *Funny.* [face a little flushed, inhibited] *What's this? You tell me.* [bed; washbowl] *What's this? Isn't this cute?* [Takes out one thing at a time, puts each back after her laconic "cute" or "funny.] *Funny.* [sink] *What's this? You tell me.* [repeats three times] Experimenter: Dresser? *Yes. Oh.* [sighs] *What's this? Tell me.* [repeats twice] *Bathtub. Isn't this a nice little bathtub?* [always puts them back] Experimenter: Shall we have some of them out? Then we can do anything we want with them. [toilet] *Isn't it cute?* [Defensive, social superficial response pattern. Looks at the experimenter quickly now and then. Leans back against bed; looks at kitchen cabinet.] *That's funny.* [She uses these categories alternately, as if in an effort to spread out to more varied reaction.] *Cute little table. Are there some chairs to it?* [Apparently *really* interested under her cover of conventional response. Picks up toilet again, flips cover back and forth.] *Cute.* [Stereotype surface over real energy. Puts part of one bed down.] *Cute . . . Oh who did this?* [When she sees torn dress on baby doll. This is first interruption of stereotype pattern.] *Cute.* [doll] *Nice.* [second doll] *Girl?* [third doll] *Cute.* [fourth doll] *Have you a toothbrush to this?* [washbowl].

Stereotypy also appeared in the photographs of Adele standing heel to heel surveying nursery school the first few days, in her concern with proper dress for different occasions, in her repetitious conversation and play during the first months, the rigid neatness of her structure when she handled the toys more actively, lack of nuances of voice, and limited fantasy. Her approach to all these situations was freer, though still constricted, at the end of her two years in nursery school.

A usual exploratory response on first seeing the toys is illustrated by the following record of Betsy.

[Business of removing clothes. Betsy then goes right over to the boxes, and starts talking about and handling the toys while still being undressed.] *A little truck. A little boy. A little girl. What's this?* Experimenter: What do you think it is? *A little bed . . . A stove.* [voice going up] [She reaches into the box for the two standing rabbits.] *See de little bunnies? Two little bunnies . . . Day faw down . . . Dresses.* [now standing up] *Here's a little car . . . The goin' . . .* [Sets up the sailor doll, the green dress doll, icebox, the long-legged fur-coat doll.] *I have a coat like that at home . . . This is the lady.* [lady doll] *Dis anodda lady.* [brown doll] *A baby. What color's the dress?* [repeats the question insistently] Experimenter: Blue? *Yeah, dis girl stand up.* Experimenter: Who is it? *Some girl. De girl is all dressed now. What's dis?* Experimenter: What? *What is it?* [insistently] Experimenter: Icebox. *Yes* [gladly] . . . *Icebox. Here's another little baby. This one stand up. He go lyin' down. He gonna fall.*

Another type of initial approach characteristic of young two- and three-year-old children is seen in the following record of Kurt.

Wassat? Experimenter: Icebox. [Note: persistent holding upside-down.] *Wassat?* [sink, chair, trunk] *It goes like this . . . Wassat? Drawer?* [initial question for communication, rapport] *I got some chewing gum.* [Repeats twice. Finds bureau, small drawer.] *Put it in there.* [twice] *Wassat? Boy. He takes a baf.* [Drops him.] *Wassat? . . . Rocking.* [rocking chair] *Wassat? Hat . . . hat to put on.* [Tries it on self, fetchingly. Puts hat on baby that was in tub.]

In both these cases we find fragmentary "functional activity" such as putting the doll into a bed, running a car along the floor without any consistent idea or purpose indicating that the child has assimilated the possibilities of the toys enough to use them in a series. In some cases a child will spend thirty minutes or more the first time he sees the toys doing nothing more than getting acquainted with the material, and then leave; in other cases five to twenty minutes of this inquiring activity precedes more organized play.

Noting the child's *choices, repetitions, rejections,* and *persistent clinging to certain toys* is the beginning of our analysis and serves to sharpen our question of what these choices and rejections mean to this child. One child (like Karin) will play actively with a baby to express her competitive or hostile feelings, whereas another child will ignore the baby as a way of dealing with similar feelings. How the child feels about the objects and events he presents in his play session, how he handles and feels about his feelings, and what the consequences of these feelings and their expression are for his personality as a whole is our concern. Here the sequence analysis gives us our clues. When Karin selects the baby we can surmise only that babies mean something to her; when she tosses the baby away, we infer that she may feel hostile or would like to get rid of it; when she follows this by putting the little girl doll into the mother's bed, we infer that it is not so much that there is anything bad about babies (Nellie was upset because they dirtied their panties) but that the baby comes between Karin and her mother whom she would like to stay close to (or perhaps possess exclusively, but that is stretching the inference).

Control may be expressed through selection (and rejection) of toys, through delimiting the activities or area of their movement, through organization of the toys, and through integration of action with the toys by means of an idea which involves implicit limits or moral values (e.g., soldiers just shooting bad people, not destroying wantonly). All of these, or any combination of them, may appear in a given child's play; or bad versus good distinctions may appear without marked concern with the first three (i.e., no obvious rejections, no limits set up by police or fences, etc., no structures such as lining up the soldiers). When a child gets stuck at one of the first three levels of control—that is, when he cannot go beyond selecting and rejecting—or when he sets up policed areas but cannot carry on activities within those areas, or organizes structures such as tracks or fences or houses, but cannot proceed to use them, this suggests that control is interfering with the integration of impulse with fantasy and activity.

The role of organization can be evaluated only in the light of all the rest of the play session. Occasionally a child will arrange a group of toys and then turn to the experimenter, asking, "See what I made?" expecting approval for his "good" achievement. Another child will set up the toys, fascinated by problems of "What will these [Lincoln logs] make?" Many children organize garages, airports, farms, barns, or houses, just as a setting for the activity which comes afterward. By no means do all children "make a world" when they are told merely, "Do what you like with the toys."

Every aspect of control, organization, and the making of structures may be influenced by typical forms of the culture in general—the shapes of houses, arrangements of furniture, groupings and patterns of streets, as well as the specific forms and patterns in the child's own home, and the intrapsychic patterns which may be projected into external forms. Such intrapsychic patterns may be derived from routines of the day projected into space or from the structure of sequences experienced by the child over a longer period of time.

Thus structures, like symbols, and sequences of play cannot be fully understood separately, or even in totality, aside from their immediate and total life history. All aspects of the patterns need to be seen in relation to recent and longtime patterns of the child's experience. Form and content alike need to be considered both analytically—each part in terms of its own implications —and integratively, with all the separate meanings seen in relation to each other and to the whole, and to the child's whole life.

TYPES OF CONSTRUCTION PRODUCED BY THE CHILD

Many children do not produce an externally organized construction at all; their play consists of acting out with the toys or talking about them as they handle them. When children do produce a construction which is permitted to remain for part or all of the play session, we ask several questions about it. First, does pattern take precedence over active functional play with the toys? Is the child chiefly interested in what he can do with or make out of the toys; that is, is he primarily interested in organization as such? If so, is he interested in the aesthetic qualities, in problem-solving, or in achievement? Or is the organization incidental, secondary to exploring or to dramatic activities or expression of fantasy? Second, what is the character of the pattern if a definite structure is produced? The following patterns frequently appeared during our experiments.

1.) *Horizontal lining up:* This appears normally in young children of two to three years, certain handicapped children, children who are dull or constricted, and also may appear in certain functional contexts when realistic patterns of the culture are being reproduced (e.g., parked cars, shipping docks, trains, etc.).

2.) *Geometrical pattern of oblong enclosure or square arrangement:* This may be functional or empty and rigid, depending on the context and what use is made of it.

3). *Lining up the toys against the legs of desks, against the wall, or along the edge of the rug:* This may go with other evidences of taking cues from the environment, or working within assumed limits.

4). *A pile and a close compact arrangement of things set on the floor and immediately adjacent to it, allowing for little space between them:* This appeared in children temporarily or more persistently constricted or inhibited. (E.g., Joyce made this sort of grouping at first, then later both her structures and her behavior loosened up.)

5). *One-floor arrangement representing a house:* This was usually made by children who were realistic and down-to-earth; the houses varied in stereotypy or originality.

All the constructions just named were generally repeated many times by the children who made them. As a rule, a child who made a square house repeated this structure in many sessions, and this child never made the compact bunched arrangement characteristic of another child. There were often close parallels between the line pattern of the constructions built with toys and analogous patterns appearing in fingerpainting, easel painting, block-building, and other activities of the same child. Examples of these activities may help to illustrate the structures.

Cecily lined up the toys using leg of desk, bed, etc., as points to determine the location of toys. The result was a neat arrangement with which she did nothing, carried out no activity, and about which she expressed no ideas.

Betsy often made a tidy four-room house, expressing no ideas about it. When it was finished she sometimes became active and enlisted the experimenter's cooperation in carrying out a dramatic game in which she was a vigorous actor, moving all over the room, with little or no relation to the house structure she made at first.

Constructions which used given boundaries (desk-line, box in which toys were presented) were built by children to whom "accepting given limits" appeared to be a general characteristic merely illustrated or dramatized in the Miniature Life Toys session. The building of clear constructions did not mean that a child was "constricted"; many children showed "areas of constriction and release" or "sequences of constriction and freedom," of which the pattern of first building a structure, then carrying on active fantasy was an illustration.

Structured objects like toys can have different meanings. Squares and other tidy structures may express rigidity when they are used at the expense of functional activity, fantasy, dramatic acting out. But when structures are first set up by way of stage-setting and are then followed by richly acted out fantasy, they contribute to the completeness of creative expression.

Organizational Patterns and Perception

Those who are working with this approach will be interested in the categories developed by Witkin and his colleagues who used a Miniature Toy play situation along with other projective methods and experimental procedures to provide data for the study of relationships between perception and personality in children. Assuming that "to a specific opportunity to play [the child] comes with personality institutions and equipment which have evolved out of his past attempts at regulation and control of these same dynamic sources of play [impulses and idea] with which he has had long and intimate association. . . . His behavior in the face of the conflicts inherent in the choices imposed, his modes of dealing in thought and action with anxiety, the confidence with which he deals with himself and the field, and his quality of awareness of self and objective realities are factors that must enter into other life operations. . . . Some players are able to deal in play with only what they can control, whether it be impulses or the objective features of the field, and can maintain a tight, integrative hold throughout the plan of the ensuing play . . . [while others] are unassertive and passive in directing their play into a logical and integrated pattern, and seem to be more mastered than master of the deeper impulse systems which demand expression and restructure the play field."[15] Such differences appeared to be similar to differences in the ego-operations of "field-independence"[16] and "field-dependence" adults and suggested

15. H. A. Witkin, *Personality Through Perception* (New York: Harper, 1954).

16. Field-independence, as used by Witkin, refers to the ability to separate a perceived object from its context. Specifically in their experiments

the desirability of studying relationships between patterns of personality expressed in play and patterns of *perception*.

Children from the ages of eight to thirteen years took part in the experiment. The play situation included a low table which served as a stage on which the child was invited to "make a play" and set the stage for it. Toys available included a variety similar to the variety of housekeeping, town, animal, and war toys already described in this chapter, together with blocks, paper, clay, and water. Both form and content were studied, but the chief aspect of play analyzed intensively was the *"organizational pattern"* or "the executive functions of the individual's ego in utilizing the play opportunity, yet keeping the play bound into an organized, rationally directed form of expression in spite of conflict-laden and deep-lying impulses stirred up by the materials or by the permissive and protracted play situation."

A seven-point scale was devised for assessing the child's pattern of functioning in executing his play.

Scale 1 For sessions in which a child played with some freedom, dealt concretely with the play materials, maintained some conscious grasp of what he played and verbalized about it, and most important of all maintained a logical mastery over the play ideas despite any irrational forces that were activated. Lack of mastery expressed itself predominantly in loss of continuity of play ideas or forms, the eruption of irrelevant and irrational material into the play operations with incomplete rational assimilation of these intruding elements, or some form of play inhibition. The theme is brought to adequate closure in the play sessions rated *1*.

Scale 3 For sessions in which spatial and ideational organization is adequate in most of the play, though minor irrational elements are discernible which interfere in the beginning or are later interjected into the play, but are given some rationale before the play closes.

Scale 5 For sessions in which the main portion of the play produces a logical developed body of forms or concepts or both, in spite of the intrusion of markedly irrational elements, which are retained and not assimilated into the body of the play.

Scale 7 For sessions in which the play attempts, but is not able to

---

it is a *visual* field from which the perceived object, sometimes the individual's own body, must be separated.

maintain, any established idea or form organization because of continual intrusion of marked discontinuities or eruptive material.

This scale was aimed to judge only the organizational and not the adjustive aspects of the play, according to the authors, and we might add that these organizational criteria do not tell the whole story when we are interested in such criteria as creative potentialities. It is pointed out that some of the play with a tight logic of organizational pattern was achieved at considerable price in adjustive terms by virtue of the sharp and often deep constraints maintained by the player over his own impulses and the detachment and wariness with which he dealt with the field.

Summary examples of play sessions given each of the successive ratings on the scale are presented. This entire discussion and analysis should be read by anyone who is studying the play of latency-age children.

For children of preschool age it is important to remind ourselves that the "highest" degrees of organization and control have been seen in children who are highly identified with adult standards, in some cases precociously academic at the expense of emotional integration, or unusually form-conscious at the expense of motor and emotional freedom. High degrees of organization and control in Adele and Edna accompanied high social awareness and response to mores, manners, and smooth social interaction patterns. While we may agree that at the adult level a high degree of organization is desirable provided it includes integration of the individual's needs and feelings, we can still recognize the different processes by which this is achieved, the price that may be paid for premature emphasis upon it. Above all, we must recognize the wide variety of personality patterns that can find a place in our culture and the different constellations or patterns of areas of structure and areas of freedom that comprise these different personalities. Cora showed an unusual interest in classifying and organizing toys in systematic ways at the age of four; several years later she was showing a strong interest in science consistent with though not required by her sensitivity to sharp perception of size, color, and form in the preschool years. The same perceptual alertness, comparable to that of Joyce, might have been utilized, as Joyce's was, in poetic expression, and may still develop in this direction. We can surmise that what steered her perceptual clarity initially into scientific directions was the organizing, classifying method of using it—a form of mastery that may have offered special satisfactions to an only child in a family of several adults, including a scientific father.

Functional Aspects of Organizational Patterns

Let us look more closely at some of the different ways in which these preschool children used structures or organized patterns. Betsy began each of fourteen sessions over a period of sixteen months by making a square arrangement which contained four neatly set-up rooms. Conventional as it was, this was not done by any other child in school at the time and was uniquely characteristic of Betsy. It is important that in Betsy's arrangement each piece of furniture was exactly where it belonged from a conventional or functional point of view during this period; for example, the bathroom furniture was arranged as a bathroom would ordinarily be arranged. The bedroom furniture was set up to make a conventional bedroom, etc. This systematic functional use of toys within a definite pattern is in contrast to the nature of the arrangement made by Kene.

Kene repeatedly set up a long oblong in which pieces of furniture were just arranged without reference to the functions of arrangement in a conventional house. The kitchen sink might stand between the bathtub and parlor sofa. At times, the arrangement seemed to be dictated by color, but this was not consistent enough to be a basis for dependable generalization. In his case also, when his clear-cut pattern was finished, he went ahead to carry out exciting dramatic play of a very active sort.

In contrast to both of these, Joyce built a structure by a process of accretion, putting a sofa or the sink next to the cribs, some chairs next to them and adding on pieces, so that the effect at one stage was that of a rather carefully arranged, tightly packed storeroom. Around the edges, however, her arrangement characteristically became looser, and although there was no intrinsic or functional value in the spacing of the furniture as far as the experimenter could see, each piece was not placed so tightly against the next one but was set out in a somewhat freer fashion. It is our hypothesis that this compact center with a periphery of looseness and freedom has an important intrinsic value to Joyce in relation to other aspects of her response to the world.

Laurel repeatedly produced definite patterns which were an expression of one controlling idea: she wanted to find beds for every single doll to sleep in.

In contrast with all of these definite geometrical patterns, which were repeated over a period of months or even years, was the approach of another group of children who *never* made geometrical arrangements of this sort and whose play with toys varied more in structural quality from one session to another than did the play of the children who made the more clear-cut structures referred to above, although the over-all style and relation to the situation was consistent.

This second group of children carried patterns of manipulation of the toys along as a vehicle of fantasy. They usually started in with "functional play" with the toys without setting up any clear-cut arrangement at all. This occurred at all ages. In fact, one of the most striking examples was that of a bright two-year-old, the youngest child in the group. There seems little likelihood that the quality of functional play which kept organization secondary to the flow of fantasy was a result of chronological or mental age chiefly. Certain children developed in this direction as they grew older and freer in nursery school; other children began with a free type of play and developed toward more definite structures as they grew older. These differences are of basic importance, probably, for the understanding of personality organization and its relation to thinking and creative work. Their full meaning can be understood only by an analysis of relationships between the appearance of these characteristics and the appearance in the same child of other analogous aspects of behavior. We will discuss these relationships more fully at a later point in this chapter.

Karin and Dusty never built a definite geometrical pattern

like those described in the first group above. Toys were spread around them and without any particular attention to the more or less disorganized arrangement of the toys as a whole. The child carried on her fantasy with a pattern of toys intrinsic to the fantasy at that moment.

Leaving aside for the moment questions of interpretations of intermediate or unstable changing patterns, we find two convenient extremes of organization with Colin's consistently fluid, imaginative responses at one end, and Abigail's clear definite patterns, often dependent on knowing what you're supposed to do, at the other end. Unlike Kene, Betsy, Laurel, Abigail, Janet, and other children both older and younger than he was, Colin never "built a house." Toys were often little more than hooks on which to hang long strings of fantasy; sometimes they were material for active dramatic play.

Constructions produced by the child will be influenced by various factors in addition to creativity: the child's perception of reality and "feeling for reality" (wanting to reproduce it, versus wanting to make his own patterns); perceptual clarity and precision; organizing ability; ambition to make something impressive; the forms, structures, and character of design in his environment generally and his home specifically; his relation to space and tendency to express his creativity in spatial terms (in addition to or instead of in terms of dramatic plots or themes).

In distinction from the space structures discussed so far we can note the implicit structure of the process or of the thought sequences in the child's play; play sequences of some children are fluid, while the play of others is tightly knit, and still other children display loose sequences with logical relationships within each sequence although the connection between sequences may seem tenuous. Firm space structures may accompany either firm thought structure or loose sequences but are not likely to appear in connection with extremely disorganized or fluid thought except as expressions of a tense effort at control.

Structures with Blocks

Certain aspects of structure appear more clearly when we inspect the children's constructions with blocks. We have not experimented with blocks alone, but we include some blocks with the Miniature Life Toys, and their use is closely related to the use of other expressive materials.

We cannot necessarily assume that the use of blocks or other relatively abstract forms to express such ideas and feelings is of necessity more distant because it appears more abstract to us; we saw instances of children whose next step after this form of expression was to move to direct verbal expression of ideas. Rather it is the child who has a talent for space organization and clear form perception, or who has identified with a parent who expresses himself this way—as in architecture or carpentry— or who for some other reason has found strong satisfaction in this means of expression, who uses it by preference, just as a musician or an artist chooses tone or color as his medium.

When children play with blocks their constructions may be dominated primarily by relatively autistic or relatively objective approaches, or a combination of these. Within the group of autistic or highly projective approaches we include the structures which are a reflection of the child's own body-image; those which serve, almost as directly as fingerpainting, to give an imprint or projection of the child's patterns of motor co-ordination; those which are a report of the child's wishes or hopes, or of his anxieties or special concerns; those which serve as a safe abstract representation of what he dare not or cannot represent concretely. Among the structures considered "relatively objective" in approach, we include the garage, farms, houses and stores which approximate the proportions of real-life buildings. Persistent interest in one structure, or idiosyncratic use of it, may point to personal concerns just as directly as do the nonrepresentational structures. Let us illustrate these differences.

Karin built a solid structure, totally different from those built by other children. Karin's building is like herself. Cecily's airy loose building is in turn more like Cecily.

Closely related to this type of projection of the child's own body-image is the type of building we find resulting from loose casual motor co-ordinations, as compared with the precise delicate manipulations of Joel and Philip.

Neither sheer body-image nor motor co-ordination alone, however, quite explain Philip's preference for curved blocks, which he used more consistently than any other child, just as he used coy, curved-posture approaches to adults. Sharp edges apparently did not belong to him, either in behavior or block-building.

Amy's tall building, to which she points with evident pride, seems to have wishful implications for her, the littlest member of a household of nine. Insecure children not uncommonly build structures which dramatize the experience of being shut in, imprisoned, of having to stick to a narrow track. Children who have moved from one place to another, or have lived in different families, may project a two-level life space, the levels being more or less closely bound together.

Occasionally a child will make a series of constructions which virtually tells us his life story. This happened in the case of Nelson, and his story is virtually an epitome of the essential experience of many three-year-olds in our culture.

First he put a car into a small cupboard on the floor, placing five large blocks in front, so piled as to make an exaggerated barrier. "I close the door; it won't come out." Then he arranged four of the longest blocks perpendicularly with a small space between each block and the next. He then removed the car and attempted to push it between the tall blocks, and when he could not do so at first, pushed ahead, making the blocks fall down. Next he leaned the long blocks against the wall in a semi-reclining position and the little car rode over them (they took it lying down, as it were). Following this, the long blocks were laid on the floor to make a track for the little car to go on. Since the car was a little wider than the blocks, one width would not quite carry it without falling to one side, so an extra width of track was added. This procedure was accompanied with expressions of the greatest satisfaction and the remark, "I'm making a road . . . *myself*." He then picked up a block, rejected it, saying, "That's no good," picked up another and a second to put at the front of the track, and pushed the car the whole length of the track, after adding small ramps to the ends as indicated.

Up to this point, it looks as if he had said, "The little boy [car] was constrained behind large barriers. He got free and

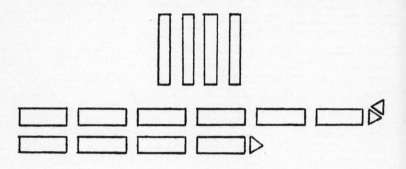

aggressively knocked down the grownups [tall blocks]. This released his own productive powers so that he was then able to build constructively a road for himself." This was the beginning of a longer sequence of activity.

It is worth noting that his behavior at the beginning of the year was that of a shy day-dreamy boy out of touch with people and objects, and that he early showed some concern about aggressive retaliation to grownups and children. The day after this block-sequence, he dramatized a similar sequence of experience-digests. He played for some time on an oral basis, sucking, drinking, then holding scissors in his mouth. This was followed by vigorous aggression against an assistant teacher, hitting her with a broom, and throwing the glass stoppers of the bottles he had been sucking earlier at her. Following this he accepted an invitation to play, threw teddy-bears with good coordination and participated at a good level for his age. This sequence, oral preoccupation, to aggression against authority, to constructive participation, seems to be related to the block-building sequence, if we see the constraint and dependence of infancy and early childhood as two aspects of the same experience.

The block-building in itself, without other data from the play session and from the life of a child cannot usually give answers to basic questions about the child. But it can pose questions; and a consideration of similarities and differences, sequences, and comparisons with the other activities of the child may give answers to questions. Thus if a child builds a tall or squat building, we cannot say, by looking at the building and knowing nothing else, that this is a tall child, or that this child has a tall brother, or is the youngest, or would like to be tall. If the child is short and builds tall, it is likely to be a wish, and if he is tall and builds tall, it is likely to be a projection of his body-image.

If the child is building in a group it is, of course, important to know who is copying whom, so that we can know whose is the projection and whose is the experiment.

Control, Organization, and Intellectual Functioning

Control, organization, and construction are sometimes considered synonymous terms, but need to be looked at separately. Normative studies of children's Rorschachs, by L. B. Ames at the Gesell Institute,[17] and by Jean Macfarlane and her colleagues at the Institute of Child Welfare Research at Berkeley, and elsewhere,[18] find periods of change from introversion to extroversion in the same child, and periods of constriction at the age of twelve or thirteen in different groups of children. This suggests that at times the developmental stage dominates the child's response to such a degree that individual differences are diminished —the child appears to be more like others of his age than like himself a couple of years before. We find similar types of response characteristic of developmental stages in the response of young children to the Miniature Life Toys: "What's this?" is fairly typical for two- to three-year-olds, while the acting out of conflicts via planes, cars, or animals is more frequent in four-

17. Louise Bates Ames and others, *Child Rorschach Responses* (New York: Paul B. Hoeber, Inc., 1952).
18. "Study of Personality Development," in R. G. Barker, J. S. Kounin and H. F. Wright, *Child Behavior and Development* (New York: McGraw-Hill, 1943).

year-olds. At the same time, individual differences and sub-cultural differences are so important that an elaborate normative check-list could be very misleading when applied to subculture groups different from the one used as a basis for the check-list, and when applied to children of grossly different I.Q.'s, sensitivities, or family experience. Consequently it is important to compare any child with himself at successive times and with others of his own subculture in order to evaluate the process set down in the play record.

A high degree of precision in organization often occurs in bright children with high awareness of form and skill in translating this into clear patterns with the toys, but casual structures do not imply the opposite. Colin, Karin, Joyce and other children with I.Q.'s of 135 to 150 did not create the precise forms characteristic of Betsy, but as we have noted, used the toys to project their fantasy directly in action. While they had a high degree of perceptual clarity, the production of forms as forms was not of interest to them. Consequently, we must be wary of tendencies in certain psychological circles to equate the degree of organization with ego-strength, form-perception, or capacity for control on the one hand, or with excessive compulsiveness or rigid defenses on the other hand. The implications of different kinds of integration of impulse and control, as illustrated by the production of an architectural structure, versus the production of a drama, cannot be dealt with by putting these on a rating scale. The builders of Chartres reveal one type of integration and ego-capacity, the creator of *Hamlet* another. What we need to watch for is this: in what terms *can* the child give form to his feelings and communicate them? And with what results for his own development?

EXPRESSIVE PATTERNS

A full stenographic record should provide not only an account of what the child does with the toys and the fantasy which is carried along, but incidental aspects of expressive behavior, voice patterns, verbal expressions, and body movements and the fantasy context of changes in these.

It is important to note body parts that are tense in contrast to those that are relaxed; variations in posture and flexibility or rigidity of posture, economy versus extravagance of movement as well as smoothness or tenseness of coordination; relation to space (centripetal and persistently centered versus centrifugal all-over exploration). Manipulation and other movements may be delicately controlled or clumsy, and efficient or inefficient. Integration may appear in wholeness or orientation—posture, leg-movement, hand-movement, eye-movements all co-ordinated versus segmental or conflicting responses in different body parts. Facial expressions may be mobile or sluggish, and varied through a wide or narrow range, with different degrees of obviousness or subtlety. Dusty's records repeatedly included comments on her grunting, sighs of apparent satisfaction, heavy breathing through her mouth, humming, singing to herself, and on her appearance of complete muscular relaxation and freedom from bodily tensions. She always seemed to be completely and easily herself, deeply centered in her activity, oblivious to outside distractions. Carla and Karin also sighed with deep contentment and usually seemed absorbed, unexcited, and free from tension.

When a situation was changed somewhat and the experimenter sat down on the floor without pad and pencil instead of taking her usual place in a chair nearby with a pad and pencil, Karin seemed less at ease than usual. (A variety of nonadaptive movements, fiddling with the back of her collar, slapping her hands, handling her skirt and pants, suggested embarrassment or possible bladder tension.) However, after the experimenter assumed her usual position with a pad and pencil, Karin again began a slow, quiet building, entirely directed to the toys, and her deep breathing against suggested her usual deeply centered activity.

Joel seemed to have a more superficial relation to the toys. His gestures and movements instead of being slow and almost integrated with the toys were dramatic, impulsive, and sudden at times.

Wide sweeping gestures throughout the hour, covering a fairly wide area, were typical of some children in their activity with the toys, in contrast to others who, like Carla, sat solidly on the floor keeping the toys within reach and not moving around.

While jerky and careless or bumptious movements in contrast to delicate and careful ones, if consistent from one situation to other different ones, tell us something about the co-ordination and attitude of the child, they also tell us something about the attitude of the child to these particular toys when behavior varies from one situation to another. Whether the Miniature Life Toys are something to exploit, something to have fun with, something to love, possess, or revere in contrast to dough or cold cream is important to know in evaluating the child's use of the toys.

Individual children handle the toys quite differently in carrying out their dramatic play. Some children move them across the floor like puppets, while others do not attempt to represent walking, standing, active behavior of the dolls, but merely do things to them by putting them to bed, giving them a ride on a boat or a horse, and the like. The puppet-like handling probably indicates a more sophisticated attitude of a child who is aware of creating a "play" and may be more common in children who watch television shows a great deal. In fact, that is one of the first indices I have observed in conscious theatrical constructing of the play situation with toys. Doing things to the toys goes along with more naïve attitudes where play is spontaneous and unconscious of theater.

Verbal Expression

Records of verbalized fantasy and of conversation with the experimenter give long sequences of two-, three- and four-year-old verbal and vocal behavior. Important extremes that suggest lines of analysis are apparent when we compare the fantasy of a child like Karin whose thinking is consistently coherent and logical in its sequences with that of Camille whose thinking at times seemed jumpy, incoherent, and followed sequences which had little clear relation to one another. We can also distinguish major clues for analysis in the persistent, central idea shown by Laurel, the handful of major ideas frequently repeated by Betsy, in contrast to the fluid and whimsical thinking of Colin. The hypothesis that the quality of thought sequences has an intrinsic relation to personality structure gains weight from an analysis of patterns discerned in other aspects of the child's behavior and manipulation of the world. Spontaneous verbal expressions, directly expressive of qualities of feeling, appeared in the records of Colin, Laurel, and others, in contrast to the adult-like crystallization of verbal structure characteristic of Abigail. These verbal expressions seem to be directly analogous to voice qualities. Fresh, original perceptions of experience and freedom of motor and emotional response, with a complete absence of tight or arbitrary organization of structure, were also characteristic of Colin, while Abigail for a long period showed much stereotypy of language, motor behavior, and structures.

Voice patterns made on phonograph records gave clear evidence of the objective difference between the wide range of tones and fluid movement within the range characteristic of certain children in contrast to the limited range characteristic of others. Voices are equally varied from Colin's rangy inflections and expressive spontaneous noises, Jay's big-boy explosions and Bronx cheers, or Camille's subtle expressiveness to Abigail's flat adult stepwise inflections. We are not surprised to find Colin inventing syllables and words to express his moods and meanings, while Abigail invariably uses conventional terms.

In discussing the child's expressive behavior, we have already referred to aspects of bodily movement, voice quality, and verbal patterns which may be clues to a child's feeling. When the child is actively engaged in fantasy it is particularly important to observe the rapidity of verbal comment, its coherence, inclusion or exclusion of the experimenter, loud dramatic talking as contrasted with whispering. Some children maintain a fantasy orientation without interruption for a long period, while others alternate clearly between fantasy and reality level; shifts may be reflected in different tones of voice or tempo or rhythm.

These expressive patterns are related in a parallel or complementary way to the patterns of handling the toys which were described earlier, to the initial attitudes and action described in the opening pages of this chapter, and to characteristics of fantasy to be discussed shortly. Observation of each helps to clarify the others.

RELATION TO ADULT IN THE EXPERIMENT

The child's feelings about the adult experimenter profoundly affect his use of the play session, and in common with any other situation, from that of intelligence tests to a medical examination or even a casual conversation between an adult and a child, a play session in which an adult is alone with the child for any length of time provides an opportunity to observe the child's relation to the adult. This may be approached in terms of several foci, those of authority and affection being essential roots of feeling toward adults. We find Abigail asking permission to dump out some toys, asking the adult to help her find what she wants, looking for patterns from the adult, acquiescing with and even echoing adult authority. Patsy, by contrast, asserts herself or questions explicitly and persists in her demands upon the adult authority with good-natured defiance, assuming she can have her own way. Karin and Dusty responsively enjoy the physical contact of holding an adult's hand or even being carried, although they do not reflect the delicious pleasure which Betsy seems to have in being actively cuddled by an adult. Claudia also enjoys physical contact of a cuddling sort, but expects a lot of playful mauling.

Colin and Laurel never show the clear-cut awareness of authority illustrated by Abigail and Patsy, but both have a friendly, sharing, social attitude expecting give and take. Camille is communicative and responsive but in an ambivalent way, turning her back on the adult during a part of her fantasy, often asking provocative questions, and reflecting a complicated form of authority-love relation with adults.

The extent to which behavior of this sort is characteristic of a child in the sense that it appears consistently, could be judged by a comparison of the child's behavior in this situation with behavior with other grownups in other situations, especially adults of the opposite sex, as well as comparison of the child's behavior with the same adult on different occasions, such as routine or "more structured" situations. Records of relations to adults in nursery school, and to other experimenters, especially Eugene Lerner, are of chief importance.

"Variable" behavior need not be inconsistent, of course; for instance, Calvin was extremely reserved and unable to confide in or expose fantasy with the experimenter or any other adults in nursery school, except his teacher on certain rare occasions; yet neighbors reported him a rollicking boy at home with his mother, gay and conversational. In such instances, the response to the adult is submerged in his feeling about the total new situation in which he found himself in nursery school. In still other cases which will be noted later in more detail, a child may show a differentiated reaction to different adults rooted in the feeling that "you don't talk about" certain things to strange adults as you do at home; or conversely, that you *can* talk about things here you wouldn't dare to discuss at home. Such differentiation must be seen in relation to what the adults at home and at school mean to him.

These observations of the quality of the child's relation with the adult are important to relate to patterns of structure which often reflect how the child has interiorized adult control, and to fantasy which may describe in representative or symbolic form the child's emotional experience with adults.

If we try to sort out the attitudes toward adults reflected in the child's expressive patterns, manipulation of the adult dolls, and attitude toward the experimenter, we may summarize.

1. Child complies with adult requests or what he thinks adult expects of him; obedient, submissive.

2. Child imitates accurately adult manner, mores, speech, habits; is consciously meeting adult expectations.

3. Child unconsciously identifies with adult and as if by second nature echoes adult inflections, vocabulary, which have often become a vehicle for self-expression.

4. Child resists, protects himself from adult, handles adult with techniques of his own.

5. Child uses his childishness, humor, coyness, charm to stimulate adult response of tenderness.

6. Child follows own ideas, impulses independently of adult;

does not bait, make demands on, handle adult; has own expressive patterns.

FANTASY

It goes without saying that even such a varied collection of toys as the first one we used would not be sufficiently inclusive to give an opportunity for all the possible fantasy subjects important to children of this age. Many children, especially girls, from two to four years old are chiefly interested in family life and activities going on in the company of parents outside as well as inside the house and play with the dolls and housekeeping materials, animals, and vehicles. However, four-year-old boys who thought of themselves as big boys were less interested in these toys and needed bigger boats, cars, soldiers, or firemen, and toys of definitely masculine symbolic value to work out their creative ideas. An interest in these toys sometimes reflects a satisfactory solution of family problems, but other children transfer conflicts to the vehicles, animals, or persons of the larger world.

We find subculture variations here; boys who see more of their fathers, as in small towns where fathers get to work in two or three minutes from home, may identify themselves as male earlier than urban boys who see little of their fathers except on Sundays. Such differences in time together, range of shared activities, etc., affect the whole psychosexual development of the child, as do sleeping arrangements, observation of sexual activity in animals, etc. In general, urban and suburban children reflect an interest in the world outside of home at three and one-half to five years of age, and may start with or confine their play to toys connected with activities in the big world.

Types of fantasy which appeared in the records of these children may be loosely divided in a variety of ways.

1. Those directly representative of reality situations, in contrast to those which are indirect or symbolic; although it is by no means always possible to draw a sharp line between the two, since purely representative fantasy may often be carried out because of special underlying symbolic value to the child.

2. Those concerned with family relationships and attendant

problems of authority, love, competition, and so on, in contrast to those concerned with physical experiences such as sailing in a boat, riding in a car.

3. Those which deal with experience at a tempo and level of intensity closely analogous to that probably experienced by the child in contrast to those which deal with experience at a bizarre level of exaggerated intensity.

These differences point to different levels or patterns of emotional response.

The direct representation of family life was a very familiar theme. Often the first things that a child would take out were a baby, together with a maid or a mother, or both. Then he put the baby to bed. Going to bed, eating supper, going to the toilet, being spanked, going on a boat or in a car, sex differences at the level of the differences between the way boys and girls urinate, were predominant themes repeated in many different children's records.

In addition to these illustrations, moving from one house to another, putting lots of people to bed, garage play, were items of experience appearing in the children's play with the toys. Any one of these common fantasy subjects, however, might become a special focus for an individual child and be elaborated in an individual way, occurring more persistently or with more content or more intense affect than was usual with other children. Individual ways of elaborating fantasy about common subjects were apt to be more charged with emotion and evidently reflect family experience particularly dramatic to the individual child; dramatic experience usually meant experience colored by an adult relationship or conflict with adults.

The child's world projected through the fantasies recorded with this method is a world of objects and relations familiar to the grownup, but seen in a new light; his amazement at the violent bustle which moving day with the Seven Santini Brothers brings to a usually ordered household, as rooms full of furniture are whooshed out of one door and into another; his puzzlement as to just where he belongs in the pattern of things when a new baby upsets the comfortable security of Mommie-takes-care-of-me and Daddy-goes-to-work; his struggle with grownups who won't answer his reasonable calls in the night when he wants to go to the toilet; and who even more unreasonably want to sleep later than he does in the morning. All these feelings are reflected in a mirror which shows how the child feels about these everyday and special wants that grownups dismiss casually or complain about unthinkingly.

Symbolic play was also concerned with experiences of intense emotional value to the child and was often centered about sex or authority problems. An outstandingly well and happy child, Candice, symbolically dramatized her own conflict between being bad and good by utilizing one doll to be the bad girl and one doll to be the good girl. Alec went through a sequence of symbolic activities suggestive of sex preoccupation preceding an explicit period of questions and dramatic play concerned with sex and punishment.

Another point of view concerns the extent to which the fantasy keeps within bounds dictated by the nature of the material available and the space in which the child is playing. Jeremy, for instance, did not adapt materials to functions other than those for which they were made, but let his fantasy accept the relations set by the materials: "This dolly's sleeping in this bed. This one can't sleep coz there's no bed. . . . He can't fall out, his feet might get caught in there." (The doll was actually a little long and its feet stuck out between the bars of the crib.) In contrast to this type of adaptation to the material, Joyce used almost every object for almost any purpose—a sink, a washbowl, a chair or almost anything handy was used for her doll to sleep on. Here again, as in the cases of all the differences in approach described so far, the child's pattern does not seem to be related to intelligence levels so much as an attitude or orientation toward things outside himself, and the character of perception. There are other indications that for Joyce things were sometimes seen in more abstract terms. The essential thing about sleeping was thus the horizontal position; the essential thing about a bed, the horizontal support which could be used to sleep on. From the abstract point of view this approach was simple and logical, although it produced bizarre results from a conventionally realistic point of view.

Self-image

Fantasy appearing in play with Miniature Life Toys of children from two to four may be expected to throw further light on the child's image of himself and his role, his relation to adults and to the routines they impose. It is not possible here to illustrate at length the varieties of self-image and attitude to adults that we find in the children's fantasies. Certain outstanding patterns will be recognized by everyone who uses material like this with young children.

1. S (subject) represents the child (doll) as compliantly participating in adult-directed routine; or as defiantly opposing it, protesting, refusing. In any case the child envisages himself as vis-à-vis the adult; it is hard for him to separate himeslf from the milieu of the adult.

2. S represents the doll as in a world of his own; ignores references to adult-directed routine; the child goes places, decides things, as if there were no grownups, or as if he had the autonomy of a grownup.

This type of distinction may point to the degree to which the child has sold out to the grownups and envisages himself as dependent. Other clues to the child's self-image come from such remarks as: "She has blonde hair like me"; "I screech when mother washes my hair"; "Sometimes I'm naughty."

This age period is the time during which clear-cut masculine and feminine roles are being developed. At two, boys and girls are hardly distinguishable in their play with Miniature Life Toys. At four, some boys appear to have interests largely dominated by the problem of achieving a masculine role; they definitely reject the housekeeping series entirely and want to play only with soldiers, racing cars and other toys of aggressive value. At four, girls are apt to play with the dolls with a new maternal quality and identification with being a mother. The four-year-old boy who rejects housekeeping toys does not verbalize his sense of his role by asserting "I'm not a sissy." He *dramatizes* it by his belligerent actions, aggressive talk, his rejection of "little things" and "girl" things. The role of "big boy," of aggressor, defender, a "guy who can shoot those bears dead" is asserted with naïve intensity at this age by the same boy who will merely kick his challenger in the shin at the age of eight or nine.

The child's image of himself appears not only in his representation of the child of his fantasy as naughty, good, independent of adults, escaping, paying back, achieving masculinity, but in his relation to the toys, as a child who can *do* things, who can give or take or have adventures, make things happen, have fun, get a reaction from grownups, get the grownups to play with him.

A basic distinction must be made between the self-image of the relatively self-conscious child who patently sees himself as loved and lovable (Joyce and Philip) or as superior ("I am Bob Important") or as dumb; and the unself-conscious child (Dusty at three years) who goes ahead pursuing her own ends without obvious self-awareness. In the Miniature Life Toy situation such a child will manipulate the toys to the completion of his own ideas without any of the coy appeals of Joyce, Philip, or Colin, or the imperious commands of Betsy.

Role and Structure of Fantasy

Content-analysis of fantasy usually needs to be supplemented by analysis of the role and structure of fantasy. With Karin a free dramatic play was completely shared with a grownup, as if the child was telling the grownup something through her play which she could not tell in another way. The coherence of the fantasy may have been functionally related to this communicative quality. Camille, by contrast, talked or whispered almost inaudibly with jumps or gaps in her thought; she was reserved in her communication in spite of the great amount of verbalization. Jeremy did not communicate at all while he was piling a dozen things on top of a doll and a crib, but was willing to reply to a question at the end by explaining that the doll was being locked up because it had been so bad! In other words, the activity expressive of the fantasy seemed to be a satisfaction of his own need to work out the idea rather than any desire to communicate, although he was willing to tell about his product finally. It is interesting that when a man familiar to Jeremy, but not present during the play with the crib, came in to question him about it, Jeremy was evasive and did not explain.

The use of definite symbolic activities such as breaking off the projected point of a pencil, rattling his foot around in a wastebasket preceding explicit elaboration of sex and discipline conflicts, suggests both a sequence of development of the ideas in Alec's mind due to possible repression and also a sequence in his security regarding communication with the adult.

Griffiths has described at length many examples of ways in which children use fantasy to solve problems which are important to them.[19] Many of the children in our present group also did this. For instance, Karin's repeated dramatic plays, centering about her relation with her father, mother, and baby sister, clearly appeared to be the objectification of a process of clarifying her own relations with them. Alec and Cecily also seemed to be "working through" problems in terms of dramatic activity.

In Betsy's case, dramatic exaggeration heightened the excitement but did not appear to be connected ordinarily with any problem-solving activities.

Emotional overflow may accompany a type of fantasy which shows less internal coherence than the problem-solving fantasy of Karin, Alec, and Cecily. This type seems unintegrated to external opportunities and values.

Some of Camille's fantasy in which authoritative females were killed off seems to have a value of direct catharsis or satisfaction of retaliative wishes rather than problem-solving value, in the sense of achieving the clarity which we can see in Karin's fantasy. The projective satisfaction of wishes also appears in Betsy's reversal of her relation with her older brother in a play where the girl was older and the boy was younger, and also in Karin's restoration of her doll-self to her mother's bedside.

Another aspect of the structure of fantasy involves the distinction between the degrees of literalness or symbolic remoteness of the drama in relation to the real-life situation in which

---

19. Ruth Griffiths, *A Study of Imagination in Early Childhood and Its Function in Mental Development* (London: Kegan Paul, Trench Trubner and Co., Ltd., 1935).

it is rooted. We shall discuss separately some of the problems involved in interpretation of symbolic meaning of material to the child. At this point, we may state the hypothesis that greater remoteness or depth or complexity of symbolism (in contrast to literal projection) may go along either with greater anxiety or with a larger degree of imagination. The more ease and assurance the child has in relation to adults, the more likely he seems to be to set out his needs and feelings in simple undisguised terms. When the child is older, the culture itself may provide symbolic patterns which express more than playful fantasy. Perhaps these symbolic patterns serve effectively the purpose of disguise; they are commonly misunderstood.

INTERPRETATION OF SYMBOLS

In children of two to five years we find a variety of sources of symbolization, many of which can be grouped under the general heading of association by similarity, or better, substitution via similarity.

1. By *similarity of form one object stands for another:* a bassinet or a bathtub may be used as a boat if you don't have a boat, or a crib with a cover on it may represent an abdomen or uterus with a baby inside.

2. By *similarity of form or behavior combined with affect:* one object stands for another when the latter is surrounded with taboos or anxiety from other sources: a snake may stand for a penis, or a bull stand for threatening father, or a tiger for the child's own frightening aggressive impulses.

3. By *similarity of function, orientation, or direction:* an object stands for something which may be beyond the scope of realistic representation: a track may express the authoritative pressure to go in a certain direction as contrasted with a fence which may express limits, keeping impulses under control; or a fire engine may express uninhibited impulse since it does not have to stop at red lights, while by contrast a locomotive, like a father, stays on the tracks.

But symbolization may proceed by part-whole, contiguity, or other relationships. A part may stand for a whole: one soldier for an army; or a whole may stand for a part, as when the boy baby stands for his penis; or a basket stands for its contents. A thing may stand for its neighbor or a more remote neighbor several steps away, or a thing may stand for something different but with a similar or the same name.

Experiences may be symbolized by the persons or structures by which they are implemented: for instance, *experiences of control* may be symbolized by *limiting persons* or by *limiting or directive structures* such as tracks, fences, platforms, cribs, play-pens, cages, etc.

Impulses and feelings may be symbolized by creatures free to express such impulses: a monkey may represent mischievous activity of a relatively non-aggressive sort; animals in general may represent spontaneous activity; tigers, alligators, or lions may represent aggressive or hostile destructive impulses.

Space patterns as well as objects may be symbolic; they may be used to represent concepts of the body, as with Dorothy, who arranged little mice as babies within a block representation of an abdomen or uterus; or more abstractly, as Erikson has illustrated, vertical phallic structures may be characteristic of boys while round womb-like structures may be more characteristic of girls.[20] Mere differences in size of anything—blocks, animals, or unidentified dolls—may represent differences between parents and children.

The same object may be used in different ways symbolically by different children, or even by the same child at different times.

A bed can be realistically a bed, even specifically, a child's bed for the child, an adult bed for the adult. Here the microcosm built with the tiny toys simply mirrors the real world.

Or a piece of plain wood can stand for a bed, and the play with this may be as realistic as the play in the first instance. A part equals the whole, and all that is needed is the horizontal something for somebody to lie down on.

Or beds associated with activities, e.g., story-times and cuddling experiences, may be assembled cozily together, not primarily to provide a setting for sleep, but to reintegrate the cozy feelings; or a bed may be used with a baby on the bottom and

20. Erik H. Erikson, *op. cit.*

may be piled high with toys to keep the baby in, because he was bad. In these instances the activity associated with objects relives an activity associated with the real objects, but the feeling is the core of the experience, not the procedure.

Or a bed may be used as a representation of an abdomen which holds baby, food, and dirt or excreta. In this case, the symbol is arrived at by similarity, using the available object to substitute for the somewhat similar inaccessible one.

The process of substitution of the similar "X" for the fantasied "A" may follow one of these lines.

A similar shape may be a substitute for the inaccessible or avoided shape.

An object with similar texture or other sensory quality may substitute for the unavailable object (soft mouse or kitten for lovable baby, or soft lovable self).

An object with similar activity patterns (fast, slow, violent, etc.) may be substituted for the intangible impulse or activity (aggressive animal for own aggressive impulse).

But also a means may be substituted for a result; an aborted action may be substituted for the completed (generally destructive) one or a mere gesture toward an object may symbolize the action which is not even begun.

At this age level especially, symbols are not rigid; the same feeling or idea may be symbolically expressed in different ways; the same object may have different meanings in different contexts (Colin's cat was an object of tenderness in certain settings, a symbol of a terrible thing that eats little things in other contexts). Thus it is *always necessary to evaluate the symbol in the specific context of the child's action, sequence of play, behavior, expressive pattern, interpersonal relation with the experimenter, in this play situation and experience in his real life situation.* Rigid symbol interpretations will lead to gross errors.

The physiognomic, poetic, animistic thinking described by Werner,[21] Piaget,[22] and others is generally based on analogies. Thinking by analogy is not identical to classic "primary process"

21. Heinz Werner, *Psychology of Mental Development,* Revised Edition (Chicago: Follett, 1948).
22. Jean Piaget, *The Language and Thought of the Child* (New York: Humanities Press, 1952).

origins of symbolization, in which the association is via simultaneity of experience, often internal and bodily, rather than perceived similarity, or is dominated by strong drives; the essential nature of primary process thinking is its *lack of differentiation,* with its resulting lack of criticism or discrimination, and the safety from reality-threat produced thereby. Safety may also be achieved by removing the symbol from the object it refers to, by reducing the degree of similarity, or by increasing the time or space distance of the context of the symbol. Thus legends of past heroes serve normal people well as a catharsis for feelings of rebellion without exposing the hearer or his neighbor to an uncomfortable "Who, me?" feeling.

The more culturally widespread and clichéd the symbol, the less we can be sure of its affective intensity for the individual, although an idiosyncratic situation is always involved; where symbols are original they emerge from the individual and personal experience of the child past or present.

It is impossible to have the experience of playing with hundreds of small children with Miniature Life Toy material without feeling considerable awe for the creative and integrative capacities of these young minds. Like poets, they often distill what have been repeated sequences of life, experienced in large segments, into the simplest patterns which could convey these sequences. Arnheim refers to the tendency to reduce experience to its basic forms as underlying art,[23] and we find this tendency in many children. Many children have a natural, untaught capacity for defining the essence of an experience succinctly. The capacity for abstraction which appears also in the child's natural tendency to draw a head in terms of its essential roundness, ignoring details, is one basic factor in the formation of symbols at the preschool level. Before the age of television and radio, when children under five were relatively free from exposure to stereotyped or clichéd visual presentations, these spontaneous, unique symbolic expressions of the design of life as the child experienced it were common. I cannot tell whether this will be true in the television age, when even two-year-olds clamor, "T-V on, Mom-

---

23. Rudolf Arnheim, *Art and Visual Perception* (Berkeley: University of California Press, 1954).

mie." It seems likely that the experiencing process will be weighted with stereotyped visual patterns mingled with, or superimposed upon, the kinaesthetically and tactually richer experience of typical preschool explorations of life.

In any case, some stereotyping takes place through the necessary standardizations of language, and the extension of language through story and picture books, and comics which children from the age of four or five now drink up. Beyond the age of five, emotional and spatial experience is heavily weighted for some children by such cultural fantasies, although some children do not reflect them in their play.[24]

Although we cannot report much direct evidence of repressed contents which symbolically emerge, it is entirely probable that such contents, gradually pushed further and further away from awareness, become in the full sense unconscious, as they would be, for example, were any of these children studied psychoanalytically as adults at the age of thirty. At the age of two to four, anxiety over weaning or toilet-training *may* have been repressed in a culture where these are foci of adult-child tension; conflicts over siblings, sex differences, punishment are often still open in a subculture where sibling rivalry, sex curiosity, anger are tolerated by parents. When this is the case we may, however, find differences between children who express their feelings as Alec did, with primitive directness, and those who express feelings only in socially approved terms. Children like Karin and Dusty who have had an unusually permissive background are more apt to be free from ambivalence and have less tendency to hide activities or words.

Instead of trying to drive all the symbolic play in the direction of stock symbolisms we find that a fresh approach to symbolism is needed. The pattern which is projected symbolically rather than in simple realistic terms is apt to be one about which there is conflict. In Western culture, where sex taboos have been the tradition, it is quite true that conflict between the child's impulses and adult authority has often centered about sex curiosity

---

24. Note the wide range of themes and degrees of utilization of cultural standardizations in the play sessions of the seven-year-olds which were reported in Biber, Murphy, Woodcock and Black, *Life and Ways of the Seven-to-Eight Year Old* (New York: Basic Books, 1952).

or exploration. In American middle-class suburban culture, where many parents have accepted the child's need to learn about sex casually, this may *not* be the focus of conflict or the source of symbolic projection, although we still find it in more conservative or Puritan groups. Correct interpretation of child symbolism demands both a large knowledge of unique patterns of individual personality and also an accurate understanding of the specific subculture in which the child is growing up; our data suggest that new symbolic values growing from specific patterns, family constellation and authority, pressures of parents, may be most important for many children. Bodily constriction and repression of spontaneous activity, confinement (in cribs or playpens which represent "cages" to children) isolation, deprivation of affection, bossing, coercion, are repeated sources of symbolic play among these children, but would not appear among children who had never been isolated, constrained, confined in "cages" or handled "objectively" to the same extent.

DYNAMICS OF PLAY SEQUENCES
IN TOTAL SESSION

We have discussed the need to study the interrelations of content, fantasy, structure, expressive patterns, and behavior during a play session. It is especially important to watch the relation between behavior during periods of free-flowing activity and behavior at punctuation points.

Play disruption, a term used by Erikson[25] to indicate the point at which a child stops his play, leaves the room, or abruptly changes the theme of the play, occurs when conflict or anxiety reaches a high point. It is to be distinguished from milder interruption due to needs that may appear during the course of an hour's play session (needing to urinate, or get a drink of water, or change one's body position after playing for a considerable length of time), and also from shifts which commonly occur after satiation of either exploratory drives or fantasy with one

---

25. Erik H. Erikson, "Studies in the Interpretation of Play: I. Clinical Observations of Play Disruption in Young Children," *Genet. Psychol. Monog.,* XXII (1940), 557-671.

group of toys or ideas. Inability to interrupt a play sequence to satisfy needs, or to shift from one group of toys to another requires interpretation: Is the child consistently rigid, or inhibited, or merely shy in a new situation? Play disruption from other than practical reasons is typically accompanied by a sharp upsurge of anxiety arising from the activation of a more or less acute conflict. The inability to shift or to interrupt play to satisfy bodily needs may be an expression of insecurity in the immediate play situation itself.

Points of shift in ego-state or level of functioning as discussed by Ekstein and Wallerstein[26] and points of climax, fulfillment, or release, also show us what the experience means to the child. Very similar content and constructions may lead to resolution of a problem with one child, or a crescendo of tension with another. The same or similar behavior may accompany very different sorts of content: one quiet child may be merely responding to the contagion of the tester's passive relaxed attitude and play out serene or matter-of-fact events of home life, while another quiet child may be constantly inhibited everywhere he goes, and play out problems which are connected with his sense of constriction.

In evaluating any play session we not only look at relationships, whether parallel or contradictory, between the different spheres of activity and expression, but we also consider the overall pattern and design of the session. Where did it begin emotionally and where did it end? What recurrent themes appeared in similar form, and what implicit relationships appear beneath superficially disparate fantasies, constructions, and behavior? What evidences are there that a significant theme is first hinted in fantasy, and finally resolved in action or vice versa? This total analysis of symphonic structure of the play session will lead to conclusions about the role of fantasy in the emotional economy of the child, and the areas which the child can confidently trust to verbal communication, or to action.

---

26. Rudolf Ekstein and Judith Wallerstein, "Observations on the Psychology of Borderline and Psychotic Children" in *The Psychoanalytic Study of the Child*, Vol. IX (New York: International Universities Press, 1954).

EGO FUNCTIONS

Since social aspects of the ego are dealt with systematically in Eugene Lerner's chapters, and specific aspects of aggression and dominance or leadership are discussed in the chapters by L. J. Stone, I shall not develop these areas here. However, certain other aspects of ego-development appear in free play sessions as in any other situation. The child has to perceive the situation and do something with it. How he perceives it and how he proceeds to come to terms with it give us some data on the resources of his ego. We have already discussed a number of these resources in talking about his capacity to conceptualize his problem in some sort of realistic or remote fantasy form, and to do something with it, and in our discussion of the constructions he makes and how they function in his total activity during the play session. We would like to select and summarize a few other items, some of which have been mentioned before, which are all important aspects of the child's ego-functioning, seen as his way of dealing with situations and with his problems.

A child may deal actively or passively with the whole play situation; a passive child is carried from one toy to another as they come, and is guided in fantasy and activity by the demand value of the toy almost completely; these children will go from one group to another, doing just the things that are obviously suggested by the toys.

A child with a strong drive to mastery will usually be more appraising at the beginning, make very selective choices of toys, and impose his own ideas on them through his ways of grouping, organizing, and dramatizing with them. This firm grip on the situation may appear either in a child who is relatively free of problems, at least of acute ones, or in a child who is actively struggling with a problem which he is trying to master.

When a child shows obvious concern with a problem, the range of his ways of dealing with it, the energy with which he works it through, the consequences of his efforts, are more important as clues to his personality development than the details of the problem itself.[27] If he can formulate his problem, project it through the toys, release the feelings accumulated around it, arrive at a fantasy solution or rehearsal for a real one, and feel relieved or satisfied afterward so that he goes on to other things, this is good evidence of his capacity to grow and to outgrow difficulties as he goes along. In our first group of children, who are now grown up, the children who were able to use the play situations in this way, have in general continued to develop well; it is usually the children who could not formulate their problems, who remained confused about them, who were blocked and ineffective in playing them out, who had more difficulty.

Ego functions to be looked for include then: appraising, selecting, organizing, dramatizing; other forms of control of the situation; control of self, including integrated emotional and impulse expression; using the experimenter; resisting intrusive questions; ability to terminate the play session and to leave the play-room; self-reliance in self-care, etc.

Preschool children are not expected to be completely independent; it is good ego-development at this stage to express warmth in childish ways and to be able to elicit it when the child wants it, whether this means a few moments of sitting on a lap, or affectionately rubbing up against a soft fur collar.

Bright children with an unusual capacity for integration often put together toys from different piles in a highly expressive and dramatic scene, accompanied by rich verbalization and sound effects. I have not seen this done by a dull child but the lack of such over-all integration is no evidence of difficulty; the presence of it indicates creative talent.

SYMPTOMS, PROBLEMS, AND SYMPTON TOLERANCE

In the slow process of growing up in American culture we have extensive evidence of the normal prevalence of symptoms and problems, that is, bits of behavior which are not approved by parents or teachers—anything from thumb- and finger-sucking to interrupting or unpredictable biting, hitting, or snatching from

27. See the following studies for evidence of common aggression and anxiety patterns in middle-class children.

other children, quarreling, or being a cry-baby. Thus *symptom tolerance*, to use Redl's term,[28] is a problem for both adults and children. It is not always easy for the child to tolerate what he needs to do when he knows the adults don't like it. Allowing oneself leeway for mild deviations, in a general context of social conformity, goes along with over-all healthy development in the group we have watched grow up. Redl calls this "leeway for regression," and it can be considered one expression of flexibility.

Indeed the many methods of achieving gratification must be considered along with ways of avoiding pain frustration—such as keeping out of the way of a cross grownup or a belligerent child, at one level, or keeping one's aspiration level within reasonable limits at another. These come together in patterns of sublimation where moderate gratification is available without risk of frustration through punishment. Such patterns of sublimation can be seen in preschool children. Yet most of the well-rounded children, including Candice, Betsy, Joyce, Colin, and Alec, indulged in periods of frankly unsublimated messing, or aggression, or mild sex play. The preschool age is too early a period to expect complete sublimation, if indeed it ever develops in anyone.

It is also normal in our culture if not indeed in any culture to have deeper problems; life involves solving, working through, outgrowing or learning to live with, a measure of strain, conflict or frustration. Children are supported in this process of growth, by the tolerance and help of grownups who care for them. Parents sometimes need help from professional people in giving this support just as they need the help of dentists and doctors in caring for the physical ailments of their basically normal children.

Signs of trouble differ in different children and sensitive mothers are usually aware of the times when "John isn't himself," "something is getting Mary down," when the child needs help in tiding over a rough spot. While the children described here all developed normally in that they kept on growing and increasing in their ability to cope with problems, and to enjoy new stages of development, they had their troubles, and their teachers gave generously of their talents for helping children to

28. Fritz Redl, *Controls from Within* (Glencoe: The Free Press, 1952).

express their difficulties, to become more clear about their experiences, to gain confidence in being themselves, and confidence in the people around them.[29]

Trouble signs, or indications that a child needed special teacher help included:

Chaos, confusion, or irritable violence in painting, block-building, clay work, or other nursery school experiences.

Extreme contrasts between tight control and explosive outbursts.

Aggression and destructiveness beyond the child's usual reaction to specific frustrations.

Overprecise, stereotyped, tight productions which were not freely expressive of a child's ideas (precision itself when combined with expressiveness accompanied intelligence or talent as with Edward).

Repetitious preoccupations lasting months where the child ordinarily worked through problems in a few weeks (apt to follow operations, absence of mother, or other marked stress experiences).

Repeated, prolonged or inconsolable crying.

Moodiness, loss of appetite, unusual fatigue or physical symptoms.

Record of a Session
with Miniature Life Toys

In order to illustrate how these aspects are seen in an actual record, one record of a play session with Miniature Life Toys is presented, with brief analysis of certain implications of the record.

29. In Volume II we discuss the effort of the staff to understand Colin's periods of anxiety and aggression, and his teachers' successful ways of helping him work through his need to prove his adequacy and strength. The movie *This Is Robert* (New York University Film Library), illustrates the efforts of his teacher to help another little boy from this group cope with accumulated tensions from a stressful home situation. Both boys have successfully weathered adolescence and are now on their way to their own professional training. In both cases, our judgment that these boys were normal, and were going through normal strains and crises was based on the result of looking at the problems they presented, in relation to the total picture of their personality development, the rich capacity for experience and growth which they both shared, their ability to use a wide range of experiences with children, adults, and materials.

Approach

[Danny had been resting in the experimental room. The experimenter came into the room and placed the toys on the floor, saying:] You can do anything you want with the toys. Danny: *Sally had a cold.* . . . [He flopped down on the floor and immediately started with the toys.] [Note his resistance to help and intrusive questions.]

Play Sequences

This little doll goes right in that box. [putting her in crib] *That's for her to lie in. There's a mirror.* . . . *A washbasin right there* . . . *see?* [He lined up two cribs, one with a mother doll in it, one with a father doll in it.] *What's this?* Experimenter: What do you think? *Kitchen.* [fixing kitchen furniture] *Here's a little chair fits in. Oh, this is a big dog.* . . . *This is a father, isn't it?* [Held the crib up, put the father in the crib.] *Have to have a bed right by everybody.* [He lined up beds, bureau, washbasin.] *Right there is the kitchen. What's this* . . . *what is it? On top of that.* . . . *Oh, do this.* . . . *See?* [He sighed.] *Oh, look here what I found.* [He picked up a bed, first put the icebox then the sink in the bed.] *Oh, it fell down. Oh, this is for there, see? This little doll to sleep in.* . . . *Looka* . . . *the doll is broken, isn't it?* [He shook the doll up and down.] *She goes in this little bed, doesn't she? There's a little chair.* [looking at experimenter, smiling] *Here's a living room* . . . *goes right there.* . . . *What's this broken off? Oh, chimney right there.* [in living room] *Here's the dog. He won't stand up. I'm going to put him back. Oh, look, the doll certainly is broken, isn't it?* Experimenter: Yes, children break toys sometimes. *Children break toys sometimes.* . . . *What shall we do? This one's broken too. Horribbblle.* [He picked up the toilet.] *Look* . . . *it's a candy-pot.* . . . *It really is a flowerpot.* [He picked up a doll, put her in bed.] *The dolls are all in bed. Here's a washbasin. Dear, dear, dear.* . . . *Here's a couch, isn't it? It goes right by this chair, right there.* . . . *Sink! Goes right like that, right against the father's bed. Say! I have a new sink! All these are jigging around my house! This goes up in the grandpapa's bed* . . . *this goes right there* . . . *goes in the kitchen.* . . . *Ooooo!* [The cabinet falls.] Experimenter: Now what? *This boy, all night he's going to* . . . *in the mirror.* . . . *Look* . . . *he's at this mirror.* . . . *Called in the night.* [Experimenter, misunderstanding:] He gets cold? *Called. Called.* Experimenter: Who calls him? *He calls himself.* Experimenter: Then what? *And the father he gets up and goes to the bathroom if he wants to.* Experimenter: Then what? *Might find the dog.* Experimenter: Suppose he calls daddy again? *Then daddy really would come.* Experimenter: Would he help the little boy, or be cross? *Help the little boy* . . . *but if he calls* [only] *four times the father doesn't come.* Experimenter: Then what . . . would he wet the bed? *Of course not!* [spreading out his hands in dramatic expressive gesture] Experimenter: But if it were dark and he couldn't go to the bathroom? *Well in the morning he would.* . . .

During this first period he seemed free, open, frank. He handled the toys functionally, but with a close compact organization. His voice had a wide range of tones, varying with his mood: "Say" came out with dramatic explosiveness at times. He also engaged in some spontaneous vocalization, twiddling with his voice, as it were.

[Following the dialogue above, he continued with the toys:] *Where shall I put this washbasin?* [He picked up a stove and two rabbits.] *Well, well, these won't stand up.* . . . Experimenter: Want help? [Experimenter fixed the rabbits so they stood.] *Give them to me.* . . . *I'm doing my house nice.* . . . [Evidently experimenter misunderstood; he asserts his competence.] *Well, wait a minute, I have to use all these yet.* . . . *What is this? Does it go this way or the other way? Table to eat on.* . . . *Put this in the living room.* . . . *Somebody eating in the living room.* [He giggled.]

[He puts two little dolls in bed.] *Two little dolls sleeping. Oh, look, isn't she cute.* . . . *She isn't broken.* . . . *Nice little doll. Somebody's arm broken off.* . . . [He laughed.] *Here's one I think could go . . . no bed for this.* . . . *Yes, there is.* [He put her in the chaise longue.]

This is going to be the chimney. [small block] *But say! whose pencil is that?* Experimenter: You can use it if you want to. *I want to write my name on paper.* [He wrote, put the pencil down quickly, picked up the bathtub.]

Oh, two tables. [with a squealy giggle] *This is s'posed to go right like that . . . oh, no it isn't. Here's the animal.* [horse] *He doesn't stay up in the night. Oh this does.* [boat] *Ferry boats always do . . . stay up in the night. They're just parked in the dock. Here's the dock. Lookit, here's a washbasin getting water on it. This is a nice house.* . . . *Oh, but the living room ought to be close to the house. Oh, a thing to show the dock when to stop and when to go.* [washbasin] *What would they do without any washbasin?* [laughing, sharing joke] *Two couches and a clo-o-o-set.* [squealed] *Oh that's a funny kitchen. I'd better move some of these things. Oh no.* [He rearranged the kitchen furniture, leaning the sink up against the toy box, lining other furniture up alongside.] *This* [icebox] *goes against the father's bed. This goes here.* . . . *That's a better kitchen, that doesn't take up so much room.* . . . *Look, the washbasin goes right beside it. In real kitchens they do, don't they?* . . . [washbasin for sink] *This is going right over here.* [He hums.] *Mind if I take this*

Actual events experienced or heard recounted by adults
are re-enacted by many children in the following scenes.

FIGURE 1 — A trip.

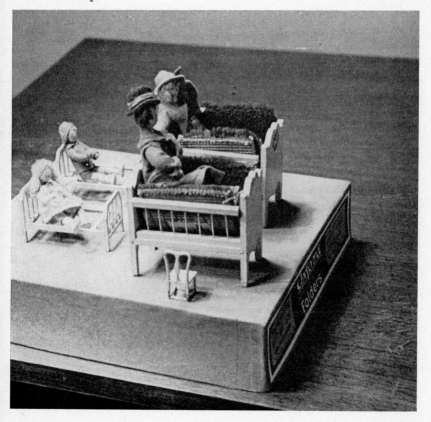

FIGURE 2 — Finding places for everyone to sleep when there were many guests at home over the weekend.

FIGURE 3 — The crushing mob at a farewell to an ocean liner.

FIGURE 4 — A war scene. A wall protects the home area from the battle area, yet the soldiers get beyond it and threaten the families.

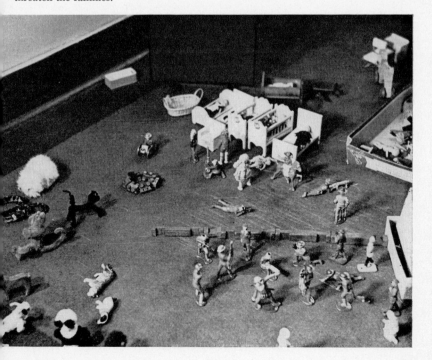

Relationship Themes

Lonely children sometimes play out longed for relationships or a desire for closeness.

Figure 5 — Florence was a left-out oversized girl in a family where the mother and son were close, and the father was not especially interested in his daughter. Her play patterns expressed a wish for family togetherness.

FIGURES 6 and 7 — Two little girls, each of whom had a pregnant mother, preoccupied with a coming baby, played out their wish for intimacy with father.

Activity-Passivity

FIGURE 8 — Some children represent people in consistently passive postures, as if the people were under the same control as the furniture.

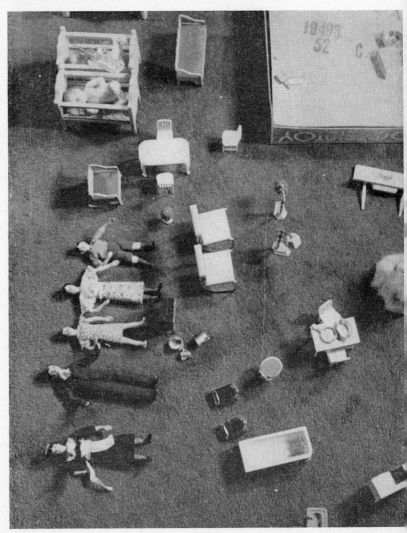

Stability of Structure

FIGURE 10 — Some children arrange a tight structure, then loosen up as they play, even during a single hour. This loosening up comes more gradually for other children.

FIGURE 11 — Edith made a formally good, but constricted and minimally functioning structure, tightly organized within the confines of a box (not done by any other child).

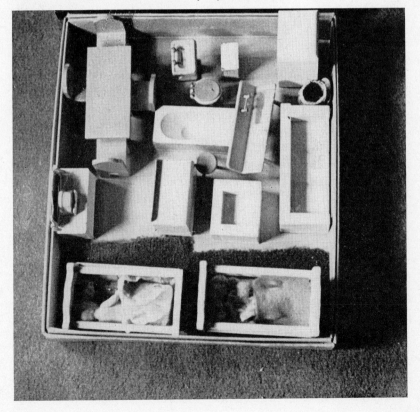

FIGURE 12 — Adele's organization is neat but repetitious and also minimally functional, with people in passive roles and no activity.

FIGURE 13 — In Candice's more flexible and functional organization of toys, children are somewhat isolated while grownups communicate.

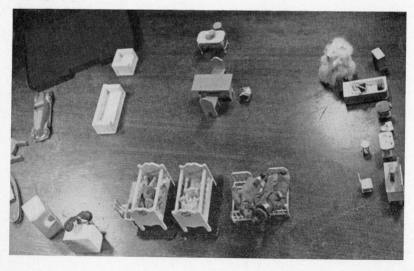

FIGURE 14 — In Kene's functional organization, mother tucks in the baby while father and son wait for her to join them.

Variations in Meaning

FIGURE 15 — A snake may be a threat to the home.

FIGURE 16 — Or its formal qualities may be exploited and it may be used as a barrier.

Blocks and Toys

Tracks, platforms, fences and other sorts of block structures are often used to express concepts of confinement, direction, control, and other nuances of authority pressures.

FIGURE 17 — Jeremy always kept people on a narrow path or track, moving ahead, but expressed a concept of authoritative control by close direction.

FIGURE 18 — Camille controlled animals within a fence which, however, offered them an open gate.

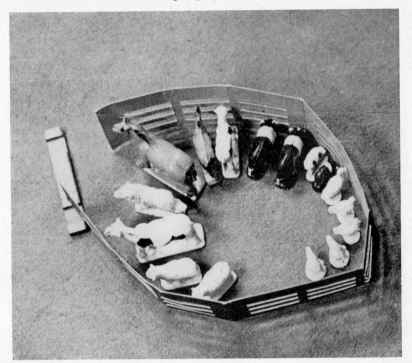

FIGURE 19 — Janet's animals were kept within a zoo-like enclosure, confined and watched by people, whom they in turn watched.

out? Oh, dear, got to have that wide kitchen. Experimenter: Why?
That's too wide. Experimenter: Why? *That's too wide. We went to
the fair. . . .* [Sings "We went to the Fair" etc., with a shy, gleeful
smile.] Experimenter: That's a grand song! Know any more? *Don't
know any more. This has to be closed because the dogs might come
in, might just br-r-r- in. The bathtub has to be upstairs where the
beds are . . . right here is the bathroom so . . . won't have to go so
far.* Experimenter: So who doesn't have to go so far? *People in the
house.* [Turns faucet on.] *O-o-o-o-w-w. Water running. . . . It'll spoil
my nice house!* Experimenter: Like to take a bath? *Yes! You know
everybody does! You know they do!* Experimenter: When do you take
a bath? *Lots of times.* Experimenter: Like going to sleep? *Why, yes!*
Experimenter: Eating? *Yes! I like everything. Can't you understand?
If you ask silly questions. Because I do eat and I like it. . . . Don't
ask silly questions. I do.* [arranging things in kitchen, living room]
*Everything is going to be turned around the other way except the
couch.* [matter-of-fact voice]

Experimenter: That's a lovely house. *Isn't it? This is the door . . .
I'd better save that until the last because that's the door. Now here's
the door. Door has to be near the bathtub doesn't it?* Experimenter:
Door has to be near the bathtub? *No, no, no.* [as if to say: You're
trying my patience"] Experimenter: So he could get out quick? *That's
the front door . . . Now let me tell you . . . When the donkey comes
backing, backing, backing he might bump into the bathtub.* [moving
the toy horse around] *Oh heck, that'll fit in . . . There is the door . . .
Room for the donkey . . . That's a dresser . . . Oh, my gee-shush . . .
Dresser.*

[The experimenter attempted to introduce a bed game to check
on the earlier fantasy but Danny cooperated in only a desultory way,
then said:] *I'm still fixing my house, you can't play the game just
yet . . . I'm not ready yet . . . Look, I broke a chair. This is going to
be a train when I get it done. The mommie's going to spank him if
he doesn't get back to bed . . . When she hears him running around
the room she'll say, "Who's that? You get back in bed or I'll spank
you so hard that you'll never forget! You get back in bed or I'll spank
you so hard that you'll never forget!"* [emphatic, dramatic voice]

This little boy . . . Smashed his toe . . . Look! Look! He's crying.
Experimenter: Too bad. [He picked up a dog.] *Wait a minute . . .
This dog should be there but he won't stand up . . . Make him stand
up.* [Experimenter fixed dog.] *There! Thank you! He sleeps on the
floor in the night, cuddled up close to the bed . . . He sleeps in the
kitchen. This boy doesn't have any place to sleep. Watchman stands
here.*

[At this point the experimenter introduced another game.] Ready
for another game? *No, no, no. I am not.* [protestingly] [Experimenter
proceeded, however, because of time limitations which made it

desirable to round out as much of his fantasy as possible. Experimenter stated the "game" of the little boy who doesn't eat his lunch and what does the mother do.] *She slaps him.* Experimenter: Then what does the boy do? *He runs away.* Experimenter: Then? *I don't know.* Experimenter: He stays home then? *He runs away some more.*

[The experimenter moved the box of toys toward herself.] *Don't . . . Don't! This is my little chair . . . Oh dear! Stop it! Stop, stop, stop!*

[The experimenter then presented the third game:] The little boy breaks his toys . . . what does the mother say? *You can go in your room and I'll shut the door.* Experimenter: What does the little boy do? *He gets up in surprise and runs away as fast as he can!* Experimenter: Then what does the mother do? [Reply not intelligible.] Experimenter: What does the little boy do? *Runs away.* Experimenter: Runs away? *Of course! Little boy better be careful because the mommie's getting up. She slaps him.* [dramatic, made-up voice] Experimenter: Slaps him? His face? *Like that. Bow wow wahhhhh. Shaking the mommie's bed . . . Great big dog. Look, what's this? Somebody's trousers?*

[The experimenter checks the fantasy:] The little boy runs away, daddy and mommie have no more little boy. What do they do? *Cry.* Experimenter: Daddy? *Cries and cries.* Experimenter: Can he find the little boy? *No.* Experimenter: Then? *The little boy comes back.* Experimenter: The little boy comes back? And gets in his bed? *Then he goes way over there.* Experimenter: Daddy goes to find him? *And he takes him back in his bed.* Experimenter: The little boy likes daddy? *Why, of course!* Experimenter: Likes mommie? *Why of course so . . . Yes! This house is going to be nice . . . Don't talk to me . . . I can't get this finished if you keep on talking to me. Where's those things?* Experimenter: Here. *Thank you very much.* [Takes living room chair, big couch.] *There's a ghost over in the corner.*

Experimenter: What does the ghost do? [Danny's answer was not intelligible, so the experimenter returned to the earlier discussion:] Does the little boy like the mommie when she slaps him? *No, of course not!* Experimenter: He gets mad? *He cries and cries. She gets him from school . . . and what do you suppose . . . He took a nap . . . and then the mommie asked him if he took a nap . . . Yes.*

[As this theme petered out, the experimenter returned to the toilet which Danny had handled in a curious way.] What is this really? *It's like a candy bowl.* Experimenter: What is this? [washbasin] *Washbasin.* Experimenter: And this? [tub] *A tub.* Experimenter: Couldn't this be a toilet? *No . . . Yes . . . Is it really? Here's the stool and a bath stool . . . Two stools.*

[The experimenter left the room for a moment, saying:] I'll be back in a minute. [Danny picked up the drawer for the bureau, turned it over and over in his hand . . . tried to fit the drawer on the sink. He picked up the toilet, put his finger into it, turned it over and over, lifted the lid several times, put it down by the bathtub. He picked up a doll, took one of the dolls out of the bed, put a mirror on a sink, and the sink fell. He put the sink to one side, the mirror on the kitchen cabinet. The mirror fell off. He put the doll in the bed, shook the crib to get a doll out. During all this time he kept up a steady stream:] *Kesta kesta kesta . . . Sink, stink, snink, sunk, steka . . . stuck, stuck. . . .* [The last words, "stuck, stuck" apparently were comments on the difficulty in getting the doll out, but they blended into the word-chain of "st" sounds. He got the doll out of the crib and waved the crib around.]

[The experimenter returned:] Tell me what that's all about. *It isn't done yet . . . The little boy sleeps with the father . . . Here's the little boy . . . With a bell. He doesn't have any place to sleep because, he's a watchman. He sleeps there.* [on the sofa] *Here's a pretty handkerchief . . . They're covers. . . . What's this?* Experimenter: A cover too. *No, it's all tied up. Untie it.* [Experimenter did so.] *Here's a little hat to go on somebody.* [He tried it on the doll.] *It doesn't go on a child, does it, on this little child. Oh, a father's hat it couldn't go on this little child, could it? I don't believe it does . . . does it?* Experimenter: Does the daddy go to work? *Of course so.* Experimenter: Does the little boy like to go with him? *Yes.* Experimenter: Does the little boy go with him sometimes? *All the time.* Experimenter: Does the little boy help the daddy? *Yes.* Experimenter: Does the daddy tell the little boy stories? *He reads them. The maid's hat came off.* Experimenter: Does the daddy take the boy piggyback? *Of course not. This is where the maid sleeps . . . Upstairs . . . Look this chair is broken right there . . .* [He put the daddy doll in the bathtub.] Experimenter: Does he like to sleep in the bathtub? *Yes.* Experimenter: Is that the daddy? *Yes . . . Here's the hat, he lost it . . . Here's another. That's the child's hat . . . A lampshade.* Experimenter: Does the little boy ever play with the toilet? [He nods.] What else does he do? *He gets on . . . Gets off . . . He's bad. Steps on a thumb tack . . . Isn't that hawwwrors . . .* [horrors] Experimenter: Why? *Just is hawrors . . . I can't talk any more because this house is r-r-r-r-r ha, ha . . . Lookit, boy's hat . . . here's his hat . . . he lost it some place . . . hat, hat.* [singing] *Well I think I'll put these things away . . . I'll put them away carefully because I do want not to smash them up. . . . I'll make a nice house.* [Picks up the toilet.] *Wait, somebody needs to go to the toilet. Open it up, flush it. . . . Where's the flush handle?* Experimenter: Guess there isn't any. *No-o-o I guess there isn't.* [Puts doll in crib.] *This be a girl. . . . She isn't broken is she? Mommie lies right next to her. I want her to lie on this bed* [Puts toys away.] *Mommie's dresser, see? Lookit. . . .* [sings] *Somebody broke the head.* [addressing the doll] Experimenter: Somebody else's turn. *I don't want to go now.* Experimenter: Some other day, etc. *I don't want to, I want to play some more. . . . I want to play some more.* [Experimenter had to open the door and lead him out.]

SUMMARY

Danny not only responded to the situation and the experimenter immediately, where other children are sometimes hesitant at first, or take time to get oriented to a new person and situation, but also began immediately to tell the experimenter about matters unrelated to the situation at hand, but which he had on his mind (Sally had a cold). The fact that he carried around with him ideas and impressions from home did not block his response to the new stimuli in the play situation. He seemed to move freely from concern with his own ideas to response to new stimuli, and while socially responsive, defended his autonomy.

Manipulation of toys: From the first moment his manipulation was functional ("This doll goes in that box, that's for her to lie in") rather than exploratory, or organizing in terms of color, size or shape. His manipulations appeared to be directed by ideas of "fitting in," what was needed ("have to have a bed right by everybody"). Within a few minutes it became apparent that his fantasy directed the manipulation ("This boy . . . he called in the night").

Structure and organization: In spite of the functional character of his manipulation, his organization "showed a close compact" quality. He arranged the toys along three sides of a square with definite "rooms": kitchen, bathroom, living room. He seemed specially concerned with whether things stood up, with the size of the kitchen ("That's a better kitchen, that doesn't take up so much room. . . . Oh dear, got to have that wide kitchen"), and rearranged objects to fit the pattern in his mind. There was some concern to "use all these." A frequent alluring smile; coy, challenging glances; spontaneous, fluid vocalizations; gleeful enjoyment of his songs and his products were an interesting contrast to his systematic organization of materials, insistence on fixing things just right. His strong dramatic emphasis on individual words was striking. Things were important along with words and people, and he had developed skill in controlling all of them and using them to conceptualize his life space and his problems in it.

Fantasy: Danny's persistent concern over the broken doll suggested an obsessive fantasy (five references to broken doll); his somewhat defensive insistence that the toy toilet was a "candy-pot" or a "flowerpot," and his use of a small block for a "chimney," although there was no hint of a roof, suggested a probable conflict about excretory functions and symbolic translation of the penis into the chimney. If these interpretations are seriously considered they must be seen in relation to the marked, if not exaggerated concern over the broken doll (to which many children paid little or no attention), and also in relation to the explicit fantasy developed both spontaneously and in response to the experimenter's "games." The persistent concern with the matter of things "standing up" may need to be set in relation to these themes too.

Danny began by putting dolls to bed, and in his case this seemed directly related to an elaborate picture of everybody in bed, little boy calls in the night, father doesn't want to get up, but does so on repeated calls. Up to this point, the fantasy appears to be representative of actual situations probably repeatedly experienced by Danny and certainly characteristic of family procedures in this culture, where busy and tired parents often resist the night demands of children for help in toileting, or punish night-time explorations.

The representative origin of the fantasy yields in importance to the systematic associations which Danny has developed around it: Horses don't stay up in the night; ferry boats do; the dog sleeps in the kitchen; the watchman is awake. A clue to the drive behind this elaboration of the problem of who is asleep or awake in the night comes from the intensity of Danny's response to the question: "What does mother do when the little boy gets out of bed?" "You get back in bed or I'll spank you so hard that you'll never forget" (repeated and spoken with great emphasis). It must be noted here that this was followed by the dramatic episode of the little boy smashing his toe and crying.

The repression already suggested, the initial evasiveness in response to the experimenter's touching off what was apparently an open and probably current conflict (punishment threats in connection with getting out of bed) may be seen as a foretaste of the fantasy of running away, which is resolved when the little boy comes back and the daddy takes him into his bed. The wish for affiliation with daddy seems to be substantiated by his response to the questions: "Does the little boy go with the daddy to work sometimes?" "*All* the time," and "Does the little boy help the daddy?" "Yes" ("the daddy's hat could go on the little boy").

The relation between father and son is sharpened by a comparison with the boy's relation to mother in the play: Mother's punishment associated with breaking off a toe; his evasion in response to the question "Does the little boy like his mommie?" ("Why of course so . . . yes! This house is going to be nice . . . don't talk to me"). There is a further hint that the daddy is non-punishing in contrast to the mother. The mother puts her hand in the toilet (i.e., does bad things like those the little boy does), but the daddy doesn't say anything to her. And further clues to sex-identification come out in the point where the girl and mother are put together to sleep. It is not quite clear whether the remark about the girl: "She isn't broken is she?" related entirely to the objective comparison with a doll that was actually broken or to a castration anxiety which seems to be implied in the repeated concern with broken dolls, the broken toe, etc.

The actual resistance to recognition of the toilet (which no other four-year-old out of the number who have played with these toys failed to recognize), together with the vocalizing of anal sounds, the insistence on making "a nice house" and vague reference to a ghost over in the corner, the little boy's self-punishment (stepping on a thumb tack) after he "gets on . . . gets off" point to further aspects of the conflict in which sex differences, anal functions, relations with parents, order in the home are all related.

Expressive patterns: Danny's vocal and dramatic spontaneity must be seen in relation both to his controlled and repeatedly revised organization of his house to make it right and nice, and to his repertoire of stalling, defensive, evasive, leg-pulling, raise-you-one, frankly resistant reactions to the experimenter's remarks. Danny did not handle the toys roughly, throw them about, cover a wide area; his handling of them was studied and orderly at the same time that it was active and free from inhibition about manipulation as such. His language was a constant accompaniment of his activity, and served to help his defenses at times; he did not, like some other children, hesitate to tell the experimenter what he was doing, or show any verbal inhibition as such; instead, language was a skillful means of communicating affects and detouring the attention of the experimenter. Both childlike and adult types of emphasis appeared: contrast the adult quality of "Dear, dear, dear" with the childlike "Oooooh," "*Horribbbllee*," "Ho, hooo, ho"; the range of pitch and sharp emphasis on individual words as well as casual singing accompaniments seemed to fit with a picture of childish spontaneity in vocalization. At times there appeared to be a burlesque quality: "Isn't that hawrors?"

The aggressive quality of many of these emphatic vocalizations seen in connection with the denying remark, "I'll put them away carefully because I *do* want not to smash them up," and the importance of the run-away theme as a reaction to punishment or aggression from adults suggests that vocalization serves the function of aggressive outlet which he does not permit himself in direct action in the presence of adults. Other children, both boys and girls, who expressed similar resistance to adult coercion, constraint or punishment, used the permissive situation offered by the experimenter to break toys. Danny hints that he would like to, but responsibly or compulsively restrains himself from doing so; a substitute or prelude to sublimation is achieved in terms of his dramatic projections and the use of his voice as an outlet for aggression.

Hypothesis regarding Danny's life space and his picture of himself: Danny, in contrast with some other children, is not primarily interested in the toys for their own sake or as objects, but for their role as part of a home setting in which people move in dynamic relation to one another. Home has a definite structure, there is a right way, there are balanced relationships which he is at some pains to achieve by correcting his first attempts at organizing the objects in the home. In Danny's mind these activities and relationships of the home go on in simple representative fashion part of the time as he rehearses the vivid episodes of daily experience. At the same time, specific objects, events and relationships carry a subtle overtone of symbolic values and implications that are not entirely clear to him. Some of these are so confusing that he puts them out of his mind or magically translates the objects into other objects with more pleasant and unequivocal associations. Thus, he can contemplate the horrible feeling which a broken body gives him, but the associated feelings about toilets are so confused that he must arbitrarily submerge them under the idea of the flowerpot. He knows that little boys are like daddies, little girls are like mommies. He would like to be even more like his daddy, and really go to work with him, and sleep with him. But for some mysterious reason, daddies do not sleep with little boys. It is even hard for a little boy to make a daddy come in the night when the little boy needs him. Daddies appear to be simple and uncomplicated, except for the difficulty that they do not always respond when a little boy wants them to. But mommies are more confusing. They scold, and threaten to punish, perhaps they will punish some day, and it would feel like getting broken (broken toe following first violent threat from mother). Somehow this is connected in his mind with the thought that maybe girls and mothers are broken, and that is horrible.

He likes his daddy in a direct uncomplicated way. He likes his mother too, but in a more confused way. Partly he wants to have comfortable relationships (a nice house), yet he is aware that something is unresolved (ghost in the corner), although he is quite clear that he does not like his mother when she punishes him. He does not feel that he should not be punished, however, for he could even punish himself (step on a thumb tack) and that would be bad enough ("hawrors"), but perhaps not so bad as real punishment by his mother.

His wish for happy relationships motivates his protest to the adult as he says, "I like everything! Can't you understand! If you ask silly questions . . ." but at the same time he would like to be more aggressive himself. At present he expresses strong feelings through strong words which he partially disguises: ("sink, stink, snink, gee-shush," with a hard g) and through almost violent accents in his dramatic speech. He can also imagine a donkey that would show more stubborn defiance than he himself does:

("When the donkey comes backing, backing, backing he might bump into the bathtub"), or a dog that could be more vigorously aggressive ("Shaking the mommie's bed . . . Great big dog"). But with all his lack of violent physical aggression he can dominate the adults with his vigorous talk and protests ("Don't . . . don't talk to me . . . I don't want to go now"). However, this is not complete release, sometimes he would like to smash things up and only his strong reminder to himself controls him ("I *do* want not to smash them up").

Implications of this record for temperament: It goes without saying that one forty-minute period will not give a complete inventory of significant aspects of a child's temperament or anything approaching it. What we are interested in is: What can we learn about Danny's probable temperament from a record like this?

It is worth noting that Danny did not show any tactual or tender response to furry animals; these animals functioned entirely as dramatis personae in the play he developed; nor did he show any mechanical interest in the way objects were put together or worked. Again they were of interest as they contributed to his dramatic activity. This is in sharp contrast to other children who might be just absorbed in the mechanical or tactual aspects of objects as Danny was absorbed in their dramatic potentialities.

We also note that Danny was not seen to relax into a deeply absorbed reverie with slow deep breathing like some children. He was alert and vivid throughout, and from the first moment included the experimenter in his situation, with every evidence of strong social interest or definite interest in adults. He commented conversationally about his first handling of the toys and was never too absorbed to hear the experimenter's remarks, as some children are. We also note that there was no evidence of concern with his body such as many children this age show by rocking, patting, scratching or other self-activities; his attention and response were to the adult and the toys as materials for imaginative activity.

We have commented on his occasional use of adult phrases ("Dear, dear, dear"); this not only adds to the picture of his interest in adults but suggests a sensitivity to nuances of tone of voice and expressive patterns that may be one aspect of auditory sensitivity. His use of songs also suggests a musical responsiveness related to auditory responsiveness (at the age of three or four, less than one child out of twenty has spontaneously interspersed singing with play with toys). This auditory sensitivity also seems to be related to his large vocabulary, his exploitation of the sounds of words for dramatic effect (*"Horribblle"*). Verbal ability and interest associated with awareness of expressions of feeling-tone appear in his use of words unusual for this age: *certainly, surprise, parked, silly, understand.* Vocal expressive patterns already referred to revealed a tendency to strong emphasis, explosiveness, and variation through a wide range of tones and of feeling.

We can summarize these observations in these terms: Danny appears to be a child of strong social, verbal, dramatic responsiveness, with basic auditory sensitivities and vocal range. His interests seem to be outgoing rather than centered on himself or his own body. This responsiveness has led to identification with adults shown in his use of adult nuances of expression, and adult control of aggressive patterns. He is not, however, an inhibited or timid child; he has used his expressive resources for outlets other than the direct physical outlets for aggression common to boys with less identification with adults.

Implications of this record for "areas of spontaneity and anxiety": It will be obvious to the reader that Danny has considerable anxiety about breaking and broken things (frequent references to broken objects, self-control about smashing things up, etc.). There is also evidence that might be interpreted in terms of castration fear: (his question whether the girl is broken, the association of punishment with breaking, the alignment of father-boy, mother-girl, and his wish to be more with father). He expressed a limited hostility response to punishment when provoked by the experimenter (doesn't like mommie when she slaps). There also seems to be a definite concern about order (critical rearrangement of the house) and a possible association of this with the problem of unbroken relationships in the home (wanting to make a nice house, self-control regarding breaking). This suggests the possibility of dependence on adults of a constraining sort, as well as the identification which underlies his use of adult phrases and wish to put the father's hat on the boy. The concern about order may be related to the curious behavior with the toilet. Anxieties are handled in terms of evasive or disguise re-actions: (running away, calling the toilet a flowerpot or candy-pot, expressing defiance via the donkey who backs into things, use of strong words and strong vocal emphasis as a substitute for direct action).

Danny's spontaneity lies in his social resourcefulness and outgoingness, his capacity to carry on active social relationships through the use of sublimated expressions of aggression and dramatic humorous communication. He makes good use of his vocal and dramatic gifts. It is not clear from this record how well these substitutes for direct action serve him; if they lead to a sense of impotence for direct action they may prove to be a source of conflict. This will undoubtedly depend on how his culture both at home and at school accepts his behavior and how he responds to further discipline at home and also to stimu-lus by boys, especially those having more open aggression.

STEPS IN ANALYSIS OF THE RECORD

Several processes are included in the analysis of Miniature Life Toy material.

1. A statement of the child's *use or uses of the situation,* approach, activities.

2. A list of the *objects chosen* and ignored by the child.

3. A list of the *significant comments* made by the child in their context.

4. A list of *the behavior units or acts* in their context. This is subdivided into body behavior; specific movements with toys.

5. A list of *the structures produced.* In some instances, a child makes one larger structure which is used as a setting for the play; in some instances, such a larger structure constantly changes with the play. In other instances smaller groupings are created; and in still others, individual combinations of toys are

used to act out fantasies, without any intent to "make something" that lasts even temporarily.

6. A list of the *emotional expressions,* direct and indirect.

7. A list of the *sequences* of units or stages through the session. Ideally a Miniature Life Toy record contains a complete sequence of objects chosen; verbalization; action with the toy and use of body and emotional expression. An attempt is made globally and with nuances to describe the shifting atmosphere, relation to space of the room, to experimenter, etc.

Each of these must be analyzed for itself and in relation to the rest, and requires an evaluation of the meaning, role, and effect of each toy, emotional expression, or act, and its part in the total sequences of the play session.

We are then concerned with problems of interpretation— some of which involve pitfalls—which arise in the following areas:

1. The selection of items to be emphasized is influenced by the cultural and individual experience of the experimenter as well as his professional frame of reference.

2. Judgments as to generalizations and inferences adequately documented in the record versus inferences based on slender evidence (frequency of occurrence, clarity or vividness, relation to context).

3. Judgments regarding the point where fantasy begins: does it begin only where objects are moved, or when images are involved, or is fantasy developing parallel with objective appraising of the toy from the moment of the first sight of it, or when it is chosen or rejected?

4. Judgments regarding the idiosyncratic value of the fantasy
   a) when the demand of the object is clear,
   b) when cultural stereotypes are used,
   c) when clichés typical of the developmental stage are used.

5. Judgments regarding the exact meaning of specific objects to the child in the context of the play situation and his life experience.

6. Judgments regarding the level of significance of the fantasy for the motivation and structure the personality, and

weight to be given to each level when more than one is involved as when a child acts out, puts on a show, is emotionally involved in it, but also handles the show at points in typical television style and follows the "performance" by calling attention to her skill. What weight do we give the threat, the counterattack, the emotional and active cathartic participation, the exhibitionism, the sense of release and mastery and achievement? One experimenter might emphasize the theme of threat and counterattack; another might emphasize the use of a culturally acceptable vehicle; another might emphasize the emotional intensity, still another the subsequent sense of mastery, together with the place of this aggressive fantasy in the total sequence.

We cannot overemphasize the potential pitfalls of ascribing assumed meanings to any child's use of a toy (e.g., horse can be feared or be a love-object, or something I want to ride, etc.). It is absolutely necessary to avoid making assumptions. A snake may be seen as a threat, a scary thing under the back porch, or a penis-symbol, or (by a two-year-old) a necklace, or a fence. Only the context, sequences, verbalization, etc., of the play, or an inquiry, with or without data from the home, can tell us. Multiple meanings are to be expected too.

These variations in what a type of person can mean to different children can be illustrated by the ways in which each of a group of nursery-school children used the Miniature Life Toy soldiers. Only five handled the soldiers realistically, objectively, and conventionally, arranging for them to shoot, but without evidence of identification; while eleven included soldiers as people with animals or domestic toys as part of life without assigning special roles to them or projecting hostility or anxiety through them. Soldiers go on trains, go to the toilet, talk to policemen, lie down, sit up, stand up, watch parades, march in parades with animals. Three children asked questions, comparing the soldiers with one another, or saying, "What can we do with it?" or, "Why is he shooting?" One boy enjoyed the soldiers without doing anything: "They're pretty." Eight children explicitly identified with the soldiers or used them as if they were themselves, shooting teachers, mother, observers, father, "everyone," maid, lions, animals, an unspecified man, the experimenter.

Eight others represented the soldiers as righteously threatening or punishing agents who shot bad people, bad Hitler, bad spiders, bad boys, cat, dog, man in the sky, etc. Two used the soldiers to "shoot me" (the child), while one expressed anxiety directly as he picked up the soldiers: "I don't want to be killed and stuff in no war." One represented animals, policemen, and soldiers as hostile, confronting each other in conflict, and another one used the cannon as a phallic symbol.

These differences in the use of one type of toy involve differences in knowledge about the soldiers and what they are like and do, as well as differences in the feeling projected through them and the individual child's need to project such feelings.

Some objects show much wider variations of meaning to individuals in a group of children even from the same subculture.

PROBLEMS OF EVALUATION

Relationship between Behavior in a Play Session and in Other Situations

In some cases it is possible to trace direct and quite clear consistencies or congruence between the organization of the toys, fantasies, and expressive behavior. We have seen how Joyce over a period of two years built a compact cumulative structure with toys occupying a solid central area, with looser relations on the periphery; her fingerpaintings also showed a solid mass of color painted close to her body, which gradually spread out to wider areas later on; in nursery school she clung to one spot during the first two months of each year, then moved around more freely. These patterns can also be seen to be related to her striking pattern of acquisitiveness: in gathering all the toys on the playground into a mass in a wagon; gathering as much flour, salt, and water as possible in the Dough experiment (see pp. 122-125); in discussing presents and more presents in play sessions during her third year; in boasting of her brothers' possessions; and finally, perhaps, in her sense of cumulating years in her boasting of her age.

Colin's voice was capable of vivid explosive aggressive expressions, which fitted his sudden aggressive attacks on children, and his fantasy of creatures of prey which attacked other creatures. Alec's brusque dumping of toys on the floor was matched by his rehearsal of a mother spanking a baby and by his own reckless attacks on other children on the playground.

But not all children express such consistent attitudes through their structures, fantasy, and behavior. Dusty's solidly integrated play with structures completely assimilated to fantasy, and body behavior equally assimilated to it, suggested a degree of coherence of personality which was belied by the unpredictable spurts of tremulous anxiety that punctuated the flow of creativity, like a sudden streak of lightning through a calm summer rain. (Spurts like these had not occurred in the group situation at nursery school.) Betsy's relatively rigid and repetitious structures of a house (which were incidentally comparable to her approach to painting, where she usually began with a border and a pattern of squares on the paper) were hard to relate to her gay spontaneity in behavior and fantasy. Kene showed a similar social pattern of initial rigidity followed by spontaneous creativeness; we saw that the latter could only appear after the former initial organization of material was accomplished. A rigid oblong house was built first, accompanied by restrained behavior, then a more functioning arrangement of boat, horse, and boy who furnished the starting point for a lively drama. Claudia's behavior and structures showed a consistent freedom the first year, and were followed by a unique pattern subsequently, illustrated by her handling of finger paint. She smeared the paint freely at first, as she had done the first year, then imposed a cross or square or other similar form on top of the freely smeared painting. Her play with toys followed a similar sequence with more organized patterns the second year.

Actually these patterns are no more inconsistent when we think of them in relation to the family experience of these children. In the case of children who showed no essential change in the structure and content of play over a year or two, we have found no major change in home milieu; children who have shown such changes have often been exposed to a major change such as a new and more disciplinary maid, as in the case of Claudia. "Inconsistencies" that seem to appear in the relation between structure and fantasy at any one time frequently make sense when we know the family experience which often contains the same variety.

Laurel, whose mother was both a warm person and a conscientious organizer of home and children's life, followed a consistent procedure in all the play sessions we had with her. She set up her housekeeping toys in a pattern representing four rooms, all neat and straight and square. After everything was well organized she burst out into spontaneous dramatic play lasting ten minutes to a half hour. This was frequently concerned with the give and take of a demanding, mischievous little girl and a tired mother who was busy or wanted to sleep on Sunday morning. Laurel was the only one (out of 326 records on nearly seventy children) who followed this sequence. Most children as spontaneous as Laurel carried along the organization of toys in direct dramatic relation with the fantasy that was expressed. A few children set up the toys in a definitely organized fashion without any accompaniment of oral fantasy.

Patterns of this sort, where organization as such is interiorized and projected by the child, are both quite different from that shown by Camille. In this preschool group she was a creative, dominant, imaginative personality full of ideas and capable of carrying a group into a long-sustained activity. Her painting was characterized by subtlety of organization and unusual nuances of color. Her play with toys always kept organization functionally subsidiary to her imaginative idea. Her fantasy revealed a great deal of rebellion and hostility toward maids and mothers. In other words she did not appear to have interiorized constraint, form, order as Laurel and Claudia did.

We referred earlier to Kene, a three-year-old boy who was only seen over a one-year period. Kene lined up the house toys in an oblong, without relation to color, shape or functional value. When this was done, he set up boats, house and a boy in an adjacent area that represented a body of water. Here, in contrast to the empty, rigid house structure, everything that was exciting went on—sailing, falling into the water, being rescued. This separation of outdoors from indoors organization does not seem unrelated to his family experiences. His mother planned, built, and furnished a house, then sold it, moved into another which she planned, built, and furnished. Away from home she and her son flew their own airplane, sailed, went to dog shows, horse shows, and other exciting events. Indoors and outdoors were very different experiences for this child.

Alec, like Camille, was a child who showed explicit concern about authority without interiorizing constraints insofar as we could tell from the projective patterns of his play. He regularly represented a baby getting out of bed, being spanked very hard until he stayed in bed. Alec himself was a lovable little bull-in-a-china-shop; he dumped out all the toys roughly, selected those needed for the fantasy of the moment, and junked the rest. His fingerpainting was a big, free, vigorous smear.

These different ways of internalizing family patterns suggest some needed correctives to assumptions about the effect of maternal tension and domination. The mothers of all these children would certainly be rated at the tense end of any scale that included a definite alternative of relaxed or easy-going behavior. Most would be rated dominating. Yet the experience and behavior of the children vary enormously. The reasons are not hard to find if we look at the total experience of each child with his mother in his home. Laurel's mother is tense and dominating, but also affectionate and playful and supporting. Camille's and Alec's mothers are tense, but also direct, honest, affectionate and understanding.

In order to understand the experience of the child we must consider not only the traits related to tension and dominance but the place of these in the total relation of mother to child, including both offsetting values and the mother's way of handling tensions. These footnotes to current methods of analysis are especially relevant where we are studying children from a normal or favored segment of the culture in contrast to the extreme and more clear-cut patterns of clinical groups.[30]

----

30. Lois Barclay Murphy, "Interiorization of Family Experience by Normal Preschool Children, as Revealed by Some Projective Methods," *The Psychologists League Journal*, IV (1940), 3-4.

Meaning of the Play Session to the Child

The question has been asked, "But don't the children ever *play?*" meaning, "Doesn't a child ever carry on fantasy activities which represent a stretch of the imagination beyond his own experience, or play for its own sake?" A glance at the summary of children's activities will give the answer: Eliminating family experiences as too obviously projective in one way or another, we may say that we have not found a preschool child who played garage man, aviator, going to South America, who did not have some important roots in his experience for this activity—either participation or in terms of identification with a relative or figure in a story. The content of a child's play with materials like these always represents something that he has taken in, however reorganized or distorted or colored it may be by his own projection of it.

At the same time, it is important to make this distinction: going off on a boat may be a representation of an exciting experience that was fun, as in the case of Kene; or it may be a fantasy of escape from the routines of adult-dominated family life, as with Joyce; or from the pain of competition from a new sibling, as with Patsy and Karin. The question whether imaginative activity concerned with faraway places, events, plans, has a value of escape, compensation, or problem-solving can only be answered in the light of other data on the child. For instance, in the case of Karin, the journey appeared along with dramatic activity covering new physical spaces in the room, in the context of a sequence of play sessions concerned with her reactions to a new baby. This was also true in Patsy's case. In neither case did the child represent explicitly what she was travelling away from. Yet in neither case had the idea of travelling away appeared before the child had a new sibling.

However, direct rather than symbolic satisfactions occurred in plenty. Joyce's delight in manipulating colored cubes and solving puzzles made sense in terms of her good form perception and color interest apparent on intelligence and Rorschach tests. It seems far-fetched to attribute any escape-from-reality element to these abstract activities in her case. They were fun both because she enjoyed color and manipulation of small objects, and because she could handle them skillfully. There was no diminution of either interest at the age of five, when increasing freedom of action, feeling, and fantasy was shown throughout her nursery-school behavior and experimental responses.

It seems equally far-fetched to overemphasize deep symbolic drives back of Eric's delightful cuttings, which were also the product of delicate form perception and eye-hand co-ordination. Children and adults alike enjoyed his products as he did, and symbolic interpretations in terms of the aggressive value of cutting seem either incidental or evasive in face of the direct pleasure and achievement satisfactions available to him through this activity.

Personality structure is influenced by the initial abilities and competences and sensitivities of a child at least as much as the sensitivities are structured by the personality needs. That is, a child who sees forms sharply and makes fine distinctions naturally may tend to develop a more cautious personality just because of his more detailed awareness. Fear may sharpen observation, but we are not confined to a one-way street in analyses of this sort.

Inferring the Child's Life Space

We have observed that the child's life space may be seen in terms of:

1. The people and objects to which he is impressionable.

2. The meaning these objects have for him in terms of his feelings toward them, how he views them, what he associates with them and how he relates them to other objects.

3. The relation of the child to immediate and remote physical space—whether he occupies or covers much or little—moves from one spot to another or remains fixed, is oriented to immediate or remote space or both.

4. The pattern of the child's responses to and withdrawal from the objective world; the bases of this in positive feelings or release, or in feelings of anxiety; temperamental bases in tempo and rhythms of inner-outer orientation.

Briefly we may illustrate these by describing Kurt. Kurt persistently over a three-year period was interested in light-fixtures, gadgets, and any mechanical objects in the room more than the toys; his interest in the latter was mild and fluid in contrast to the persistence and vigor of his response to and manipulation of lights and gadgets. Apparently the background for this fixation was the fact that he had been alone a great deal in his infancy and the chief object of interest at the age of eight or nine months was a light switch which he could reach from his crib. Definitely integral to this interest was his space-behavior; going from one corner of the room to another, climbing on tables and desks or under beds, if these were in the way of getting at lights. He never mentioned objects outside of the room and his home, never referred to faraway places. His attitude was primarily manipulatory and there was never any explicit verbalization to indicate what fantasy meanings this interest had for him. The only hint of anxiety was in the compulsiveness and perseveration of his interest, which often seemed to make it hard for him to be free to respond to anything else.

The problem of the child's life space is in part a problem of figure-ground relationships in experience, and this has important implications for problems of interpretation of the child's fantasy-projections. Just as we guard against inferring facts directly from data gathered in parent conferences, it is even more necessary to be cautious in making the bridge from the child's attitudes to events. A prolonged fantasy about spanking may reflect repeated spankings, or a background of no spankings which provided a ground against which the experience of another child's spankings or a single experience of spanking stood out in sharp relief.

In relation to this same problem of figure-ground aspects of experience we may ask: what does the experience of free play with toys in the presence of a permissive adult who puts you through no paces and gives you little stimulus mean? If you have been craving release from coercion it may be an exciting novelty; if you have enjoyed released play in similar situations it may be a familiar pleasure. If you have enjoyed directed play with a great deal of satisfying adult suggestion, it may seem empty. According to these different values, you will as a three-year-old respond to the situation, and the experimenter will have to judge meanings of this sort accurately if she is to make valid use of the material. For instance, when Camille smashed up dolls, and Philip let himself go with gusto and squeaking delight as he put all the wooden toys into a bathtub of water, were they experiencing familiar or new forms of excitement and release? Clues to the answer may be found in subsequent responses; the same gusto repeated over a long time is less likely to be seen as response to a first-time release situation. If a marked settling-down occurs, it may be more likely that the release was a new experience.

Inhibition or control may be a general attitude assimilated by identification with a controlled parent or sibling, or a specifically taught manner as it was in the case of Janet, whose mother constantly spoke of wanting her child to have lovely manners; or a general attitude of reaction to a boisterous, relatively uncontrolled family; or an expression of fear or hostility in one specific situation, not characteristic of the child in other situations.

We have noted that in order to evaluate the behavior of a given child in a given play situation it is necessary to compare it with behavior in the nursery school group, and at home, and to relate it to what is known of family structure, parents' values and conscious emphases, and parental patterns as felt by the child. When we can do this, we can see the serene and adaptable charm of Kene and Candice, both only children, as the reward as it were which they offer their parents for the uncontested love and security they are given. Both children at the age of two and three years were never seen to be defiant, self-assertive in ways that might conflict with the desires of parent or teacher, although both were freely assertive in creative and constructive ways acceptable to and enjoyed by adults and children. Both were popular with children and adults alike. In both cases, Miniature Life Toys gave clues, along with Rorschach, to sources of possible strain or conflict resulting from their sensitive adaptations to unseen boundaries intrinsic in attitudes of the adults.

Summary of Miniature Life Toy Play

At the preschool stage, play tells us how the child functions in his own medium, at his own tempo, with his own balance of autistic, adaptive, creative responses.

It shows us the depth and coherence of these responses, the quality and function of structuring, the level of conceptualization, the level of symbolizing, the design of affective release. It also shows us the affective pattern of rhythmic up and down or crescendo to releasing climax; crescendo to climax with guilt; splash with diminuendo.

It shows us something about the balance of pleasures and anxieties, and where the important areas in each may be found.

It shows us what he is doing with his problems: observing, or liquidating, or by-passing, or denying, repressing, or compensating.

And it suggests with what consequences he does this: relief, clarity, vagueness, or confusion.

Finally it shows us something about the weight of the problem in the total affective-cognitive picture or the total picture of his personality.

An over-all outline of this sort does not do justice to the need for a sensitive weighing of nuances of the child's behavior, which must go into every appraisal of a play session. A furtive glance at the experimenter after an abortive gesture toward a toy subsequently ignored may be more revealing than fifteen minutes of representative "safe" play which uses conventionality to prevent expression of real feelings. A record of "aggression" is incomplete if we have no indication whether it is for excitement, or a means to an end, or a reaction to frustration, and whether it is followed by satisfaction, more aggression, anxiety, restorative behavior, or constructiveness.

Sequences of details and over-all sequences of the total play session give a basis for evaluating the meaning of each item. Generalizations are made on the basis of recurrent items, and of related, including opposite areas. A flock of migrating birds may herald spring, but so does the presence of one robin, two crocuses, and melting snow.

If the child's exposure is wide enough, limits outside of which variations do not occur may also form the basis of conclusions, but we cannot ascertain such a frame for the child's behavior if we have not seen him in situations where he is free and happy and situations where he feels anxious or insecure or frustrated. We have to be cautious about assuming limits to his potentialities in other environments unless a range has been tested.

Within this range, we look for relationships between variations of behavior and varied internal and external situations (fatigue, hunger; being with an adult male, or female, or older or younger children, etc.). Distinguishing a transitory mood from a developmental stage, or a persistent inner core, or a semi-universal pattern in the subculture (or a coalescence of the latter two) requires comparisons of the child with himself in different situations, and with other children of his age in the subculture.

We do not know whether the "negativeness" of two, the "creative overflow" of four, the "constriction" of twelve, so widely documented in our culture, also appear in the rest of Western culture, or the Near East and the Orient. To what extent are these basic developmental phases in personality; to what extent are they products of interaction between phases of development and the special impact of our culture?

As we clarify the areas of release, by comparing expressions, behavior, constructions, and verbalized fantasy, we come to the point at which we can define the terms in which the problem is being stated, and being solved, or handled. Behavior may tell us the latter, while the child's construction tells us what the problem is; or both may mingle. The relation between what is *overtly* or directly expressed, as contrasted with what is *covertly* or indirectly expressed will clarify the areas with which the child can cope. Time orientations are sometimes impossible to judge except by comparisons with the reality situation; penned-up wild animals were Richie's rehearsal for a control which he did not yet show in nursery school.

VARYING USES OF THE MATERIAL

The uses of toy-centered versus relationship-centered play become clearer when we look at the situation of the shy or anxious or very young child, who may feel threatened by a situation in which he feels that demands, which he is afraid he cannot meet, are being made upon him by a strange adult. The quiet, seemingly passive suggestion, "You can do anything you like with the toys," focuses the child's attention on the objects, away from the person of the experimenter or therapist, and often frees him for explorations which he could not make if he kept on trying to meet expectations of interpersonal interchange.

Children who are ready or even eager for contact with the adult will, like Trudi and Deborah, maintain it in this context; others will develop it through or after achieving some satisfaction with the toys. But children like Camille, who prefer to turn their backs, or like Jeremy, who play silently at first, still communicate to us much of their feelings and perception of their world, which, if we are concerned either with teaching or therapy, can be used to help their relationships. Toy-centered play is neither a substitute for nor a hindrance to relationship-centered play, but a method which produces its own helpful results, and is at times a stepping-stone to more social give and take.

Published investigations based on play sessions similar to those with Miniature Life Toys have usually centered on play with dolls, in order to elicit conflicts regarding family relationships and aggressive wishes toward parents or siblings. Recent studies of perception, using the Miniature Life Toy approach among others, have been chiefly interested in the structural aspects of the child's play. Clinical uses of similar materials are concerned primarily with the child's conflicts.

Actually, the material from records of play sessions may be analyzed in an almost infinite number of ways, and a "complete" analysis of one play session lasting an hour can take ten times as long to complete or more, if a thorough study of it is made.

The type of analysis will depend on the use to which it is put, and the questions the examiner wishes to ask.

He may be chiefly interested in the child's relation to authority, in which case he will pay attention to ways of structuring and limiting, or patterns of control in behavior, expression, and play structure, as well as his ways of dealing with authority figures such as parents, policemen, etc. Or he may be interested in the child's development of sex-role, in which case he will note the choices of toys (distinguishing those usually chosen by boys as compared with those chosen by girls), type of activity with toys (nurturant versus mastery or aggressive activities), indications of specific concern with sex-differences in body, or in functions such as going to the toilet, evidences of "feminine" interest in clothes, etc., versus "masculine" interests in mechanical objects and motor activity.

If he is interested in emotional tone of family relationships, he will observe not only the direct indications of these through noting activities and emotional quality of response to dolls, but also to family-substitutes, such as mother-horse, baby-horse combinations, or daddy-car, baby-car combinations, or even the child's handling of blocks in terms of big-little, protective or other relevant structures.

If he has special interests such as the child's relation to doctors or response to hospital experiences, he will add toys and blocks which permit the elaboration of feelings or concepts and fantasies related to these experiences.

In other words, by selection of toys, or by the plan for analysis of the data, the experimenter will abstract the information he wishes to have about a given group of children.

Since this is a flexible approach, which is relative to the family and subculture experience of the child, scoring will have to be done relativistically also, comparing a given child with others of his group or a relevant control group.

CHAPTER 3

Sensory Toys

Statement of Purpose

PLASTICS AND SENSORY TOYS were used to elicit evidence on the range and richness of response to stimuli from different modalities characteristic of different children. This area of study needs much more work. The range of sensitivities of an individual child acts as a sieve or net for environmental stimuli, and determines the scope of the impact from the environment which the child must absorb and integrate in order to act. By the same token, it determines the range of sources from which he learns, the resources from which his fantasy life is nourished, and the directions in which he can turn for compensation when frustrated. It also determines the areas in which needs, frustrations, and traumas are most likely to develop: a child with relatively little oral drive will be less likely to be seriously disturbed by oral deprivations than a child with strong oral drives. Similarly a child with strong responses to tactual stimuli may crave contact more urgently than a child with less interest in and response to contact. Such differences also affect deeply the interaction between the child and his environment, especially the mother; a contact-loving mother will be frustrated by a child who does not respond much to contact. A mother with strong food preoccupations will be frustrated by a child who is easily satiated. Musical parents will be gratified by a child to whom auditory and rhythmic stimuli are exciting. All of the later developments built on the foundations of early sensory responsiveness will be important for the pattern of interests and vocational choices which are available to the child. Responsiveness in general to sensory stimuli from the environment is thus an important aspect of the capacity for spontaneity and for the range of gratifications open to a child.

In the large group situations of nursery school it is not always easy to tell the difference between the severely constricted or anxious child who has no adequate relation to children or materials, no satisfying experience of his own, and the child who engages in little or no group or manipulative activity, but who has a vivid capacity for appreciation, analysis, reflection, or personal emotional experience which will be expressed in social ways later.

The difference between the two patterns can be of great importance. The first may be a traumatized shut-in child whose lack of rapport with reality precedes serious withdrawal. The second may be a "well-adjusted introvert," or a child who will later be more outgoing, but is at present in a "drinking-in" phase. He may simply have a different timetable for social development, or social interaction may not have the value for him that it has for other children.

We are sometimes confused too about the difference between children who are socially active and who also have rich sensory and intellectual experience to contribute to the group, and children who respond to the group but have little or narrow experience capacity, in sensory and intellectual terms, and therefore little fresh stimulus to offer the group.

All of the procedures with plastics give an opportunity to observe the responses of children in these categories: Amy, Dusty, and Eric are examples of children whose social activity was limited when we studied them, but who showed lively response to plastic materials. But dough and paints call for action and do not discriminate between passive appreciation and active release. It is true that Miniature Life Toys also reach these children, but play with the toys does not always yield "rich" results; it is most revealing with the "good projectors," the imaginative or verbal children, or those who "act out" fantasies. Children with capacity for rich sensory or emotional experience are sometimes slow or inarticulate, unable to "project" actively, although they can respond at the simpler appreciative levels called for by sensory toys. Early difficulty in response may be due precisely to the difficulty of integrating all the child takes in or responds to. Some of the multisensory children like Joyce needed a longer time to produce creative or active results than "motor" children who did not respond to so many aspects of the environment. L. J. Stone accordingly prepared a toy sequence designed to clarify the areas and patterns of response to sensory materials. Materials were selected in terms of their probable appeal to preschool children rather than in terms of rigid scientific categories.

Procedure

The materials are covered and out of reach. When the child enters the room he is told that "There are a lot of surprises. I'll give them to you one at a time and you tell me when you are ready for the next one." The materials that the child has seen are not taken away. They are presented as follows:

1. Tapping bell (rings when top knob is tapped)
2. Music-box
3. Strip of fur (white, about 3 by 7 inches)
4. Copper mesh ball (for scouring pots and pans)
5. Colored sticks (flat, about the size of tongue depressors with a hole in one end)
6. Colored skeins of wool (small sample size)
7. Kaleidoscope
8. Acetate black "hair" (cuttings from dictaphone records bunched together in hair-like mass; marked chemical odor)
9. Wax dust (resembling colorless, pulverized, dry gelatine)
10. Excelsior (made of colored cellophane)
11. Humming top (musical tone while spinning)

12. Color top (primary colors blend when it spins)

This situation, then, provides a series of objects designed to make their appeal primarily in sensory terms and including a variety of tactual, visual, and auditory values. The child's spontaneous comments on, and uses of, each object are noted, as well as his response to such questions as: "Do you like how that feels?" "What's the best thing you've had so far?" These results are examined in relation to various problems. An attempt is made to note whether the child responds to the *Ding-an-sich,* sensory qualities of the toys, or whether he requires organization and "meaning"; and to see which sensory avenues are of most significance to him and what meanings he attaches to them. It is also important to watch special points such as aggressiveness (the child is invited to throw the wools "as hard as you want") and orderliness (as shown, for example, by the compulsive insistence on putting things away).

With a procedure like this it is obvious that many chance factors might affect the child's response. Shyness at the beginning of the experiment may inhibit a positive response to an object whose intrinsic sensory value is definitely positive; inattention toward the end of the experiment might similarly mask the child's more stable responsiveness. While different inner states of fatigue or resistance may affect the child's response to the situation as a whole, responses to specific toy materials in this sequence may also be affected by varying functional contexts in which they are presented. The music-box, kaleidoscope, and tops, for instance, call for an active approach on the part of the child, actively directed toward getting specific results. The fur, cellophane-excelsior, and dust can all be either passively enjoyed or incorporated in a larger fantasy. The latter materials involve less risk of infringing upon rules (it would be more serious to throw the music-box because it might break). From this point of view, the passive and safe pleasure of rubbing the fur might be expected in the case of shy children who want to avoid risks. We are therefore summarizing this exploration with method as an illustration of an area which needs much more work.

Results

Clear-cut types of response to sensory toys may be described in the following categories:

1. *Direct sensory pleasure*
   (a) polysensory: enjoying color, sound, tactual experience with exuberant delight (e.g., Colin).
   (b) relatively monosensory or bisensory: enjoying tactual experience deeply, not much interest in others (e.g., Claudia) and enjoying visual and auditory stimuli without much interest in tactual materials (e.g., Joel).
   (c) nonsensory: chiefly interested in what can be done with the toys or in a social orientation to the situation, rather than in the sensory experience of the objects or materials themselves (e.g., Adele or Abigail).
2. *Derivative sensory pleasure*
   (a) e.g., Jay, who gave considerable evidence of chiefly anal values in tactual satisfactions rather than primitive sensory values.
3. *Strong defenses against sensory pleasure*
   (a) conventional attitudes, inability to make use of "less structured" material (dependence on accepted or authoritarian patterns of response), anxiety regarding messiness, etc.

Responses to Sensory Toys

The following detailed records illustrate differences between two children; one showed limited freedom to respond to sensory stimulation, the other was delighted by sensory stimuli of many kinds.

RECORD OF ADELE

Experimenter: You can sit in that little chair. I have some toys to show you, etc. Maybe we'd better take your jacket off. *Maybe I'd better.* [Experimenter helps her with jacket; she spends some time unbuttoning snowpants, slow, evidently not eager to see things. Finally gets things off, sits down in small chair.] Experimenter: Now I'll give you the toys. *You tell me. . . .* [mumbles]

[Experimenter brings out bell.] *Cute.* [before she has time to see what it really is or can do] [Experimenter's comments: Conventional response used as defense, verbal sop to adult?] [Experimenter rings bell.] Experimenter: Want to do that? [She bangs it hard, blinking, sets it down.] *Now . . . Play with other thing.* Experimenter: Do you like it loud or soft? [Experimenter rings bell loudly and softly.] *Soft.* [without conviction] [Experimenter's comments: Just because an answer is expected?]

What's that? [as experimenter gives her music-box] [Sits with legs stretched out, slumped in chair.] Experimenter: Like that? *Cute.* [expressionless comment] Experimenter: It's called a music-box. Know why? [No response.] Experimenter: Guess. [Shakes head, eyes down, turning handle.] Experimenter: Does it make music? *Mmmm.* [mumbled] Experimenter: Which is better? *This.* [music-box]

[Experimenter brings out fur.] *Scarf . . . isn't that a nice scarf?* [Experimenter's comments: Positive response to clothes.] *Mommie has one home.* [She holds it out at arm's length, looking at it, smiling.] [Experimenter starts to rub it on her face; she draws away, saying:] *Mommie has one.* [Experimenter's comments: Looks rather annoyed as if to say: "Here I'm telling you something sensible and you're interrupting me with this face-rubbing nonsense."] Experimenter: What would you like to do with it? *You put it on.* [quickly, indistinctly] Experimenter: You put it on. *No.* [sneezes] Experimenter: Handkerchief? *No.* Which is nicest? [She stretches leg and rings bell with her foot. Experimenter understood this as an attempt to point to music-box with her foot.]

Experimenter: What is it? [copper ball] *Don't know . . . do you? . . . fence.* [Handles briefly, sets down.] Like how it feels? *No.* Which is nicest? *I like this.* Bell or music-box? *This.* [Picks up music-box, turns handle, sets it down.]

[Experimenter holds hair. Adele goes over and puts her hand on it.] *Cute.* [Experimenter's comments: Say-something-and-get-it-over-with.] Experimenter: Could it be hair? [She fingers it, touches the container.] Smell good? *Hmm.* Like how it feels? *Don't want . . . don't like it. . . .* You don't like it? *I do.* [Experimenter puts it on floor. Adele kicks at it.]

[Experimenter shakes sticks out on floor.] *Cute . . . those are cute. . . . What are those? You better play with them.* Experimenter: What will you do? *What do you do with those?* [Experimenter's comments: Needs clear, familiar function.] Experimenter: Anything you want. [She picks up nail.] Want to break one? *Mmmm.* [mum-

bles] Or shall I? *You. You break one.* [Experimenter breaks one.]
Want me to break another one? [No response.] You give me one . . .
what color? *Red.* What color is this? *Orange.* Which is the nicest color?
[Adele squirms around on chair.] Experimenter: Shall I break it?
[Experimenter breaks. Adele blinks.] *Bang.* [expressionless] Experi-
menter: Now you break one. *No.* Fun? *What's that noise?* Radiator.
Now what do you want to do? *Another one.* [toy] Experimenter:
Do we have to put these away first? [Adele shakes head.] Experi-
menter: Shall we leave them on the floor? *Mmmmm.*

[Experimenter shakes excelsior out on floor.] *Cute. We have
. . . home . . . Christmas trees.* [Picks some up; throws it awkwardly.]
Experimenter: What's nice about it? *I like it.* What do you like about
it? Is it pretty? What color do you like? *Blue.* [sitting back in chair]
[Experimenter's comments: This expresses her attitude.] Experimenter: Like how it feels or how it looks? *Looks.* . . . Experimenter:
What will we do with it? Put it right here? [on floor] [Adele nods
head.] Experimenter: Which is the best? *This.* [Taps bell with
foot.]

[Adele sits with hand in lap, half smiles as experimenter shakes
out wools.] *What are they for?* Experimenter: Whatever you want.
[Adele gathers them into pile.] *You play with them, will you?* [Ex-
perimenter's comments: Smug, withdrawn, not "letting go."] Experimenter: How? *Just play with them.* Like the colors? Which is
nicest? *You play with them.* [pushing pile with foot] Which is nicest?
[Adele indicates pale green.] Nice and soft. . . . You could throw
them at people, etc. . . . *Hit.* [Experimenter throws some at her, she
throws back at him with embarrassed smile.] Experimenter: Shall
I throw more at you? *No.* You throw more at me. [She throws.]
Experimenter: Shall I throw some at you? [She shakes her head.]
Hide them in there. [Buries two or three wools in pile of excelsior.]
Where are those wools? [Experimenter "looks" all around room for
wools. Adele sits in chair holding foot on wools buried in excelsior.]
[Experimenter's comments: Her role is very passive and unimagina-
tive. She could have gone on for hours.] [Experimenter finds wools.
Adele giggles.] *Now some more. . . . I hide them. . . .* [Puts foot
on wools, looks at experimenter expectantly. Experimenter "looks
and finds" again. Adele smiles and repeats the process twice more.]

[As experimenter examines horn, Adele says:] *What is that? Huh?
Cute, isn't it.* Experimenter: It's broken. [Experimenter tries to blow
it. Adele's mouth twists in blowing gesture as she watches him. Experimenter leaves to look for another horn. Adele picks up excelsior,
pulls at it, drops it. Goes to door, opens it, looks up toward garden
and down steps. Experimenter returns.] Experimenter: I couldn't
find it.

[Experimenter turns the kaleidoscope for her.] Experimenter:
Look through it. *I have one home.* Experimenter: Do you know what

it's called? [Adele shakes her head.] Kaleidoscope. Isn't that a funny name? [No response.] *I think that's pretty.* [as experimenter turns it for her] *I want something else.* Experimenter: Do you like the one at home? Do you play with it much? *Mmmm.* [mumbling, wiggling around on chair] [Remainder of record not given.]

Comment

Manner: At no time did Adele seem really released, or seem to be throwing herself into anything. She was always guarded, slightly anxious occasionally, particularly toward the end when she directly manifested eagerness to leave. At other times she showed a kind of swaggering bravado. There were moments when her smile seemed genuine, but usually it was merely polite or forced. She characteristically commented that everything was "cute," etc., without meaning it.

Sensory Interests: However, experimenter did not have the feeling that any of these things would have had much appeal, even if she had been at ease. She was not one of the children open to stimulation and keyed to the surroundings. Her primary needs seemed to be social acceptance, and everything else was secondary to her.

The only things she responded to at all genuinely, however briefly, were the excelsior (possibly because it reminded her of a Christmas tree) and the top which she seemed to like for a while, although she didn't want it repeated. There was distant (constricted) contact with the bell, using her foot to tap it.

She had a way of smiling or nodding: "Yes, that's fine. What's the next thing and when do I go?" The same kind of nod that a rather intolerant adult would show a child.

This limited response could hardly be due to general insecurity, since although she was ill at ease and self-conscious, at times she was able to dismiss the experimenter with "Don't do it again" very easily, and was able to give instructions: "You better button this."

The only time she seemed to be really interested, and then in a rather strained way, was during the game of hiding the wools, which apparently could have gone on endlessly. Here her interest seemed to confirm the fact that sensory appeals were meaningless essentially, and that the game appealed because of its social nature. The color top also appealed to her the first time.

Adele feels happy and safe only when she is in a conventional situation with people she knows, and knows will respond to her plain "wholesome" interests which are largely expressed in terms of social and large-muscle activities of a galumphing kind, or definite school jobs such as puzzles and painting.

Use of Materials: There was a poverty of intellectual or imaginative use of the materials.

Orderliness: She did not care about putting things away. This was part of her refusal to become really connected with any of the things; she persisted insofar as she could in maintaining a spectator role.

RECORD OF COLIN

[Experimenter brings Colin over from school.] Experimenter: Colin likes the snow. Abigail doesn't like snow. [This was an aside to recorder but Colin picks it up.] Colin: *But I do.* Experimenter: Why? *Maybe she hates it.*

[Experimenter offers chair to Colin.] *I want to sit on the bed.* [Experimenter gives him the bell. He turns it over, examines it, fiddles with knob; experiments with it, ringing it hard and softly.] Experimenter: What is that? Let me show you what it does. [Experimenter taps bell lightly. Colin taps it with palm of hand, then thumb.] *That's a telephone bell.* [He bangs it hard and shoves bell into experimenter's face. Experimenter takes it and gives him music-box.] Experimenter: Do you like the bell better hard or soft? *Soft.* [softly]

[Colin watches experimenter, all eyes, interested, eager. He turns the handle of the music-box.] *What is this?* Experimenter: Music-box. [Colin examines pictures on music-box which show frogs playing violin.] *Violin.* Experimenter: Who's playing a violin? *A frog.* Experimenter: Do you like that? *Yeah.* [turning handle] Experimenter: Does it say the same thing when you turn it the other way? [Colin turns it the other way.] Experimenter: Does it say the same thing? *Uh huh . . .* [Too much absorbed in music-box to give proper consideration to experimenter's question. He puts down music-box, picks up bell, whacks it with jerky motion.] Experimenter: Which do you like better? *This . . . Music-box.* [mouth open as he plays it]

What's this? [puts fur around his neck] Experimenter: Who has something like that? *Mommie doesn't.* Experimenter: Doesn't she? *Yes she does.* How does it feel? [Colin rubs fur on his chin with a blissful look. Offers it to experimenter.] Experimenter: You can put it over there with the other things. Which do you like best? *This and this and this.* [Points to all the things he has seen.]

What is it? [copper ball] Experimenter: What is it? Like how it feels? [Colin feels it, squeezes it.] *No.* No? *No.* [Rubs it on his chin and throws it toward experimenter.] *Play ball with it.* [He throws and catches it quite expertly.] Experimenter: Okay. [They toss it back and forth.] Experimenter: We could play ball with any of these things, couldn't we? *No.* Could we play ball with this. [copper ball] *Hate this.* Experimenter: All right, put it over here. [Colin plays with music-box again.]

[Experimenter puts hair on couch. Colin touches it.] *I like to feel this.* [Buries hands in it; pulls it into shreds; enjoying feel and resistance of it.] Experimenter: What does it feel like? Like how it smells? [When experimenter asks him this he sticks his face into it and makes a noncommittal remark.] Which is nicer, fur or hair? *This.* Experimenter: Which. *Fur.* [Experimenter tosses the hair to him.] *I want to put this away.*

Experimenter: Ever see one like this before? Have you one at home? [kaleidoscope.] *No.* [Colin kneels on couch, peering into kaleidoscope. Experimenter turns it around. Colin takes kaleidoscope away from experimenter and turns it over, looking into big end.] Experimenter: See something from that end too? Which is nicer? *This.* [big end] *You can hang it up too.* [pulling at loop of string and looking up at experimenter with a big grin] Experimenter: See what happens when you turn this. *What?* Experimenter: What? [Experimenter turns it for him, Colin peers into it.] *Squiggling things!* [enjoying his consonants in warm appreciative wonderment] Experimenter: Turn it like that. [Colin turns it.] Experimenter: What's the best thing so far? [Colin offers kaleidoscope to experimenter.] Experimenter: You can leave it there. Which is best? *Bell.*

[Colin hops off end of couch. Experimenter lets sticks fall on floor.] *What are these?* [Starts picking them up; starts to put them in box. Conversation takes place while he is putting them away; when they are all in the box he is done.] Experimenter: What are you doing? *Putting them in the box again.* Experimenter: Do you have to put them away before something else? *No.* Experimenter: Is it all right to leave them around on the floor? *Here are some broken.* Experimenter: You want to break some? *No, there wouldn't be enough.* Experimenter: Enough for what? *To go in the box.* Experimenter: What's the prettiest color? *All of them.* Experimenter: What color is this? *Purple.* Experimenter: Yes. *Yellow.* Experimenter: Yes. *Green.* Experimenter: Yes. Could you just leave them there? What do you want to do with the broken ones? Throw them away? *Uh huh.* Experimenter: Put this on the bed now?

[Experimenter lets cascade of wools fall to floor. Colin's eyes "pam" up and down, excited, eager for new surprise, taking it all in.]

Experimenter: Which color is best? *This one.* [red] Experimenter: This or this? [green or gray] *This.* [green] [He squeezes wool, rubs on face; starts to put them away:] *Look you can squeeze them!* [Squeezes; rubs on face; seems to like it.] Experimenter: We can throw them at people, etc. Want to throw some at me? [Experimenter throws some at him.] *Throw a lot!* [throws handful] Experimenter: Now I'll throw some at you. [Experimenter throws some at him.] *No! I don't like it.* [But Colin throws big bunch again, not hard, at experimenter, when assured that he can do it and experimenter will not.] Experimenter: Shall we leave them lying around? *No.* Experimenter: Why? *Because somebody might step on them.* Experimenter: You step on them. [Colin does.] Do you like to? *Yes.* Experimenter: Have to put them back? [No response.] Experimenter: What is the nicest thing? *These.* [pointing to all toys on couch] Experimenter: Which is the very best? *This and this and this. . . .* [pointing to all on couch: ball, music-box, fur, copper ball, kaleidoscope] Experimenter: How about these on the floor? *I don't like those.* [wool, sticks, hair]

[Experimenter brings out humming top. Colin is crawling around on couch. Experimenter spins top.] Experimenter: Listen. [Colin watches, and listens—enthralled.] *Give it to me.* [Takes top of top from experimenter and tries to wind it.] Experimenter: What are you doing, Colin? [No answer; brings top to experimenter.] Experimenter: Have you one of these at home? *No.* Experimenter: Want me to wind it? *Yes.* [Walks over to arm-chair.] *Me sit down too.* Experimenter: Okay, here's a chair. [Gets him to sit down in nursery school chair. Colin is trying to wind top and having a hard time with it.] *You do it.* Experimenter: Want me to do it? Oh, the spring came out . . . have to get another top.

Experimenter: Ever see one like this? [color top] [Colin watches absorbed, mouth open, lip curled. Breaks into a smile and suddenly reaches out to stop it and take it from experimenter.] What is it doing? [as he starts it again] *Making colors.* Want to hold it? [Colin takes it, holds it, looks attentively and suddenly reaches out and stops it.] *I'll make it go fast. I want to hold it.* Experimenter: Does it make your arm shake? Like that? *Yeah.* [Holds face close to top as it spins; then he stops it.] *I want it again.* Experimenter: All right. *One—two—three—four—five times!* [Experimenter spins it for him again; he holds it.] Experimenter: Which top is better? *This.* Experimenter: Why? *Because that top's broken.* [humming top] *I want to hold it.* Experimenter: Do you like to hold it or shall we put it on the floor? [when it's spinning] [No response.] Which, Colin? *Uh huh.* Experimenter: Hold it? *Uh huh.* Experimenter: Okay. Enough now? *Two more . . . Three more . . .* Experimenter: Which is the best thing? [Colin turns to pile of toys on couch.] *This and this and this.* [pointing to all of them] Experimenter: Which is best? . . . Just one. *This* *and this and . . . this.* Experimenter: Want to go to the toilet? *No.* Experimenter: All right, this is the last time. [Experimenter winds top.] *I want to see more.* Experimenter: That's all there is. Shall I put it on the floor? *No!* Experimenter: all right, you hold it. [Spins top again. Colin holds top, drinking in color, holds it and watches it even after it has come to a full stop.] *Once more . . .* Experimenter: Last time. [Experimenter winds top again.] *I want to hold it.* [Top spins . . .* Colin still has same absorbed interest.] Experimenter: Like those colors? *Uh huh.* [more interested in top than in answering experimenter's question] [Again Colin lets it come to full stop before giving it up to experimenter.] *Now put all the things away.* Experimenter: Can't we just leave them here, lying around? *Does this belong here?* [putting things in box] *And this and this . . . ?*

Comment[1]

Colin showed real sensory appreciation. He was the most generally responsive, drinking in all sense impressions and seeming to enjoy all of them. He seemed to enjoy all the things, whereas other children had been more selective. It was not just a matter of inability to make a choice when he said he liked everything: "This and this and this . . ."

Quite orderly: definite notion that everything should be put away broke down in the face of the wools which were scattered in wide disorder.

Refused to break sticks.

Teacher "pumpings" on these two children will give the reader a basis for making his own comparison of the play session data with teacher's observations of responses in nursery school.

ADELE

Adele doesn't know what sensory interest is. Her concern with things is how you use them; what you are supposed to do with them; what's acceptable; what's expected. Doesn't let loose on anything.

Painting: Entirely imitative, except when ridiculed by other

---

1. In Volume II Colin's multisensory response is discussed at greater length; it was intimately related to the development of rich fantasy and creativity. In later years he wrote poetry, played in the school orchestra, acted and sang in operettas.

children; then she makes an effort to make something different.

Color: Not especially aware of color. Aware of clothes, not because of texture, but because they're different. Aware of her own and other people's clothes: "I have a new scarf . . . pretty color." Very superficial. Having a new thing appeals to her. Said to her mother: "Why do you wear those slacks?"

Form: In block-building she will take the blocks out; has no plans; usually imitates somebody else's building.

Music: Unmusical; never heard her sing spontaneously.

Food: Drinks with dispatch. Her mother says she will eat anything. The only way her mother could get her to stay home from school was by promising to take her to Schrafft's.

Kinaesthetic: Getting some place as a result of effort; no particular enjoyment of motion.

COLIN

Pretty sensory; no guilt.

Clay: Very able to enjoy free sensory use, with imaginative running comment: "This is a sna-a-ake. I think I'll make two snakes . . . and a worm and an alligator."

Sounds: Keen, aware. He makes noises himself, beating blocks together.

Color: Sensitive to color. Quite a lot of fun in piling colors on top of each other to see what happens. Vigorously takes two brushes in each fist and paints that way. Free. Calls it: "Messy, messy, messy."

Tactual: Probably is the most avid sandboxer; a mudder too.

Form: Does not mean a lot to him.

Music: Very musical in solo situation.

Food: Good eater; lip smacker. His dramatic play is often full of food. An ardent gum chewer.

Kinaesthetic: Very swingy and slidey.

He is an all-around constructor-destructor—acting out all his ideas—not especially inhibited by anything.

Inspection of these records suggests the following hypotheses:

1. Responses to the wide range of sensory qualities of the

environment as sampled by these materials may be the result of

(a) Constitutional thresholds for positive or negative response to each modality of sensory experience and even to specific kinds of experience within a given modality.

(b) Conditioned and (or) canalized responses, including both positive reinforcement by the culture and negative or blocked responses in certain areas.

(c) Repressed anxiety or conflict which may lead by the age of three to inhibition of spontaneous pleasure in one or more areas.

2. Anxiety may be experienced and sustained by a child in a variety of ways:

(a) Segmentally, and (or) peripherally as a "fear," which does not produce generalized personality effects and may not be serious if sustained by a personality of wide satisfactions and spontaneous interests. That is, the child has localized fears (e.g., fire-engines) which do not interfere with great delight in life generally.

(b) A generalized and (or) central worry about certain classes of experience such as being left alone, getting dirty or messy, being lost in amorphous, unstructured situations which interfere with the child's capacity to respond to large areas of experience.

(c) Diffuse insecurity against which defensive compulsions have been set up which do not leave the child open for free-floating pleasure in response to unstructured materials and experiences although the child gets satisfaction out of conventional, ritualized, proper experience.

(d) Generally inhibiting fear without defenses or compensatory areas of freedom and satisfaction.

3. Areas of anxiety are more or less threatening as they confront further cultural disapproval or acceptance.

4. Areas of spontaneity are more or less satisfying as they confront cultural acceptance or resistance (mud; music; tricycles).

Even in a three-year-old child it is impossible to unravel constitutional and cultural factors in the development of these different ways of experiencing. Colin's mother was obviously a person of greater appreciations, while Adele's mother was a person of predominantly social and executive interests. But Colin's mother contributed chromosomes as well as an attitude toward life. Other experimenters will have to solve the problem of the relative weight of both influences in the quotient for spontaneity, and richness of experience.

The following summaries will further illustrate the range of responses of different children to the various modalities of sensory stimulation.

Claudia enjoyed tactual and smell stimuli while visual and auditory stimuli were almost meaningless, though she preferred the humming top to the color top. To the bell and music-box she said respectively, "Let's have the furry one," "Let's have the next one," and she enjoyed the "nice furry" scarf and other things that seemed to her to be soft. It is possible that this tactual preference may have been accentuated by visual difficulties recognized later which had not been diagnosed during her preschool years; she also enjoyed physical contact with people.

Carla's auditory and visual (especially color) interests were strong. She liked to bang the bell. With the color top she said, "Do it again . . . I like it . . . do it again . . . let me do it . . . give me something to take home . . ." as she watched, holding her breath and smiling with pleasure. She seemed to like the motion of the top as well. But she showed no tactual interest except in exploratory and functional contexts; the colored wools were valued for their decorative possibilities, to put on the Christmas tree, not for the soft furry quality which Claudia felt in them.

Cecily was outstandingly interested first in auditory, then in visual objects. She commented discriminatingly on the music-box and was enthusiastic about the bell, which she watched closely, eagerly asking, "How do you do that?" In response to the humming top, which she enjoyed as much as the color top, she said: "Both tops are better." She was excited by the kaleidoscope, peering into it with interest and exclaiming, "I want another!"

But with tactual stimuli she squirmed, or seemed impatient: "What do you do with it?" and "What's it for?" The fact that she was orderly at first, then messy afterward, and seemed comfortable only when definite functions were implied in objects or when they had definite structure, suggests that some of her inhibition to or rejection of tactual objects may have been primarily connected with guilty feelings about their amorphous or mess-inducing quality, while visual and auditory areas were free from such conflicts.

Patsy showed clear likes and dislikes within a general responsiveness to all forms of stimulation. Her visual responses were stronger than her tactual ones. She was, however, not abandoned to sensation, but more interested in doing things with objects. She was interested in how things worked and in manipulating them, and was somewhat creative with materials. She like noise, and rough-and-tumble play which the phonograph-record dust stimulated, reminding her of "Sa-a-a-a-nd." She liked the bell better than the music-box; liked the pink wools best; liked fur but disliked hair, enjoyed winding the tops but not the music-box—perhaps because there was nothing more for her to manipulate or do with it. The motor-manipulative aspects of objects predominated over their sensory value for her, in short.

Camille was deeply responsive to sensory stimuli of all sorts, visual, auditory, tactual, especially everything which had aesthetic values to her—the "pretty things" she saw in the kaleidoscope, the "pretty" excelsior cellophane, the "pretty" color top. In the case of all these objects the color and movement in color was especially stimulating to her. She said, "I love that!" when given the fur, and smiled responsively, enjoying the music-box. The colored wools overstimulated her, so that her controlled behavior at first changed to violent, gleeful, destructive messiness, but she was able to shift to a throwing game.

Joyce liked auditory, visual, and the soft tactual stimuli; she rejected the hair. She built a house with the sticks after teasingly threatening to break them. She loved the humming top: "Beautiful! Do it again." She seemed to be seeking sensory stimulation of an aesthetic quality, and was at the same time more provocative than the others, delighting in teasing threats to the adult.

Both Joyce and Camille developed subsequently in creative as well as active directions—poetry in Joyce's case and dramatic work in that of Camille; both enjoyed sports.

The boys had equally clear-cut reactions. Alec was definitely interested in color, tactual experience, and smells, but had a limited auditory interest. The color top was especially stimulating to him: "When's it going to stop? Let me hold it now. I want to do it again. You wind it up again, I'll spin and you grab it." Here the movement combined with the color was exciting, but the movement of the humming top produced much less of a response. Curiosity, and some aggressive anal and sex implications, seemed to be involved in Alec's feelings. He broke one of the sticks quickly and did not use the rest in any way except to poke one at the experimenter's mouth.

Calvin was the least responsive child of the group with the sensory materials. He seemed suspicious of the music-box, stoical with the fur, played gingerly with the copper ball, thought the hair didn't look like anything, pulled apart the colored excelsior and gave a shred to the experimenter, but seemed to enjoy the color in the kaleidoscope, the wools, and the color top. His visual preference seemed clear, and the fact that he shook the cellophane and sprinkled the dust around seemed to point to a covert need to toy with destruction and messiness, the inhibition of which was shutting him off from the other sensory experiences.

Joel was especially responsive to auditory stimuli, and ignored or seemed uninterested in tactual experiences. Manipulative interests, kinaesthetic and intellectual interests were strong and he had considerable curiosity. He wanted to know what was in the music-box, wanted the humming top repeated—"Beautiful!"—and was equally interested in the color top, smiling excitedly and exclaiming, "Say! See if it spins any more!" He wanted to return to the music-box after playing with some other things; to him the music-box was "an oriole singing, a boy playing the piano." He was not interested in the amorphous stuff, and liked the unstructured materials only when they lent themselves to being structured. His attention span seemed brief, but perhaps he got everything he could out of the primitive materials in a short time and since they didn't lend themselves to his interests, shifted to others. In later years he was interested in music and as a college student, psychology.

Jeremy had definite, not intense sensory interests, especially in color and texture; he was equally interested in structured and unstructured materials, and recognized areas where order was desirable without being preoccupied with it or being inhibited by it. He liked the bell loud and swung it with a large whole-arm movement, suggesting that it gave an outlet for motor interests as well. The fur was "pretty." He rejected the copper ball as "bad." With the sticks he made a house and an airplane, and when a suggestion to break one was given, excitedly burst out, "Break them all up!" The colored wools and color top excited him especially and stimulated fantasies of fire. The phonograph-record dust stimulated fantasies of spilling and getting on people's feet, then rejecting the mess because his mother didn't like him to make a mess in her room; finally he just played with it: "I make it nice and sawf." The intensity of the fire fantasy suggested that he has a problem about spilling over into undifferentiated primitive feelings when he gets excited.

Jay responded spontaneously only to the color top, colored wools, and kaleidoscope; he rejected the music-box as a "baby thing," and other amorphous things with, "Don't like that." He warmed up slowly, with considerable defense against spontaneity, followed by an aggressive release of excited admiration and pleasure especially at the color top. A forced laugh, and "swell boy" pattern were expressions of the "front" that was his defense against indulgence in spontaneous enjoyment of a wide range of sensory stimuli. In school later he was a member of an orchestra, but teachers complained that while he did everything well he lacked originality.

Kene showed a spontaneous and unadulterated delight in almost all the toys and materials, in all modalities and degrees of structuredness, with a deep warm appreciation of visual, auditory, tactual stimuli, easy uproarious enjoyment of the materials, and no concern with putting-away, no anxiety about tossing or throwing.

Thus, at the preschool level, some children are free to respond to, enjoy, and utilize a wide range of sensory experience, while others are narrowed either to specific modalities or to certain kinds of items within a modality. These tendencies depend on thresholds which have developed presumably as a result of interaction of initial or constitutional thresholds with the child's experiences in his culture, including parental stimulation or prohibition of behavior in response to different modalities or to specific activities with certain kinds of things in one modality or another; and to parental encouragement or discouragement of exploratory activities in general. A child like Jeremy, who had a tendency to become extremely excited when overstimulated, might arouse in some parents a generalized prohibition against excitement, and the exploratory activity which could lead to it. We know that Colin was capable of wild excitement and abandoned feeling, which was evidently tolerated by his family; and also know that his multisensory responsiveness was supported by the varied interests of the family, in music, life in the woods, sports, boating, gardening, home activities, and books.

It would not be possible to say at this point that one or another type of selection or shaping of responses in different modalities is related to "adjustment." Jay's dependence on structured form for sensory interests could support an interest in music in his later childhood years, which gave him satisfying outlets, and at the same time kept his interests within the range of what the culture could comfortably accept. Claudia's lack of response to visual and auditory stimuli narrowed her interests as compared with the range enjoyed by other children, but her high intelligence gave her the material for a good development. Camille's wide sensory responses led to an interest in artistic and dramatic activities which took her to a school for art instead of to college. In general we can infer that the pattern of responses in different modalities provides a basis for important aspects of the personality development, values, and interests of the individual; our culture has room for many different sorts of persons and activities, vocational and avocational, and both a unisensory and a multisensory person can find a place for himself in the culture. Difficulties arise at certain stages, as when in some elementary schools a child with a strong interest in form and visual design, for instance, and slight interest in motor activity, like Stanley,[2] confronts the demand of the peer-culture for motor skills not in his repertoire. By high school or college age the intellectual and creative skills natural to such a person are in greater demand and roles suited to his pattern of interests are available.

The range of modalities to which the child responds readily is thus an important determinant of the impact of the environment, the stimuli which reach him and his tendency to be over-stimulated, enriched, or indifferent to them. It selects the menu of experience and doubtless also provides avenues for sublimation or release. Whether or not a multisensory child "adjusts" will depend partly on whether his intelligence, motor skills, and other equipment for integration afford him adequate ways of dealing with his rich impressions. Whether or not a unisensory child is adjusted may depend partly on whether verbal, motor, social, or other outlets are adequate to handle the needs which he cannot sublimate in sensory or artistic ways as readily as could the multisensory child. Obviously in each instance many other factors such as the patterns of instinctual drives and autonomic response can play a decisive role in shaping the patterns and quality of experience, its meaning and what the child does with it.

We must therefore be wary of assuming values for adjustment in one or another constellation of thresholds or competences in different modalities as such, but rather watch these to see what they are contributing to the design of the developing personality, and the place it is making for itself in the culture.

---

2. See Chapter 15.

CHAPTER 4

Dough and Cold Cream

IT IS ORDINARILY SAID that paints and fingerpaints are releasing to children and are apt to stimulate rich fantasy. This is true at the older levels, but the two- and three-year-old child is sometimes too busy getting acquainted with the possibilities of the medium. Paints are a new object to him at first, with new visual and tactual experiences which he takes in gradually. He does not give out, frequently, until he has absorbed the medium and achieved some mastery of its potentialities for him at that stage.

Casting about, therefore, for a medium with less new-experiences or reality-orientation than paints, we began the use of a flour-salt-water mixture, and later changed to cold cream.

Research Assumptions and Aims

It was anticipated that sticky, plastic substances with which the child did not ordinarily play might serve several purposes.

1. Since the material appealed intrinsically to tactual interests, it would reveal the presence or absence of such interest, and specific qualities it took on in different children, some of

whom might exploit the tactual possibilities aggressively, others more tenderly or delicately.

2. Since current suburban mores are generally strict against getting dirty or messy, the opportunity to handle this type of material would reveal to what extent a child was coerced by taboos, to what extent he was free to use the material in his own way; the anxiety that attended his inhibition if he was not free, and the types of defenses involved in maintaining his inhibition.

3. Since the material would be new, it would add data to the picture which we wanted to build up of the child's spontaneity; freedom to explore in a new situation; and his pattern of response, of handling his insecurity if he was not free. Since data on this third point were acquired in most of these situations with toys, animals, materials different from the familiar ones with which the child played, the results will not be discussed in as much detail as results pertaining to the first and second points.

4. Since the material did not have formal associations, it might release free fantasy.

The procedure was simple. The materials were placed in the pan on the floor, which had been covered with an oilcloth or newspapers for protection. The child was merely told, "You can play with this today." If he did not begin to play within a couple of minutes, the experimenter began to play with the materials, feeling the ingredients, mixing a little of the material. If the child did not respond to this illustration of possibilities, the experimenter proceeded to make a cake and invited the child to do so too. If the child began of his own accord to explore the material, no suggestions were given. Running notes were taken of the child's handling of the material, his attitudes, conversation, and demands. The child was permitted to leave when he wished.

Varieties of Response to Dough

From the point of view of the range of responses elicited from the children, results were better than expected. Joyce loved to feel the flour, salt, and water separately, giving evidence of marked sensitivity to nuances of texture. Colin joyfully scattered flour all over the place, squooshing, slapping, pounding ingredients and dough with abandoned delight, and made a cake and a "tower." Christopher and others, by contrast, were interested only in what could be made with the dough, forms and objects to be constructed taking precedence over the sensations to be gained from handling the materials as Joyce and Colin did.

One boy was reminded of the analogous pleasures of mud and remarked wistfully, "I can't dig in my garden . . . there isn't any place for myself," and then worried about the stuff he had spilled on his shoes.

Another little girl whispered "I can't" at first, and approached the dough almost tentatively. She ran her hand in a gingerly way through the mess, and did not squeeze the dough until the experimenter had done so. However, when she did, she squeezed *very* hard, with a kind of aggressive violence which no other child showed. After more play she volunteered, however, "I don't think it's nice." Yet when the experimenter started to put away the pan, she resisted: "I'm not all finished yet." She shook her hands through the mess saying, "Gooey, gooey, gooey!" She squeezed, made balls of the dough. But at the end, after she had washed her hands, she said, "I never want to do that again . . . why did you do this to me?" Her expressive face appeared "mildly horrified and puzzled," wanting rapport at the beginning; after being released by the experimenter's example she was definitely aggressive with the paste, in contrast to the other children, and then seemed to develop a sense of guilt as she went on, apparently feeling this was naughty. Among other comments made in the context of cleaning up after the dough, she said, "My mother spanks me if I'm naughty . . . I cry so the neighbors hear . . . sometimes I scratch her and she spanks me."

This type of anxiety and hostility was released directly and indirectly in connection with other materials such as celluloid dolls, housekeeping toys, etc., and should not be regarded as a specially unique result of the dough experiment as such al-

FIGURE 20 — One child gets in "all over" with reckless, abandoned delight.

though "messy" materials naturally release hostilities associated with repression of messing tendencies.

Most striking among the differences more directly sharpened by the dough-play were differences between children who enjoyed the amorphous sensory experiences which the dough offered and those who were cheerfully absorbed in forms and objects to be made with the dough; those who were gentle in contrast to the aggressive splashers; those who were free to explore it without adult example versus those who were inhibited; those who played with it within a limited area and those who knew no bounds, not even those suggested by the protective newspapers or oilcloth on the floor.

Varieties of Response to Cold Cream

While the dough proved provocative and revealing, it was a mess to clean up, especially after children like Colin, who indulged in a field day and got the kitchen, where it was used, thoroughly spattered and sticky. In the interests of finding other materials that might serve similar purposes both cold cream and mud were tried.

Cold cream has tactual quality and can be spattered; it was also used to smear and paint with in a way in which the dough was not used. However, it is *one* material, not three in contrast to the flour-salt-water arrangement prepared for the dough, so that it did not bring into sharp relief the sensitivity to nuances of tactual sensation characteristic of certain children. Nor could cold cream be adapted to the formal uses of pie-making, etc., like dough and mud. Cold cream released anal associations more frequently than had the dough. The fact that it did not invite objectively-oriented discrimination (as between flour and salt) may underlie its value for release of fantasy. For the moment, anal aspects of the uses of all three materials will be set aside until we have looked at some records.[1]

---

1. Records will be quoted in more detail for this procedure than for dough.

The following excerpts illustrate the use of cold cream by children who did not expand into verbal fantasy directly.

Amy enjoys cold cream for its own sake: she kneels down in front of the jar, takes the lid off, regards the cold cream with quiet pleasure and astonishment. After experimenter's suggestion (You may play with it), she pokes her forefinger slowly into the jar, and draws out a minute blob of cold cream, bends her finger in the palm of her hand and placidly rubs it in between fingers and as far as finger is capable of reaching. Leisurely puts finger forward and brings forth another miniature blob of cold cream, scrapes and re-scrapes finger in clenched fist over and over again. She grins at experimenter radiantly. She squooshes and smooths left hand against right with a glowing smile at the contact of one hand against the other. She "washes" hands together, her tongue sticking out. With a very deep-rooted interest and absorption, secures still another blob of cold cream and smooshes hands together. With her eyes starry she grins and digs into the jar more forcefully than before, lifts out a large blob, tongue out, spreads cold cream on her wrist, adds another blob, squooshes it on her hand, and with more rapid tempo secures two blobs in succession, really getting into it now. After some time at this sort of activity she has done a very thorough job on both arms. She scrapes two ridges of cold cream on both hands, and attempts to pick it off her overalls when a blob falls on them. More scratching, pressing, rubbing are followed by slapping, which produces small splatters of cold cream.

[Kurt came into the room, stood staring down at the jar of cold cream, circling warily around it.] *What's dat?* [repeatedly] [He dropped to his knees, tried to unscrew the top of the jar:] *How do you open this thing?* [After he had opened it he looked at it inquisitively:] *You know what this is?* [Experimenter explained that it was cold cream. Kurt dipped two fingers into it, smeared in rather scratchy finger strokes in three different areas on the oilcloth, asking:] *What do with it?* [He then asked other questions about the oilcloth and why it was there. He smeared it with his right hand on the right edge, with his left hand waving loosely in the air, smeared a finger around the top edge of the jar, swishing the cold cream around inside. This was typical of his activity during the rest of the session.]

In contrast with these children, whose response to the cold cream was in terms of sensory delight and manipulation, Philip carried on a constant stream of associations, both suggested by and remote from the material he was playing with:

Philip, half listening to the experimenter's explanation, knelt on the oilcloth . . . lifted off the top of the jar, lightly pressed his finger into the cold cream, taking out a very small blob, then another. He wiped it off the fingers on his left hand, working it into his right hand with his thumb. He clasped the remainder of the blob between his forefinger and middle finger, pressed a blob on the oilcloth, pressed a finger in the center, the cold cream sticking to it. He dug his forefinger in twice and slapped his finger against the cold cream.

[He picked at a thread in the cold cream, dug his hand in the jar, spread the cold cream brought out—first on the oilcloth and then smeared it more freely on his hand, and rubbed his fingers off on each other.] *Need to take care of the tail of this thing.* [referring to the thread] Experimenter: The tail of what? *The cat. Molly and I will be cats . . . I always have fun with Molly.* [Experimenter and Philip continued talking informally about what Philip did, about his birthday and picnic.]

[Then he pulled out a huge load of cold cream, raising it in his hand.] *Look how much I got this time . . . Quite a load!* [He inserted his hands into the jar, drew them out completely covered.] *Making gloves.* [holding his hands up; the weight of the cold cream makes it lean to one side] *I don't mind if it is lopsided . . . Whoop . . . Whoop!* [taking out more cream, more excited] *Need to take all that stuff out . . . Haa haa haa haa haaa!* [Bubbling, gurgling with laughter, he seems to expand physically, his chest puffs out.] *Look at that cream! Look! Look!* [His breathless, beaming laughter continued, he crowed, permitted a ball of cold cream to fall off his hand, stared down at it, then up at experimenter:] *I hate that piece.* Experimenter: Why? *Because it dropped off . . . Will it come out by itself?* Experimenter: I don't know, you can see. [He turned the jar upside-down, shook it, not very disappointed when it did not come out, then took out more.] *Woo! Look how much I got this time!* [He held a huge amount cupped in both hands, then dropped it on the floor and looked up elatedly.] *This time I take a lot—it's going to make a big pile that I need . . . It's a tail and a mouth and everything! There's not much left.* [peering into the jar]

[He dug out a huge ball, dropped it.] *This will drop off . . . I'll let it drop off . . . I bet it's going to make a hole in the board . . . I bet it will get awful sticky!* [in happy anticipation] *These little pussies right here . . . Boom . . . Boom. I bet I hear Molly . . . Why didn't you come at resting time?* [All these remarks came out directly on top of each other with very little space between the ideas. After a few more comments on Molly, he burrowed into the jar again.] *Look how much came out this time!* [cupping his hands and holding a huge ball of cold cream]

Woof! Says the big goose. . . . . Get this piece off! [He leaned forward shaking his hand limply from the wrist.] *I said to that piece "Get that off! Get that off!" I say it again.* [ominous whispering] Experimenter: Then what does it do? *Come off, it came off this time.*

[He wiped his hands on each other very vigorously.] *Look what I did . . . Get that off . . . It came off . . . I took it off with my fingers . . . Oh it didn't come off yet!* [He stirred the cold cream in the jar.] *I have to get more of this stuff . . . Mmmmmm . . . Have to get some more . . . A lot some more . . . I'm getting very lucky.* Experimenter: Why? *Because I want to . . . Because I like it . . . It came off.*

Philip's type of association pattern represents a very different sort of fantasy from the explicit and focused variety carried on by Dusty.

[Bringing her right hand into use, still covering a relatively small area, she dipped two fingers into the jar, spreading the cream on the oilcloth.] *See this is a great big running brook.* [She dipped her left hand in, pressed her right hand against the left, bent over the cold cream, and rubbed it horizontally.] *This is the rest of the running brook . . . Great big running brook . . . Great big running brook. Isn't the running brook big? Isn't it? It's not very deep. It's the running brook that whirls people way down to the bottom . . . Great big running brook. . . . It whirls like this . . . It whirls round and round.* [rubbing her finger in quick circles over the surface of the cold cream] *I have to take a whole lot to make a great big running brook. One day the donkey ran into the running brook and the running brook overflowed really. I have a toy donkey because I'm not big enough to have a real donkey. . . . See, I'm making a bridge right now.* [She plopped a large blob of cold cream in the middle of the oilcloth.] *You have to stay on this bridge because the bridge doesn't go whirling round and round . . . Then I make the running brook kind of bumpy.* [She slaps the cold cream with her hand, creating a wave-like effect.] *This is the place where the people go . . . See them running up the stones? I'm making a running brook.*

Eric's fantasy has still another aspect of taking its departure from the observation of the texture and quality of the plastic medium, and also suggesting a strong anal excitement in play with it.

He immediately dug into the cold cream, took out a large handful, smeared it on the oilcloth, then took out a second handful and added it to the other. Smeared with the right hand vigorously in circular motions, switched to overhand strokes for a second or so, dug in for a third handful, spread it and the other cold cream already on the oilcloth all across the bottom of the oilcloth. He skittered back to the jar and took out a fourth handful, continued wild free smearing process, kneeling on the floor, not the oilcloth, apparently to have more room on the oilcloth.

[He grunted as he reached the far area, looked from one hand to another and squooshed them together.] *This is a river . . . No boats go over it . . . It's just a river where you get milk from . . .* [After further playing he giggled quietly, sat back washing his hands with the cold cream, then laughed, shrill genuine laughter, rippling up from a low register to a shrill piercing register.] *Can you see the river?* [He laughed again shaking, buried his head on his knees, rocking back and forth.] *This is where the milkman gets milk from!*

The excitement and extreme laughter were probably stimulated both by the attention of a little girl who looked in at the smearing, by the fact that it was the first real spring day and all the children had been hilarious out of doors, and possibly by the fact that this was the first experience with this material and one of the first Eric had had with this kind of material at all, since he had refused to come with this experimenter before. It is also important to note that some concern with soiling his pants had been reported by his mother, so that the actual process of smearing probably had more anal symbolic value for him than for the other children discussed here.

A similar hilarity with explicit anal associations appeared in the record of Jay, who also had refused for a long time to come to the experimental room with the experimenter.

[At first Jay ignored the cold cream. Experimenter carried on some conversation with him, and let him warm up by playing with a balloon. The conversation led to laughter, then Jay rolled into the cold cream before he saw it.] *What do you paste with it?* [misinterpreting its nature] *Gooo Gooo Goooooo!* [He got a handful of the cold cream.] *That's Goo Gooo Gooo!* [hearty, bubbling, delighted, delightful, infectious laughter] *Goosh . . . Goosh! . . . Make a house with this! Ooooooo look at me! Wheee! Gooosh! Now you want to look at me!* [After more explosions of this sort he wiped his hands on a towel.] *Wow! That's fun! Goosh, that's fun. Dooo doo that's fun! I smell doo doo in the panties. Woosh! Does painters have their hands like this? Goosh!* [He rubbed and swished it in both hands.] *Do doo in the panties. I see panties up in the air . . . This is fun!* [He made a sound of mock disgust as he squirted goosh on the floor.] *Squirt it in here? Shall I? Oink! I love it! I said, "I hate it." Goooosh!*

Jay's enthusiasm continued for some time, but with no new ideas or qualities of response, so that it is not necessary to continue the record here.

USE OF COLD CREAM SITUATION FOR PLAY INTERVIEW

As in the Miniature Life Toy experiment it is sometimes desirable to use situations like this for interview or conversation with the child, to get additional information which may not appear clearly in the play session itself. Some examples of this procedure with children who were distinctly responsive to the cold cream are given here.

[Philip gave the experimenter an opening:] *If you were home my mother would see just what you do.* [Experimenter followed up the lead:] What do you think she would do? *I think she would yell at me!* [No fear here, more to be regarded as a joke.] Experimenter: What would she say? *She would say, did I get that full of it?* Experimenter: Would she be cross? *Yes . . . She would cry.* Experimenter: When does she cry? *I don't know. She really doesn't cry . . . My father doesn't really cry. I just hear a sound from crying.* [wisely] Experimenter: I suppose she cries sometimes. [as if to reassure him that adults do; that it isn't something strange] What else makes her cry? *I don't know. My father just spanks me . . . Spank me . . . Spank me! . . .* Experimenter: Why does your father spank you? *I don't know. . . . I'm making a lot.* [It's hard to side-track him.] Experimenter: What do you do that's bad? *Boo!* Experimenter: Do you make a mess at home? *No.* Experimenter: Jump around? *No.* Experimenter: Make noise? *Yes.* Experimenter: I bet you do! *Do you hear me? I make Miss Gray and Miss Molly my friend. Miss Molly? She's a girl . . . Woooo. . . .* [spreading cold cream vigorously; much intake of breath, sheer delight] *You know why I'm doing this? So I can put in that cold cream. . . . It's warm on this thing, you know it?* Experimenter: Yes. *Look . . . Look at my leg! . . . Now lookit the other side of my . . .* [displaying both sides of legs] *Now watch me pour this!* [Turns jar upside-down, rolls it about in cold cream.] *See that stuff . . . See the way it's cleaning.* [vigorous body movements] *Wooop . . . Wopppp . . . Look what came out of the jar. . . .* [Scrapes cold cream into lid of jar.] *Isn't that funny? Get in . . . Get in the top . . . Darn . . . Get in* [lifting cold cream in hands and piling it on] *Get in! Get in! Get in! Get in! Get in!* [voice soaring and dropping] *Get in, Tootsie . . . That isn't nice to say* [coyly to experimenter]. Experimenter: Get in Tootsie isn't nice? *Tootsie is nice.* Experimenter: Why isn't "get in" nice? *You must say "Please get in . . . Please come in," open the door and they say "Hello" and they come in.* Experimenter: What else isn't nice to say? [no answer] Experimenter: What is nice to say? [Philip very busily "washing" hands] *Do you mind if I get my shoe in there?* Experimenter: What do you think your mother will say? *Look . . . Now how we going to get that off?* [viewing shoe with distaste] Experimenter: What do your big sisters do when you get spanked? *I don't know . . . Somebody comes along and says "What's the matter Philip?"* Experimenter: Who says that? *I don't know.* Experimenter: What do you say? *I don't know.* Experimenter: Do you say "My daddy spanked me?" *No.* Experimenter: Do you? *No.* Experimenter: Does it make you feel good when somebody comes along and says "What's the matter with Philip?" *Yes.* Experimenter: Make you feel better? *Yes and I get a tissue . . . I get a tissue . . .* [mutters something about "friends"] *Alice* [his sister] *isn't my friend. She switches me all the time.* Experimenter: Switches you all the time? *Yes.* Experimenter: Why does she switch you? *I don't know. She just wants to.* [continuing to spread cold cream on the oilcloth area thickly covered with cold cream] *See the way we get it up. . . .* [pushes jar with lid] Experimenter: Who else spanks you and switches you? *I don't know.* [good-natured evasiveness] Experimenter: Is Alice your sister? *Look on my shoe . . . Haaahaaa* [gleefully examining shoe which is marred by cold cream] Experimenter: What's your other sister's name? *Doris.* Experimenter: Does Doris switch you? *No . . . Not all the time. Sometimes.* [debonair] Experimenter: What does she do? *It was warm.* [rubbing oilcloth] Experimenter: Does Doris play with you? *Yes, only if I'm a good boy.* Experimenter: What does she do if you're bad? *She just comes along and scares me.* Experimenter: Which do you like best, Alice or Doris? *Doris . . . Doris is the best all the time.* [Experimenter mentions playing with something else.] *Yes, I'd better get washed up and then play with some more.* Experimenter: Play with some more what? *Some more that stuff.* Experimenter: Really? *Yes.* Experimenter: Well you could do that. I tell you what, maybe we might play with the toys for a while. You haven't played with the toys for quite a while. *Why don't you get two sets?* [Experimenter aids Philip in cleaning up.] Experimenter: Who gives you your bath, does Doris, or Alice or Mommie? *Sometimes mother . . . Sometimes Jim.* Experimenter: Who is Jim? *Do you know who our maid is?* [wide, expansive smile] *Cora.* Experimenter: Cora? *Yes.* Experimenter: Is she nice? *Jim is Mr. Morris.* [Belated response to question, entirely spontaneous without having to be reminded. Mr. Morris is Philip's father.] Experimenter: Mr. Morris is Jim? Is your maid as nice as Doris? *Yes . . . She's the nicest dimple!!* [gurgling, jokey manner] *She has the nicest dimple!* Experimenter: Who has? *The maid . . . She just looks sweet! This morning I just hugged her and switched her this morning!!!* [joy too intense to describe] Experimenter: What does she do when you hug her and switch her? *She feels nice . . . And she feels warm!* [voice caressing and rolling over words] Experimenter: She feels nice and she feels warm? *She feels flowers and she feels lights and she feels everything!*

MORE VARIATIONS
IN RESPONSIVENESS TO COLD CREAM

Cold cream, like every other medium, is not equally appealing to every child. Colt looked at it and walked away: "I don't like it." Then he asked questions about the use of the oilcloth, paper towels, etc., and asserted that he liked toys to play with. When the experimenter asked if it was naughty to play with this stuff he said, "Yes . . . waste it," then later rationalized, "I can't do it cause somebody put mercurochrome on my thumb."

On the other hand, different children may be released in different ways by a medium. All degrees of caution, slow orientation, and exploratory use of the cream were found in the records of children. Colin and Alec were extremely free with it, getting it all over themselves and the oilcloth, without regard to clothes, shoes, or anything that might be messed up by it. Both of them were active and aggressive, enjoying big splatters and dropping gobs of it on the floor. Colin got it in his hair and all over his face when he was three years old, and at four he covered his head with it so that he looked like a clown in the circus. Both also enjoyed the tactual experiences it offered, and slapped, squooshed, scraped with the cream—Colin showing more range and ingenuity in this form of exploitation of the cream.

One or two other types of reaction are worth illustrating. Several girls played with the cold cream, smearing it, feeling it, rubbing it; then, after an initial smearing, made a definite patern in the cream. Claudia drew fences, streets, squares and the like as she did later with finger paints. Adele used it like sand or mud, attempting to make cakes, without regard to the special quality of cold cream that makes it difficult to give it any stable structure.

Interest in molding and playing with feces is one manifestation of sensory, tactual, texture interest and appreciation. The effect of heavier repression, in such activity, may be generalized, and may be extended to repress later interests in the whole area of texture and actual activity while among other children who do not meet harsh responses, tactual appreciations develop normally.

Thus the relationship between anal interests and such activities as those with cold cream would be not one in which the feces is primary and everything later represents feces, but a relationship that is determined by all of the relevant inhibiting influences imposed by mother, nurse, *et al.*

If we find a rejection of such materials, as in Colt and to some extent in Claudia, we may be justified in asking whether there was a strong repression of anal interests in the past, although the positive expression of interest in such materials is not necessarily connected with anal activities.

There *may* be a relation between the two kinds of activities and materials, even where there is positive interest (e.g., Jay). Again we might expect that the connection is one that has been imposed by adult pressure, and there may even be an extra delight in the experience because of the previous taboos on pleasure in anal explorations.

Basically the interest in feeling textures, in squooshing, or whatever is involved in handling gooey materials, is in terms of their own values as sensory stimuli just as running can be fun for the function-satisfaction alone.[2]

Summary

Dough and cold cream were studied originally with the intention of getting away from the objective orientation induced for many children by the color and relatively new experience of paints and finger paints. Obviously, this purpose was realized only in part. Suburban children brought up in streamlined apartments or model houses are not so familiar with either dough or any other messing-around experience as one might expect. For most children the opportunity to play with "goo" was a novel one.

At the same time, children had had enough experience with

---

2. Animal experiments are now demonstrating the importance of free sensory experience for the development of intelligence. See William R. Thompson, "The Inheritance and Development of Intelligence from Genetics and the Inheritance of Integrated Neurological and Psychiatric Patterns," *Proceedings of the Association for Research in Nervous and Mental Disease,* Vol. XXXIII (Baltimore: William & Wilkins, 1954).

trying out messing at home so that the situation had different meanings: some had associations of severe taboo or punishment attitudes from adults; others had along with this, or milder experiences of disapproval, memories of extreme delight possibilities in this experience.

Moreover, the material itself, "relatively unstructured" though it was, had its own qualities which clearly elicited much of the behavior typical for this situation. The high plasticity of the cream, the fact that it can be completely dominated, yet is not easily amenable to the creation of specific forms (as is clay); the extreme permissiveness of the situation, heightened by the fact that it was a situation ordinarily associated with taboos, are all relevant to the type of responses we have seen.

With all the wide variations, from one child to another, which are apparent in either the play with "relatively unstructured material" like cold cream, or "relatively structured material" like Miniature Life Toys, each medium has its own range, which is related to its own qualities as a medium. This suggests the importance of using fundamentally different types of material to get different facets of the fantasy life of the child.

In the records given, different types of response within the range of responses characteristic of cold cream can be distinguished.

1. A child who has not experienced strong taboos, who accepts the situation as completely permissive, and experiences it as undirected by either the adult or the form of the material, may find himself on a roller-coaster, as it were, of experience, with the roller-coaster type of experience of freedom from time-space forms.

2. Another child, more inhibited and unable to slide along easily in the formless experience offered by the cold cream, may make an initial compulsive effort to get beyond the taboos within him, and experience an explosive burst of freedom, with incoherent associations and feelings. He behaves like a person who is drunk, and for perhaps the same reason; that his usual patterns of behavior are broken when he is released from his inhibitions, like the novice under the effect of a little alcohol.

3. Another child, who reacts overtly less than the first two,

may nevertheless find the experience one rich in appreciation. This is the child who responds to other tactual experiences richly, and who enjoys the milder sensations of sliding, smoothing, softness which the medium offers.

In these different patterns of response we can distinguish different emphases on the perceptual, motor, and creative aspects of experience in different children; whatever the predominant emphasis of an individual child, we find that the rapid restructuring of the perceptual field made possible by a medium of this degree of plasticity presents a combination of affective nuances, conative structures, and perceptual patterns relatively free from stereotyped habits, and integrated at a pre-differentiation level more primitive than those apparent in the records of Miniature Life Toys.

CHAPTER 5

Personality Appraisal Through Painting

by TRUDE SCHMIDL-WAEHNER

MOTOR, VERBAL, AND DIRECT emotional expression are differentiated to a greater degree in the preschool child than his graphic expression through drawing or painting; not until the age of four, or sometimes five, does a child frequently paint forms and objects which an adult can recognize. Yet the years before representational drawing and painting are achieved are full of expressive experimentation which produces rich records of the child's impulses, and yields material very useful for structural or form analysis.

The paintings used in this study were made during the course of everyday nursery school life without any of the special arrangements which a more formal research plan would have required. The intention was to avoid any interference with normal school routines. The nursery schoolroom was equipped with back-to-back standing easels, each of which had a shelf with supports for six bottles of paint: red, yellow, orange, green, and blue were almost always available, with brown or black as the sixth color. The children were allowed to dilute and mix their own paint when they wished to, and received help when they wanted it. Certain children mixed paint in bottles, others mixed it on paper; still others kept colors separate, and thus did not have so many to work with. Standard unprinted newsprint was used for the painting surface. Children began on their own initiative and were permitted to paint one picture after another, stopping when they wished.

Under these spontaneous conditions a number of incidental factors could influence the result. Dribbling on the steeply slanting easel could produce shapes not intended by the child and implied that he was not concerned in keeping his brush dry enough to prevent the dripping. Black was not regularly included in the colors available to the child and its use is therefore hard to evaluate. The children had no choice in the size or shape of paper or in the size of the brush they used. They were not pressed for comments about their paintings, so that there is no record of associations; and no notes on imitation, spilling, or special outside stimulations were made. A more thorough study would have been possible had there been such records.

The value of children's pictures as psychological material lies not only in the major and easily classifiable elements such as color and direction of line or preference for blots versus lines, but also in the unique configuration of the individual child's painting. We cannot, therefore, limit the process of interpretation to a mechanical scoring of psychological factors such as intelligence, control, and emotions, but must take into account the many concrete formal qualities which appear in the paintings of a particular child. In my interpretations of children's drawings and paintings I have developed a tentative scoring system through a series of intensive studies and experiments with small groups of children.[1] Before presenting the version of this system which I found valuable in analyzing the paintings of the children in the Sarah Lawrence Nursery School, I will explain the theoretical assumptions on which it is based.

In studying sequences of children's pictures from a formal point of view, we can experience the changing relations be-

---

1. "Formal Criteria for the Analysis of Children's Drawings," *American Journal of Orthopsychiatry*, XII (1942), 95-103.

tween drives and controlling factors within the ego, not only in their quality, but even in their quantity. The latter is reflected in the number of repetitions of different form-elements within a series of pictures by the individual child in comparison with the average frequency among the age group studied. The individual expressions of intrapsychic dynamics, which are so directly observable in children's paintings, provide a basis for inferences regarding specific personality characteristics. These inferences can then be formulated into a general description.

In a child's creative production there are conscious intentions as well as unconscious fantasies and demands in varying layers and configurations; and, in addition to both of these, there are the results of outside and incidental stimuli. The task of analysis must include discriminating between these inner and outer, conscious and unconscious influences so far as possible.

In the process of developing my approach I made preliminary analyses of the paintings of six children which were given to two nursery school teachers and to the psychologists who knew the children for matching; the descriptions were matched to the names of the children and, in addition, specific statements were compared with the teacher's and psychologists' knowledge of the particular child. These comparisons helped me further to formulate and revise my system for analysis. In this preliminary study I found that it was possible to describe the following aspects of a child's personality: adjustment, type and range of personality as to capacity for experience, intro- and extraversiveness, constriction, delayed development, fixation, and regression to earlier phases. I could make inferences as to conflicting impulsive and repressive tendencies, intelligence in general, and the specific manner of thinking—whether abstract or concrete, vague or clear, systematic or unsystematic—the balance of or preference for work on a large scale or interest in minutiae; sense of order; vigor, carefulness, independence, flexibility, impulsiveness, integration. Depressive trends, anxiety, and aggression were also described.

In order to understand the meaning of what a child does with painting from the age of two to the age of four, we need to look at the stages of development of drawing and painting in its earliest phases, and even its background in the psychic development of the infant. At the beginning, there is a purely kinetic expression consisting of scribbled loops and circles, and, if liquid materials are available, of more or less formless smearing which also involves "haptic" or touch experiences. In this first phase, visual perception takes little part in the creation of "forms"; in other words, the created form is a result primarily of motor and tactual activity.

In the second phase the child discovers what he is doing. Visual perception is combined with motor activity, and he begins to play with the forms which up to now occurred by chance. He comes to prefer certain forms and to avoid others.

In the third stage the child discovers some similarities between the forms with which he has been playing and objects in the outside world. Forms arrived at through his playful experimentation are interpreted as objects after he looks at them. This is the first step connecting his own imaginative world with the real world around him. As this stage matures, the child intentionally employs forms which have some similarity to outside objects, and he repeats and connects them. In other words, the picture begins finally to have some representative content.

The child sometimes goes through the last two phases very rapidly. For instance, one child painted a blue spot with fringes. Looking at this form he said, "That is the sun." Within the space of an hour or two he took yellow paint, repeated the form, and said, "Now I'm going to make a real sun!" His first interpretation and his first intentional use of form for the representation of a real thing thus occurred on the same day. He was a rather advanced child; in other cases the same development might take weeks or months, or even longer. Of course this development takes place to a great extent in the unconscious, and we can see only the final result in the child's expression. Therefore, if a child takes the final steps as rapidly as did the child in the above-mentioned case, we cannot determine actually how long it took him to develop up to that point. However, on the basis of our observations we can say that between the ages of two and three children usually go through the first two stages only; the last stage should be reached by the age of four. Children who are delayed in their emotional development, fixated to an earlier stage of development, or regressing to such an earlier stage, show it in their paintings; they cannot proceed to more advanced phases of pictorial expression or regress to former ways of expression.

Now, to push the analysis of development of form experience still further, we must consider its very earliest beginnings in the development of the infant. Here we can only offer a hypothesis on the basis of inferences from our observations. The newborn infant, with his dispositions inherited from past generations, is confronted with the outside world. He experiences his world through his sense organs in two different ways: passively, through perception alone; and actively, through movements. Perception is necessary for absorbing the outside world and receiving communications from it; movement is necessary for communicating something to the outside world. Perceptions are transformed into movements, and movements give rise to more perceptions. Both perceptions and movements are necessary to satisfy vitally important needs, to gain pleasure, and to avoid painful experience. Certainly not all the experiences of the child are of a voluntary or a pleasurable nature. Certain demands are made on him which mean giving up some pleasures or tolerating some discomfort. Therefore all sensory experiences and the sense organs themselves are involved in both pleasurable and disagreeable associations. The number and intensity and quality of such associations, and the balance between them, will shape the functioning of the sense organs and help to determine the degree of spontaneous activity in their use.

At first, the world of the child is dominated by parents or parent-substitutes. The parents, particularly the mother, are the ones who satisfy the child's vital needs, cause pleasure through love, and also make certain demands. The behavior of the parents, consequently, determines to a large extent the form and amount of pleasure associated with the senses.

One can define three contrasting types of parental behavior, which occur in all variations and combinations and are modified by the special qualities of temperament and interests of the parents. First, the parents may accept the child as he is, love him with little or no ambivalence, and make their demands only for the sake of social adjustment and at the right developmental stage, when the child is ready to cope with such demands. He will develop responsibilities but he will not be overloaded with them. The disagreeable experiences do not exceed the pleasurable ones. The child learns to control himself to a certain degree, but on the whole preserves a great amount of freedom and develops flexibility. Secondly, the parents may reject the child or be strongly ambivalent toward him; both attitudes occasionally appear in the form of overprotection. Strong rejection or ambivalence are shown typically in either of two ways: the parents may make too many demands without regard to the child's developmental capacities, in which case he has to exert too much control, becomes paralyzed in many regards, and on the whole shows delayed emotional development and rigid preoccupations; or the parents may show too little interest and neglect the child, in which case he may not develop sufficient control. In both cases, the child is left alone and without help in solving his problems of adjustment, and his development will depend mainly on the amount and quality of his natural tendencies and his experiences. Thirdly, the parents may accept the child on the whole and he may fulfill a large number of their demands; but some parental demands represent not only conformity to a social necessity but to the parents' personal problems, involving their own anxiety, and are consequently tensely imposed, as may be the case with toilet training. In such instances the child is likely to develop certain rituals or compulsive tendencies in particular directions along with a more flexible and normal development in many other respects. The relation of the child's impulses to the controlling factors will form the pattern of the child's character.

As we have said, the first communications of the child are movements. The first attempts at form-creation are applied to movements. Grasping and all other bodily movements which carry out specific functions require shaping of movements, and the predominance of certain movement patterns will be determined by the proportion of pleasurable experiences associated with them. At the beginning the child can express himself only by very few and very simple movements. Gradually his movements become more developed and greater in number. They are combined in complex patterns, and some of them are subordinated to others; through repetition, patterns of habits are formed. Refinements and differentiations take place, and finally some of the movements lose most of their personal meaning and become mere traditions of the body.

During this development a process of symbolization goes on: certain forms perceived or transformed in movement will have symbolic significance for every normally developed child; other forms will have symbolic significance for only a particular individual; some forms which are symbolic to a certain degree for every child will be strongly symbolic for one child.

Thus we can observe in the child's very first attempts to draw circles and loops, or to smear spots on a paper with paint, that he approaches the new activity with a series of previously established habits of movement connected with form attitudes which are determined by the amount of spontaneity and control at work, and by the amount and kind of symbolic meaning which movements have accumulated.

The first circles and loops show a greater or lesser degree of regularity in the pressure of line and the distance between them. Different tendencies in distribution are apparent, such as keeping within certain boundaries or neglecting them, preference for or avoidance of the center, vividness or rigidity, narrowness or wideness of distribution, preference for lines or spots, preference for or avoidance of colors.

The slowness or speed with which the same kinds of loops are made by different children varies considerably. The severely controlled child is apt to draw very slowly a kind of loop similar to that which another child draws quickly, but the difference can be seen in the quality of line.

We can observe that the variety of forms on a page and size of format (or sheet chosen for painting), of form-elements, and of colors in a sequence of drawings, differ in different personalities. Naturally in the more advanced stages the evaluation of time taken and of choice of size should not be interpreted without relation to other form attitudes, as, for example, size and shape of forms, their relation to each other and to the whole, the presence or lack of details, and other form attitudes. Small and tiny sizes are more significant than large ones and are more related to constriction than largeness is to aggression, especially if confirmed by other constrictive factors, as, for example, a preference for forms which are small in relation to the whole sheet. A flexible, rich personality makes frequent use of all sizes. Also, it is more natural to prefer form-elements which are large or medium-sized in relation to the whole sheet. A preference for only small form-elements occurs frequently in depressive personalities, especially together with small pictures and symmetrical arrangements or some other constrictive factors. When it comes to interpretation, a preference for small form-elements is more significant than a preference for large and medium-sized ones, because it is rather unusual. Sharp, short, scattered strokes or points arise from aggressive impulses.

Vivid distribution combined with balance is a positive factor, expressing a vital, spontaneous, flexible, and well-controlled way of experiencing. A reliance on symmetry indicates a lack of flexibility and frequently appears in depressive or constricted individuals.

In general, human movement in drawing has at times a different meaning from the M in Rorschach. Human movements in drawing occur sometimes as expressions of a wish by persons who have no movement in Rorschach. The qualities of movement (curves, vivid details in line, vivid distribution, and differentiated rhythm) are more comparable to the movement-element in Rorschach. These are the elements which presuppose the capacity to make a human figure in motion. Such qualities occur even in pictures by little children who are not yet able to draw human figures, and are indicative of a capacity to sublimate. The representation of human figures and animals develops much later, but should begin between four and five years of age. In the drawings by individuals with narcissistic preoccupations, lack of or preoccupation with human figures is frequent.

These are some of the most important factors on which my

interpretations are based; I have analyzed a chronological sequence of drawings of each child according to the following categories.

RELATION TO FORMAT[2]

Ma	Painting or drawing completely to the margin of paper or beyond it.
Ma Di	Tending to paint to the margin but with occasional distancing of form-elements.
Di Ma	Measuring up the space well, distancing the form-elements in relation to format, with occasional touching of the margin.
Di	Keeping a distinct distance from margin.
Ng	The feeling for size and proportions of the whole sheet is neglected; all form-elements or a large part of them are too small in relation to space. Ng should not be judged separately, but together with the proportion of the form units within the picture, with distribution and balance.
E	Emphasis on framing, not being satisfied with the given margin, but emphasizing the frame by making another one, "putting the whole thing on a stage."

SIZE OF FORM-ELEMENTS[3]

l	Large.
m	Medium.
s	Small.

MOVEMENT-ELEMENTS

H	Human movement.
A	Animal movement.
SM	Secondary movement elements or qualities of movement.

(a) Positive: vivid details in line, curves, vivid distribution, differentiated rhythm

(b) Negative: symmetry, rigid distribution, rigid uniform rhythm

---

2. Size and proportions of paper, and time taken, could not be evaluated in this study.

3. More exact definitions of form-elements—for instance, of what I call *large, medium, small*—are given in the paper cited in Footnote 1.

Curves and Sharp Edges and Angular Forms

$$\left.\begin{array}{l} + \\ \pm \\ \mp \\ - \end{array}\right\}$$ Denote the range from many curved or angular forms to none at all.

Vivid Details in Line

+   Vivid details in the form of the line as well as in pressure of the hand in drawing.

±   Tendency to vivid details.

∓   Slight tendency to vivid details.

×   Meticulous elaboration of vivid details.

      The occurrence of vivid details is not very frequent and can be called an original element.

Differentiated Rhythm

+   High degree of differentiated rhythm.

$$\left.\begin{array}{l} \pm \\ \mp \end{array}\right\}$$ Tendency to differentiated rhythm.

      Differentiated rhythm is a very positive factor, which occurs infrequently. It is the repetition of similar forms with little deviation in direction and in distance.

Rigid Uniform Rhythm

      This element occurs in feeble-minded, stereotyped, psychotic, and compulsive neurotic types. Its significance depends on the combination with other form-elements and on the frequency. It is important whether lines, shapes or colors are the elements repeated.

      The tendency to copying or tracing should be observed, but could not be evaluated in this study.

DISTRIBUTION OF FORM-ELEMENTS

v   Vivid distribution, form-elements being distributed in relation to diagonal axis.

r   Rigid distribution.

h   Horizontal distribution in relation to horizontal, vertical, or centrifugal axis.

vt	Vertical distribution in relation to horizontal, vertical, or centrifugal axis.
c↑	Centrifugal distribution in relation to horizontal, vertical, or centrifugal axis.
c	Form-elements grouped in or around center.
L, R	Emphasis on left or right side.
E↑, E↓	Emphasis on top or bottom of picture.
n	Narrow, overcrowded distribution.
w	Wide distribution.

These scorings are partly an evaluation of the *balance*. E↑ and E↓ occur frequently as an over-compensatory element in cases of inferiority feelings. E↑ may be a kind of wish element: "I'm not free enough, I'm clumsy, heavy." E↓ may indicate being afraid of losing footing. The significance depends greatly on the connection with other form-elements and also on the relation to content.

Balance of Distribution

In this category the distribution is judged more quantitatively, a consideration of form-elements as related to weight of masses "filling a page."

+ ± ∓ −	Indicate the degrees of equilibrium of form-elements,[4] from well-balanced to unbalanced.
(+)	Balance which is achieved only as a result of center or rigid distribution.
∓ −	Infrequent, and for this reason of important negative significance.

Symmetry

+	Full symmetry.
± ∓	Tendency to symmetrical arrangement.

---

4. In a standardized study this criterion should be considered together with the choice of size of form-elements and also with time.

QUALITY OF LINES

Variation of Pressure (cf. Vivid Details in Line)

th	Thin lines.
e	Energetic lines.
w	Weak lines.
c	Rigid contours.
a	Lines repeated anxiously.
r	Rigid lines.
l	Lines applied in a relaxed, loose way.

ORGANIZATION OF FORM

U	Unity achieved in the whole picture, a good combination of parts (criterion related to distribution).
up	Parts of the picture contain good units.
cn	Group of details or little parts are well connected.
cl	Collected details or little parts are arranged near to each other in a group, but are not connected.
sep	Parts are clearly separated from each other, have sharp forms.
sc	Details and small parts are scattered over the whole sheet (criterion related to distribution).
r+	Show adequate or inadequate relations to representa-
r—	tive content; can be scored only if there is any content.

ORGANIZATION OF CONTENT

it	Content of picture was determined in advance (intentional).
ip	Content of picture was not determined in advance, but was interpreted as such afterward.
ip ch	Change of content during procedure of painting or drawing.
xp	Expressionistic.
abstr	Abstract, geometrical forms.

COLOR

Color represents the emotional attitude of the individual toward reality, very much in the same sense as in the Rorschach test. Choice of color, avoidance and fear of color have to be considered. Furthermore, form-color (F-C) relationship is important. Choice of definite single colors (e.g., black, white, yellow, red, blue), and of mixed colors is scored.

F-C+   Very good form-color relation.
F-C±   Normal form-color relation.
F-C∓   Slightly less than normal form-color relation.
F-C—   Bad form-color relation.

Preference for linear expression (L) instead of representation by color spots (Sp) is also scored.

L Sp   Linear expression preferred to color spots.
Sp L   Color spots preferred to linear expression.

COPYING, CHANGING OF FIRST CONCEPT,
FREQUENT ERASING AND DESTROYING OF PICTURE,
AS WELL AS THE CONTENT AND SUBJECT OF THE PICTURE

The content is of special importance for interpretation when human figures are represented. It throws light on specific emotional problems of the individual, rather than on a definite personality structure or form of disturbance.

PERSPECTIVE

Perspective does not occur at the preschool level.

The most essential of these form-elements are listed below according to their significance in regard to extroversion and control.

Extratensive factors	*Factors of Control* (Introversion)
painting to margin	keeping distance
large form-elements	small form-elements
centrifugal distribution	emphasis on center and centripetal distribution
scattered or wide distribution	narrow distribution
lack of balance	— — — —
large curves	lack of curves
preference for spots	preference for lines
smearing	separating colors carefully
vague forms	rigid sharp forms
lack of forms	lack of color
glaring color-scale	pale or dark color-scale
preference for red and yellow	preference for blue and black
color variety greater than average, with average or reduced form variety	form variety greater than average, with average or reduced color variety
	or
	form variety greater than color variety

Each painting was checked for each item on this scale. If possible I scored at least fourteen paintings by each child for each year, in chronological order. In exceptional cases when the child was less productive, I was forced to try an analysis on a smaller number of pictures. In some cases I found it interesting to focus my attention on certain periods in the total sequence of time, in addition to the regular fourteen paintings.

The following personality descriptions were based on the individual configuration of scores, by single pictures and by sequences of pictures. For the reader I have indicated some of the most obvious form attitudes and scoring configurations on which the personality description was based.

Personality descriptions were written on the basis of the analysis of form qualities. Then in groups of five, teachers were asked to match the descriptions to the names of the five children whose pictures had been analyzed. After the matching had been done, I discussed with the teachers their observations of the children and followed this with my own "post-matching comments" which are included here at the end of the personality descriptions.

Based on Alec's first year at nursery school—from age two years, five months to three years, two months

Remarks on Scoring	Personality Description
Keeps Di except in one picture (No. 13 completely black). Frequency of Di is unusual. No variety in size, uses only large form-elements; no vivid details in line or outline.	This is a strongly self-centered boy with an "I can show what I am" attitude; he is almost provoking in his attempts to compensate for great insecurity. He is not without self-control, perhaps even too much at times; he can be resistant, but also self-critical.
Spots more prevalent than lines and curves; few movement elements. F-C combination negative. No form attempt, distribution in center of sheet going through almost all pictures.	

Based on paintings of second and third years—from age three years, five months to five years, five months.

Center distribution continuous. It is interesting that in the first picture he starts with center distribution and then covers this with partly rigid, partly scattered disruptive distribution; also the contrary procedure takes place. Interesting also in picture number 4, the outspoken center-distribution combined with movements and sharp zig-zag forms; sharp edges in other pictures.	He can be very aggressive and even destructive; in a conflict atmosphere, he would fight against himself and other people. I suspect he can be furious and wild and harsh.

Factors of Control	Factors of Release	
Di	Large form-elements	His extroversive and introversive tendencies are in conflict. His self-assertive tendency is so strong that it may lead to unbalanced actions; he is certainly not cooperative where he is insecure. He is intelligent but not adjusted to reality; there is only slight improvement here in the third year.
Blue, green	Red, yellow	
Center distribution	Scattered distribution	
Frequently no balance		
U, up, ip, r+		
F-C relation negative		
sep, slight form		
attempts		
Stereotyped rigid patterns, few movement-elements		He is likely to become rigid when fighting against his own disruptiveness. All the above tendencies are corroborated by many form-attitudes which point in the same direction.
Scoring through all three years shows marked deviation from the group average.		

POST-MATCHING COMMENTS:

On the whole Alec's scoring shows very strong contrasts, the same "black and white" attitude which he shows in his behavior.

He shows factors of extreme constriction and self-centeredness, as well as those of aggressive outgoingness; i.e., many Di, a large amount of center distribution, and treatment of black, which is conspicuous as compared with other children in the group, on one hand, and a large number of large form-elements, scattered distribution, and negative balance on the other. The same contrast can be found in the color selection. In Alec's case I found a strong parallel with the Rorschach.

Based on Jay's paintings for one year—age four

Remarks on Scoring

sep striking; F-C relation quite good. High C variety; frequent vivid distribution; no Ma; mostly Di Ma and Di. U and up present. Sp>L. Concept building, several H. Not sufficient F+; many movement elements. Many large form-elements, mostly lms, but also quite a number of s, F-C and sep.

Short strokes (occasional), yet not scattered and interestingly combined with good F-C relation and sep.

This impression is not derived so much from any particular scoring elements as from the whole configuration.

Movement elements with differentiated rhythm.

Personality Description

Jay is probably rather skillful. He is also emotionally responsive, vital, outgoing, active, flexible; he could be excitable but not uncontrolled. However, he has more intellectual control than emotional balance. He has superior intelligence yet does not use this intelligence completely. On the whole he is the more healthy and pleasant narcissistic type. He thinks on a large scale, yet very concretely.

I am not sure whether he is overtly aggressive; it could be that aggression takes another form. He is not careless. I believe that the whole pattern suggests a child who has ambitions and who is dynamically striving to satisfy them. He is not yet free from inferiority feelings which he probably would not like to admit.

He has an active fantasy and creative capacities.

POST-MATCHING COMMENTS:

Jay's scoring shows a picture of definite control with underlying excitability: lack of Ma on the left side and rigid uniform rhythm on the right side. The short strokes suggest a capacity for aggression. There was almost no disagreement on the part of the matchers in this case.

Based on Stanley's paintings for one year—age four

Remarks on Scoring

Concept building, many U, up; very many movement elements: excellent form attempts; very rich variety. Usually l, m and s.

Vivid distribution, usually loose, but occasionally goes to both extremes (wide and narrow); however extremely good balance score. Great color variety, contours. More spots than lines, but more Di than Ma. Interesting black contour around sun. Movement-elements in high degree, especially differentiated rhythm. F-C relation.

Personality Description

Stanley is highly intelligent, has both abstract and concrete thinking in subtle nuances, with a rich, dilated personality, not banal or flat.

He has a very responsive temperament, but represses his excitability and also probably his aggression. He has a high super-ego. He has lots of drive and energy as well as lots of control and is altogether rather well-balanced.

He has creative and original capacities.

He is skillful and more spontaneous than pedantic; neither superficial nor flighty. I cannot evaluate the black which occasionally appears.

POST-MATCHING COMMENTS:

Stanley's scoring is rich in the middle and both sides. He has great variety in all form-elements and a high response to color. He also shows a high amount of secondary movement-elements. There was almost no disagreement among the matchers in Stanley's case, except that it was noted that Stanley's extreme verbalization did not show up in a pronounced way in his scoring.

CHAPTER 6

The Child's Reaction
to the Rorschach Situation

by ANNA HARTOCH

[Editor's Note: Anna Hartoch made completely "blind" interpretations of these Rorschach records collected from 1937 to 1942. She never saw the children she described. At first I made the Rorschach records myself, in an exploratory way, since I knew of no other work on two- to four-year-old children, and had to experiment with procedures. As the work expanded, L. J. Stone and the teachers cooperated in the making of records. The number of times a child was given the Rorschach depended on the material obtained, the cooperation of the child, etc.

[While Anna Hartoch's analysis and interpretation always emphasized "how the child experiences the stimuli of the cards" and "what he is going through" as we see in her sequence analyses, this process approach always rested on a firm base of Rorschach scoring as indicated in her complete report. For the purposes of this book it seemed more important to give complete samples of analysis of a few cases, with the summaries of the children in nursery school, than to give a larger number of end-product interpretations without the data and process behind them. Anna Hartoch had an extraordinary capacity to integrate a sensitive empathy and penetration to the child's experience with a deep understanding of relevant dynamics and a firm *grasp of the technical problems of scoring and integration of scores into a unified living picture of a child. Her contribution is still timely, perhaps more so precisely because additional work has been done and the professional group concerned with young children will be able to view her contribution in a deeper perspective.]*

Introduction

THE RORSCHACH TEST represents Rorschach's attempt to analyze the functions of perception and comprehension in order to draw conclusions, from individual responses, regarding the characteristics of the entire individual psyche. According to Rorschach, the process of interpreting the ink-blots—that is, of finding objects similar to them—is basically the same as the process of comprehension in everyday visual perception, occurring when we identify some object perceived as a tree, a house, a friend, etc.

The difference between everyday comprehension and the comprehension of the test plates lies chiefly in the fact that the ink-blots are strange and unfamiliar in appearance, and that in most adults it takes a conscious effort to find objects similar to them; most adults remain aware of the fact that the ink-blots neither really are nor represent the objects which they see in them, whereas in our usual comprehension of objects perceived we are not aware of such an effort and have no doubt as to the identity of the object perceived.

For a child, also, the factor of strangeness and unfamiliarity exists. Nevertheless, the child is more accustomed to discovering and naming surrounding things for the first time. The young child has not yet acquired the cliché, the set pattern in which, to a large extent, the adult perceives surrounding things. For most children, therefore, before school training, there is less conscious effort to find many already defined objects, especially since they have a small vocabulary and small variety of associations at their disposal. Most things still have a subjective meaning. The distinction between detached apperception and spontaneous recognition of identity of the presentation with the thing perceived takes place later, and is probably stimulated by school training.

For the same reason, the child does not distinguish as sharply as does the adult whether the objects which he sees in ink-blots really are there or represent his own discoveries; the child is much more directly concerned with the objects perceived and has not yet developed an intellectual approach separated from his feelings. We do not find self-critical remarks as to whether the objects seen are really those which they should be; nor do we often find interpretative remarks which are made from an observer's viewpoint, such as those we usually find with adults who discuss the picture from an aesthetic, critical, moralistic, or literary viewpoint. In children's reactions we find a much more outspoken relation to the cards; also more blocking, failures, and repetition than is usually found with adults.

The Child's Reactions to the Cards

The child is not asked to react to a single card but to a series of ten cards. This involves a continuous effort. It is emotionally difficult for the young child to keep his uninterrupted attention on a series of ten cards at one sitting.[1]

The child sees the cards for the first time and has to invent phrases denoting their similarity to known forms. This requires a different approach from that used in looking at a picture. In the latter case he discovers again what the adult has told him the picture means, and so he may let his imagination go, growing from the basic idea which the adult has set for him. Not so in the Rorschach situation. Adults have given him no orientation; he is left alone with his own imagination and with the associations he has at his disposal. He must get used to this new situation.

Every card presents new surprises for the child. It would be easier if all ten cards were like the first one; then he could get

---

1. In our work at the Sarah Lawrence Nursery School we never forced a child to persist through the whole series after he ran off or actually left the situation, although his mild protest was usually ignored unless repeated. If a child ran away we let him go, and then brought him back to the cards after a period of rest or play; we felt that forcing or coercing an unwilling child to a task created an atmosphere which distorted the results (assuming that a preschool child could be coaxed or coerced, which of course was not always possible).—Ed.

used to them and could go on undisturbed. In the Rorschach situation he does not come to a restful "Now I know" conclusion. The cards are not only generally strange and unfamiliar, but they also present their own rhythm and excitement pattern. The child is taken through many emotional stages by the changing pattern of stimuli.

With the first card the new orientation is not an easy task. Already somewhat accustomed to the strangeness of the picture, the child is faced in the second card with some red color spots combined with black forms. Red is much nearer to emotion, to experiences like fire and blood; the young child who is unprepared for this sudden change either becomes excited or shocked by the new event. The third card keeps the black and red color and is therefore something more familiar, after the first red impression in Card II. Card IV is the darkest card of all. It is not only complex but black, and this stimulus often creates in the child a new surprise, or even fear. This is the point at which some children experience a "darkness shock," and either fail to respond or, wishing to get rid of the sensation, stop looking at the cards. The fifth card presents no new surprises; it is also a dark card. But the form is clearly defined; it is a card in which it is easy to follow the given lines and to relax. Some children, however, cannot do so because their previous experiences, especially in Card IV, are still much too vivid. In some the previous red shock, or dark shock, or both, may find its culmination point in Card V, where everything breaks through. Card VI is difficult to interpret as a unit. It is intellectually the most difficult card to interpret and has, moreover, sexual implications, which may lead to involved reactions. Card VII is light, vague and open. To many children it is a delight. In some it causes a feeling of uneasiness because of the open form and the incompleteness they experience in it. The vagueness leaves some too much in the air; others feel as if they were emerging from darkness to light. Card VIII is the first full color plate. This requires that the child again adjust to a new situation; some children need time to forget that the black color is no longer there; some feel great excitement because there is so much color; some cannot see anything which might be called similar to what they have seen around them; some find the most intensely interesting achromatic color and form combinations. Card IX is also full of color. But the spatial division in Card IX is less distinct than that of Card VIII, and the child is taken still further into the full tropical coloring. For some children this is an experience which resembles being blinded by strong sunlight. It is too much for them. They give up or want to give up. Others become aware in this card, more than in the previous cards, that color overwhelms them; a retarded color-shock appears. Others react more distinctly to this colored card than to the first one. Card X looks like a picture book to most children. They find familiar forms of animals with great ease and enjoy the variety of forms. Others are too shaken by previous experiences; they react in a stereotyped way or not at all because they have already given up at one difficult step or another.

It is the intensity of experience and the inner sequence which we must constantly bear in mind in order to understand what the child is going through.

The Child's Reaction to the Experimenter in the Situation and the Psychological Role of the Experimenter During the Performance Proper

The child undergoes the previously described stages emotionally, and must at the same time accomplish the task of recognizing objects, persons, and scenes similar to those he has come across in his daily life. It is even more than recognizing, since he has to reconstruct each shape and to name it according to his own discovery. He is not alone in this situation. There is somebody with him, showing him the pictures, taking notes of what he says and how he behaves; an authority is present. The child transfers to the cards all his expectations in relation to the adult, e.g., fears and wishes, intensified by the emotional quality of the different card-stimuli, the shock character of which has been described. The relationship to the authority figure enters into this whole rather complex situation. The cards are unfamiliar to the child; it is also an unfamiliar experience to discover that there is not an accepted name for everything, that there is nothing right or wrong, and that the adult's role is not to tell him what this or that means, what the thing is called, since this role is not relevant in the Rorschach situation. This brings about another factor of uncertainty for the child, and at the same time an element of possible activity, spontaneity, and creativity, since the child is the only decisive factor in the situation. In order not to introduce too many unfamiliar features into the Rorschach situation, I think it advisable that the experimenter who shows the cards to the child be a person with whom he is familiar, possibly his teacher.

But the teacher also represents authority. The teacher is usually the person who answers the child's questions and represents the adult world. Although she is familiar to the child as a person, the teacher's role in administering the Rorschach—the fact that she does not answer questions, does not decide what is right or wrong—is not familiar. This puts the child into a new situation with the familiar teacher.

For the teacher, too, the situation is unusual. She should give the necessary instructions to the child, make the arrangements as easy as possible for him, but must first of all be the recorder of the child's response to the cards. The greater the child's concentration, so that all his reactions may be transferred to the cards, rather than to the teacher, the better. The ideal situation is one in which the teacher wholeheartedly respects the reactions of the child to the cards, in recording them verbatim as far as possible, and in trying *not to interfere with the child's positive reactions or with his blockings*. One might describe this as passive collaboration on the teacher's part. Undoubtedly much of the established relationship will enter into this process. The more the teacher is aware of her own reactions, especially of her authority relation to the child, the more easily will she find the way to this indicated collaboration.

From the record one can see much of the teacher's relation to the child. This is an interesting approach to the relationship of teacher and child, and I found it very instructive to draw certain conclusions about the teacher. To give a few examples:

it seems very hard for some teachers to find themselves in a situation with a child in which the child should not be helped or encouraged too much. One can observe here how difficult it is for some personalities to let the child actually be independent, act independently, and even be blocked independently; this last is especially hard for some teachers. They feel as though the Rorschach situation were an examination; when they are very fond of the child, or consider him very bright, they cannot bear to let him fail. Actually, blockings are quite frequently nothing to be afraid of, being due to the rather involved situation which has been described. The over-solicitude, or over-helpfulness of a teacher often interferes with the situation.

There is another element which makes it hard for some teachers: actually the teacher does not know which answers are best; in fact, the child often sees more vividly and spontaneously than the teacher herself. The Rorschach procedure is but little concerned with verbal content; *how* one sees and identifies the cards is the essential part and the verbal expression is of secondary importance. In most situations the teacher is superior to the child, especially in being able to verbalize much more than the child; but in this situation the child is the equal of, if not often freer than, the teacher in capacity for real experience and response to a variety of stimulations.

The Influence of the Mood

Everything in the relation of the teacher to the child and his role during the Rorschach has its importance. Nevertheless the child's relation to the teacher is only one expression of his attitude to authority in general. I am often asked whether the results are different if different people give the Rorschach to the same child, and how much the results are influenced by the specific mood and momentary feeling of the child at the time the test is given. Generally I find that the stress on these two factors is exaggerated; the child's experiences in the three to five years or more of his life, his way of meeting the demands placed upon him by himself or others, and his manner of reacting emotionally, are deeply rooted, and often predominate over the mood at the time, or the response to a sympathetic or unsympathetic adult. Thus if one regards the personality picture as a structural unit, a Rorschach expert will be able to look through a child's consistencies and variabilities within his Rorschach and see from their relation to the score and its meaning whether the changes are superficial or are more deeply related to the structure. This will become clearer when I explain somewhat more about the method, and give examples of specific cases.[2]

On the other hand there is this to say: the child is more expansive in a good mood, more blocked in a bad mood; it is advisable always to have two or three records from a young child over a period of several months or a year. Thus the mood, insofar as it is a changing influence from day to day, is not so important, does not influence the Rorschach fundamentally, unless a so-called "mood" is really the beginning of a trend or is a manifestation of a more deeply rooted real change in the personality structure.

Methodological Aspects

SETTING

The procedure should be as informal as possible, but should not allow opportunity for the child to divide his attention between test and play at the same time.

For a child of this age the over-formal situation of being taken into a strange room with a strange person can be ideally overcome when the nursery school teacher is also the tester. She can choose a good moment to present the test in the familiar playroom, or at the edge of the playground, if the child is reluctant to leave the group entirely. At ease in familiar surroundings, and with the full attention of the familiar teacher, the child can give free cooperation in the test situation.

The child can sit on the lap of the experimenter, kneel on the floor, or sit beside the experimenter. It does not matter. The main thing is that the child should feel at ease.

---

2. See pages 165-80.

METHOD OF PRESENTATION

There are not many instructions to be followed. One of the best ways of introducing the cards to the child is: "I have some pictures you haven't seen. Wouldn't you like to look at them? What do you see?"

One card after another is presented to the child in a definite order. The child may handle the cards in his own way; he can keep each one as long as he likes, can turn it or give it up entirely. The child gives the signal for a new card. The person giving the Rorschach should not interrupt the performance by any questions or requests for more answers.

Young children often have difficulty in going through all ten cards in one session, and, as already indicated, the child should not be forced to finish the test. At the next suitable occasion the test should be continued at the card where the child left off.

What a child sees in the cards and what the child tells about each card is taken down verbatim. The responses are written down for each card separately. It is also very helpful to get as many observations as possible, coupled with the record of responses. This behavior record should be directly related to the responses and to each card, but should be kept separately. The observations comprise a full description of how the child talks: his moods, gestures, pauses, his tempo of speech, his facial expressions. The approximate time the child takes for the whole performance, and for each card should also be noted, but the child should not be aware of any timing.

As the Rorschach expert has to reconstruct each response in terms of what was primarily perceived by the child, it is important to know to what part of each card the child was responding in each case. With young children this is often open to question, and cannot always be answered definitely. Doubtful responses, however, often become clarified when they are seen in the light of the entire record. One can also arrive at important conclusions when the child fails completely to respond to a given card. This also will become clear later. When the child gives a doubtful response, it is ordinarily useful at the end of the test to go back and ask the child directly, "Show me the . . ." (whatever he has seen). The person who gives the Rorschach has to go even further at some doubtful points, investigating so as not to lead away from what has mainly influenced the response. This is the so-called inquiry.

THE CHILD'S EXPERIENCE OF THE INQUIRY

When the person who gives the Rorschach again goes over those responses which present some difficulty, he should ask the child to help him to recognize them. In this task the teacher is back again in a much more familiar position of authority: she says to the child, "Show me this, that. . . . Where did you see it?" This situation necessarily puts more pressure on the child. Many children (and adults, too) feel resentment at this procedure. They feel they must justify each little thing they said before, and those who have gradually come to feel at ease, and confident that they can decide upon everything they wish to say, feel now that this freedom has been taken away. For these reasons I do not think that the inquiry should take the form of a second, controlled test; I do not think that the person who gives the test should go over each response once again. The inquiry should be limited to those responses which are in question; the child who takes the test should not be made to feel that he must "justify" or "prove" whatever he has seen. As long as the child can be of some help to the experimenter, the situation takes another form, namely more the character of cooperativeness and helpfulness. The more the experimenter knows about the score and the possible meaning of the score the less inquiry will be necessary.

With very young children, especially of three and four years, it is often difficult to conclude what the child actually has seen before. As the inquiry situation is so different from that of the performance proper, everything that is said in the inquiry by younger, or even by older subjects can be taken at face value. With very young children I find one factor in the inquiry situation especially interesting: children will often change the subject and will not come back to what they saw before in the same card. But usually there are a few responses which are consistent, that is to say, which have been given before during the performance proper. I consider them as more significant than those with a more flighty quality. The interchangeable responses are also interesting, especially the cases in which the child becomes confused by other cards. New or additional responses in the inquiry situation should be considered in the light of the difference between this situation and that of the performance proper. With some children the responses may be freer in the original situation, where the child uses all the initiative, while with others they may be more free in the inquiry situation, where the child is under some pressure and works according to questions and rules set by the authoritative person.

NOTES ON BEHAVIOR

In the Rorschach record of a young child, notes on behavior play a much greater role than do the notes on the behavior of an adult. The child's behavior has not become so patterned and conventionalized as the adult's behavior. The most valuable material on behavior during the Rorschach is that which gives the exact place in the Rorschach at which the particular behavior occurred. The child's special observation of certain cards, or special responses to them, give additional information which, according to experience, the experimenter can use as a valuable aid in the interpretation. That does not mean that the behavior observations can be used as a separate unit for additional information; but it is of importance to compare them with the scores, with the stimulus value of the specific card in question, and with the place which the particular response has in the subject's whole dynamic process. The behavior notes should be interpreted as little as possible at the time when the person gives the Rorschach to a child. They should be minutely detailed— that is, descriptively—especially those of which the child is not aware, such as voice intonation, facial expression, typical gestures and movements, etc.

Aside from the task of careful observation there is another difficulty, a technical one. It is a difficult task to give the Rorschach to a child who may be sitting on the teacher's lap, to get correctly everything that the child says and sees in the cards, and to get, in addition, the previously mentioned behavior notes. I find it quite practical for the teacher to write up the behavior notes fully *after* the performance proper, and to note during the performance proper only a key word; that makes it easier for her to keep up with the record, which is the main task. These technical difficulties vary with different children, and the more practice a teacher has the more easily she will overcome them.

THE RORSCHACH
AS A CONSTRUCTIVE PLAY SITUATION

The child creates in the Rorschach a vital relation to persons or things, and discovers in this procedure phenomena which have a special meaning for him. He makes decisions, selects according to his own plans, not according to any given standard of right or wrong. He may also feel frustrated and disappointed, insecure and afraid, so that he cannot take part fully in this discovery. Thus the Rorschach situation is an especially productive situation.

It is not in any sense a make-believe situation. Full justice is done to the meaningful processes of experiencing; the inadequacy of the verbal expression plays a minor role. Things are recognized and taken for what they are, in their form and essence, rather than in the name or formula attached to them. What actually moves a child, what he can express and what he cannot express, where he is open or repressed will come to the fore through his Rorschach. Therefore this situation gives the teacher an unusual chance to be with the child as he really is. The teacher, in following this creative process, gets a new approach to the child. The child is spontaneously telling the teacher about himself, and the teacher, through her natural respect, curiosity, and cooperation, is *with* the child. This situation in itself is very helpful in creating full confidence between teacher and child. Take the case of a shy little boy who, in a nursery school group, had been unable to come into satisfying contact with either the teacher or group despite several weeks of school. A Rorschach was given to him by his teacher. After this mutual experience there was an immediate change of relation; confidence developed between the child and the teacher which enabled the boy to begin to make real contacts in the group.

Another example: a little girl who had always been very sensitive to criticism, and had also had difficulties in feeling free with the group and with the teacher. I interpreted the Rorschach record of this girl made by her teacher, and pointed out several symbolically important associations and their meaning to the child. The teacher developed an understanding of this child, and in a kind of private language made use of some of the symbols which meant so much to the child. The child felt that the teacher understood, even without talking about it much, and this created a new basis for understanding and cooperation.

Whatever application can be made depends on the group, on the child's individuality, and on many other factors. But what is emphasized here is the possibility of making the experience in the Rorschach effective in the daily life situation, especially with the teacher and the group.

The following records include examples of my method of analyzing Rorschach records of preschool children. The analyses include a sequence analysis of the record of two contrasting boys, Jay and Stanley, and the integrated personality picture of the child derived from the scoring and sequence analysis.[3]

Stanley

SEQUENCE ANALYSES OF TWO PROTOCOLS[4]

(1) AGE—4:9
(2) AGE—4:10

CARD I (1): *Well, I can't tell—I don't know what that looks like. I don't know what it could be.* [Apparently he needs a little time to

---

3. See Volume II for scoring procedure.
4. These two records will be considered together since they were taken within one month's time.

become better acquainted with a new situation. He does not jump immediately, spontaneously into a new situation.]

I (2): [When he sees the cards again one month later, he starts in a similar way:] *I don't know . . . I guess that would look like some . . .* [and then:] *I guess that that might be a puff of smoke.* In the smoke response it is striking how impressionable he is and how occupied with getting the mood, the unformed quality; how shy he is to formulate what he sees, and how he just follows his mood without any intellectual aim.

CARD II (1): [After his *I don't know* in the first card, in this one he immediately says:] *Oh, that looks like a fire blazing. It just looks like a fire blazing. . . . Outdoors, a little bonfire blazing.*

II (2): *That looks like smoke and red flames. That's all I think about this one.* Experimenter: What is this down here? *That's some more flames sticking out.*

CARD III (1): *That looks like a fire, too, outdoors, a different shaped fire burning. That's all.*

III (2): *I think that looks like people cooking bacon on a fire.* [The experimenter asks several questions, to which he replies. On the question of whether they are men or women Stanley says:] *They are men, they haven't long hair, you can see that they don't have long hair.*

It is striking how he is able to differentiate the color values and how he is fascinated by them. In the first record he seems almost exclusively preoccupied with color. In the second record he also sees very colorfully; this time not only the fire but also the black smoke. Perhaps the familiarity with the card contributes to this much more complete interpretation of the picture. There is now a familiar quality in it; he creates a scene where two dark men stand against the fire, and he combines movement, color, good form, in a very artistic way. He sees these figures as in a picture, but he creates this picture with his own eyes. It is a very productive, selective process.

CARD IV (1): *Smoke that looks like just smoke.* [then he adds:] *We could make these things with paint. We could . . . With gray paint.*

IV (2): *I guess that might be another puff of smoke.*

In both responses to this card he is overwhelmed by the blackness. In Card IV (1) he saw smoke for the first time, and now he sees it again. In looking at these cards his eyes seem to be following the way the smoke drifts upward. He apparently does not want to change it in any way but just watches it appreciatively.

CARD V (1): [His reaction to Card V is similar to Card I (1):] *Why, I don't know. I can't think what it looks like. I don't know what it looks like.*

His failures are different from those of most other children. When the picture does not move him to a certain response, then he just doesn't force anything. This comes out very strongly in the inquiry, when he is asked: "Is this a butterfly?" and he says: "It doesn't look like a butterfly." He rejects everything in the inquiry which he has not seen with his own eyes before. For instance, on IV, when the experimenter suggests: "Fur rug?" he answers "No"; on III the experimenter asks: "Two men dancing?" and he again says "No"; on I the experimenter asks: "Is this a butterfly?" and he reiterates "No." He does not make any concessions or compromises here.

V (2): *I guess that would be a black spider.* [Asked why, he answers:] *Because it kind of looks like a spider there. Those two are little horns. . . . And those wings.* This response [like Card III (2)—*People cooking bacon on a fire*] is rather decisive and definite. It is one of the few responses which does not merely give way to the impressions and moods of the colors, but has a definite form; although here, too, the mood seems to play a role.

CARD VI (1): *Why, I don't know about it. . . . These things just look like smoke. I like colored pictures better: all colored nice cards.*
It is striking that in the first record after the differentiating black-red responses and impressions, there is to be found only the one smoke response to Card IV. Between Card IV and Card VI there is a lack of variety, even a certain stereotypy, compared to his reactions to the color in Card II and Card III. Especially in VI it seems that Stanley is somewhat oppressed. He is not free to leave it. He wants to get rid of it, but does not know how. He is apparently under a certain fearful strain—not being on top of the situation, but buried under it.

VI (2): *That might be another puff of smoke. . . . And a bird flying by. That's all of that.*

This reaction is similar to Card VI (1); it is a smoke stereotypy and a somewhat better technique and verbal routine of how to shape and repeat things. *A bird flying by* is a new association. He is somewhat freer than a month ago, but one must not forget that he is now in a situation which he already knows and in which, therefore, he is somewhat more skillful.

CARD VII (1): *That looks like nice white clouds . . . White silk. Like clouds, that's what it looks like. Now you show me something else.*

The white-silk-cloud effect which he gets from this card after the dark ones is very genuinely felt and originally seen. It has a poetical quality.

VII (2): < *Those might be white clouds.* [The experimenter turns the card (>) and asks:] Why is it better clouds this way than that? *Because if it is this way* (>) *the clouds are better.* Experimenter: What happens when we turn it this way? (<) *Then there would be less of smoke. Lots of smoke this way.* (>) . . . *Just clouds this way* (<). He is very much aware of the light and shade and apparently much interested in it and its quality. There is a certain freedom in the way he lets himself go with it, rather like a bird, sensitive to where the wind goes, where the light and shadow is, but absolutely dependent on the outside stimulus.

CARD VIII (1): *Oh, that looks like something pretty good. That's pretty near all the pictures. I can't think what. Now I've got an idea. That looks like a rainbow. Now I'm ready for something else.* He apparently is in a very stimulated mood, and it is again striking how able he is, how sensitively he composes the color values.

VIII (2): *Oh, I guess that's a rainbow. A bear climbing up the mountain.*

CARD IX (1): *Oh, that looks like another kind of rainbow. That looks like a rainbow too.*

IX (2): *Oh, I guess that's just the rainbow and some deers. And that's all I can see.* [After some questions from the experimenter ending with: Is the deer lying down? he answers:] *No, climbing up.* Experimenter: Climbing up what? *This is the mountain.* Experimenter: Did you see him climbing up before or did you just notice it now? *I saw him in the beginning.*

CARD X (1): *That looks like nice colored things. That looks like four rainbows.* It is interesting how highly original concepts like rainbow appear at the same time with stereotypy and lack of variety. It is as if he was taken by this impression; the impression "has him" so to speak, and he is not able to come away from it. Again the external influence preoccupies him intensely.

X (2): *Oh, those are beautiful. I didn't know they had those colors all in a picture. This seems like a lot of things. Rainbow, fire smoke. All the rest of that is smoke.* [After some more questions, ending with: "Why is this smoke and this rainbow?" Stanley says:] *Because I see a little of it different blue color—different blue.* Experimenter: This too? *No, that's a little animal . . . That's his eye, nose, and leg.* In the colored plates of the second record he has the same original rainbow combinations in all three cards. But he seems more skillful in repeating them, and at the same time in each of the plates he gives one more popular animal response. There is more verbalistic routine, more technique in expressing it, but at the same time he cooperates more, is not so caught by his own impressions as he was the very first time he saw them. He is more at ease in a familiar situation.

PERSONALITY PICTURE OF STANLEY

AGE—4:9

AGE—4:10

Stanley is very impressionable and highly receptive. His receptivity is directed toward stimuli from outside and is genuine and strong. He has a great respect for everything, and is eager to find out about life's hidden and nameless secrets, the mysteries and the contrasts that he finds. His attitude is somewhat like that which one finds in persons in the Orient who sit and wait until something evokes a response from them; he is passive but ready to receive impetus. One could call his approach a creatively passive one. He is very patient inwardly; stillness and slow growth mean a lot to him. He is also filled with a sense of wonder and discovers the world with it. This sense of wonder, the real great basis for all creativity, which unfortunately has been lost in so many human beings, is alive in Stanley and is the great motivating power of his life. He has an enthusiasm for the things that surround him, and therefore he has a great variety of sensory impressions from which to draw. It is as if he responded to qualities of shading, vagueness, achromatic colors, indefinite variety rather than to decisive inflexible forms; as if he created a world of contrasting beauty and taste all by himself. He insists on what he sees and he creates a world according to his views. He does not live in fantasies, however, like Betsy or Camille. He actually sees the differences in tone, the nuances in reality, and he penetrates deeply into a thing in order to discover which nuance brings about an altogether different effect. What he sees he takes into himself, and he can work with it. The outside influence stimulates him, opens him, moves him, and enriches him; but he follows his own rhythm.

There is a conflict in his personality, however. He lives and creates for his own pleasure; he needs to discover the world without interference from anybody else, thus erecting a barrier between his intense experiences and the people surrounding him. Yet at the same time he needs reinforcement, he needs to feel that others sustain him. His difficulty is that he cannot or will not sufficiently bring to the fore the full amount and implication of his unique approach. Possibly he keeps it for himself because he fears that he may be misunderstood or laughed at. He fears that he might be considered different, that these are not the things he is expected to say. He feels too weak and not sure enough of himself. He approaches people verbally to a large extent and hopes to meet their expectations in so doing. With this verbal approach he defends himself, he conforms and makes concessions to others. He tries to get their favor and he hopes to be left in peace when he submits this way. His verbal efficiency serves to get the support he needs, to get protection and safety. Thus, throughout his approach one finds the following contradictions: He hides his intelligent, original and highly differentiated approach, his discovering attitude toward life which is really the motivating power for his assertion. And he brings about a compromise whereby he is on the defensive, working out many things on a verbal basis in order to appear the way he is expected to be, so that he will be accepted and protected. This compromise solution does not help him to become as independent and strong as he could be. He is strong in being able to look at the world so independently, spontaneously, and courageously, but he himself renounces the benefit of this original and creative approach by his conforming verbalistic appeal to the adult. He has not yet experienced sufficient assurance so that he can assert himself directly through his own forces. The more assurance Stanley gets that he does not need to be on the defensive and to make compromises in order to get protection, but that he will be recognized and appreciated for what he is, the freer and more secure and strong will he become and the less afraid. He should be encouraged to accept his being different as something that he does not need to hide, but to put into action and set to work.

Stanley is highly gifted and enjoys the variety of the world with an immense richness. He has promising gifts and talents and will bring out still more of them when he gets the constant understanding and encouragement he needs.

Jay

SEQUENCE ANALYSIS OF PROTOCOL

(1) AGE 4:1

CARD I: [Jay starts with the question] *What's that?* [frowning] *I don't know what this is.* [Then he says:] *A fly.* He sees the whole thing as a fly. The frowning expression continues for Cards II and IV. I think this has something to do with acting like a grownup and trying hard. That he does it in Cards I, II and IV shows that these are particularly difficult for him in the beginning. It is hard to say what really reminds him of a fly. It may be the feelers and the middle form, but it doesn't seem too good an answer, because he gives it up in the inquiry and sees the plate as "A flower." It may be that he really sees the feelers in the performance proper and feels threatened or attracted by them and changes in the inquiry to a more beautiful concept.

CARD II: *A Dog.* [again frowning] It is interesting that he sees only one dog; apparently this dog is attached very closely to the other one, so that both to him mean one. He doesn't react to the red at all. He is apparently influenced by the strong big solid impression.

CARD III: *A ducks.* Again it is interesting re the question of plural-singular that these two figures are seen as "A ducks." He sees these two figures as connected. He neglects the red. He sees the biggest and most obvious part in Card III as well as II as standing there like a rock, i.e., the dogs as well as the ducks.

CARD IV: [He frowns and sees] *A horse.* There is no indication as to whether he sees the whole as a horse or the animal's head as a horse, or whether he might see the middle figure as a horse with a person on it. Anyhow, he again sticks to the most solid, safe, strong ground, sparing his words and going ahead, without seeking approval for his response as most children would. He feels on the right track now.

CARD V: The same is true of his response here, *Butterfly*. What is important is that in II, III, IV and V there are very good forms, good mental achievement and all of them are popular or near popular with a popular quality. It implies that he is very cooperative and that he participates in a common task and has good common sense.

CARD VI: Possibly Jay has turned the plate. It may be that the original upper part reminds him again of the fly and that the things sticking out bother him and that he prefers to have the round form uppermost. He sees a *flower* in it. In the inquiry he sees the *stem*. It is striking that this flower association starts a series of associations in the next plates of less prosaic, matter-of-fact, and creature-like beings.

CARD VII: He now starts on associations of more emotional quality. It may be that he now feels sure that he stands on solid enough ground to give way to this side which is not so utilitarian. It is also interesting that he starts with this approach in the card which is the most difficult to interpret. He turns this card also and sees *snow*. One gets an impression that the dirty quality of the gray and white colors impresses him and that in this plate where he doesn't see a given form-pattern before him he is free enough not to have to give a definite form in his response either. It is also interesting that he is most free where the stimulus from the card is less definite, when little form is prescribed—but here his ground is pretty unsolid, uncertain. His answer has artistic qualities, well observed. It is in great contrast to his intellectual achievements. These emotional responses have a more abstract quality than his intellectual concepts.

CARD VIII: Jay sees this as *grass*—probably because of the blue color.

CARD IX: *Grass again. Two grasses.* Here it is probably the green color which causes this response.

CARD X: In the inquiry he sees Card X as *grass* too, but in the performance proper he sees it as *flowers*. The association *grass* is similar to the association of *snow*. It may be that the question of ground plays a part in his role pattern. It is striking that in the uncolored cards he sticks to good precise form and avoids repetition of content in the different cards. His reactions to the colored cards are entirely different. He does not react to form at all, but exclusively to rather smooth and peaceful color stimuli. What this contrast means in his personality will be shown in the Personality Picture of Jay at four years, one month.

PERSONALITY PICTURE OF JAY

AGE—4:1

Jay is attracted by strength and would like to appear strong himself. Probably he identifies himself with the authority of his father or that person who represents authority, and he tries very hard to be accepted by him. He has first principles and concepts and prescribed examples or images which he wants to follow. Everything is prescribed for him and his aim is to become like the adults, and especially like the authority image.

He has suppressed all emotional life to such an extent that he is preoccupied in forming a solid, safe, and sober ground on which to stand. His approach is not very spontaneous and it has little room for his own wishes. He seems somewhat tense—a little bit like a horse in blinders. He is not flexible and continually has to measure up to a standard—his standard of efficiency. He is prosaic but decisive. He wants everything right and exactly the way the grownups expect a matter-of-fact boy to be. He can be that way only when he renounces many things, when he does not allow himself to be uncontrolled and relaxed, and when he keeps himself constantly within his limitations. This makes him more one-sided, more wooden and less lively than he could potentially be, and it also develops his intellect in a static pattern. He is strongly dependent on his authoritative model and gets his security from it; thus he cannot move freely as he constantly must get approval over and over again. This situation calls for aggression in him, especially when he is not entirely approved of. He is not simply a tame, docile, and submissive child; strength, efficiency, and manliness really have become his aim and goal. He wants to have the same attitude toward those weaker than he that his father or the most authoritative person has toward him.

He does not seem prepared for unforeseen emotional situations. At first he acts tentatively and cautiously, but when he is acquainted with adult expectations in a particular situation he adapts easily. However, his approach is generally gradual and somewhat retiring, showing a not entirely conscious aversion to a powerful and immediate emotional experience of life. This may have its origin in his anxious admiration and fear of the powerful authority.

His drive for superiority as a means of establishing his security seems to have considerable significance. Perhaps he has felt the superiority of the powerful authority without feeling permitted to oppose it directly. There is a certain attitude of detachment towards this authority, but it by no means excludes a genuine object-relation and interest in persons. It is rather the detachment which is to be found in a slight retreat from emotional participation, a process of retiring which then permits him to look down on others, sometimes as a humorous, sometimes as a sad observer. Superiority which is thus gained by retreat is of course not a real superiority, and he gets no real benefit from it, so in spite of all his efforts he is still frustrated. He has justified to himself his wish to be superior, and therefore feels that he has a right to assert himself. But his fears prevent him from asserting himself directly, so he uses an oblique, indirect way.

He is rather susceptible to influence, even when it evokes strong aggression, but his intellectual control and discipline and discriminating judgment bring him back to a more reasonable adaptation.

He can also retreat from the demanding, powerful authority-restrictions and indulge in emotions; these then take on the quality of a certain luxury which he permits himself only apart from the rush of the world. There in his refuge he will not have too many disappointments. However, the intellectual pole is much more predominant than the emotional pole, and it is important for those who are working with him to know that the latter is there and to try to get a better integration or connection for him—perhaps even to stress the emotional part.

SEQUENCE ANALYSIS OF PROTOCOL

(2) AGE—4:6

CARD I: Jay starts with the first plate immediately, without any questioning, and brings everything together in a combinatory way:

Some leaves on a big tree and *Stem and branches*. He is very much concerned that everything should belong to the main root, and this attachment is very much expressed in this response. His intellectual achievement is even better here than that shown in his response to this plate in the first protocol.

CARD II: He sees *a butterfly and a bee and a wreath.* In the inquiry he pays special attention to the wreath; he gives up the butterfly and the bee. He is again very methodical in the way in which he includes everything, and in the way things must fit together. It is possible that the red color enters in the butterfly association and in the wreath also. His response is more elaborated than it was five months ago. It may be that he has to stress very strongly his need to be included, and that he attains his sense of belonging through being a part of the wreath, as he did in Card I through being a leaf on a tree.

CARD III: He says *That's a smiling face, and a nose, and a eye and a mouth.* It is not quite certain, but probably he sees only the usual upper head. What is striking is that he sees concretely only one face, nose, eye and mouth instead of the usual two figures. He does not try to combine the whole at all. In Card II, similarly, he did not see two animals, but *a butterfly and a bee and a wreath,* so that the wreath becomes the connecting form. He does not refer to color at all. His hesitation to face the two figures that are usually seen contrasts with the fact that he sees a *smiling* face. I suspect that it has to be a smiling face. He seems very dependent on the good will and encouragement of a person, and gives expression to this need in this somewhat compulsive response.

CARD IV: He sees *leaves,* and on the bottom middle projection: *No, a puppy dog's face.* In the inquiry the rest is a *wreath.* Leaves and wreath are probably used in an identical way. They seem to be used as something which keeps things together and are in contrast to animals and human beings. Since this plate is often coupled with some fear because of the blackness, one might think that he is again much concerned about being sufficiently included in a close family group, and that he really feels successful in this struggle at this time. This may refer not only to his family, but also to his nursery school group.

CARD V: *Butterfly.* Apparently he feels more secure. It is the most conventional, easy situation. He repeats the butterfly response given to this plate in the first record.

CARD VI: *That's a big leaf somebody picked.* He saw *a flower* in the first record. The leaf form is very well seen. He is impressed by the size—it is a big one. But one gets the feeling that the leaf does not belong anywhere, that it is alone, left hanging in the air.

Card VII: He sees the card again as a *part of a wreath*. In the inquiry he says *a crazy wreath*. To the question: "Anything wrong with it?" he says: *It doesn't have a ribbon*. [When the experimenter shows him the second plate and asks:] Does this have a ribbon? Jay answers *yes*, and means the red top and bottom. Apparently he is somewhat worried about the open top. It may also be that he goes on somewhat from Card VI—*a big leaf that somebody picked* and *a part of a wreath*. In both responses: *a big leaf somebody picked* (VI) and the *wreath* that *doesn't have a ribbon* (VII) there is an expression of something hanging in the air—an impression that he feels the lack of the harmony he is looking for. This suggestion is especially based on his uneasiness because both sides are not connected in VII. He is not a child who gives his imagination free rein and who creates a fantastic ribbon or connecting line to the wreath. Nevertheless, he cannot leave the fact that it is only a part of what he wants to be a whole. We must remember that he had seen *snow* in this plate on the previous test. There is a similar abstract emotional quality here in the *part of a wreath* association, and a similar uncertainty about the solid ground; but there is more shape and form in the second record.

Card VIII: There is a great change in his reaction to the first colored plate. He is more concrete now, seeing a *Butterfly—kind of a funny butterfly*. Probably the color plays a role since an abstract response is not given. This might mean that he has a less retiring disposition in a new situation and that the outward stimulus helps him not to retreat so much. The *butterfly* response has a more concrete participation than the abstract *grass* response in the first record.

Card IX: He sees again *a funny wreath*. Here again he reacts in a rather abstract way. The stimulus of this card is more interwoven with color and it has the most intense quality. Again we find indications of his retiring and retreating, and of his need to stick to an abstract whole—his wreath concept. He seems to cling to the roundness of the form, to be a part of it, without doing anything about it—almost as if he were allowing himself to be entwined.

Card X: Again he reacts more concretely. He sees *some butterflies*, and then corrects this: *No, spiders, butterflies, bees, ants, and a wasps*. The experimenter comments that "He had very recently been intimately involved with a wasp." This reaction to Card X is the most participating of all his color reactions in the first and second records. He dares to get a closer look at different animals, even those that hurt. He sees more form-elements and includes the color in these animal associations.

In summary, one may divide the responses from the viewpoint of whether he sees a concrete living thing only (Cards III, V, VIII, X), an abstract, lifeless thing only (Cards I, VI, VII, IX), or whether he sees both together (Cards II, IV). Note that from V on he is outspoken, either abstract or concrete.

PERSONALITY PICTURE OF JAY

AGE—4:6

Jay has developed intellectually: he is even more decisive and can meet new unforeseen emotional situations with greater ease. He is also more cooperative and probably more trustful. He feels himself more capable of managing situations and of asserting himself the way he is expected to. He is surer that he will live up to expectations; he is even less aggressive, and rather in harmony with himself. Consequently, he is more charming. He wants very much to protect this security, and if it is threatened then he can become stirred up and will react sharply. It is as though he wanted to be left in peace and would defend his peace. This may sometimes make him attack before he is attacked. This is a different kind of aggression from that which he showed before; his earlier aggression was that of rebellion. Now he wants to keep what he has.

Thus the nuances have changed here and there, and he has become happier and even more outgoing. But he has not become more independent; he has not gained more initiative. He has rather made peace with himself, has resigned himself to the acceptance of things as they must be. And he has gotten this ground on the basis that he is not looking for other things any more; he wants to feel now that this attitude is his, his possession, and that he has a firm hold on it. If someone attempts to break through this, he can put out his claws and become quite aggressive—but only then.

SEQUENCE ANALYSIS OF PROTOCOL

(3) AGE—5:11[5]

CARD I: *Bird. I see toads . . . and black . . . A frog . . . And birds . . . I don't know what else. A leaf . . . That's a whole leaf, isn't it?* Good accurate form. Jay is still occupied with problems of singular and plural; still sees a combination of concrete things first, and more lifeless things at the end; still has a need to bring everything together.

CARD II: *Another whole leaf . . . Red, black, red . . . Red, black, red.* More red shock than at four years, six months, because there is no association to color, only color naming and the lifeless whole leaf association.

CARD III: *Red, black, red . . . And gray.* A kind of failure. He counts only colors. He is much more afraid and less spontaneous than at 4:6 when he saw the *face* on this plate.

CARD IV: *Black and gray . . . I think that's upside-down. Eyes, nose, mouth, ears, teeth. These aren't ears too. . . . I bet our kindergarten is having fun now. We're having fun now, we're in the first grade room. I want to go.* He starts with color enumeration, black and gray. He sees only rare details, eyes, nose, mouth, etc. Sees no face, doesn't put it together. He is apparently afraid, and the remark at the end about fun in kindergarten is a conventional phrase he uses to relieve an apparently difficult situation. He is much more inhibited than at 4:6.

CARD V: *Butterfly. I'm all finished with that. It's a butterfly.* Butterfly response indicates that this situation is easy for him, and is the same one given in the first two records.

CARD X:[6] *Oh! Oh! Leaves . . . Blue, green, yellow, red, gray.* This *leaves* response is a lifeless one for this plate.

CARD VI: *Oh sure, that's a frog.* This is more concrete. His response to this plate is more alive than at four years, six months.

CARD VII: *I don't know what this is . . . Some kind of butterfly . . . I don't know what it looks like. An ant, a bug . . . Crawling through some rocks.* Butterfly and *bug crawling* are two concrete responses showing a movement tendency. He tries to make a place for himself, using the place on the plate which is most enclosed for

5. Jay was then in kindergarten.
6. The order of presentation was confused here by mistake.

this, but he tries hard to get through it. It is as if he experiences the feeling that "These rocks are too big and they may shut me out entirely," as if there were not enough air to breathe.

CARD VIII: *Leaf . . . Gray, blue, orange, pink, pink. And two tigers, they're climbing on the rocks, leaves, I mean . . . Colored rocks.* He sees more in this card than at four years, six months. He reacts more to the stimulus of color; there is more movement tendency, but this is somewhat threatening too—the big *tigers* and *rocks.* He combines better; lively figures even do something lively—a good development. But he is much less an extrovert than he started out to be at four years, one month.

CARD IX: *Orange, green, red, gray. . . .* He enumerates colors very well, but cannot make anything out of the plate. When not on safe ground emotionally he cannot bring out form, not even the abstract forms of former records. It is as if he would like to do better with the colors (cf. Card X above), but didn't dare. He started out at four years, one month, to be self-assured, but now he is not. He is more childish in his enumeration of colors than he was at four years, six months. He is not on an altogether direct level. There is some deterioration in his courage to act on his feeling; he is more on the defensive. He will still participate, but something must have happened in his relationships with human beings. It may have a merely temporary effect, however. He needs stability—every external instability makes him more unstable.

PERSONALITY PICTURE OF JAY

AGE 5:11

Jay is now more in the picture himself. He still seems to feel that his whole life and happiness depend on forces outside his influence. Whereas previously he felt quite sure of being able to control these forces and of being able to make them peaceful and conciliatory, he now feels that he cannot control them. The authoritarian forces which seem to him invested with such power over his life have been pushed somewhat more into the foreground. As a consequence, Jay has more difficulty now in feeling protected; he finds it harder to arrive at decisions of his own. He tries to placate those in authority and pacify them with conventionalities. But he also feels that things are expected of him, things toward which he would not be naturally inclined. He is more like a tamed animal which does what his trainer has taught him to do, but is also ready to break out at any moment or just to stand still. He no longer seems to feel that he is regarded with such good will; he seems rather to have experienced the fact that the overpowering forces may have become malevolent. I suspect that perhaps he is now being treated in a rather rude and rough way, which may have shaken his confidence in others. And he experiences a failure in himself because he cannot avoid the precarious position in which he finds himself and for which he blames others.

His development since the age of four years, one month, is somewhat as follows: He has never had the experience that he could really influence others, that through his own activity he could change situations and thus his own life, as, for example, Colin does.

The general picture seems temporary and there might be reality conditions to account for it. However, with all these different nuances, one sees a trend in his personality development from four years, one month, to five years, eleven months; this is the tendency to a certain retiring, a sit-and-wait dependency. In this basic passivity there is a danger that he may become a "chameleon," changing color, reacting too much to circumstances. This would be a pity because he has a capacity to establish a place for himself and to express the right to like and dislike things on his own account. There is still a fine quality in his nuances of feeling, and he has a rather hard time trying to make things right for everyone. Fortunately he has now come to the point where he wants to have some fun for himself. At least in this last record he is not too willing to conform—is no longer trying to do so well. It is as if he says "You can expect everything when I get love and protection, but you will not get anything when I do not get that."

CHAPTER 7

Conclusion

Contributions of the Methods

WE ARE OFTEN ASKED whether the methods outlined in this section will disclose anything which would not be apparent from observation of the child in everyday situations. The case records reveal an extensive overlap, as a matter of fact, between the data collected from the experimental methods and those available in the teachers' records. However, even in these cases, we found the Miniature Life Toys pointing up more clearly the conscious disingenuousness of Joyce's feeling about enuresis at the time her mother discussed the problem with the parent consultant; and similarly we found an elaborate projection of her feelings about her new dog in relation to her feelings about family routine and adult authority. There was a projection of two selves, one identified with forbidden outlets and the other identified with acceptable ones in Candice's Miniature Life Toy record. And both children gave a more complete picture of their feelings and preoccupation with enuresis and illness respectively in the experimental situations than appeared in group play situations in school. Fresh aspects of known problems, sharper revelation of attitudes, greater elaboration of them, and new insights which enrich observation of the child in the group have occurred in the experimental situations as we developed them, when these were compared with the reality-oriented behavior in the group.

The scientifically oriented reader may still be puzzled about the character of this procedure in which the experimenter remains passive or follows the child instead of determining focus points for the child's response. Both free and controlled procedures have a place in the study of child personality. Strictly controlled procedures provide clear answers to specific questions formulated initially by the experimenter. Free procedures often provide the experimenter with a whole battery of questions he would not have known enough to ask. Play-pen and crib trauma, isolation in sleeping and the longing for companionship, the meaning of animals and fire engines as exempt from culturally imposed routines, are examples of new insights the children brought us in their free play. More controlled procedures might, if it seemed desirable, now check frequencies of these attitudes and elaborate the contexts in which they occur, and their different meanings in different parent-child relationships.

DIAGNOSIS OF PERSONALITY DIFFICULTIES

The teacher tends to diagnose personality difficulties in terms of inadequate relations to materials, to other children, or to the usual activities of the nursery school, or in terms of inadequate body functioning. Nonparticipation and excessive annoyance of others are among the first things that disturb a teacher, along with nervous habits, enuresis, or excessive oral habits such as thumb-sucking or nail-biting, or more serious psychosomatic difficulties. Shut-in children whose contacts with the group have been inadequate are often unwilling to come to play with the toys or plastics. This was true of Christopher, Calvin, and of Stanley and Eric for many months. In itself this extreme caution about new situations is diagnostic, but does not tell us much more. Some children, however, whose relations with other children are difficult, reveal a degree of integration and creativeness in play with toys which points to possibilities of improved relations with people and objects at a reality-level.

Other children show comparable patterns of inability to carry through tasks and ideas once begun or flighty, indecisive approaches to objects and people, both in group situations and in individual play with toys. In other cases, the freedom from the usual coercions of group life reveals tendencies toward potentially dangerous symptoms such as schizoid types of thinking or violently charged emotional conflicts which do not appear in the group situation.

In still other cases the fantasy elaboration of an idea reveals conscious and sometimes amusing motives responsible for behavior which might have been interpreted in terms of unconscious conflict (Joyce's dramatization of the bed that was never, never going to get dry).

Since many of the materials used for the exploration of areas of spontaneity and pleasure (including sensory toys, plastics, etc.) were also new materials in the form in which they were presented to the child, they provided an opportunity to observe the child's response to such attenuated insecurity or anxiety as might be present in the protected nursery school environment. Data from these sources should be related to observations in other routine situations such as the medical examination, the posture photograph situation, and intelligence test situation,[1] all of which afford an opportunity to observe ways of handling initial insecurity along with opportunities to observe later resistance to the sometimes frustrating authority of the adult.[2]

Outlines of items to be watched for will give the reader not only alternative implications of choice of toys and objects, and of structures, but aspects of temperament directly inferable from behavior.[3] A complete summary of observations of a child will then describe what kind of child this is, and how he deals with

---

1. One full record of a child, presenting data from all these situations, is included in Volume II.

2. Cf. Eugene Lerner's studies. The reader will find other aspects of spontaneity in L. J. Stone's records of play with balloons and records of play with other children in trios.

3. See Appendix I.

his experience, as well as the content and quality of his feelings. Such outlines are not, however, intended as short cuts or substitutes for the student's own careful observation and weighing of his material. They are based on records collected to date, and are representative therefore only of predominantly Eastern metropolitan children. They are intended to extend and to stimulate the students' awareness, not to harness it.

ASSUMPTIONS ABOUT INDIVIDUAL TEMPERAMENT EXPRESSED IN PLAY

We have seen that a child's free play uses and thus expresses the child's whole self, as we observe his intellectual responses (that is, observation, organization, and integration of the play materials with his fantasy and creative ideas); his emotional range, intensity and pattern of inhibiting and releasing his feelings; his bodily behavior and use of himself in space, his manipulative skills; his social awareness and techniques. His alertness and emotional response to different sensory aspects of the environment—visual, auditory, texture, kinaesthetic—are equally observable in a play situation which contains stimuli of all of these kinds. For lack of a better term we may call the total intellectual-sensory-emotional-motor description of the child in a play setting a description of "temperament." This does not, however, separate genetic or constitutional factors from the many subtle or gross habit patterns which have contributed to his present make-up. It simply emphasizes that we are interested in the total child as we see him at play, and not just in his problems.

While masses of evidence regarding individual differences in intelligence have been accumulating for forty years, we are still limited in our grasp of individual differences in temperament. In the field of intelligence, despite the apparent contradictions growing out of recent arguments, we have a solid basis for believing that differences of the sort represented by intelligence quotients of 100 and 150 are partly due to genetic factors. Many a child's I.Q. may be raised twenty points by improvement of environment from a poorer than average to a better than average status, but genetic factors provide a ceiling or ceilings which cultural or environmental forces cannot pierce. We also readily grant such differences in aptitude as appear in musical, arithmetical, or artistically talented children, although our measures of their abilities are less adequate. But when confronted by similar differences in temperament, let us say, in enthusiasm-for-music quotient of 100 versus 150, or a resistance-to-trauma quotient of 100 to 150, or a laughter quotient of 100 to 150, many people reverse the emphasis and place heavy if not entire responsibility on the environment. Even if the loyal geneticist points to marked differences in the same family, the environmentalists will say, "But no two children in the same family *have* the same environment." We can agree heartily that they do not, but this conclusion should not paralyze our efforts to get a clear idea of the interactions, combined influences, and results of genetic and environmental factors.

We assume that genes are important not only in relation to eye color, stature, and I.Q., but in relation to every aspect of the constitution of the child as shown by different techniques at different levels of observation: blood pressure, stability of physiological rhythms, metabolism, susceptibility to organ weakness; tempo, ease of laughter and of crying, grace of coordination, finesse of small-muscle coordination, degree of affective response to sensory and pain stimuli, and so on.

A few references to relevant research will indicate the empirical basis for these assumptions:

Pratt, Nelson, and Sun have demonstrated objectively many differences in activity and reactivity in new-born infants; and have found significant differences even between infants in utero.[4] Differences in the time of appearance of new patterns of coordination, such as holding head up, grasping, sitting up, smiling, are definitely established in the work of Bühler,[5] Jones[6] and others.

Emotional and personality differences have been less adequately explored. Among the important pieces of work, one by

---

4. K. C. Pratt, A. K. Nelson, K. H. Sun, "The Behavior of the New Born Infant," *Ohio State Contributions in Psychology*, X (1930).
5. C. Bühler, *The First Year of Life* (New York: John Day, 1930).
6. M. C. Jones, "The Development of Early Behavior Patterns in Young Children," *Ped. Sem.*, XXXIII (1926), 537-85.

Washburn deserves special consideration.[7] Washburn observed fifteen infants at four-week intervals during the first year of life and found enormous differences in their responses to stimuli for smiling and laughter. She organizes these differences into types: the parvi-expressive versus the multi-expressive, marking off the difference between children of low and high responsiveness; the risor-expressive and depressor-expressive point to children who smile easily in contrast to those who cry easily, while the ambi-expressive children do both.

Harold Jones's measurements of psychogalvanic reactivity have suggested three types: those who show marked behavior reaction but slight psychogalvanic deflection; those who show the reverse, that is, marked psychogalvanic deflection without great behavior changes; and those who show both.[8] Macfarlane's studies of infants point to clustering of reaction patterns: children who have temper tantrums, eczema and other external reactions to disturbance seem to be best understood as "peripheral" reactors; children who show a great deal of fantasy, stomach upsets and other "internal" reactions are understood as "internalizers."[9]

It is important to note that when Washburn followed up her earlier study of infants, she found that the "parvi-expressive" groups as infants appear at six years old to be introverted in contrast to the multi-expressive group.[10] From an increasing mass of data of this sort we can conclude that while it is true that a child educated for it from birth may by the age of six or sixteen be a Catholic, or a Presbyterian, or a Communist for life (though he may *not*), it is also very likely that you cannot, taking any child at birth, make him an Edison or a Toscanini. Neither can you make a passionate child of myriad responses into an emotional imbecile, or an emotional imbecile into a genius of sensitivity.

Still we know too little about temperamental differences in

7. R. W. Washburn, "A Study of the Smiling and Laughing of Infants in the First Year of Life," *Genet. Psychol. Monog.*, VI (1929), 397-537.
8. Harold E. Jones, "The Retention of Conditioned Emotional Responses in Infancy," *Jnl. Genet. Psychol.*, XXXVII (1930), 485-98.
9. Jean Macfarlane, "Study of Personality Development," in R. G. Barker, J. S. Kounin, and H. F. Wright, *Child Behavior and Development* (New York: McGraw-Hill, 1943).
10. Personal communication.

children to know what to take into account.[11] Only by watching children over a period of years to see *within what limits* changing environmental demands and satisfactions bring changing behavior, and *in what terms* the child remains unmistakably himself, can we begin to define, botanist-like, this and this and this kind of child.

It seems reasonable, then, to carry the implications of data like these further and to project a hypothesis which research can gradually substantiate, reject, or refine. It is assumed that just as we can probably speak of general and specific factors in intelligence, we can also speak of genetically determined general and specific factors in temperament. The general factor would be the high or low affectivity (as measured perhaps by the psychogalvanic reflex, behavior indices, etc.) or tendencies to inner or outer reaction. Specific factors would be low thresholds for delight, humor, pain, traumatic sensitivity; toward sensitivity to certain types of experiences — tones, colors, touch sensations, muscle experiences, rhythm, formal details or gross patterns.

This list is merely suggestive. It is assumed in the case of intelligence, if we find outstanding arithmetical ability, verbal skill, or problem-solving ability, that genetic factors play a large part, whatever the contribution from a dynamic study of the child may reveal. Similarly, when a child shows outstanding sensitiveness to nuances of musical tones, persistent delight in all tactual experiences from fingerpaints to fall leaves, special pleasure in stories or pictures, sensitive accurate rhythm, or feeling for detail or organization, it is assumed that biological differences underlie these areas of response just as clearly as they underlie differences between the child who learns to read at three and the child who learns to read at eight, and that such biological differences are modified—stimulated or repressed or directed, etc.—by the child's earliest experience.

We come then to the possibility of conceiving of the organism at a biological level in terms of areas of low and high thresholds for response, or simply, of *different* thresholds for response. These areas of response afford the initial direction for

---

11. But see forthcoming studies by Sibylle Escalona, M. Leitch, and their colleagues.

the "canalization" which Gardner Murphy, following Janet, describes as the explanation of the formation of patterns and interests.[12] In our experience, bi-focal and multi-focal types are quite as important as the cases in which a predominant sensory, muscular, emotional, or rational emphasis appears; but the frequency with which we must admit multi-focal bases for development need not blur the picture of the "kind of child" we are dealing with.

These patterns have importance both in relation to adjustment and to maladjustment. A "sensory" child blocked in satisfactions in his main area may turn to thumb-sucking, for instance, not simply as a regressive reaction but as a pattern of satisfaction in the only area in which he can obtain his kind of satisfaction. "Motor" children, on the other hand, are more likely under pressure and tension to show motor distortions than are sensory children.[13]

These patterns of low thresholds are important for more complex behavior as well. I have found that verbal children who were not active expressed sympathy in verbal terms, active children in active terms, emotional children in emotional terms. These were not always mutually exclusive, but in many cases were nearly so. The capacity to "get the feel of things" may be based on a pattern of low thresholds for kinaesthetic response or for maintaining sensitivity to cues from all modalities; the same pattern may underlie the tendency to "identify" predominantly in relations with others, while a "motor" drive may be related to a more superficial kind of limitation; and similarly a verbal tendency underlies a preference for learning via explanations rather than "getting the feel of it."

How can we relate this point of view to an approach to the study of child personality? Discussions of personality development of young children have inevitably been skewed by emphases emerging from the particular ad hoc adjustments to problems of children confronted by the clinicians or teachers who

---

12. *Personality: A Biosocial Approach to Origins and Structure* (New York: Harper, 1947).

13. Hypotheses of this sort will be documented in a book on temperament and children's ways of coping with their problems, now in progress, by Nelly Tibout, and Lois Murphy.

are carrying on the discussion. Thus in the nineteen-thirties awareness of the fact that two-year-olds have so recently developed the capacity of locomotion led to an overemphasis by nursery school educators on large-muscle activities and their role. This often left out of account the wide differences in need for or interest in these large-muscle activities. Similarly the fact that infants who have been deeply frustrated in basic functions of feeding and eliminating bring serious problems to the clinician has led to an emphasis on oral, anal, and genital functions as the core and foundation of personality development. Experience with normal children does not encourage us to feel that either of these emphases provides an adequate framework for describing personality development. Few normal children present a picture dominated by a large proportion of traits of directly anal or oral derivation. Many children have personalities with striking foci of their own, including "anal" or "oral" characteristics which have interacted with other traits. They call for a reformulation of the theory of personality development in terms which will make it usable in relation to all children, not only the extreme types. Erikson has shown how the important residue from infantile preoccupations may be the mode of functioning, seen as intrusion, retention, assimilation tendencies which give orientation to the personality.[14] We could add that early preferences for different zone and mode responses share with persistent and transitory experiences the responsibility for the emerging patterns.

We could get further help in this direction when we stop to look again at the child seriously as a total organism. We saw that oral pleasure, even if the term oral is used to comprise all sorts of mouth pleasures and all sorts of passive receptiveness, is but one of a group of sensory areas of satisfaction. Some children, even as infants, are more delighted, comforted or stimulated by visual or auditory stimuli and others by varied tactual or skin experiences. For those children oral functions become important or dominant only when so seriously blocked that they are *forced* into predominance over the child's original areas of intense interest and responsiveness. For some children, if not

14. Erik H. Erikson, *Childhood and Society* (New York: W. W. Norton, 1950).

severely frustrated orally, small-muscle manipulations of fingers and hands may be most exciting even from infancy, while others enjoy most the rhythm and motion of their bodies in kinaesthetic terms, and still others enjoy vigorous large-muscle activity persistently, regardless of whether they are at the locomotor stage.

Similarly, for some children objects are of predominant stimulus-value while for other children human beings or faces always take precedence. For some, language is in and of itself important and exciting, a medium of expression as well as satisfaction of needs, while for other children it is merely a means to an end. Dramatic activity is early and persistent for some children, while it is incidental and an aspect of a "stage" for others.

In the animal world we can accept individual differences easily. Any animal breeder recognizes the weakling or runt of a litter, the high-strung puppy, the timid one, the bold aggressive one, and has for decades successfully developed strains contrasting sharply in temperament. We do not always appreciate comparable differences in children.

While temperament has many aspects, the areas of sensory satisfaction are emphasized here chiefly for the reason that it seems especially important to get at this most neglected area in order to round out our approaches to child personality. But individual differences in all other areas—affective, motor, manipulation, cognition—are equally important.

ROLE OF GRATIFICATION AND OTHER AREAS OF STRENGTH IN PERSONALITY DEVELOPMENT

A second hypothesis regarding forces contributing to development is that in studying personality with a view to better understanding both for its own sake and possible sources of breakdown, it is important to get a balanced picture of weaknesses and strength.[15] We see about us traumatized children and adults. When some of them become neurotic or psychotic it is

15. This point of view underlay my first discussion of "Areas of Security and Insecurity" at the Lewin meetings in 1938, as well as my study of sympathy in children begun in 1932. It is noted in the observation that most of our study of personality has been skewed by an overemphasis upon destructive or problem tendencies, and that valid predictions cannot be made until children are seen in a balanced frame of reference.

easy enough to point *a posteriori* to the difficulties that lay behind. We do not often enough check ourselves with the obvious comment that Tom, Dick, and Harry have been exposed to similar traumata and did not break down when Robert did. Why not? The relation between these balancing, releasing, control factors and the defense mechanisms may come close to a picture of the "structure of health."

One answer may be sought in the "offsetting factors," the areas of spontaneity, work, satisfaction and joy that fence off anxiety for some people; another in terms of "safety valves." Another answer may be sought in terms of "control" and skill.

The control referred to here includes both intrinsic, spontaneous integrating control and the coercive self-control known as will power. Control in the former sense is closely related to the spontaneous capacity to manipulate, or "handle," modulate, and release emotions. "Ways of handling" anxiety or conflict are as important to observe as its total amount, or the extent to which it is offset by positive areas of satisfaction.

"Ways of handling" anxiety are presumably closely related to total character structure. That is, we may ask whether anxiety drained off either in gastro-intestinal upsets or in crying may have less likelihood of cramping the style of the individual as far as day-in-day-out freedom for fresh perceptions and thinking and feeling are concerned, than anxiety drained into compulsive or rigid patterns of behavior. If so, we can take our choice between a poet with an upsettable stomach or a Puritan with a limited world of response.

I began with the assumption that *the balance of areas of anxiety* (tension, inhibition, etc.) and *areas of security* (gratification and spontaneity) would be a major indication of a child's capacity for healthy development. An inspection of the data on a small group of the children with whom we have been in touch over the years from 1937 to 1954 is the basis for a reformulation of this hypothesis and of the concept of healthy development.

We can now say that of these children who have all developed extremely well, *no child was completely free of conflicts or developmental problems*. Among these normal children, five to our knowledge required special help from parents or others at some point where they were bogged down. This help included changing from a school when the child was unhappy to a school where the child was better able to take hold; in one instance, special help from teachers; in another instance, suggestions from a psychiatrist who was a friend of the family, and in one instance, therapy.

In all these instances the children had strong areas of satisfaction which have carried through from preschool to college years; these areas of satisfaction (music, creative writing, art, etc.) have contributed to the child's strength. Areas of satisfaction were not enough to enable the child to withstand severe stress from external or internal sources (hostile teachers or developmental conflicts).

The ability to respond quickly to help, whether this involved an environmental change or personal help from teachers or parents, involved *flexibility and resilience* which our original frame of reference did not emphasize, and which appeared even in the most disturbed child in the group.

This flexibility and resilience may be looked at as expressions of a *drive toward growth and health which asserts itself in children who feel supported by the people important to them.*

In addition to the flexibility and resilience which appeared in the quick response to help, these children showed varying degrees of *capacity for integration.*

To understand the child's efforts toward integration and his ways of handling his problems we must go beyond the balance of areas of satisfaction and areas of anxiety to the relationships between these and their place in his total pattern of life and growth. Areas of satisfaction may be substitutes or compensations for deprivation, or they may provide sublimations for frustrated drives, including the aggression that is not expressed directly, or they may be peaceful islands which permit the child to mobilize his energy for direct efforts to solve problems.

When Catharine's little brother arrived before she was two she developed a great interest in purses; tried to cover up his penis with any handy small tube; became interested in tummy-buttons: "I have one, you have one, Mommie has one, baby has one"; clung to her own bottle; and spanked her doll-baby. Later, she became very protective of her little brother, much of the time, mothering and watching over him.

Thus her "interests" were spontaneous, self-healing techniques which helped her through play to liquidate her rivalry and loss, and progress toward an identification with her mother. The behavior described above pointed not only to her problem but to her versatile efforts at its solution.[16]

SPECIFIC PROBLEMS: RIGIDITY

We have already given some illustrations of the use and implications of the term "constricted" or "rigid," one of a group of concepts important in the study of relationships between spontaneity and anxiety in personality organization. We noted in the chapter on Miniature Life Toys that Betsy's geometrically organized house, with its four rooms neatly arranged, old things and broken things excluded, looked on the surface like a very rigid pattern. Yet her expressiveness and dramatic freedom showed real spontaneity as well. After repeated intelligence tests, it was very clear that sharp form perception was an outstanding characteristic of her mind. The geometrical form of organization in and of itself could hardly be called rigid. But the fact that this form was repeated in her initial approach to situations over a period of a year and a half, virtually without change, pointed to an area of rigidity, confirmed by her difficulties in adjusting to the new situation of nursery school, her concern with change expressed in themes of "moving," and by postural rigidities apparent in photographic records. Thus, the process of checking the rigidity hypothesis with other data, both positive and negative, served to pin down the area and limits of rigidity and to suggest clues to why formal structures were satisfying patterns for her to begin with in playing with Miniature Life Toys.

The chief importance of the distinction between *relatively* "structured" and "unstructured" material relates to the type of

---

16. A more complete exploration of balancing, releasing, sublimating, controlling techniques used by a child will appear in the study of Colin in Volume II.

information desired about the child. Relatively "structured" materials and methods are necessary to focus the child's behavior so as to give "Yes" or "No" answers. Relatively "less structured" materials and procedures are fertile in affording clues or substantial evidence for qualitative aspects of the child's use of his life space. Their only advantage is that the selection of a constant equipment of materials and the exclusion of the range of stimuli by observing behavior in a suitable room provides data which can be compared from one child to another with some validity, if evidence regarding the child's attitude or view of the situation is taken into account.

Whether the material be toys, clay, or balloons, certain basic aspects of the child's approach will whittle out their own indices and doubtless use their own vocabulary. But regardless of the particular terms used, observations will include references to behavior related to the following extremes of categories.

Form	intrinsic to material	*vs.*	extrinsic (arbitrary)
Organization	functional	*vs.*	artifact, discrete
Patterns	emergent	*vs.*	imposed
Sequences	fluid, spontaneous, flexible, fresh, free	*vs.*	static or abrupt, step-wise, discontinuous, stereotyped, rigid, repetitious, constrained
Construction	creative, intuitive or integrative	*vs.*	mechanical, rationally manipulated, disassociated

Behavior with materials may also be related to the child's patterns of handling his body in the experimental situation, among which are the following:

high tonicity	*vs.*	low tonicity
relaxation	*vs.*	tension
free, fluid movement	*vs.*	inhibition of movement, postural rigidities, jerky behavior
adaptive, flexible	*vs.*	compulsive, forced
trunk-centered	*vs.*	extremity-centered
deep breathing, sighs of contentment, etc.	*vs.*	attenuated breathing
wide vocal range	*vs.*	monotone or step-shifts
resonant voice	*vs.*	nasal or throat-constricted quality

In a few extreme instances, which may be considered "pure types," a child may show response to materials and behavior which follows all the patterns on one side of the above charts. Karin, Dusty, and Colin, for instance, at this age handled materials in a consistently functional adaptive way and this behavior could be described solely in terms from the left-hand columns above. Adele, by contrast, showed extreme rigidities, tension, extensor-compulsions, lack of spontaneous functional handling of material, flat voice—a maximum of characteristics listed in the right-hand columns above. She was one of the most rigid in a group of thirty-five children among whom she was seen. Alec, by contrast, showed points of great originality and intuition along with qualities of tension and rigidity. Many children display a changing balance of areas of freedom and areas of rigidity, constriction, compulsiveness (or other reactions to anxiety) at different developmental stages or in response to different life experiences.

It is significant that most children in this group usually showed patterns from both of these columns: areas of rigidity and areas of freedom, periods of originality and considerable use of imitation or creativeness based upon periods of imitation. In many cases the distinction between mechanical procedures which appeared to observers to be healthy, as compared with those that seemed indicative of inhibition and loss of free creativity, could be seen in terms of the extent to which patterns had been deeply interiorized in such a way as to prevent responsiveness to new ways of doing things. In the case of Nancy, a basically imitative adult-like child, the patterns seemed to everyone to be real vehicles for expression; while in Adele's case they remained external and stereotyped, and constantly interfered with spontaneity. Both children had I.Q.'s of between 120 and 130, so that differences in intelligence as measured by I.Q. can hardly account for this difference in rigidity, and certainly not for the difference between both of these children and the "creative" children, some of whose I.Q.'s were considerably lower than this.

The distinction just made between the behavior of Nancy and Adele, in terms of the manner in which patterns are assimilated, points to a basic difference between the "functional" and "rigid" groups as a whole: the extent to which emotion and the ideo-motor activities are integrated. In a creative child like Karin, they *have never become separated,* and the easy "natural" flow of response from stimulus to emotion to reaction seems to be the basis of the striking "integration" that all observers felt in her, in Dusty, in Colin, and their like. In more externally patterned children who develop by submitting to adult directives which may be *later* digested emotionally (holding emotional response of their own temporarily in suspense), an equally convincing soundness may result if the child is not submerged by patterns too forcefully imposed to be emotionally assimilated. Without emotional assimilation, we find the child helplessly approaching each new experience, lost until he has the "right answer," the right pattern. He may be incapable of achieving his own spontaneous insight or clarity of ideas regarding the possibilities of a situation or of connecting any clarity which he discovers with action indigenous to himself. We are apt to think of these qualities of integration, spontaneity, and rigidity as resulting from certain types of handling, and undoubtedly the treatment which the child receives at different stages is of great importance. An opportunity for free exercise of autonomy while the child is mastering locomotion and manipulation before the age of three years can give a foundation which later restrictives could destroy only with difficulty. However, we do not usually pay enough attention to the enormous differences in the ways in which different children respond to similar cultural pressures.

Adele, with her inability to make any spontaneous response to a new situation and materials, seems flattened out like a sheet. Alec's disorganized and easily disturbed sensitivities, if more extreme, might deserve the term "culture-shocked." In contrast to children like these two, who have felt the culture as violent in different ways, a child like Colin moves through life chiefly urged by his own drives, casually tasting or using the culture as it meets his individual desires. Candice, in contrast to both of these groups, makes serious use of the forms around her without being driven by them. She is a good example of a "culture-assimilating" child.

The "culture-blocked" child finds the forms and patterns to which he is exposed to be insuperable obstacles to his spontaneous expression. In their various different ways, then, the children we have mentioned are overpowered by, or relatively indifferent to, forms which the culture supplies, or, like Candice, can assimilate forms without losing their integrity.

Undoubtedly, qualities of "energy," "drive," "resilience," "vitality," "vulnerability," and thresholds for "psychic balance" or "disintegration" are involved here. The relation of form to experience in the child's expression can thus be seen from the point of view of specific intellectual and temperamental differences which affect the assimilation of form. Here it is possible to make three major distinctions around which the nuances of different patterns may be grouped. First we may see a group of "cortical-dominant" children. Regardless of I.Q. (their intelligence quotients range from 100 to 160), they are children whose activity or thinking is primarily "intellect-directed." In extreme cases where the child seems to have no integration at all of emotional processes with intellectual ones, he may be "intellect-bound." In vivid contrast to these, we see children whose thinking and behavior is consistently colored by emotional or autonomic responsiveness. In the case of Camille, the autonomic overflow seems to occur within the limits of certain situations and not in others, so that it is almost as if she turned a switch to carry the overflow down a spillway maintained for the purpose. Alec's overflow, and also that of Colin, cannot be charted so easily. In fact, in the case of Colin we rarely find the intense autonomic spilling-over characteristic of Alec and Camille, but often a whimsical quality in his play and in his thinking, suggesting that cortical activity is consistently flowing down the beds of little creeks and rivers cut by emotionality.

In contrast to the extreme "cortical" child for whom form, intellectually assimilated, appears to have little integration with experience or personal feeling and impulses, and the "autonomic child" who has not been able to absorb enough form to direct and make use of emotional sources of creativity, we find that children like Karin and Dusty seem to illustrate an unusual balance and integration of cortical and autonomic function, with the result that form and feeling flow together. This rare degree of intellectual-emotional integration is different from the intellectual-emotional parallelism of other children who take on forms and make use of them intelligently and who also retain considerable freedom for fresh emotional experience, but do not integrate these two capacities. Our culture makes use of both types of intellectual-emotional patterning; both may be healthy; but when anxiety mounts it is handled in different ways. Disturbance is expressed differently in different types of children, but with the common element that growth is interfered with.

PART II

Experiments in Group Play and in Readiness for Destruction

by L. JOSEPH STONE

CHAPTER 8

Introduction

Use of Group Techniques

THE DISTINGUISHING FEATURE of the procedures to be described here is the use of several subjects simultaneously. A variety of aspects of personality can be studied with such techniques by suitable modifications of procedure, of which I shall describe but two or three. In all the procedures, three children (occasionally the number has been varied) are brought together in the experimental room: thus, the fundamental characteristic of all the situations is their *social* nature. This is so obvious as to be misleading, unless we emphasize that we have been concerned primarily, not with group effects but—as in all the methods discussed in this volume—with specific individuals in specific situations; in this case, with the individual in a fairly complex social situation.[1]

The aspect of personality which I have been most interested in studying through a social play situation has been the quality of each child's relations with his fellows. It has been possible to

1. Of course, the presence of the experimenter in all our play situations introduces an important social factor. A distinction, however, exists in view of the sharp qualitative difference for children between their contemporaries and an adult.

observe these relationships under somewhat better controlled conditions than the free play situations and, with the specific procedures employed, to achieve considerable clarification of some of the personal dynamics underlying the problems that are designated by such (almost hackneyed) terms as "dominance and submission," "leadership," "sociability," etc.

The observations that one may derive from the procedures under discussion are applicable to the entire cluster of problems suggested by these phrases, viewed in individual rather than group or statistical terms. I do not seek to offer new concepts under these headings, but rather to demonstrate techniques for observing an individual child in a social context.

In our exploratory work with procedures using small groups of children, we have already found that the social context serves especially well to illuminate at least two other important "regions" of the personality. For preliminary purposes I may refer to these as "freedom and rigidity" in social situations, and the social facilitation of fantasy production.

In developing a procedure for the study of leadership and social relations, situations were set up requiring all the children to shift from one role to another, and from one play context to another. It has been extremely illuminating to observe the phenomena produced by the imposed requirements to shift, quite apart from their meaning to the problem of leadership. It would be most satisfactory to describe these phenomena "operationally" (and I shall do this below), since it is difficult to label them without using terms which, through their popular or psychological connotations, obscure rather than clarify their meaning. I may designate them, for want of a better term, as phenomena of *social adaptability* or, more accurately, phenomena of adaptability within a social context. I am concerned essentially with the "flexibility" or "rigidity" with which the child meets each demand to shift. Clearly observable and apparently structurally significant differences between children appear. Although, of course, it has not seemed sensible to divide all children into two classes, *rigid* and *flexible,* it has appeared feasible to stamp some children "flexible" or "rigid" or even (structurally speaking) "fragile," on the basis of observations in the play situations to be described.

It has also been possible to study the fantasies of individual children to advantage under social conditions. The "let's pretend . . ." nature of the games used has secured the children's whole-hearted interest and readiness to create "dramatic play" (i.e., play which is not merely motor activity for its own sake). For many children social situations seem to facilitate fantasy, so that the stimulus of the give-and-take with other children may release fantasies that might otherwise be rather guarded, particularly from adults. In general, the nature of the fantasies revealed may not differ sharply from those produced in various individual play situations (especially Miniature Life Toys), but with certain children they may be expressed more freely and directly. It is also true that certain children are more released in the individual type of play. Thus it has been useful to compare the way specific children work out wishes of focal significance using inanimate materials with the way in which the same wishes may be elaborated when the child has to deal with real people (his playmates) as protagonists. When group dramatic play is undertaken for the general purpose of revealing the child's unique personal world of experience and relationships, it may be readily modified to show the special significance for each child of specific roles, such as mother, father, baby, grandfather, etc. The adult may suggest a variety of games ("Let's play house," "Let's play store," "Let's play doctor," etc.) in order to tap different levels or areas of the child's experience.

The three aspects of personality I have referred to do not, of course, exhaust the possibilities of work with small groups, nor do they exhaust all the data in the protocols obtained.[2] They are, however, the aspects which received most analysis, and for which it is possible to offer some suggestions to those who wish to adopt these techniques. Although the procedures may be modified to emphasize one or another of these "trait-complexes," or aspects of personality, it is a fault—or perhaps a virtue—of the

2. This discussion is based on approximately twenty experimental sessions involving some twenty-five children in various combinations.

group situation that it is impossible to limit the procedures sufficiently to elicit information on only one aspect at a time. This is something that can be accomplished only in an analysis of the *results,* which means that the data of any of our group experiments may be analyzed according to *several* heuristic schemes rather than only one. Therefore, one may, in effect, be performing several experiments at once: the protocol of a given experimental session may be analyzed to bring out essential information in regard to any or all of the personality aspects we have just described. We may also regard each of the three aspects in turn as the main subject in our analysis. A single group experiment thus yields several kinds of information on several different children (a nine—or more—fold "table" of results), a fact which accounts for the greater difficulties in recording and analysis, and the occasional necessity of employing more than one recorder.

Before describing the procedures in detail I shall discuss briefly some of the problems of control and recording which are inherent in group experiments, as distinguished from the other techniques and experiments described in this book.

CONTROL

It is well to accept at the outset the impossibility of completely controlling certain of the aspects of the group situation. Of course, as in all projective techniques, the subjective meaning of the situation is different for each child—and constitutes, in fact, the dependent variable one is studying.

Beyond this, however, is the inescapable fact that each child is *part of the stimulating situation for every other child;* since a child can never be a similar part of the stimulating field for himself, the situations cannot be equated for all members of the group. Nor is simple mechanical rotation of the choice of subjects sufficient to insure control of this factor. It might be suggested that for two main subjects, "A" and "B," we employ the same additional subjects "x" and "y." But the situations Axy and Bxy are different situations, and the different social stimulus values of "A" and "B" make "x" and "y" to some extent different children in the different situations. Thus, in this respect complete control can only be approximated.

The situation directly preceding the experiment frequently can be ignored in experiments using single children, but is likely to be more important when several children are drawn from the same group. Different states of temporary tension, of attraction or repulsion between the specific subjects selected, are very likely to be carried over into the experimental scene. Other characteristics of the total situation may be controlled as rigorously as desired. The experimenter may keep constant the physical setting, the toys or other materials that may be introduced and—at least within rough limits—the timing and content of his own conversation and instructions to the children. The activities of the children can be controlled very grossly as far as the major theme is concerned. They can also be controlled negatively—for example, by preventing fights—to the extent that it is desirable to do so in the given situation. The experimenter must achieve his ends, beyond this degree of control, through the use of much the same techniques that are used by the skilled nursery school teacher. Judgment, subtlety, and the ability to act promptly on the basis of reasonable inferences must be demanded of the experimenter in his handling of the procedure and his analysis of the results. He must always be prepared to deal with the irruption of uncontrolled or unexpected variables so that they will interfere with his planned procedure as little as possible, and so that he may take explicit account of them in analyzing the results.

RECORDING

In virtually all the methods described in this volume, and in general with most projective techniques, it is necessary to have a full stenographic record of everything the child says, and as complete a description as possible of all of his actions and expressive behavior. Without this information a full use of the experimental procedure for the understanding of the specific personality being examined is impossible. In ordinary (nonprojective) laboratory procedures it is possible to analyze the situation in advance in such a way that recording is necessary only at predetermined key points in the procedure. In a great many of our procedures—notably, for example, the Miniature Life Toys—most of the analysis necessarily follows the experiment, and it is not usually possible to predetermine the points at which behavior significant for the understanding of this personality will appear. Even with techniques such as Blocking Game Number 2,[3] where it is possible to predict the moments when indicative behavior is most likely to appear, the nature of all these studies, directed to the understanding of single persons, is such that it is never possible to state that for any subjects certain portions of the procedure will *not* produce significant behavior. Recording, then, begins to take on many of the aspects of court reporting, with the added difficulty that it requires not merely mechanical speed and skill but judgment and sensitivity on the part of the observer. When several children are present at once, the recorder's task is many times more difficult.

In the records of our Group Play experiments something of the quality of the interpersonal relations must appear in addition to sequence of talk and action among three children, and therefore a new dimension of events must be included in the record. It is obvious that one cannot obtain a complete record of the subtler phases of the subjects' behavior because of the necessary division of the recorder's attention, or unless a second, or sometimes a third recorder, is present to help record specific aspects of the procedure.

We have found it helpful to prepare the notebook for recording in four parallel columns, beginning with the main subject and ending with the experimenter, so that the words and actions of each may be recorded appropriately without wasting any time in identifying the individual. Abbreviations (even abbreviations of shorthand) for commonly used terms and objects in the experimental field are also helpful time-savers. Frequently the recorder's greatest difficulty is not in setting down actual words or obvious locomotions and activities, but in noting the subtler characteristics of movement and expression which serve to con-

---

3. See pages 303-333.

vey the child's mood and the emotional import to him of the events taking place. It is usually safest to set down some cue word or phrase along with some marginal indication that will readily catch the eye and not risk the danger of falling behind the whole action in seeking the *mot juste*. Immediately after the experiment the recorder can look for these cue signs and, while the events are still fresh, elaborate the description as necessary. Unless absolutely necessary in terms of the experimenter's time or the possibility of working with a particular group of children, it is best not to record a second group experiment until the first has been transcribed. The process of transcription at its best necessitates elaboration and clarification of the notes, and if a second record is made before the first has been written up, there is a very noticeable confusion and displacement of events as a result of the mutual interferences between the two rather similar sets of remembered items.

Aggression and Destruction Games

The approach described in Chapter 10 is an exploratory technique which has taken its specific form and direction under the influence of the leads provided by the subjects themselves. At its inception the experimental procedure consisted merely of confronting a child with a number of balloons, giving him freedom to explore and play with them. On the basis of general observation, it seemed likely that the child's mode of approach and handling of this material might be revealing in a multitude of ways. For example, *sensory interests* might be shown in response to the color of the balloons or to the tactual experiences or sounds produced by rubbing them. Something of the child's *temperament* might be shown in his manner of play: a child might be easy or hesitant in his approach; vigorous and active, or cautious and reserved in playing with the balloons. It was soon clear that the balloons (which could be regarded in so many different ways) were important for almost all children chiefly as *breakable* objects. It was equally clear that to some children they represented objects-to-be-broken while to others they were definitely objects-*not*-to-be-broken. As it stands at present, the procedure has been developed largely for its value as an indicator of what we may term for the moment "destructive tendencies," and to differentiate finer gradations of attitudes than merely willingness or unwillingness to destroy.

CHAPTER 9

Group Play Techniques with Special Reference to Leadership

Procedures

EACH OF THE GROUP TECHNIQUES has been frankly an exploratory device rather than a means of testing specific hypotheses. Hypotheses, however, have grown rather directly out of our observation of children in these situations, and after detailing the procedures I shall attempt to indicate in the next section some of the directions in which our observations seem to lead.

In this section I wish to describe in detail the actual techniques used. They may be employed, as I have said, merely for the purpose of understanding individual children better; and a description of the techniques may suggest uses or modifications for any purposes which the reader may have in mind, and quite apart from the theoretical implications and insights which their use has brought to the writer.

Potential Leadership Game[1]

The children who are to be the subjects are brought into the room together, with at least the implication in the experimenter's behavior that he regards them not merely as three individuals but as a group, a unit. In my own use of the technique up to now, three children have always been used, although modifications are possible. At the outset, the experimenter attempts to establish a friendly, but withal mildly authoritative, atmosphere. This helps to polarize the group, and makes it possible to compare adult-directed with later spontaneous activity. Instructions such as these set the tone: "Now everybody sit down here, and I'll tell you what we can all play together." Depending on the atmosphere of the group, which the experimenter must sense, he may consciously increase either his friendliness or his authoritativeness, so that the emotional tone at the outset is roughly comparable from one group to another.

When the children have settled down, the adult suggests the initial activity. This should be one that is appealing to the children so that they will fall in with the suggestion not only readily but eagerly. The procedure used with almost unfailing success with three- to five-year-olds is, "Now we're going to play house." After the initial suggestion has been made, the experimenter attempts to withdraw from authority and active direction as quickly as possible. The opportunity is thus provided for any one of the children to take up the adult's suggestion (or reject it); to select and assign roles for himself or for other children; and in this way to exercise initiative and authority and assume a more or less dominating imaginative role. It may be necessary for the experimenter to use additional instructions and suggestions: "Who do you want to be?" "Who wants to be the . . . ?"

1. This title may be regarded as an arbitrary and merely descriptive designation, conveying the suggestion that it is possible for any of the three children, at any time, to assume the functions of a leader if he is able and wishes to do so, in distinction to the second, or Imposed Leadership Game, described later. The use of the term "leadership" in the title does not mean that the technique is not useful in considering other aspects of personality.

"What is . . . going to be?" When the game is under way the children are also given access to the toys which have been in view but out of reach. If the adult has not been included in the assignment of roles by the children, he may ask after a time, "What shall I be?"

This first portion of the game of playing house is permitted to continue for approximately five minutes. The time is only important in view of the fact that a number of units make up the game and one does not wish to tire or bore the subjects. It is not desirable, however, to terminate any portion of it when the children are in the midst of something very interesting, or at any time when it will be felt as a major intrusion by the adult. There is an opportunity after the game has been initiated to note such events as the acceptance or rejection of the adult's plan, to see which children assign roles to others, and whether such roles are accepted or rejected, to see whether the adult is included or excluded, to find out which children actively select the toys, to see which roles seem to be most desirable and with what content they are invested, etc.

The following toys were used: 3 quarter-blocks, 1 thin half-block; 1 large truck, 1 small truck; 1 naked doll, 1 dressed doll, 4 doll dresses, shoes, etc.; 6 pieces of cloth for "blankets" etc. There is no need to use precisely this group of objects. It is desirable, however, to use toys which have some relevance, or at least suitability, to the games to be played; which are interesting and somewhat different from the toys the children use every day in the nursery school, but not so new and fascinating that they will dominate the psychological environment.

The next unit of the experiment, while still "playing house," is introduced when the experimenter says, "Now everybody change. Everybody play you're somebody else. Who do you want to be, etc." If necessary, the experimenter may exert gentle (verbal!) pressure on children who try to maintain the roles they already have, but as before, he should tend to withdraw from the situation as soon as the children singly or as a group begin to work it out.

Here it is of interest again to observe the content of the play during the next five minutes, much as during the first unit.

There is in addition, however, the opportunity to observe each child's response to the suggestion of *shifting*. It is of interest to see whether the child is rigid and resistant to change, or flexible in accepting the new order of things; and if the latter, to look for indications which will show whether he is merely accepting adult authority (perhaps unwillingly) or is really adapting himself to a new situation and making the most of it. (Such an indication might be the sullen relinquishing of a role as compared with immediately dropping it and actively selecting a new one for himself.) It is also interesting to compare the meaning of the first and second roles in terms of their authoritative content: is it easier to drop the role of baby for that of mother, or vice versa?

The next portion of the game which is introduced after a second period of approximately five minutes involves still greater shift. Not only are the roles to be dropped and new ones adopted, but the experimenter introduces a new frame of reference, a new game. The "playing house" period is usually terminated by the following instructions: "All right, now we're all through playing house. Everybody sit down and I'll tell you what we're going to play now." Sometimes, of course, it is necessary to take a few moments to see that the first game has really tapered off and the children are really ready for something new. When the subjects are in readiness, the experimenter introduces the second game. "Now we're going to play store. Who wants to be what?" The first and second units of the second game are then played exactly as described for "playing house," with the selection and assignment of roles, the shift from the first to the second unit with the adoption of new roles, and the actual playing of the game for approximately five minutes under each set of conditions.

In the final unit of the procedure opportunity is offered the children to set up their own framework. "Now we can play something else. Whatever you want. What shall we play?" After a game has been selected and agreed upon, the experimenter again sees that roles are explicitly selected or assigned for each child and as explicitly accepted or rejected.[2]

---

2. The plan of procedure is outlined in Appendix III.

Here one may observe who determines the choice of the game, to what extent he is able to secure its acceptance by the other children, and to what degree it continues as "his" game. It is also interesting to note the extent to which the nature of the game is determined by the patterns the adult has established during the preceding units, and to what extent the child's imaginativeness and creativeness may overcome this fixed pattern or make a really new use of it.

This procedure, then, involves playing consecutively three different games, of which the toys and "props" are relatively unimportant and of which the major content must be drawn from the children's own fantasies. During each of these games the experimenter may observe the social relationships of each child. These are revealed particularly in the selection of specific roles, in attempts to impose or accept or reject such assignments, and in the social content (authority and status aspects) that each child uses in developing his roles. The child's conception of himself and his social status is still more critically tested when he is suddenly required to shift to a new role. The experimenter is also afforded the opportunity of observing the flexibility, creativeness and resourcefulness of the individual in a social setting: the acceptance or rejection of the experimenter's program, the content of the role he plays and the devices he uses to obtain the roles he wishes or to assign roles to the others. Moreover, the content with which he invests each role and each game reveals his picture of the world in which he lives. Thus, daddies may be ephemeral commuters or fonts of authoritarian pronouncements; stores may be pleasant haunts to which people are paid (change) to come and make purchases ranging from trucks to lettuce.

Below is a sample protocol which may suggest the atmosphere maintained, and give some hint of the possible ramifications produced when real children are really playing.

SUBJECTS: Alec
Camille
Colt

PLAYING HOUSE

Experimenter: Now everybody sit down. We're going to play house. Alec: *This could be all house!* [breathlessly, indicating whole room] Who wants to be what? Alec: *I want to be the mother.* Camille: *No, I am, because you're a little boy and little boys can't be mothers.* Alec: *And what could he be?* [pointing to Colt] Colt: *I'll be the daddy and he'll be the grandfather.* [indicating Alec] Alec: *No, I want to be the big brother.* Now what things will we need? Alec: *All of them.* Now who are you? Colt: *The daddy.* And who are you? Alec: *The big brother.* Alec's the big brother—and who's Camille? Camille: *The mother.* What does the mother need? Camille: *Child.* [pointing to doll] [Camille then sits quietly and confidently, not going after things, expecting them to be brought. When experimenter offers her a doll, she asks for a different one, having specific idea of what she needs.] Camille: *No. This one.* Alec: *I want a child.* This one? Alec: *Yes.* What does the daddy need? Colt: *I want a child.* Alec: *I need this and this and this.* [grabbing all cars] Camille: *I've got to have some.* Alec: *I need these.* [lies down on them, hiding and protecting them] Camille: *Well, I need some.* [getting them away from Alec] What shall I be? [No answer; Alec and Colt quarreling. Colt hitting Alec.] Alec: *We need all these things. You can't have any.* Camille: *Yes, you can play with one. I'll let him have this . . . And this one.* What can I be? Alec: *The grandfather . . . And this be the work . . . I have to go to work . . .* Colt: *I have to go to work too. I have no car to go in. I could use that yellow chair.* Alec: *But we could make believe it's Saturday once.* Want to make believe it's Saturday? Camille: *They go on Saturdays.* Colt: *But on Sundays they stay home.* Camille: *But the mommie has to do the work.* [Camille is very busy as the mommie, sitting on the couch, sorting clothes.] Who's the big boy? Camille: *You are, Alec. Go to school.* Alec: *Okay.* [He goes off to opposite side of room toward door, chanting rhythmically:] *Work, work, work.* [making rhythmic scrubbing movement on floor near door] Is that what you're doing in school? Working? Alec: *Yes.* Camille: *He has to stay in school eight minutes.* [Then, to Alec:] *You have to stay four more minutes.* [confident, not self-conscious] Colt: *When can I go?* [looking to Camille for answer] Camille: *You're the daddy. You're in the office. Work, work.* [Colt goes through similar scrubbing motions as his work in the office.] Colt: *Work, work, work, work.* Camille: *Now you come home . . . I'm putting on the dolly's little nightgown.* What does the mommie do? Camille: *The daddy stays to work some more . . . Until ten o'clock at night.* [Note her discrimination between Colt and Alec.] And what does the mommie do? Camille: *Now you come home. I'm putting on the dolly's little nightgown.* [Alec comes home. Colt lies down on the floor.] Colt: *What's this for? What's under here?* [Breaking down to his customary attention-getting pattern; is looking in back of curtain.] Alec: *What is this?* [lifting curtain]

Now we're all going to be something else. Alec: *I'm going to be the mother.* Camille: *I'll be the big sister.* Alec: *And I'll be the mother.* Colt: *This . . . This is my baby . . . What shall I be? Oh, I know what I'll be . . . I'm . . . I'm a lady.* Alec: *Yeah . . . I'm the mother . . . I'll be the mother . . . I'll have all these things.* Use all those things you're sitting on. Alec: *Yeah, I don't want to change because I need these.* [Alec lying on back on couch. Camille comes over toward him, giving him something.] Colt: *Where's my dress? Why did you bring two dresses?* I thought we might need them. What are you now, Camille? Alec: *I'm the mother.* Alec's the mother. What does the mother do, Alec? Alec: *I'm the mother.* What are you, Colt? Colt: *I don't know what I am. I want to be the father. I'll be the father, the daddy who takes care of the big brother.* Who's the big brother? Colt: *Camille is.* Camille: *No, I'm the big sister.* Colt: *Okay. I take care of the big sister. Okay Camille?* Camille: *Yes.* Colt: *I take care of you, Camille.* Alec: *Now you take care of me, coz I'm the mommie.* Who am I? [Camille ignores this and goes on with a new idea:] Camille: [sitting up brightly] *Oh . . . Somebody has to be sick! Do you want to be sick, Alec?* Alec: *Yeah. I'm a sick child.* Camille: *Don't forget I'm sick and you have to take care of the whole house, don't you?* [to Colt] *Ha!* [with satisfaction] Is everybody sick now? Camille: *Yes. Please don't get near us very often.* Can't you get near people who are sick? Camille: *No. Coz my real father . . . Really home . . . Really has the gripped, and I can't even go in his room.* Who shall I be? Colt: *You can be the child.* Alec: *You can be the child in this house.* Colt: *And scare us!* [All three laugh gleefully. Camille and Alec lying on the couch.]

PLAYING STORE

Now we'll put all these things away. Everybody sit on the couch again and I'll tell you what we'll do now . . . let's play store. Camille: *Okay. I'm going to be the woman who writes down things.* [She gets herself a pad and pencil and soon ensconces herself in solitary glory on the swivel chair that was supposed to be in the corner, out of reach.] Colt: *I'm going to be the man and I can have apples and corn-flakes.* And what is Alec? Camille: *Alec's the mother who stays—oh, he needs one child. He stays there with the child.* What are you doing in the store, Camille? Camille: *I'm writing down things.* Colt: *And don't forget you're the mother and I'm the daddy. And I have to give him orders, coz I'm the man who gives them to you.* Where are your groceries? Colt: *I need more groceries.* Now what happens? [because nothing is being done with these roles] Camille: *Pretend the house is on fire!* ["Cagey" look; realizes that she is starting things? Definitely leading away from the adult-determined structure to something of her own.] Alec: *What can be the fire?* [looks pleased and happy] *You be the match and I'll light it up!* [running around, excited] [This seems to fit in with Alec's previous concern with fire extinguisher. Not set off by this, possibly because he was more concerned about adult.] Alec: *You be the match and I'll light it up . . . Get the house on fire!* [Alec drags experimenter over.] Colt: *I'm the fireman!* [Alec and Camille jumping around. They are using it as the basis for a lot of excitement, whereas Colt is structuring it in a more intellectual way.] Now the fire's out. What shall we do? I thought we were playing store. Alec: *You're the match and I light you.* Am I lit now? Camille: *Whenever that's on—it's a fire.* [pointing to the light] [Alec is generally and loosely excited and trying to get Camille to go along. Camille falls in with this but uses the general disorganization which she has done so much to create for doing other things that she would "like to get away with." She also tries to impose a kind of order of her own on the situation, specifying the conditions for the fire, etc.] [In the process of lighting, Alec seizes experimenter's hand, pulls him over toward couch, and then waves experimenter's arm in the air. Camille is very much excited herself now. She scribbles on the wall with the pencil.] Camille: *This is all the smoke!* [Camille shows quite clearly that she's doing something that is forbidden; eyes experimenter to see whether she will get a rise out of him.] [Alec runs over to door and puts on light; screaming, flushed. Is quite out of control by himself or anyone else.] Alec: *It's on!* [Experimenter turns off light.]

PLAYING A NEW GAME

We have time for just one more game. What shall we play? Alec: *The light's on! The light's on! Camille, the light's on!* What shall we play, Alec? [Note that Alec is trying to rouse Camille now, just as she had got him before.] Alec: *Let's do another fire! You be a match again! It's blazing! It's blazing!* [tense, high voice; waving hands] [Colt makes several rather futile attempts to join the other two; they tend to ignore him.] Colt: *I'm the grocery man.* [holding pad and pencil] [During part of the preceding period he was circling around desk, trying to take one of experimenter's pads, and searching persistently for a pencil. Interesting because clearly not part of the activity of the other two; Colt tries to make a place for himself within the framework that the experimenter had set up, although that was pretty well broken down by now and experimenter had even said, "You can play whatever you want."] [Colt, fiddling with measuring rod:] *I'm glad it didn't burn my measuring thing over here—see?* [Alec is attracted by this. Goes over and says:] *Look where I go— I go up to here.* [A competition is developed between Colt and Alec. Experimenter suggests that they measure back to back. Experimenter judges them as exactly the same height. Colt wasn't quite willing to take this. Alec wanted to measure on experimenter, who was crouching.] Alec: *Mr. Stone, stand up straight! I go up to here!* Camille: *I go up to here!* [really a good deal over where she came to on experimenter] *On your hand!* [i.e., arm] Alec: *Let's stand on the chair.* Time to go now.

Imposed Leadership Game

The Potential Leadership Game is suitable for studying several aspects of personality including that cluster of characteristics which we may refer to for the moment as "leadership." Each member of the group is faced with a series of opportunities to assume leadership which he may grasp if he is able. Failure to assume leadership might mean that the child was unable to do so, or merely that he had no great wish to do so. The Imposed Leadership Game was devised with the intent of thrusting the role of leader on each subject in turn. Here each child is placed in a position of automatic authority, bolstered by adult support, so that he is given the maximum opportunity to lead and direct the other children if he can and will do so. The situation is so arranged that this opportunity is clearly accepted or rejected by the child while the experimenter keeps at a minimum any opposing or interfering tendencies of the other subjects.

As in the previously described game, the experimenter brings the children together into the experimental room and asks them to sit down, thus polarizing the group and aborting tendencies to develop other interests in the room which might interfere with the experimental program. As soon as the children are ready the experimenter announces, "Today we're going to play a game where everyone has a turn to tell everyone else what to do." As soon as he is sure that all the children understand this, the experimenter asks, "Who wants to be first?" He designates as the first leader the child who first responds, assuring the others that they will also have turns. He then announces that it is "——'s turn," and the child is reminded that he is supposed to tell the others what to do. The experimenter withdraws as much as possible from the situation, if necessary asking the "leader" what he wants to play and what each child is to do.

The first child's period of leadership is permitted to last for approximately five minutes. During this time, if he meets with resistance the adult supports him, reminds the other children it is his turn now, etc. Or, if the child is vague or has withdrawn into solitary play, he is prompted again to tell the others what to do. The period of time may be reduced if the child is obviously unable to marshal the group and if there is danger of confusion and disintegration of the group situation.

The materials placed at the children's disposal were: 6 blocks of assorted sizes (3 quadruple units, 2 units, 1-unit lath); 2 toy soldiers and stretcher; 3 feet of thin clothesline, 12 toy clothespins; dolls, doll dresses and clothes as in the Potential Leadership game, and sometimes two or three small cars and trucks. The materials were selected with the intention of providing some range of possible activities, and with the wish, again, to avoid having too many toys in the situation or toys so new and fascinating that they would become the determining stimuli.

The experimenter terminates the first child's game at a suitable point after approximately five minutes: "Everybody sit down again and I'll put all the toys back on the table." When the children once more reach a state of near-equilibrium, the experimenter adds: "Now it's somebody else's turn to tell everyone what to do. Who shall it be now?" The experimenter selects the first of the other two children to respond, and the second unit proceeds as the first.

The third unit of the game follows precisely the pattern of the first two units, except that the experimenter always announces the remaining child as the leader.[3]

In the event that each of the leaders in turn has merely

---

3. The plan of procedure is outlined in Appendix III.

played with the toys and "told off" the other children without achieving any group play, the experimenter may start the whole game over again. This should be done only if the children are not too tired, and if the experimenter has good reason to think they are mature enough to be capable of more than parallel play. If this is so, the experimenter proceeds as before, with the additional instruction: "Now I want you to think of a game everybody can play *together*."

A sample protocol is offered below.

SUBJECTS: Betsy
    Colt
    Colin

I. FIRST CHILD THE LEADER

[Betsy runs into the experimental room ahead of the others. Runs straight to desk where toys are. Experimenter brings in Colin and Colt.] Betsy: *I want the soldiers!* Now everybody sit down on the couch. We're going to play a game where each person has a turn to tell everybody what to do. Who will be first? Betsy: *Me!* Colt: *Me!* Betsy's turn. Tell everybody what to do, Betsy. Betsy: [to Colin] *You take the ball and bounce it. Colt is going to play with the soldiers.* What about you Betsy? [She is wriggling around on the couch. Finally she lies down.] Betsy: *I go to sleep.* What are you playing? Betsy: *Playing with soldiers and I'm playing too.* [She is lounging on couch, just watching.] Colt: *Oh, my fing broke!* [stretcher broken] Betsy: *Going to do what I tell* . . . [She slips off couch, goes to desk.] *Can I use these clothespins?* Anything you want. Are you telling everyone what to do? [Betsy and Colt at desk, looking at toys. Colin bouncing ball around room.] Colt: *This is what Mr. Lerner had.* [holding up doll to experimenter] [Colin takes soldiers. Betsy down on floor with clothes, clothespins, ball. She folds clothes into a neat pile, largely ignoring the other two children.] Are you telling everyone what to do, Betsy? Betsy: *Nope!* [briskly]

II. SECOND CHILD THE LEADER

All right, everyone sit on the couch . . . Betsy: *Get back on the couch.* [to Colin] Colin: *I want the clothespins.* Colt: *Mr. Stone, can I have the ball next turn?* [Betsy is lying back on the couch. Colin, sitting on couch quietly; looks tired.] Whose turn next? Colt: *Mine.* All right, it's Colt's turn. [Colt gets off couch slowly, smiling. Goes to desk; gives Betsy a soldier, Colin the Russian doll. Betsy gets off couch, playing on floor.] Colin: *I don't want it.* [hurling it to the floor] *I want the clothespins.* [Colt gets the clothespins, gives them to Colin.] Colt: *All of them?* Colin: *Yes. And I want clothes too.* [Colt goes to desk, gets clothes, stumbling over Betsy. He gives clothes to Colin, then goes back to desk. Tries to take dress off doll, to get more clothes for Colin.] Colin: *How do you hang this up?* [clothes-line] [Experimenter puts up clothesline.] It's Colt's turn to tell everyone what to do. Colt: *I have to have this.* [Colt takes armful of blocks from the desk. Colin and Betsy hanging up clothes on line. Colin sniffling. Colt on floor with blocks.] [Clothesline sags. Experi-menter picks it up, interfering with Betsy's work.] Betsy: *You're in our way!* [impatiently] This is Colt's turn. [Betsy and Colin, hanging clothes, pay no attention.] Colt: *The ball is under the bed.* [Colt says this directly to experimenter. Makes several attempts at contact with adult, letting the children go their ways.] You can get it. Colt: *How?* [Colt crawls under the bed and out again.] Colt: *I went under the bed!* Are you telling everyone what to do, Colt? Colt: *Yes.* Betsy: *We know, Colt, you don't have to tell us.*

III. THIRD CHILD AS LEADER

Now another game. Everybody sit on the couch. [Betsy takes down clothes. Colin standing by bed quietly. They get on couch. Betsy starts bouncing with gleeful giggling, then Colin bounces.] Everybody sit down. It's someone else's turn. Betsy: *Everybody sit down . . . Everybody sit down.* Now it's Colin's turn. Tell everyone what to do, Colin. Colin: *You play with the ball.* [to Colt] *You play clothes.* [to Betsy] Betsy: *I don't want to play clothes.* Colin: *And soldiers I want to play!* [Colin gets soldiers, gets down on the floor with them.] Colin: *What are these doing?* [soldiers with stretcher] Colt: *If anybody is wounded they put them in the wounded bed. This guy is wounded and there's the soldiers carrying him.* Betsy: *Can I do the clothes?* This is Colin's turn. Are you telling everyone what to do, Colin? Colin: *Yeah.* Tell Betsy what to do. Colin: *Betsy, you play clothes.* [Colin and Colt on floor with stretcher. Betsy brings over clothesline for experimenter to tie up again.] Colt: *Make the soldier lie down on the bed.* Betsy: *Now you hold it there!* [ordering experimenter to hold other end of clothesline] [Colin lying half on his side, playing with soldiers. Betsy at clothesline. Colt standing by bed, watching Colin.] Colt: *What're you going to play?* [to experi-menter] What do I play, Colin? Colin: *Play holding that.* [Glancing up, then going right back to the soldiers. That is, telling experimenter to do just what he is doing.] What does Colt play? Colin: *Ball.* [Colt is bouncing ball against mirror in door. Rather wild, excited gleam in his eye as he does it. Betsy is very busy hanging up clothes. Ball bounces on Colin's head. He goes on playing with soldiers.] Colt: *What's inside here?* [shaking ball] Is there something in there? Colt: *Yes.* [Colt throws ball. It bounces and rolls under the couch again. He goes after it.] Are you telling everyone what to do, Colin? Colin: *Yes.* Colt: *What are you playing, Mr. Stone?* Colin told me to play holding this. Colt: *How do you play holding that? You're playing clothes.* [to Betsy] Now everybody sit on the couch. [Experimenter starts to take down clothesline; Betsy protests.] Betsy: *No! No! No, you can't do this!* [Experimenter takes line down. Steers Betsy over to couch, Colt makes a lunge at Betsy, who squeals. Experimenter separates them. Colin at desk looking at toys. All three get on couch. Betsy starts bouncing, then Colt joins in.] Everybody sit. [Four or five times. They are busy bouncing, squealing.] Everybody sit down, Betsy! Betsy: *My name is not Betsy!* [provocative, challenging]

IV. PLAYING TOGETHER: FIRST CHILD AS LEADER

Now this time we'll have a game that everybody can play to-gether. Who will be first? Betsy: *Me!* What will the game be, Betsy? Betsy: *You play clothesline. And I'll play clothesline.* [That is, a game she wants to play—no roles for everyone. Betsy gets off the couch, gets the clothes. Colt gets clothes. Colin throwing ball, it goes under the couch; he crawls after it.] Betsy: *Someone do this . . . Get more clothes.* Tell people what to do, Betsy. [No response.] Betsy: *My clothes—I got them first.* Colt: *I want some more clothes.* Betsy: *I had them first.* Tell everyone what to play, Betsy. [Colt takes the ball. Colin gets soldiers again.] Colt: *I have to bounce it up to the ceiling.* [The ball falls on Colin, he throws it without looking at it. Colt comes over, starts hanging up clothes with Betsy. Colin on floor. All quiet for a moment.] Colt: *Is this a new toy?* [soldiers] Yes. Colin: *Ah! It's new!*

V. PLAYING TOGETHER: SECOND CHILD AS LEADER

Now everybody sit down. [Experimenter taking down clothes-line.] Betsy: *I'll do it!* Now it's Colt's turn. [Colt in armchair, where experimenter had been sitting. Adult role?] [Experimenter gets him over to couch where Colin is sitting, Betsy is lying down.] Colt's turn. Colt: *Colin, you and I are going to play clothes.* [trying to "get in with" Colin, sloughing off Betsy] [Colt goes over to desk.] What will Betsy play? Colt: *Betsy will play with the ball.* Betsy: *I want to play clothes.* Colt: *No.* Betsy: *Give me the ball.* [The ball rolls under the couch, Betsy and Colt scrambling for it.] Colin: *I want to play car.* Not today. Tell everyone what to do, Colt. Colt: *I did.* Colin:

I want to play cars. I haven't any here today. Colt: *There are some in the cabinet.* Tell everyone what to do. [Colt hanging clothes. Colin at the desk. Betsy comes over to Colt.] Betsy: *I want to play too.* Colt: *You're not going to.* [smug expression] [exercise of power negatively, against Betsy] Are you telling everybody what to do? Colt: *Yes.* What shall I play? Colt: *Holding up the string.* What will Betsy play? Betsy: *Soldiers!* What will Colin do? Colt: *Has to play ball. Tell him to play ball.* [Colin gets the ball, comes over to the clothesline and drops it on the line. Colt hanging clothes, does not seem disturbed.] Betsy: *I'm going to break this.* [soldiers] Colt: *You're not going to break this clothesline!* [Colin pounds Betsy on the head with the ball. She hits back at him with a soldier. He pounds her quite hard but looks very calm and unemotional.] That's not a very good game. Colin: *I know a game.* It will be your turn in a minute.

VI. PLAYING TOGETHER: THIRD CHILD AS LEADER

Now everybody sit down on the couch. I'll put the toys away. [Betsy and Colin climb up on couch, bounce up and down. Experimenter starts to take down clothesline. Colt protests vigorously. Colt then goes over to the couch. Tries to get on and into bouncing game but falls off. Betsy hops off couch, sits in armchair.] Everybody on couch, Betsy. [Colt and Colin tumbling over each other on the couch. Experimenter tries to unscramble them. Then Betsy gets in the middle of it. Experimenter untangles her; she goes back to the armchair.] Now it's Colin's turn to think of a game everybody can play together. [Colt gets clothesline.] This is Colin's game. What shall it be, Colin? Colin: *A great big train. Colt's the caboose. Betsy's the coal car. And I'll be . . .* [hesitating] Engineer? Colin: *The engine.* Colt: *You be the caboose.* Colin: *No. You're the caboose. And . . .* [trying to think of something for experimenter] Shall I be the freight car? Colin: *Yes.* Tell everybody what to do. Colin: *Hitch on.* [to Betsy] *Get in back of Colt!* [Colin first, Colt holding on to his shoulders, then Betsy] Colt: *My snowpants are falling down.* [Whining tone. Experimenter fastens them.] Colt: *I go in the back.* [Experimenter hitches on, they go parading around room.] Colin: *Choo! Choo!* Betsy: *Choo! Choo! Choo!* Colin: *All the cars climb up on the windowsill.* [Colin leads train up on ledge of window. Betsy looks at experimenter questioningly; a sort of "Is this going to be all right?" look. Colt crawls from windowsill to desk. Colin follows, then Betsy. They sit in a row on the desk, enjoying it.] Colt: *I'll play Mr. Stone. I'll write.* [taking pad and pencil] [Colt writes; Betsy watches him closely. Betsy tries to get pad and pencil, he refuses to give them up. Colin gets down to floor via armchair.] Where's the rest of the train? Colin: *Come on, coal car. Come on, Betsy—er—caboose. Hitch on.*

Family Play with Interview

The procedure to be described here was developed by Dr. Lois B. Murphy, and while derived partly from the Potential Leadership Game has been modified to emphasize the value of the group technique for fantasy production. The experimenter's instructions and the toys selected have been prepared with the purpose of releasing dramatic play in the area of family relations, more explicitly than in the Playing House portion of the Potential Leadership Game. It differs also in providing a less definite control by the experimenter over the content of the game in order that the children's fantasies may range freely toward the problems that are crucial for each of them. In addition, the experimenter, where and when it seems appropriate to do so, employs a modified and casual "interview." This is never permitted to destroy the framework of the *game* characteristic of the procedure, and in Dr. Murphy's hands it has been skillfully interwoven with it.

The experimenter brings the children into the experimental room and invites them to play house and to select roles. No emphasis is placed on the social value of any role over any other, nor is there any concern with the assignment and rejection of roles except as revealing the emotional significance of the roles to the child. The children are permitted to change roles spontaneously as they wish during the game. The experimenter plays the game with the children, usually filling in a key role which has not been adopted by one of the children.

The toys are limited to a large baby doll with clothes and a "wetting" doll. Much of the dramatized fantasy is thereby automatically focused around the treatment of the "baby" (who may, however, be either one of the dolls or one of the children) and the highly moral questions that inhere for the children in feeding and toileting.

Sometimes extensions or variations of the game are introduced—often at cues offered by the children, and sometimes to get at specific questions that seem relevant for one or more of the particular subjects. A common variation is playing "doctor."

Questioning is introduced when opportunity affords in terms of what children are playing, and the paces through which they are putting the dolls. Such points as the following may be taken as suggestive rather than exhaustive:

INDEPENDENCE:

Who feeds himself?
Who puts on his own clothes?
Who wipes himself at the toilet?

PARENTAL AUTHORITY:

Who spanks?
What do you do when you're naughty?
Who is the most important—mother, father, nurse or doctor?

FEELINGS:[4]

Everybody is happy sometimes. What makes you happy?
Everybody gets scared sometimes. What makes you feel scared?
Everybody gets mad sometimes. What makes you mad?
Everybody gets sad sometimes. What makes you sad?
Everybody feels ashamed sometimes. What makes you feel ashamed?
Everybody feels proud sometimes. What makes you feel proud?

PARENTAL ROLES:

What do mommies do?
What do daddies do?

The experimenter's permissive attitude and participation in make-believe creates a situation very different from that in the

---

4. This is an adaptation of Eugene Lerner's Emotional Response Inquiry. These questions can be cautiously expanded by the experimenter, with plenty of support for the child and a shift to other topics of interest if anxiety threatens to mount.

usual clinical set-up. The presence of the group is not merely facilitating in the sense of producing more fantasy and supplying stimuli for elaborating it, but serves materially to reduce anxiety which direct questioning of this sort might otherwise arouse.

The framework of the procedure is deliberately a loose one, making it possible for the experimenter to follow the leads of the children. It thus gives the experimenter great scope and necessarily depends greatly on his skill, since he must be able to judge where and when and how much to participate in the game so that the results will be fruitful and yet represent the children's and not the experimenter's fantasy world. It will be obvious to the reader that even this framework may be modified if other aspects of the child's world are to be investigated, particularly by changing the initial suggestion of what to play and by substituting other toys for the two dolls.

Representative Findings

In this section, I should like to present samples of our findings merely in order to indicate some of the special values of the technique, and to suggest some of the directions in terms of theory imposed by the empirical findings. Mainly because I have carried the analysis further in this field, I shall stress the "leadership-ascendance-submission" complex at the expense of other areas of personality which may also be approached by the group techniques that we have used.

LEADERSHIP:

I may introduce the concepts I wish to develop here with an example from the record of the Potential Leadership Game session which was given on pp. 214 *ff*. The reader's attention is drawn particularly to Camille, whose techniques for leading and directing the other members of the group seem noteworthy.

At first she sits quietly and confidently, announces the things that she needs—dolls, etc.; waits for the adult to bring them to her, and does not pay much attention to the others as they compete for the privilege of "going to work in the office." Finally, they decide it is Sundays that "*They* (fathers) stay home," and Camille begins to take charge of the situation. She speaks confidently, unself-consciously. The others spontaneously accept her as leader, even when she discriminates between Alec and Colt. She deftly and smoothly breaks up the incipient quarreling between the two boys, clears up the partial confusion of roles, and definitely polarizes the group around herself, securing unquestioning compliance with her ideas.

In unit "Playing House" note how swiftly she reorganizes the situation when she decides to do so—by inserting an attractive idea—"somebody has to be sick."

In the subsequent units of the game, "Playing Store," etc., Camille establishes her priority even more definitely. Colt and Alec not only do not object, but seem to welcome this. From the protocol above, it can be seen how skillfully and effortlessly she assumes the lead. She is able to maintain leadership and at the same time accept the pattern imposed by the adult, even to the shifting of roles. In other words, she maintains her authority through her own skill and ability to direct the other children even when she adopts a role that does not embody inherent authority.

Camille's extraordinary ability to assert and maintain a position of leadership may also be seen in the following extract from an Imposed Leadership Game played four months after the one recorded above. The reader's attention is again drawn to the techniques she employs to establish her control over the other children, and her ability to direct them completely, even though to their own great satisfaction.

SUBJECTS: Camille
Alec
Cecily

Whose turn will be first? Alec: *Mine!* [quickly assertive] All right, now Alec tell everyone what to do. Alec: *Okay.* [Alec's eyes are fixed on the toys and he goes right over to them, paying no attention to the other children.] Tell everyone what to do, etc. [Alec starts talking about the toys; fails to direct the other children who crowd next to him as he paws at the toys.] What are you going to tell everyone to do? Alec: *This is what I'm going to do.* [Alec continues playing with the toys; apparently content with establishing his rights to them and not concerned with social leadership.]

What should everyone else do? Alec: *Cecily be the baby.* [He says this mechanically, without looking at Cecily, and continues to play with the toys.] Cecily: *No.* Alec: *Then you be, Camille.* [Camille takes advantage of the opening, and begins to take charge. Says rapidly:] *No. The last one that says "I don't want to" be the baby.* [She says this quickly herself, followed belatedly by Cecily.] Camille: *You have to, Cecily!* Cecily: *No.* Camille: *The last one that says "happy birthday" has to be.* [She makes up the rules very rapidly, babbling along to get it all out, then shouts:] *Happy birthday!* [Camille is enjoying her game and the spontaneous but legalistic form more and more.] Camille: *The last one that says "Mr. Stone," Mr. Stone.* [emphasizing this] This is Alec's game. [Reminded of his position, Alec starts to assert himself once more, but is completely caught up in the pattern Camille has established.] Alec: *Happy birthday!* [shouting] [The situation is now completely under Camille's control. She throws herself down on the couch, giggling and laughing, then starts singing, holding her arms high over her head and dancing about. Cecily and Alec follow her lead.]

Now everybody sit down and I'll put everything back on the table. [All three sit down, waiting expectantly.] Now it's someone else's turn. Camille: *Mine!* [Camille leads them off on an abortive game of ring-around-the-rosy, ending in all tumbling on the floor, giggling and squealing.] Camille: *Come on, people! Now we play one by a time and squirm all over the place.* [There is a sharp directorial ring in her voice. She stands near the door. Cecily and Alec wait for her instructions.] Camille: *Now go over to the sofa. Quickly to the sofa. Now, quickly, quickly to Mr. Stone! Now quickly to the chair!* [She continues standing at the door, others hurling themselves around the room at her command. Cecily follows instructions rather slowly, her eyes on Camille. Camille hurries her up with:] *Quickly!* [Then she calls:] *Run, Alec. Run back to the sofa. Don't you do it too, Cecily. Now you go to Mr. Stone, Alec. Cecily and I go to the couch. Now Alec, run to the chair before I do.* [She goes on in this fashion, adding new variations for some time.]

Camille's control over other children in these situations is obvious. It is clearly she who provides the ideas that activate the other children and that are accepted by them. She occupies a position of obvious prestige in their eyes, and they accept not only her explicit instructions, but are swept along by subtler suggestions that she offers. These are facts directly

227

ascertainable from the behavior records even in the partial form presented above. Difficulty and confusion arise only when we depart further from the concrete behavior and wish to use general-descriptive or classificatory terms such as "ascendance," "dominance," "leadership," and the like.[5]

For our present purposes let us take as the most general term the word "ascendance" and delimit the field which it denotes as a situation in which one individual tends to determine the activities of the group. His "power field," so to speak, is larger than those of the other members of the group. However, a great variety of dynamic patterns may produce the same ascendant-submissive relations, and there has been repeated recognition of this inadequacy of the ascendance-submission concept.[6] Maslow, for example, has analyzed the concept of dominance in terms of social relationship, behavior, and self-evaluation.[7] Anderson offers the concepts of "domination" and "integration."[8] The difference between them is fundamental, and is described primarily as a difference of *techniques* employed by the ascendant individual; of behavior to be observed in ascendant-submissive relationships. *Qua* techniques, domination, and integration are clearly different, and there is no doubt "that there is a psychological difference between snatching a toy out of a companion's hands so as to play with it oneself, and asking the companion if one may borrow the toy for awhile."[9]

However, Anderson also makes a distinction on the level of motive: "Domination is characterized by a rigidity or inflexi-

---

5. The most satisfactory general introductions to the literature in this field may be found in: P. Pigors, *Leadership or Domination* (New York: Houghton Mifflin, 1935); A. H. Maslow, "Dominance-feeling, Behavior, and Status," *Psycholog. Rev.*, Vol. 44 (1937), 404-29; G. Murphy, L. B. Murphy, and T. M. Newcomb, *Experimental Social Psychology*, Revised Edition (New York: Harper, 1937); H. H. Anderson, "An Examination of the Concepts of Domination and Integration in Relation to Dominance and Ascendance," *Psychol. Rev.*, Vol. 47 (1940), 21-37.

6. Murphy, Murphy, and Newcomb, *op. cit.*, p. 522.

7. Maslow, *op. cit.*, p. 405.

8. Anderson, *op. cit.*, and H. H. Anderson, "Domination and Integration in the Social Behavior of Young Children in an Experimental Play Situation," *Genet. Psychol. Monogr.* (1937), 341-408.

Similar distinctions are made by Bogardus (autocratic and democratic); Pigors (domination and leadership); Parten (bully and diplomat); and others. Most of my objections to Anderson's analysis apply equally to these.

9. Anderson, *op. cit.*, p. 22.

bility of purpose; by an unwillingness to admit the contribution of another's experience, desires, purposes or judgment in one's determining of goals which concern others." Integration, on the other hand, "designates behavior that is flexible, growing, learning. It is an expression of the operation of democratic processes." This distinction is important, but a demurrer must be entered to the assumption that the *techniques* labelled "dominative" and "integrative" bear a one-to-one relation to the *motivations* given the same labels—or that these motivations are exhaustive. Thus we can imagine an individual whose motives are those of "domination," but who is sufficiently adroit not to use simple dominative techniques. Machiavelli's Prince might be a person whose purposes are always dominative but whose techniques frequently can only be called integrative. Nor is it necessary to seek for such behavior only in the exalted realms of *Machtpolitik* or in purely hypothetical individuals. Camille's behavior, described in the two excerpts from the experimental protocols above, seems to fit such a pattern. On the side of technique, she clearly and deftly uses both dominative and integrative techniques as they seem best suited at the moment, but there is also definite internal evidence that her purposes are by no means the high-souled ones of wishing to "make the most of individual differences . . . bring out the most differences in a group, and therefore reveal to the group a sounder base for defining common purposes."[10] Thus we can see that it is necessary to distinguish sharply between motive and technique, even though in actual behavior such a distinction is arbitrary. The motive may be the social good or self-aggrandizement; the technique may be direct or indirect.

Still a further distinction at the level of motive appears necessary from our observations. Some individuals may wish simply to direct and control others, as a goal in itself. The use that will be made of others becomes secondary. Such a person, too, may use integrative *or* dominative, indirect or direct techniques (although he is much more likely to employ the former), and his motives, too, may be one or the other at different times (although they are likely to be integrative only by the accidental

---

10. *Ibid.*, p. 32.

coincidence of social good and his temporal goals). Such a person may be an "operator" instead of a "cooperator." Potentially, or in terms of his basic attitudes, he is capable of being a tyrant, but because of the situation or because he is not simpleminded and direct in his techniques for control over others he uses the techniques of the "cooperator" or "helpful guide."[11]

Theoretically, it would seem useful, then, to think of (at least) three *motives* for ascendant behavior, which may be named *directive, assertive,* and *integrative.* By directive I refer to the wish to control and direct and "operate" people. By assertive I mean the desire to meet one's own ends, to have one's own way; which may involve (incidentally) asserting oneself over other persons. By integrative I wish to designate the idealistic desire seen by Anderson to make the most out of a social situation for its own sake; for the sake of the group and neither for the purpose of asserting one's own goals nor the pleasure of controlling other people. The techniques that are employed may be called *direct* and *indirect* (rather than dominative and integrative), avoiding the confusion with motivating factors. The meaning of these terms is defined by Anderson's distinction between integrative and dominative—insofar as he limits the terms to techniques.

After noting the source and technique of the individual's ascendant behavior, it is still necessary to decide whether it has been successful or not. If it has been, we call the individual a "leader," especially if he has been successful repeatedly. Thus, leadership is a more or less permanent state of ascendance secured by direct or indirect *techniques* applied by individuals with *motives* which are social or self-assertive, or which arise out of the wish to control others for its own sake.

Let us now proceed with the other concrete instances observed in the framework of certain of our group play techniques. We have seen Camille as a leader with distinctly directive motives, interested in the manipulation of other individuals, remarkably able in the appropriate employment of direct and indirect techniques for so controlling them. We may illustrate

---

11. P. Eisenberg, "Expressive Movements Related to Feeling of Dominance," *Arch. Psychol.*, No. 211 (1937), 67.

the distinction between "philohegemonic" and "social" motives by referring to the behavior of Candice. Both children were capable of using indirect techniques, but Candice showed a genuine ability to yield to the other person's point of view and a genuine interest in the group for the group's sake and the game for the game's sake.

Subjects: Candice
           Carla
           Joyce

Who will be first? Joyce: *Me!* Candice: *Me!* Carla: *Me!* All right, Joyce, you make up the game. Tell everybody what to do. [As Joyce starts doing so, Candice says:] *Then Carla's and then mine.* [As Joyce sets to work hanging up clothes and telling the others what to do, Carla sits down, holds the doll, staring at it. Then she starts hanging clothes herself, ignoring Joyce's suggestion.] [Candice watches Joyce and waits for her cue.] Joyce: *You be the maid.* Candice: *Me?* Joyce: *Yes, you be the maid.* [Candice accepts this and she and Joyce play in free and friendly fashion, Candice following Joyce's lead while Carla continues by herself.]

Now whose game is it? Candice: *Me!* Joyce: *Me!* Carla: *Me!* Now it's Candice's turn. You tell everyone what to do. [Candice hops off the couch, gets the clothes and the soldiers. Puts them all on the couch. Says to Joyce and Carla:] *Play with those.* Joyce: *I want to be the baby.* Candice: *All right, baby, play with those.* [giving her some toys. Joyce accepts them.] Candice: *I'm the maid and Joyce's the baby and Carla is the nurse.* [Joyce falls in with Candice's suggestions. Carla continues in her self-isolation. Joyce is busy with the soldiers and stretcher. Candice is lining up clothespins on the couch.] Candice: *I'm making a little bed and they can sleep there. Now isn't that nice? Look what I did.* Who's the baby? Joyce: *I am.* Candice, are you telling Joyce and Carla what to do? Candice: *Yes. You be good children now because mommie is going out.* What's Carla? Carla: *I'm the mommie.* Candice: *Well, she can be the mommie too — or the maid. Mommie is going to hang up clothes.* [She goes over to the clothesline; Carla is already there.] Carla: *I'm the mommie to have to hang up the clothes.* How many mommies are there? Candice: *Two mommies, and Joyce is the baby.*

This is integrative behavior if ever there was any! Candice is able to accept the ideas of others and use them; is primarily interested in keeping the peace and enjoying the game. She can accept the role of follower without feeling so self-assertive that she feels thwarted and subordinated in this situation. On the other hand, as a leader she has shown (in this game and elsewhere) that she is neither assertive in maintaining the prerogatives of her own role or deeply concerned with manipulating the activities of other children. At the same time, out of her "social" motivation she is able to offer ideas and to maintain some group structure and unity.

Sheer assertiveness as a motive and complete inability to use any but direct, ego-protective techniques is shown by Carla. The excerpt on p. 000 shows her concern with having her own way, doing the things that she wants to do and having the toys she wants to have; her almost complete indifference to the other children, except as they threaten her private sphere of activity. This excerpt is a continuation of the preceding one. During the time that Joyce and Candice were the leaders Carla merely announced several times, without reference to what the others were doing, that she was the "mommie," and ignored suggestions from either of the other children.

The distinction between Carla and Candice, and Carla and Camille is clear. Carla was not interested in the other children, either for social reasons or because she liked to direct them, which were the motives of the other two. She was intent on her own pattern of play and maintained this actively or passively, depending on the circumstances. A person such as Carla is concerned with ascendance only as a means to some other end, and then adopts the most direct devices. Carla corresponds to Anderson's dominating child who seizes the toy that he wants. When he does not feel interfered with, such a person may well adopt the role of not dominating others, but yet not permitting others to dominate him.

Now it's Carla's turn. [Carla goes to the desk without a word and starts playing with the toys. The other two sit on the couch talking together, waiting.] What does everyone do, Carla? [No answer as she plays with the dolls.] What do you do when it's your turn, Carla? Carla: *My turn.* [belligerently] Who is everyone? Candice: [helpfully] *No one.* Carla, who is everyone? [No answer.] Carla, who is everyone? Carla: *I'm the mommie.* You're the mommie, and who is Joyce? Carla: *Wait till I tell you . . . Some more . . . I need some more . . . Give me another clothespin.*

I may give the impression that only children (or adults) of the "philohegemonic" or "social" modes can be skilled leaders successful in the use of indirect techniques, and that those motivated only by the wish to assert their own goals are limited, like Carla, to the use of crude, direct techniques. Colin, as an example of a child who belonged in the "assertive" class is an interesting refutation of such a conclusion. He was interested neither in the furtherance of the interests of the group, nor in other people for their own sake. Nevertheless, he was capable of directing and cajoling people to his ends in a manner almost as skillful as that of Camille. The Imposed Leadership Game was particularly useful in revealing such capabilities; for while Colin, and others like him, may have shown no interest in seizing the opportunities offered in the Potential Leadership Game, the enforced authority brought out the latent skills. The reader is referred to Parts III and VI of the sample protocol (pp. 220 and 222).

It will be seen that Colin is content at first to give each one a satisfying occupation, taking into account what each had been interested in doing before. From this point on, he ignores the other children, and when reminded by the adult to "tell them what to do" he acts as before, looking up to see what the others are doing and then ordering them to do it.

However, in Unit VI he is the only child who grasps the idea of "playing together," finally accepting the responsibility and developing a train game. Note also his inclusion of everyone including the adult. Moreover, when there is some tendency to disintegration, he marshals the group with "Come on, coal car. . . . Come on, Betsy—er—caboose!"

Thus, although in general Colin's is a *laissez faire* policy, he is able under some pressure to exercise leadership skillfully and successfully. Under the instructions to play a game "together," he evolves a good plan and is able successfully to attract the others without domineering, in spite of clashes between Betsy and Colt, The other children respond to the appeal of his idea and his smooth, uninsistent techniques.

From the point of view of techniques, the important point is that without specific pressure this kind of child does not show leadership, but to let it stand at that is misleading, for although he is free of any strong drive to control others, he is able skillfully to direct them under the appropriate conditions.

From the point of view of society as a whole, it is useful to know about potential leaders of this sort. If such a person can be helped to identify his own aims with those of the group he can be an effective and valuable leader and is likely to be less dangerous than a person who likes to manipulate others for the fun of it.

The Potential Leadership Game serves to emphasize the fact that *skill* in leadership—roughly identified as the ability to use a variety of indirect techniques which appeal to the "followers" —must be distinguished from any of the other factors that we have discussed. In intellectual pursuits it is obvious that interest and even the possession of good study habits do not suffice for high achievement unless there is a high level of intelligence— just as a high intelligence level alone is insufficient without adequate motivation and the possession of special skills or tool techniques. In the same way, it seems possible to differentiate out the "ability factor" in leadership. The separation, of course, is not perfect. The linkage to particular "tool skills" is more evident, in the case of leadership, since it is only indirect techniques that will assure success (where there is no extraneous prestige factor to bolster the authority of direct commands). But unless a child (or adult) can sense which specific techniques would be successful and has the other special abilities required, *indirection* as such is of no value, nor is any intensity of the "philohegemonic" or of sheer assertive *motivation* likely to produce actual leadership.[12]

TEACHERS' JUDGMENTS

I have presented several instances in the preceding excerpts of children of varying degrees of skill in leadership using more or less direct techniques, and with their ascendance stemming

---

12. Some progress has been made in defining the requisite characteristics and abilities. See Murphy, Murphy, and Newcomb, *op. cit.*, and Pigors, *op. cit.*

from apparently different motives. The analysis of leadership outlined above (which arose directly out of the findings with the Leadership Games) seemed to be capable of general application outside the limits of the special techniques in the framework of which it was created. Moreover, it was desirable to determine whether the results of the experimental situation agreed with the same children's behavior in the nursery school. Consistency of behavior in the narrow sense is of no importance here, but the characterizations we have developed go deeper than mere incidents of behavior and are attempts to describe deeper "structural" characteristics of the personality. Thus, we should expect congruence between our characterizations and those of other observers. To determine whether this is true it is necessary merely that a comparable framework be given for these observations and that the observers be skilled and thoroughly familiar with the children.

For this purpose we prepared an outline for discussion— rather than a questionnaire—embodying the theoretical analysis of various kinds and sources of ascendance which have been offered above. For the purposes of the present methodological survey, it will suffice to present the teachers' characterizations of two of the children whose experimental excerpts were described above. The reader may compare these with the indicated findings under experimental conditions in those excerpts.

CAMILLE (Summary by E. Beyer)

Motives for Leadership: She is primarily focused on *people;* she is rarely absorbed in any activity aside from her leadership role, and is rarely alone. At the same time, she is *assertive* and *aggressive.*

Leadership Devices: A master of all techniques! Molds people to her ends. Always interested in what *she* wants. (Contrast Candice.) She can be highly devious; an *instigator* of people. She is capable of exploiting her vassals, always perfectly clear as to her own motive.

Ability to Lead: A "four-star" leader.

CANDICE (Summary by M. Gay)

Motives for Leadership: Not a *calculated* leadership; leads because she has ideas and drama. Loves to *organize*: to manage groups and keep all members happy and busy. Likes to lead, but if it doesn't work out, can *abandon* that role. Capable of dividing leadership or assigning leadership to others.

Leadership Devices: Rarely uses *direct* techniques; never imposes too much. She leads by exuberance, ideas, and social warmth; by her understanding of children and appropriate activities. Can also *follow* and conform to others' leadership. *Selective* about whom she leads; may try everybody, but usually people she likes.

Ability to lead: A "three-star" leader (if Camille is a "four-star" leader).

One more word might be added with reference to the age level of the children with whom the preliminary work has been carried out. We can fully confirm Pigors' statement that "it can easily be shown that *children exercise some leadership-authority over each other as early as four to five years of age.*" Two- and three-year-olds in general are so content with parallel play that only momentary polarization in terms of ascendance-submission is likely to appear. But even with such young children we find occasionally that "the child who directs attention towards some mutually agreeable way of satisfying a common interest in play . . . becomes the center of action." Some emergence from egocentricity, as defined by Piaget, is thus a necessary prerequisite for leadership. But the contention that leadership is impossible in the preschool years[13] seems to imply too long a period of total egocentricity or the assumption of extraordinarily elaborate criteria for leadership.

RIGIDITY AND FLEXIBILITY

The value of the Imposed and Potential Leadership Games

---

13. Represented, for example, in G. E. Marica, "Conducerea la copii," *Rev. Psihol.*, Vol. 1 (1938), 417-37. (Cited in *Psycholog. Abstr.*, Vol. 13 [1939], Ref. No. 4405.)

for the study of "rigidity" or "flexibility" of a personality has been mentioned already. It will be sufficient to suggest how the experimental results have helped to formulate a few of the problems in this field, and to limit the discussion to the social aspects of rigidity and flexibility, or—phrased more accurately —to note some of the effects of rigidity and flexibility on the child's functioning in social situations.

Most relevant to the preceding discussion is the relationship between leadership *ability* and rigidity-flexibility. Some mention has already been made of the fact that children who have a similar drive toward ascendance, and even similar armament in techniques, may yet vary in their ability to control other children. Variations in ability to understand other children's motives and in the rigidity-flexibility aspect of personality account for some of these differences.

Particularly in the Potential Leadership Game, rigidity-flexibility may readily be seen as willingness or unwillingness to accept the *shifts* of role and of play content which are imposed by the adult. A "rigid" child—rigid for whatever reason —will resist such shifts and show an inability to accept them, while a "flexible" child will make a free and plastic use of the variety of opportunities offered in the game. The flexible child may either accept the entire situation as it is presented by the adult and function within it, or may persist toward goals of his own while shrewdly making use of the situation imposed by the adult and molding it to his own purposes.

Camille and Candice have both been described as successful leaders. Both were very adept at the use of indirect techniques, and the ability of both is dependent largely on their flexibility, which is demonstrated in the excerpts cited above. Camille was an outstanding example of a child who found no difficulty in accepting, and at the same time turning to her own ends, all the adult's suggestions. With effortless ease and deft techniques she maintained a position of leadership even when her dramatic role was superficially inappropriate. Candice, too, presented a picture of extreme freedom and flexibility, although hers was the kind which rarely carries with it the maintenance of ulterior goals of her own, and involves an acceptance of the game for the game's sake. She showed great ease and ability to reciprocate, and readiness to use the ideas of the adult and the suggestions of the other children.

Betsy, on the other hand, was a child so concerned with maintaining a specific identification that it was almost impossible for her to shift to a different role when so requested by the adult. Such rigidity has extensive implications for personality structure; in terms of leadership, specifically, it hampers and limits a child by emphasizing a defensive assertiveness.

SUBJECTS: Betsy
        Alec
        Laurel

[In Unit I, "Playing House," Betsy selected the role of mother, taking the lead in choosing a role and presenting ideas for play, but was most interested in the other children from the point of view of keeping them out of her way. She gets rid of Alec by telling him impatiently: *You have a business,* which "business" takes him away from her part of the room. She also announces that she, as mother, is *too busy to tell the big sister what to do.* She occupies herself with household tasks.]

Now everybody be somebody else. Laurel: *I want to be the mother.* Betsy: [vehemently] *I'm the mother!* We're all changing, Betsy. Betsy: *No, I'm the mother.* [When it becomes perfectly clear that she cannot retain the role, she consents to be the big girl. Announces:] *We don't change toys.* [Betsy turns to the new "mother" and says:] *Mother, I'm doing ironing of clothes and can't come down now.* [This is exactly what she had been doing as the mother before.]

Thus, having resisted change as much as possible, when finally accepting it she made it clear that she has accepted merely a *nominal* change, and that the big sister is practically indistinguishable in activities and prerogatives from the mother.

Now we'll play something different. Betsy: *No. I want to play house again.* [Note her resistance to change.] Let's play store. [Betsy finally accepts the situation, but immediately molds it so that it will be as similar as possible from her point of view to the previous situation. Alec is permitted to be the store man. Betsy announces:] *I live.* [i.e., "I'm playing house"] [Thus she continues in her role as housewife, even to the extent of quickly getting busy with the baby, and announcing:] *I'm busy. I can't go to the store now. I'll go to the store later.* [From time to time she says, as the others play store:]

Don't wake the baby up. She's sleeping. [Thus, she succeeds in fencing herself off again from the others, and is extremely successful in maintaining precisely the same role with which she started.]

[A little later, apparently feeling assured that she will be permitted to go on with the maternal role, she is freed to the extent of incorporating this role in the "Store Game." She has reverted to being the "great big sister"—the one who has all the maternal prerogatives:] *Now I've got to put the baby to bed. Mr. Stone, you're the father and he's* [Alec] *the storeman and she's* [Laurel] *the mother and I'm the big girl. And I'm going to buy something.* What are you going to buy? Betsy: *First I gotta take the baby. Okay, mother?* Laurel: *Mmm.* Betsy: *Pretend the baby is sick.* Laurel: *The baby is sick.* Betsy: *You have to go to business.* [to experimenter] [Betsy goes to Alec's store.] Betsy: *Here's money. Here's money.* Alec: *Thank you.* Betsy: *I want this. I need a dress for the baby.*

Note that within the safety of her role, the near permanence of which seems to have been acknowledged by the others, she has taken a successful venture into leadership and made creative use of the framework supplied by the adult. At this point, however, the other children took up her lead very actively. Laurel came to the store to buy some things, and apparently Betsy felt threatened again. She immediately reverted.

Betsy: *Our baby is sleeping! Don't wake her up! Give me that! Don't wake the baby up, Mr. Stone!* [She did not, following this, take any other active part in the game, but was content to continue in more or less solitary fashion, acting out her own private game with the doll.]

In this excerpt it can be seen that when the whole framework of the situation fits Betsy's wishes, and the prior pattern of her interests, she could be a successful leader. Under these circumstances she produced interesting ideas which were accepted by the others and which permitted coherent and consecutive play. Any *shift* in the framework, however, paralyzed her and reduced her to a level of mere assertion. She wished only to be unhampered. She did everything in her power to re-orient the situation in such a way that she could continue unchanged in what she was doing. All interest in other children disappeared, suggesting that it was secondary throughout. She was unable or unwilling to direct others in the altered situation.

We are forced to the conclusion, then, that this was a child who could be creative and active, and even mildly sucessful as a leader, *within the limits* of a certain very specific kind of situation, but one who was rigid in the sense of being unable to carry over these abilities to a fresh situation.

Abigail presented an example of a child with still greater potentialities for leadership than Betsy, but perhaps even more dependent on a familiar pattern. For Abigail, a solid, familiar and comfortably conventional setting was necessary for adequate functioning. The patterns of "right" and acceptable behavior had to be clearly discernible. It will be seen that during the first part of the experiment, Abigail made no attempt whatever to take charge of the situation. Significantly, the few points at which she asserted herself seemed to be occasions on which she felt that she was assisting in carrying out the adult's plan.

SUBJECT: Abigail
              Carla
              Cecily

Everybody sit down and I'll tell you what we're going to do. [They all sit quietly, nobody says anything.] We're going to play house. [All three children continue to sit, looking expectant but saying nothing.] Who do you want to be? Carla: *I be the mommie.* [in her customary, assertive fashion] [No one else says anything.] What will everyone else be? Abigail: *And she'll be the daddy* [Cecily] *and I'll be the big sister.* [She says this in a helpful tone, looking at experimenter but does nothing about it, although Carla has gotten up to pick out the things she wants in her role as mother.] What does the sister do? [Abigail still sits on the couch. She shrugs and says nothing. She is curling her tongue restlessly; has a polite and puzzled smile. Experimenter's impression is that the situation is still unclear to her and that she is not committing herself.] . . . We're going to play store. [Abigail opens her mouth wide, brightening up. Experimenter's impression was that she was responding less to the attraction of the store, which did not mean very much to her, than to the adult's enthusiasm.] Who will be what? Carla: *I want to be the mommie.* Let's play store now . . . who wants to have a store? Carla: *Me!* Abigail: *Carla wants to have a store.* . . . [helpfully] Carla: *No, I want to be the mommie.* [Again, after this helpful introduction, Abigail retires to the background for a time.]

Up to now, she had obviously been most concerned with orienting herself in relation to the adult. Many of her comments were addressed to the experimenter, and she spent a good deal of time watching him. She was not simply and casually herself, but was obviously trying to find out the right thing to do. This is also suggested by her turning to the other two children to see that they are "in order" at the beginning of the experiment, and her several attempts to act as a mediator between the other children and the adult. During the "Playing Store" Unit, it becomes necessary for the adult to undertake to operate the store. Carla repeatedly went through the process of making the purchases. After such a pattern had been established, Abigail was able to become active: she imitated the pattern and elaborated it. But her dependence on an established routine was further emphasized when she insisted on being called Mrs. Blank (Carla's name) rather than Mrs. Dash (her own name). This is the first indication, then, in this experiment of the extent to which Abigail is dependent on routine, and the extent to which routine *frees* rather than hampers her. This conclusion is substantiated in Unit III, where there is free choice. At first she was completely baffled, but then asserted control by establishing an exact imitation of familiar playground procedures.

What shall we play? Abigail: *Let's play ring around of rosy . . . Come on, Carla, come on Cecily!* [She corrals all the children briskly, directs them to form a circle, holding hands, and leads them around. They all fall down, laughing.] Abigail: *Now let's get up again . . . All up! Wait, Carla, I'm not up yet. Now when we fall down make a somersault. . . .* Carla: *Let's play again.* Abigail: *No. No.* [She thinks awhile.] *Now let's play farmer in the dell.* What do you want to play, Cecily? Cecily: [submissively] *Farmer in the dell.* [Abigail continues directing the group, and now even instructs the adult, telling him to be "in the middle" for this game.] . . .

Thus, once Abigail felt secure enough in the whole situation, she asserted herself in the usual way in terms of a comfortably routinized situation, and one in which she could take the role of the adult.

The following portion of a record of an Imposed Leadership Game shows vividly how Abigail's rigidity may have acted to prevent her from being a successful leader.

241

SUBJECTS: Abigail
           Colin
           Jay

[During the first part of the game, each time experimenter says:] Whose turn is it going to be this time? [Abigail cries:] *Mine!* [but she is too late] [Colin, who was first, was content with deciding to be a "daddy" himself and to play with all the toys, paying little attention to the other children. Abigail seems quite displeased, and refuses the role of the "sick baby." She announces:] *We have to go back* [to the nursery school] *soon for music.*

[When it was Jay's turn he decided to play "trucks." As he was assigning roles, Abigail said with apparently humorous resignation:] *I suppose I'm going to be the sick baby!* Jay: *Abigail is the four-year-old child.* [almost as though he recognized her strong dependence on reality] [The game disintegrated under Jay's direction, and Abigail spent most of the time away from the other two, wrapping up the baby doll. Finally she withdraws altogether and sits on the window sill.] Everybody sit down and I'll put the toys back on the table. [They sit down on the couch and bounce up and down.] Now it's someone else's turn. It's Abigail's turn. Abigail: *Now you all sit down. You're the sick baby.* [to Colin, obviously retaliating for his assignment of this role which she disliked earlier in the game] Colin: *No, I'm the brother.* [Abigail is definitely thwarted by this resistance. She knows no deft way around. She and Colin quarrel and slap each other over the assignment of the role.] Jay: *Can I be the father?* [Note his acceptance of her authority, according to the rules.] Abigail: *You be the sick baby.* Jay: *No, I don't want to. I want to be the father.* Colin: *No, I don't want to. I want to be the grandfather.* [quite emotionally] It's Abigail's turn to tell everyone what to do. Jay: *I'm going to be the father.* Abigail, you tell everybody what to do. Who am I? Abigail: *Nothing.* Colin: *He can be the baby.* Abigail: *We don't need any baby.* Jay: *Yes, we do.* What do you say, Abigail? Who is everybody? [Abigail is becoming peeved since she is unsuccessful at telling everyone what to do.] Abigail: *Nothing.* Colin: *Yes, we are something.* Whose game is it? This is the last one. Who wants it? Abigail: *I don't.* [At the end of the game, she announced that they would play "High Stepping Horses," a familiar nursery school song and pattern of dancing. She proceeded to direct them as much like the teacher as she could.]

Abigail was unable (and in this respect typifies one kind of rigid personality) to combine different patterns and routines, but was successful only when she could take over a ready-made, familiar routine and substitute it bodily in the situation, as she did at the end of the game. Unlike the more successful leaders whom we have described above, it was difficult for her to face opposition and resistance and get around it.

Thus, the necessary alternatives for her were clear. Either she could run the thing in her way—the rigid, routinized way— or she withdrew entirely. This behavior is highly consistent with what was observed on the nursery school playground. Abigail was nicknamed the "Assistant Director" of the nursery school because she took such an active part in maintaining all the regular routines. The long-time sequence of her introduction to nursery school was exactly that of the fifteen- or twenty-minute experimental period. She directed the first several days of nursery school to establishing relations with the adults. She spent most of her time sitting close to the teacher, walking around with her when she shifted from place to place, and from this point of vantage, surveyed what the rest of the group was doing, soaking in the mores and standards of the new situation. Her first ventures away from the protective nearness of her teacher were in the most thoroughly conventionalized aspects of the nursery school: the routines of dressing and undressing, having fruit juice, putting away toys, etc. Even when most emancipated, however, after she had been in school for some time, she obviously was most secure and felt freest within such a safe framework of familiar patterns. She had very little to do with the boldest and most conventional spirits among the children (such as Camille and Colin). At all times she kept a watchful eye over the activities of the other children (particularly those she felt she could control) and consistently anticipated the teacher's intervention in situations which did not seem right to her.[14] Within this safe, routinized area, and with the safer, more conventional children, she was generally accepted as a leader and initiated and sustained a good deal of play.

Children like Abigail are extremely instructive in revealing some of the possible relations between rigidity-flexibility and the ability to be creative and constructive. Such a person may be

---

14. Her moral approach to the problems of aggression and destruction can also be seen in her activity with the balloons recorded in the following chapter.

quite at a loss in the absence of familiar conventions and by this token is unlikely to be an innovator. At the same time that a person of this kind is frustrated and made relatively powerless by unstructured freedom, he is liberated by the constraint of convention. While a child like Camille may be bored and irritated and functionally inhibited by routine, the Abigail kind of person is creative only under those conditions. The psychiatrist has long been familiar with the individual who seems to demand limitations which would be thwarting to others; who is literally most at ease under the most rigid restraints. There seems to be little doubt that the function of routine for such a person is the reduction of anxiety. This is clearly connected to compulsiveness, but it is particularly advantageous when the compulsive acts are culturally approved. It is the conservatism of great insecurity, and represents a deliberate avoidance of the dangers of new experiences by an "escape into reality."

There is an apparent opposition between routine on the one hand and creative activity and free use of imagination on the other. Yet it is obvious that real creativeness (that is, creation which is sufficiently acceptable socially so that the creator is not considered mentally unbalanced) depends on some acceptance of the modification of originality through conventional patterns.[15] Really great music, for example, must not merely conform to the rigid conventions of musical traditions, but must transcend them. Thus, a person like Abigail, for whom the forms are of primary significance in themselves, is less likely to achieve a creative use of her imagination. For everyone, routine and convention serve the purpose of reducing conflict; of reducing the necessity for taking thought of each separate act. Convention is a time-saver and a means for achieving security. But when it becomes too important in itself we find definite danger of "personality constriction," possibly because the underlying anxiety (rather than the conventionality in itself) is too great to permit real productivity. Each individual must find a balance between unfettered imagination and rigidly automatized patterning of behavior.

15. J. L. Moreno, "Creativity and Cultural Conserves—with Special Reference to Musical Expression, *Sociometry*, Vol. 2 (1939), 1-36.

The problem here is very similar to the evaluation in the Rorschach Test of the significance of the proportion of Form responses. For future investigation and analysis, we could also take account of the relation between flexibility and suggestibility. The "strong" personality which we value as "good" is characterized by forcefulness, integrity, and a certain consistency of goal-seeking. It thus involves a degree of rigidity; but rigidity may also appear in forms of negativism, obstinacy, and lack of adaptability which we call "bad."

CHAPTER 10

Aggression and Destruction Games: Balloons

Procedure

THE FUNDAMENTAL PURPOSE of the experiment is to provide a setting in which the child may project his destructive impulses.[1] Therefore, the essence of the procedure lies in meeting two very simple requirements: (1) to present a large number of *breakable objects* (I have employed only balloons for this purpose up to now), (2) *to provide a graded series of opportunities to break* them, such that the point in the experiment at which the child responds, and the manner in which he responds, may be determined and compared with the responses of other subjects. The actual procedure is flexible and depends to a great extent on the experimenter's judgment of the child's attitude from moment to moment. As is the case with most projective techniques, it is more important to keep these intangibles as constant as possible than it is to maintain a misleading objective control over less relevant but measurable variables such as time, position of the subject. etc.

---

1. This term is understood in the most general way for the present. More detailed discussion of its implications may be found in the theoretical section of this chapter.

Let us consider, for example, the attitude of a child at the beginning of an experimental session. It is essential to make each child feel as completely at ease as possible, but to do so the experimenter may find it necessary to use very different techniques with each child. He may be fairly aloof with one, he may put his arm around another, or try to induce another to laugh before he starts the experiment. The exact procedure and the time involved must necessarily vary and much obviously depends on the judgment of the experimenter, since his task is not to follow a fixed experimental plan, but consciously and skillfully to manipulate a situation while keeping certain major ends constantly in view.

It has been found desirable always to carry out the experiment either in a room entirely familiar to the child or one in which the furnishing is very simple. Such a room can be quickly explored and provides relatively little invitation to "escape from the field"; and at the same time, it assures the dominance of the balloon stimuli. The room itself should present no threats to the child and should be associated with pleasant experiences. This was true in the case of the experimental rooms used at the Sarah Lawrence Nursery School and the Vassar Nursery School; although the rooms were very different, each was associated for the child with the pleasant procedures of all the experimental situations he had known, and was entered eagerly. In no case was the experiment undertaken until this was true.

The experimenter too, must be a friendly, familiar, and unthreatening person. Therefore, none of the procedures should ever be attempted until the child has become acquainted with the experimenter in nursery school situations. To assist in creating an easygoing impression the experimenter always avoided authoritative relations with the children in routine nursery school situations.

INTRODUCING THE CHILD TO THE SITUATION

The experimenter invites the child to come and play without informing him of the specific situation. He attempts to converse with the child freely, and to reduce as far as possible the distance between child and adult. The child is invited to enter the experimental room, and the experimenter closes the door and sits down in the background. As soon as he enters the room, the child is confronted with a large number of balloons of different shapes, sizes and colors.[2]

THE EXPERIMENT PROPER

The experiment proper is considered to have begun as soon as the child enters the room, although in some cases, particularly where the subject is timid, he may not choose at once to acknowledge the presence of the balloons.

Because of the necessary adaptability of the procedure, a rigid outline cannot be given here. Rather we may summarize by indicating the primary characteristics of behavior that may be elicited, and that are watched for; and by describing the critical phases or "choice points" that may serve to elicit the crucially important behavior. We may emphasize once more that the introduction of each "choice point" depends on the experimenter's judgment of the child's previous behavior and attitude of the moment. For instance, it will be obvious that the procedure for a child who breaks a balloon at the very outset must be different from the procedure adopted with a child who merely looks at them.

The crucial aspects of behavior to be watched for are essentially the following:

1. Does the child break a balloon or not?

2. If he does, at what point in the procedure does he do so? How does he rationalize or excuse breaking?

3. How many balloons does he break, and at what point does he break each?

4. Whether he breaks a balloon or not, what is his emotional approach to the idea of such destruction (including the question of whether he treats it as a "moral" problem)?

---

2. The number and the specifications of the balloons used have been altered several times, apparently without appreciably changing the situation. At present we employ 4 spiral balloons, 60″ long, 3 round balloons, 10″ in diameter, and 3 round balloons, 5″ in diameter.

5. What is his apparent emotional response after a balloon has been broken?

For the eliciting of behavior that will permit him to answer such questions about the child, the experimenter must keep in mind the following "choice points" as essential portions of the procedure, so designed as to provide the subject with a *graded* series of opportunities to be destructive. If a child does break a balloon at any of these points, naturally the procedure is abbreviated and to some degree modified. In order to show it in full, I have outlined the "choice points" below in terms of the procedure to be followed with a child who consistently refuses to permit any balloons to be broken. It will be evident that he might have broken them, however, at various stages, either spontaneously; after the experimenter first invited him to do so; after the experimenter urged him to do so; or only when the experimenter offered, himself, to be the agent and to break the balloons for the children.

Introduction of Idea of Destruction

Immediately after he enters the room, if he does not do so spontaneously, the child is encouraged by the experimenter's words and actions to play freely with the balloons. Throughout this "warming-up" time the adult tries to establish easy, casual relations with the child. During the early period of the session he also tries to find out how familiar the child is with balloons.

After the child has played with balloons for a time (roughly two to five minutes, depending on how long it takes the child to "warm-up"), the experimenter introduces the idea of breaking the balloons, ordinarily by such a series of remarks as the following. "Do you like balloons?" "Is it fun to play with them?" "Would you like to break one? You may if you want to." As I have indicated before, many children would have introduced the idea of breaking balloons by themselves by this time. Occasionally children start breaking balloons without any verbal overtures; some children remark that they would like to break them; others introduce the idea negatively or indirectly: "I'm afraid I might break one."

Urging Destruction

In the example that we have selected, the child refuses the suggestion to break the balloon. The experimenter may urge the child again, and then try to question him as to his reason for not breaking the balloon: "Why don't you want to break balloons?" "Is it fun to . . .?" "Is it naughty to . . . ?" In cases where the child *has* accepted the suggestion, a similar series of questions is used to try to determine the child's attitude following a destructive act; whether he is casual, or guilty, or fearful, or released. He is then invited to break more balloons.

Urging Indirect Destruction

The next step in the procedure is to provide the child with an opportunity to break the balloons indirectly by having the adult break them for him. When the child refuses, a similar series of questions is used: "Why shouldn't I break the balloons?" "Is it fun if *I* break the balloons?" "Is it naughty for *me* to break the balloons?" With children who accept the suggestion that the adult break the balloon, the experimenter makes an attempt to involve the child more directly by asking him to "help"—step on the balloon with the experimenter, etc.

Emotional Response to Destruction

With a child who refuses every suggestion up to this point, a final attempt is made both to urge and to reassure him, by telling him that these are the experimenter's balloons, that there are many more, that it is all right to break them, etc. If the child still steadfastly rejects the idea, the final step may be accidentally to break a balloon at a moment when he is not looking. (This is not done if the experimenter deems that it would produce too much anxiety.) The child's response to this is noted and he is immediately questioned to determine what degree of responsibility or guilt he assumes: "How did that happen?" "Did you do it?" "Is it fun when they break?" "Shall we break some more?" etc.

Occasionally there is a genuinely accidental break. When a balloon breaks under these circumstances, the experimenter must adapt his procedure accordingly, either questioning the child as just indicated, or reassuring him.

Whenever a balloon has been broken, the experimenter tries to see if the child is willing to break more. The number of balloons a child is willing to break may be quite as significant as whether he will or will not break them at all.

When there is any willingness to break balloons, the experimenter tries to determine if the child is as willing to break large as small balloons and whether, after the balloon is broken, the child wants to save the pieces, throw them away, or disregard them. Frequently an anxious child, after breaking a balloon, will hastily try to "dispose of the evidence." In some sessions the experimenter makes small "bubbles" from the fragments of a broken balloon, and suggests that the child break one of these. Very often the behavior is significantly different in response to the "bubble."

Before the child leaves, the experimenter is careful to see that he has a chance to play with the balloons freely as in the beginning, and to see that he leaves in good humor and with continued good rapport with the experimenter.

Following the experimental session, it is useful to observe the child's subsequent behavior in the nursery school situation, as well as his attitude toward the experimenter next time he sees him.

The total time varies from child to child, but generally is about fifteen minutes.

Methods of Analyzing the Records

Throughout the session an observer behind a one-way screen records in shorthand all the conversation between child and experimenter, and, as fully as possible, the behavior, expressions, and tone of voice of the subject, along with a minute-by-minute notation of the time. The record is as full and as *interpretive* as possible. Immediately after the session the experimenter dictates a summary of his impressions of the child's attitudes throughout the procedure, and as complete as possible a record of the child's behavior in coming to and leaving the experimental room. Since the recorder's notes are partly interpretive, they are gone over by the experimenter as soon as possible after the experimental session, and any questions or disagreements are noted at once.

Conclusions are drawn from the *totality* of the situation. The full written record and the experimenter's impressions are taken together, and the evidence consists of the child's verbal responses, his tone of voice, his actions, his facial expression, his posture, and any other indications of eagerness, guilt, strain or emotional tension and not merely the number of balloons broken. The conclusions are partially controlled by agreement between recorder and experimenter: and by the degree of consistency within the total record and between the results of the experiment and other data about the subject.

On the basis of such evidence, conclusions are drawn regarding the child's destructive impulses and attitudes toward destruction in terms which apply specifically to that child. No rigid classification or typology is employed. However, a half-dozen kinds of response described below give some indication of the range of possibilities of behavior in this situation, and suggest the mode of description and analysis that is used.

A QUANTITATIVE CLASSIFICATION OF THE RESULTS

As illustrated in Figure 21 below, at one extreme is the child who breaks *all or most of the balloons* (Response V). At the other extreme, behaviorally, is the child who *refuses to break any balloons,* or to permit the adult to break any (Response I).

Between these extremes is the child who *may break one or two balloons* when it is suggested by the adult (Response III). We may add two more intermediate steps in our continuum of ways of responding to the situation. One of these is the child *who breaks a number of balloons* (Response IV). Falling short of the other extreme is a group of children who refuse to break balloons, but *permit the adult to do so* (Response II).

It is from a consideration of all the results (with some fifty children) that I have arrived at a more dynamic classification of the findings in terms of motivation and emotions. Even without regard to some of the theoretical considerations that I shall introduce in a moment, it may readily be seen that the child who does not break any balloons because he enjoys playing with them tremendously, and has no wish to destroy what are for him valued objects, is to be considered on quite a different footing from the child who is basically very eager to destroy, but sets up prohibitions and inhibitions on moral grounds.

[Colin immediately picks up the small blue balloon and flings it in the air.] *Balloons! And a blue one, and a yellow one and a white one!* [Throws them gaily, kicks them, etc. . . . Bursts out laughing.] . . . [Five minutes] *It bounced down on my head!* [Jumps off couch again, flings the round blue balloon in the air and bats it around the room with great enjoyment and energy.] Shall I break one? *Ha, ha, ha!* [This is just a joke to him. He collects all the balloons, and sits down holding them tenderly.] *I'll take care of them.*

[Abigail enters, sees the balloons; turns to experimenter and smiles:] *Where did you get them? Will they break?* [She plays with the balloons gingerly, frequently turning to the adult.] [Three minutes] You could break them; do you want to? *How?* [At the same time she visibly shrinks from the idea and shakes her head.] *If you step on them?* Yes, you could do it that way. *I don't like the sound of breaking.* Do you want me to break one? *No. You mustn't.* Is it naughty? *Yes, my mommie* . . . [Her voice trails off and she sits down at some distance from the balloons, her hands folded and her brow furrowed.] Did your mommie say it was naughty? *Yes. No. Yes!* [as though seized by an inspiration] *I asked her and she said "No, it's it's not nice," and I said, "Oh, okay, I won't break them"* [she looks directly at experimenter] *and don't you break any either!* [vehemently] [Significantly, the next topic she turns to involves a policeman as the central figure.]

There can be no question of the fact that there is a basic psychological distinction between the behavior of Colin and of Abigail, although objectively each refused to break any balloons.

A similar distinction may be made among children who break many balloons, falling behaviorally at or near the point we have labelled Response V.

[Camille enters and inspects the balloons, holding her hand to her head somewhat coyly. Sits down on the floor, still coy.] You can play with them. What would you like to do with them? *I'm not going to tell you. I'm afraid I'll bust it.* [looks up archly] *Put my foot on it and it'll go smash! You can blow it right up again, won't it?* [Two minutes] [She inspects and examines them. Decides which are hers and which are experimenter's.] Do you want to break one? *Yes. Try to shoot it: step on it!* [Inside one minute she has stamped on and broken every balloon, shrieking and giggling; very tense, almost ferocious expression, especially around mouth. Is very concerned and tense when experimenter asks:] Is it naughty? [Looks at experimenter anxiously:] *Will you cry?*

[Kene picks up a balloon as soon as he enters the room; friendly but unconcerned with experimenter] *Balloons!* [He plays with them freely, tossing them in the air, shouting. Tells experimenter to catch the ones he throws.] . . . [One minute] Would you like to break some? *No, coz I like balloons.* [Continues to play as before.] . . . [Two minutes] You can break them if you want to. *Uh huh . . . I'll break that one.* [He steps on it boldly.] *Bang!* [He is pleased and excited by the noise. Grins, jumps up and down. Proceeds to break several more in the same way.] . . . Is it fun? *Uh huh!* [eyes shining; grinning broadly] Is it naughty? *Uh huh!* [perfunctory; engrossed in trying to break a long balloon. Later he denies it is naughty.] *Makes an awful noise!* [He says this smiling in a tone of approval.] [Breaks all but two. Is bored; asks for other toys.]

The comparison of these children shows Camille preoccupied from the first with a destructive impulse. When it is released she is avid and nearly vicious in its expression. Kene, on the other hand, can enjoy breaking in precisely the way he enjoys tossing the balloons about; his response is very similar to that which may be observed in some adults on roller-coasters: enjoyment of excitement, and the savoring of mild trepidation.[3] One further fact is shown so clearly by these examples that it is worth pointing out here: psychologically, Camille seems closer to Colin than to Kene, although by crude quantitative measures this would not be clear; similarly Kene's response is more like Colin's than it is like Camille's. Such facts as these necessitate the more sophisticated type of analysis indicated below.

A DYNAMIC CLASSIFICATION OF THE RESULTS

Our attempt in this reclassification is to consider not only the overt and quantitative results, but also the attitudes implicit in

---

3. This is a response that seems best explainable in terms of Dumas' theory of emotions.

the child's total activity. The dynamic factors that most interest us are:

1. The strength of the impulse to destroy.
2. The strength of the restraints against destruction, mainly:
   (a) fear
   (b) "moral" inhibitions; interiorized adult prohibitions
   (c) fondness for the objects.

We have already suggested that there may be considerable overt destruction without any strong *destructive impulse* as such (as in the case of Kene above); our attempt is to try to deal with the drive or impulse to destroy, and not merely with the fact that a certain number of balloons has been broken. It is important to make it clear at this juncture that in some children this impulse, regardless of its strength, appears to be a very significant ("central")[4] trait; for others it may be peripheral. On the other hand, as has been indicated already, some children may display no overt destruction, yet may give evidence of a very great readiness or impulse to destroy. The very presence of considerable guilt and the evident psychodynamic necessity of maintaining very strong moral restraints permit the inference that there must be some strong impulse requiring restraint Usually there is considerable internal evidence in the record supporting such an inference, as will be seen in the case of Alec.

[Alec walks in slowly, looks at balloons and says at once, challengingly:] *I'll step on one.* All right. *Will it break?* What do you think? [No answer.] Would you like it to break? *No.* Is it fun? [No answer. At this point he changes the subject; in Kurt Lewin's term he "goes out of the field."][5]

[This pattern was repeated with minor variations no fewer than eight times during the ten minutes that the experimental session occupied. He repeatedly broached the idea of breaking the balloons; refused to do so himself; denied that it was fun, and insisted that it was "naughty." Finally:] *It isn't nice . . . It isn't nice to break anything and don't you.*

[When experimenter "accidentally" broke a balloon Alec was extremely tense: he paled, gasped, looked tragic. He hastily grasped at the idea of the "accident" and said it was "All right" but he care-

---

4. G. W. Allport and P. E. Vernon, *Studies in Expressive Movement* (New York: Macmillan, 1933).

5. *A Dynamic Theory of Personality* (New York: McGraw-Hill, 1935).

fully picked up all the fragments and wanted to get rid of them all, and verbally introduced the idea of restitution:] *Now you have to blow up one.* [He then announced that he wanted to go.]

To schematize visually the relationships which appear to exist we may use a scale as a portion of our more inclusive schema. The scale, labelled Responses, is influenced by the strength of the desire to destroy (the upper vector) and also by the strength of inhibitions against destruction (the lower vector, Figure 22). For example, the case given previously, of the child (Camille) with a very strong impulse and practically no inhibition of such an impulse shows behavior falling near the extreme of explicit destruction (Figure 23). For the middle groups various degrees of the destructive impulse and its inhibition tend to produce a median amount of actual destruction (Figure 24). Consideration of the extreme case where there is very strong inhibition to destruction (as in the case of Alec) necessitates a further complication of the schema. It has been observed that maximum inhibition (meaning not merely absence of destruction, but evidence in the record of a strong feeling against it) is associated with strong destructive impulses. In this case, however, the *explicit* behavior is not ordinarily a simple resolution of these forces, but is totally determined by the inhibiting vector. At the same time, there is evidence of *implicit* destruction in fantasy or verbally, and to demonstrate this, it is necessary to add a parallel scale indicating implicit behavior (Figure 25). In most of the preceding cases we may assume little discrepancy between implicit and explicit behavior. Here it is suggested that the explicit and implicit behavior are polar opposites.[6]

Margaret Mead suggested, after reading the manuscript of this chapter, that there must be another case in which the basic impulse is nearly nil, but where social pressure functions in the opposite direction: that is, inciting the individual to a "proper," "manly" aggression. With this in mind, we inspected the records and found that the case of Jay seems to fit this

---

6. Fundamentally this is but a generalization of the basic Freudian principle of the dynamics of motivation. It is further consonant with this view in implying an increased tension and a less stable equilibrium where both the original impulse and the inhibiting forces remain strong.

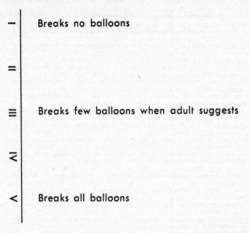

Figure 21—QUANTITATIVE SCALE OF RESULTS

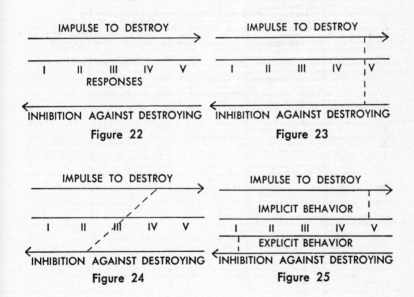

concept perfectly. It is necessary to point out that superficially Jay appeared so dashing and conventionally vigorous a boy as to receive such nicknames as the "All-American Boy." At the same time, the Rorschach clearly indicates that this was largely a false front, and that Jay was very busy living up to expectations while he was fundamentally a very different person. In the balloon experiment, it is noteworthy that he sought rationalizations to permit himself to break balloons, and broke a great many of them, but for each one had to work himself up to the necessary pitch. After he had broken the balloons, there was no trace of guilt, but rather a feeling of satisfaction and accomplishment. This is a motivational scheme directly opposite to that we found in Alec.

Dr. Mead suggested that the culture provides upper and lower limits for aggression: there is a point at which one is no longer permitted to be aggressive (in our culture, for example, not hitting a man when he's "down"); and a point at which one *must* be aggressive ("You can't take that lying down").

The foregoing diagram does not attempt to show some of the further interrelationships that are involved, such as the obvious dynamics interrelating the upper and lower vectors.

It should be emphasized that the device suggested above has grown out of the consideration of the results obtained from the experiment, and that the logic of these results seems to be succinctly stated in it. However, it is always essential to consider the entire record of each child, and to try to grasp the dynamics of the individual case. It is not only possible but desirable to do so without trying to follow any standard formula for analysis. The schema is not offered as such a formula, but is merely an attempt to make explicit some of the ways in which we approach the case record, and to illustrate some of the forces that seem to us to be operating and to be visible in the raw material.

Further Use of Concepts

An attempt partially to validate several of these concepts was made in the form of a species of questionnaire, submitted to the teachers of the Sarah Lawrence College Nursery School, who had known the subjects for one to two years. The questionnaire consisted, actually, of an outline presentation of the schema for understanding aggression, much as it has been developed above, but modified to refer to everyday behavior and not merely to the experimental situation. The teacher's task was to fit each child in the nursery school into this pattern. However, in each case the teacher presented her views as fully as necessary showing what modifications or qualifications were necessary in "classifying" each child, and giving supporting evidence.

In two very important respects the research up to this point was fully justified by the mere fact that the teachers were able to make use of the outline-plan, since this demonstrated that the analysis was not only meaningful to the experimenter, but that it was both workable and translatable.

We reproduce below the questionnaire as used, since it serves here to summarize the analysis developed above, and to apply it to everyday situations.

Questionnaire
on Aggression and Destruction

It seems insufficient merely to try to label a child as aggressive, or hostile, or destructive, without noting as well the emotional tone that attaches to his behavior. Consideration of this, in turn, seems to throw some light on the roots of the behavior in question.

I. AGGRESSIVE BEHAVIOR

A. Sources of Aggression: Taking into consideration, for the moment, only aggression (*person*-directed hostility), the same behavior could arise from:
1. Avid, deep feelings of aggression that seem always to be on tap; that seem to be a part of the personality of the child. These may arise largely as a response to some continuing, frustrating aspect of his life space, and thus seems all out of proportion to the occasion on which it is seen.
2. A direct, freely emotional response to a specific situation.

3. Seeking a way out of a distasteful situation. Usually found when the child lacks more appropriate techniques.
4. A purely imitative response to someone else's suggestion. The stimulating aggression may have been directed at the child or at a third person.

Each of these pictures of aggression is complicated first of all by quantitative gradations even shading off into *non-aggressive behavior*. Thus the aggression may be more or less *restrained*, more or less *prompt*, more or less *direct*, and, most important, more or less *intense*.

B. Modifiers of Aggression: More frequently, however, *ambivalent* or *non-aggressive behavior* is the result of the introduction of other specific modifying factors, most commonly, perhaps, (1) fear, (2) guilt and prohibition, (3) liking the person who would be the object of aggression, or (4) possession of other techniques for meeting the situation.

  1. Fear or timidity may cause the child:
    (a) to repress his aggressive response, producing
      (1) an unaggressive response
      (2) an ambivalent, inconsistent response
      (3) a more aggressive response at another time or toward another object
    (b) to increase the intensity of this response, thereby
      (1) increasing the aggression
      (2) causing a *panicky* aggression
  2. Guilt and prohibitions may cause the child:
    (a) to repress his aggressive response, producing
      (1) an unaggressive response
      (2) an ambivalent, inconsistent response (often with moralistic verbalization)
      (3) a more aggressive response at another time or toward another object
      (4) guilty behavior accompanying or following aggression (verbal comment, reparations, etc.)
      (5) accidental injury of others
      (6) *self*-directed aggression
  3. Positive affect toward the individual who would be the object of aggression may similarly modify aggression.
  4. Possession of other techniques for handling situations that might provoke aggression ordinarily may cause the situation to be resolved differently.

C. Modes of Expression of Aggression: There are also various ways of *expressing* aggression and hostility:
  1. Direct, physical
    (a) hitting
    (b) biting

      (c) scratching
      (d) kicking
      (e) spitting, etc.
  2. Direct, verbal
  3. Indirect, physical
      (a) directed at some*one* else
      (b) directed at some*thing* else
  4. Indirect, verbal
      (a) directed *at* someone else
      (b) getting help from other child or adult, "tattling"
D. Other Characteristics of Aggression: Additional points to be considered might be the most frequent *occasions* for aggressive behavior, most frequent *objects* of aggressive behavior, whether the child is usually on the *offense* or *defense,* etc.

II. DESTRUCTIVE BEHAVIOR

A precisely similar outline applies to destruction (*object*-directed hostility).

From the point of view of methodology, it may be added that the type of questionnaire used—if indeed it may be so termed—was found far preferable to a more rigid form. The teachers who filled out forms did not feel uncomfortably and arbitrarily restricted to a "yes" or "no" that might not tell the whole truth about the child. It is our view that getting the whole truth is quite as important as getting nothing but the truth, and most questionnaires do not provide for this.

It will be noted that aggressive and destructive behavior were both considered in the questionnaire. It is remarkable that there was an almost total lack of destructive behavior reported by the teachers in this group of children; at the same time we have already noted a comparatively extreme amount of such behavior in the experimental situation. Moreover, a large amount of aggressive behavior is noted by the teachers in the same children's nursery school activities. This tends to confirm the view we have suggested that aggression and destruction arise on the same dynamic foundation and that family and social (nursery school) pressure is more rigorously directed against destruction. In the experimental situation the explicit withdrawal of these restrictions produced a blossoming of such behavior precisely among those individuals who show hostile behavior against persons in the (relatively) aggression-permitting nursery school situation.

In order to give some idea of the nature of the results from the questionnaire, and of the kind of agreement found between these results and the experiment, a presentation of one subject is given below. The teacher's summary has been considerably abbreviated, but not altered.

SUBJECT: Alec

Experimenter's Summary

Initial remark about breaking: *Will it break?* Initially accepted idea of breaking. Rejected it when brought face to face with it. Evidence of strong aggressive impulse, strong and relatively insecurely established "moral" control.

Teacher's Summary (E. Beyer)

Aggression: The most aggressive child.

Source and Nature of Aggression: The first category is clearly descriptive of Alec—(avid, deep feelings of aggression). His aggression is deeply felt, always on tap. It is unpredictable, and out of proportion to the situation of the moment.

Modifiers of Aggression: Apparently there is no guilt whatever. Sometimes, however, punishment seems to be a goal—implying unconscious guilt?
No signs of fear.
Possibly some *accidental* injuries to others, but deliberate ones overshadow them.
Liking someone never stops him.

Forms of Aggression: Hitting, biting, scratching at eyes, etc. Always physical, always direct.

Occasions for Aggression: Unpredictable: frequently disputes over property or plaything.

Objects of Aggression: Calvin, Adele, Jay, Colin. Usually on the *offense.*

Destruction:

Source and Nature: He would probably like to destroy more than he does. (E.g., he saws viciously with his jaw rigid, body tense, hammers the daylights out of nails, annihilates clay—all with a blank-tense expression.) The source of this seems to be the same as that of aggression.

Modifiers: He is not afraid, he is less guilty, if anything; this is an outlet he expects to be allowed—and it seems a healthy one for him. He seems almost relaxed at the end of such times, he heaves a sigh and is quiet.

Occasions: Destruction does not seem to follow periods of tension.

Source 1, Modifier 2.[7]　　Source 1, Modifier 2.[7]

---

7. See questionnaire above.

PART III

Experiments in
Active Play Techniques

by EUGENE LERNER

CHAPTER 11

Introduction

Introduction

THE FOLLOWING ACTIVE PLAY TECHNIQUES were developed for
the purpose of observing and experimentally testing certain
personality characteristics of preschool children[1]—with an eye to
varieties of the contemporary American ego in the making. A
series of play situations was devised in which the experimenter
played a standardized and very active role throughout. As a
"participant-observer" in play situations, he then proceeded to
watch the young child in action as a directed and personified
unity. Such personified unity in action can be plainly observed
in terms of such statements of children as: "I want this," "I don't
want this," "This is mine," "Mine is nicer," "Can I keep it?"
"You shan't play with this," and through the accompanying more
overt forms of behavior (locomotions, manipulations), and
psychomotor tensions (facial expression, tone of voice, gait, and
posture).

There are certain difficulties in applying such *controlled* or
standardized play techniques. For instance, the experimenter

---

1. Blocking Techniques 1 and 2 were most fully developed by Eugene
Lerner before his death interrupted his research. Other techniques reported
in the 1941 Monograph, but not further developed were: Gratification Technique, Marionette Technique, Motivation Technique, and general Diagnostic
Play Technique. These are illustrated in Volume II.

cannot prevent unpredictable tangential behavior of his subjects. Children may ask such questions as: "Where did you get this toy?" "Can I take it home?" or "What shall I do with it?" These are then staved off through "standard" statements such as "What do you think?" "What does it look like?" "Guess." But such procedure colors the atmosphere between the experimenter and the subject—sometimes as added and experimentally unintended frustration, sometimes as additional, equally unintended gratification. The next child who does not start with such incidental behavior until relatively late in the experimental interaction or does so not at all, obviously functions in a total context which is anything but controlled or strictly comparable. Children respond and define the relationship between the experimenter and the subject quite differently in different cases—and so they ask a lot of spontaneous or incidental questions, a few or none at all; early, toward the end of the game or never. And, of course, the comparable absence of overt tangential-idiomatic behavior in two or more cases does not necessarily mean that the interpersonal atmosphere between the experimenter and the subject is strictly comparable: children may abstain from overt tangential behavior for different or even diametrically opposite reasons.

This difficulty would confront the experimenter whenever he is present in the research situation—even if one and the same experimenter's states of fatigue, hunger, resultant tempo, and expressive behavior could really be held constant from day to day, from subject to subject. "Personal equations" cannot be directly computed for given experimenters, as in the subject-object relations of an irreversible sort (e.g., the reaction time differentials of astronomical observers). The nature of interpersonal subject-object relations is highly indeterminate and elusive, resulting in data which would be highly specific for given experimenters and given subjects. Just as in clinical and everyday observations, the young child's ego is thus reflected through a limited series of unique interactions between specific, unknown individuals. From such data, one could only generalize from the particular to the particular, or within and about each particular case as such.

Some psychologists go so far as to suggest that the latter, generalizing within and about each particular case, is the *only* possibility for scientific personality study, under the circumstances. According to Floyd Allport, a large sample of the behavior of a single person would be sufficient for discovering "laws of individuals"—"as long as the generalization made from this sample . . . is made to apply to this one individual's behavior and to *no other*" (italics mine).[2] From the standpoint of the active play techniques here reported, such agnostic limitations on research analysis are not necessary. Self-comparisons of the same child in a great variety of situations and *cross*-comparisons of large samples of his behavior with those of other children are both needed. After all, every child, no matter how "unique" (postulate), represents a certain irreducible minimum: the zoological species and the cultural series in concretely individuated form. The unique "ways of seeing life," the "private worlds of feeling and meaning," are of necessity located in an intraspecies continuum. Just because we plan to study idiomatic internal sets as such more intensively than we can through large-scale, cross-sectional application of psychophysical methods, it does not follow that we must drop the postulate of differential similarities. We can simply apply it in *new* directions, in total study of child personalities who can never be considered apart from their zoological (interspecies) and cultural (intraspecies) moorings. We are looking for *new* forms of differential similarities here.

But grossly standardized behavior of the experimenter in active play techniques suggests a certain emphasis on external similarity of the stimulus. Does this not imply identity or close similarity of *responsiveness*—unwittingly anticipating what the experimenter *wants* the stimulus to mean, rather than what it *might* mean to the subjects? Are we not back to the old stimulus-response fallacy—away from projective principles?

The Rorschach ink-blots are not changed for every subject. The ten plates are standardized and presented to the subject in uniform sequence, and the test instructions are roughly stand-

2. F. H. Allport, "Teleonomic Description in the Study of Personality," *Charact. and Personal.*, Vol. 5 (1937), 203 ff.

ardized. In order to scrutinize selective responsiveness as such, it is often desirable to hold gross external variations in the stimulus to a minimum—otherwise we might literally not know when and how internal sets or "private worlds" can be identified, in the first place. Of course, qualitatively and quantitatively different responses to the *same* external stimulus are not the only possible clues to idiosyncratic mental sets. Qualitatively and quantitatively similar responses to *different* external stimuli represent yet another type of clue. The point is that in devising and applying the active play techniques in question we are aiming for the former type of evidence on selective responsiveness—in basic harmony with the main principles of the Rorschach method. Instead of providing a set of standardized ink-blots, we offer a set of standardized play situations which the subjects can then define and respond to in the idiomatic manner most congenial to them. "Tangential" behavior, this partial index of attitude to the experimenter as such, can then be handled on the same basis as in the Rorschach situation: through grossly standardized auxiliary instructions. If skillfully applied, there is no *a priori* reason to assume that such auxiliary instructions need to interfere with the basic idiomatic responses of the subjects any more than they apparently do in the Rorschach situation. Standardization of research procedure in this sense can be a necessary condition of verifiable insight into selective reponsiveness of the subjects, without necessitating sacrifice of insight for verifiability of data or vice versa.

For purposes of this study, the ego is considered as that aspect of personality which is more or less consistently evoked in specified interpersonal relationships—or (if not in the actual presence of another human being) at least with close reference to such bio-social contexts. Thus considered, it is the *"I:Not-I" oriented organization of all segmental behavior systems, which is characteristically mobilized in face-to-face interactions with other individuals.* It is assumed to be the observable outcome of adaptive integrations—as the compound function of socialization (past, present, and anticipated inter-individual contacts).

The *ego-patterns,* of which I shall speak later on, are, in turn, the *specific modes of evaluating conduct* in any "I:Not-I" situation experienced with reference to at least one other human being. They presumably reflect the more or less unified totality of self-feelings or self-ideas (ego-values). They are selectively mobilized in response to direct stimuli (internal somatic processes, external objects and events), and to direct interstimulations (acts of other persons).

In devising the specific techniques discussed below, there was one further assumption. It had to do with a *balanced* approach to the young child's ego-organization and ego-development. This assumption briefly amounts to this:

Given an individual child's selective manner of handling on the one hand his failures, defeats, frustrations, and on the other hand his successes, victories, gratifications, one ought to be able somehow to define such ego-organization in the making.

In terms of any changes or constancies over shorter or longer periods of time, *the combined frustration-gratification profile is what the investigator is after*—rather than a one-sided frustration profile or gratification profile alone.

The frustration part of the research rests on the simple assumption that the essence of frustration is interference or blocking of the organism in action. It is assumed that self-feelings are inevitably mobilized and heightened to a varying extent and in varying form in any interstimulations—and perhaps especially in frustrating situations because of goal-reinforcements or other modifications of threatened goals. Such heightened self-feelings in action are inferred from a certain intensification of given modes of conduct: by increased and characteristic self-references and, correspondingly, by increased "you-references" or "they-references," as a matter of vocalizations or verbalized self-conceptions; by characteristically intensified manipulations or locomotions (grabbing, holding on, hiding away, moving toward or away, etc.)—as well as through certain changes in psychomotor tensions (facial expression, tone of voice, gait and posture).

The earlier mentioned "activity" of the experimenter can be related to the problem of activity and passivity in earlier play research and play therapy. As applied to widely different problems of child behavior, the brilliant use of play techniques by Piaget and his collaborators, Moreno, David Levy, Kurt Lewin and his associates, Melanie Klein, Erikson, and others of the psychoanalytic school, suggests the possibilities of play techniques of decreasing activity on the part of the experimenter— roughly in the order of the enumeration above. Piaget's now classical experimental verification of some of Durkheim's moral sociology (in terms of children's attitudes versus their actual practice of game rules in playing marbles)[3] provided the background for these techniques in child research. David Levy's equally classical pioneer work in so-called release therapy provided the background from the point of view of play therapy.[4]

Special methodological mention must be made of the "post-session clinics" which accompanied the play experiments. Partly as a teaching technique, partly as a research technique, the findings of every experiment were discussed by the experimenter with Miss Marian Weber (the research secretary), and the various psychology students who observed behind one-way mirrors. Many points of descriptive and interpretive interest could be captured and highlighted in this fashion, which would have been far more difficult to locate otherwise. Through such "post-session clinics" (immediately after the experiments), the questions and insights of both beginning and advanced psychology students became available—in active give-and-take with those of Miss Weber and the experimenter.[5]

3. J. Piaget, *The Moral Judgment of the Child* (Glencoe: The Free Press, 1952).

4. "Release Therapy in Young Children," *Psychiatry,* I (1938), 387-90.

5. Acknowledgments are due to the following psychology students at Sarah Lawrence College as active collaborators in this connection: Ann Barnard, Mabel Carter Carrow, Virginia Blodgett, Jean Hammond, Avery Harder, Susan Pattison, Mary Rice, Mary Jane Rust, Ann Wolfson, and Bobette Wiley. The enthusiasm, sensitivity of observation, and continuity of leadership contributed by Miss Marian Weber in such post-session clinics cannot be adequately acknowledged.

CHAPTER 12

Blocking Technique Number 1

Aim of Technique

IT IS ASSUMED IN PSYCHOTHERAPY, especially through the emphasis of Freud and his followers, that frustrating experiences generate hostility and conduce to some expression of hostility. Accordingly, it is a well-recognized practice of psychotherapists to provide relatively artificial opportunities for substitute expression of hostility in attempting to reach or cope with patients who, in the face of serious frustrations in the past, are considered to have had inadequate outlets for direct release of their hostility.

Turning this psychotherapeutic principle into more positive form, we may assume that it may serve as a basis for differential diagnosis and prognosis in the study of normal children's personality organization. Thus, broadly speaking, it is a plausible hypothesis that a less inhibited or less severely (traumatically) socialized child will, given a frustrating experience, express hostility more directly or "freely" than children who are more inhibited or more excessively socialized into "nice" conduct patterns. The study of what Rosenzweig proposes to call "frustration-tolerance"[1] is, then, the primary aim of this particular play tech-

1. S. Rosenzweig, "A General Outline of Frustration," *Charact. and Personal.*, VII (1938), 153.

nique. While planning to look for different forms of hostility release we need not consider ourselves bound *a priori* to a necessary connection between frustration and hostility, nor to any other postulate (Freudian or otherwise) in terms of a necessary link between frustration and regression, invoked in the recent work of Lewin and his associates.[2] We think it is desirable to get away from an essentially "explosive" picture of frustration reactions. Instead of looking for one gross shot of frustration and an "explosive" reaction thereto (in the form of heightened or lowered performance and achievement), the plan of this play technique is to administer experimental frustration *gradually, repetitively—in different forms,* and *in progressive* dosages. The aim is then to look for partial, immediate, as well as delayed, reactions of the child—when relatively not blocked, when potentially, partially or completely blocked, when gradually versus suddenly blocked. This implies a distinction between *phases or sequences* of the frustration process—in terms of various *kinds* of simple primary frustration (excluding compound frustrations of the conflict sort). Assuming a number of possible main varieties in frustration response (and not just a variety of *hostility* reactions), we intend to verify just how a given child will start, continue, and finish in a wide, eclectically conceived, continuum of frustration-tolerance.

As for any qualms about "real" frustrations versus experimentally produced frustrations in play situations, we consider that in *playing* with preschool children we probably approximate "nearness to life" situations or "life-likeness" of meaning as closely as we ever do later on, when dealing with older personalities. It is not necessary here to analyze the reasons why playing is such a valid medium of self-expression and communication for nursery school children. When spontaneously engrossed and then blocked in game situations, the young child's natural tendency or ability to assert, defend or otherwise do

---

2. R. Barker, T. Dembo, and K. Lewin, "Experiments on Frustration and Regression," *Univ. Iowa Studies in Child Welfare* (1940); "The Effect of Frustration upon Cognitive Ability," *Charact. and Personal.,* VII (1938), 145-150; "Frustration and Regression: an Experiment with Young Children. Studies in Topology and Vector Psychology II," *Univ. Iowa Studies in Child Welfare,* XVIII (1941).

something about his immediate spheres of influence (ego-spheres) will be surely invoked—a fact equally well known to parents, nursery school teachers, and research observers.

Such attempts at ego-demarcations or the ability to assert and somehow defend "natural" ego-drives, the extent to which opportunity to do so will be utilized and the style in which it is done—all these forms of active and passive "frustration-tolerance"—may be assumed to involve certain core aspects of the child's personality. As will be seen later in some detail, such non-peripheral clues to child personality involve variables or factors variously termed ascendance-submission, masochism-sadism, aggressiveness-sympathy, egocentricity-reciprocity, competitiveness-cooperativeness. We propose to scrutinize the various techniques of ego-demarcation or forms of active-passive "frustration-tolerance" which given children resort to when experimentally blocked. Such active and passive techniques of ego-demarcation may be identified at first behavioristically according to whether a given child's frustration reactions are judged to be more or less emotional or rational, definite or ambivalent, direct or indirect (substitutive), stable or volatile, expanding or contracting, friendly-empathic or hostile-projective, rigid or resourcefully flexible. When seeing the child blocked or "under fire" and gauging his frustration reactions in terms of such behavior continua, we may confidently expect to learn something about his all-round *vitality* (his tempo, his over-reacting or under-reacting in out-go and absorption), *resourcefulness* (repertory range), and basic, idiomatic *adaptive style* (including so-called extraversion-intraversion problems).

The aim of this play technique, then, is to verify

1. the child's characteristic techniques of ego-demarcation—in marking off his spheres of influence (ego-spheres) in response to graduated and repetitive frustration situations, including indirect and direct intrusions, competitions, deprivations, exclusions, prohibitions, and obligations;

2. the range of intensity and diversity in such ego-demarcations: how far will the child go—how soon and what repertory of diverse techniques will he display, to begin with, in what sequence, with what degree of flexibility;

3. the degree and characteristic style of general activity or passivity in "frustration-tolerance" here.

Description of Technique

The general idea of this play technique is to give the child successively various toys with which he can play without interruption, but only for a short while. The experimenter then proceeds progressively to "intrude," "compete," "deprive," and "exclude." In addition to going through such series of motions in seven successive toy-units, the experimenter "insistently" gives the child one and the same stick to "play with"—after arbitrarily "putting away" the previous toys and before giving the child the next toys. The child thus gets one and the same stick (switch-like branch) intermittently no less than seven times.

In the first five, or so-called "single-toy units," the child gets attractive new toys each time: Mickey Mouses, Donald Ducks, toy trucks, toy telephones, and a Popeye doll respectively. The number and quality of these toys are such as to facilitate and provoke ego-demarcations during the progressive "intrusions," "competitions," "deprivations," and "exclusions." Thus, there are 3 *identical* Mickey Mouse dolls; 2 Donald Duck dolls—1 *big*, 1 *small*; 2 toy trucks—1 *big*, 1 *small*; 2 toy telephones—1 *clean*, 1 *"dirty"*; and 1 Popeye doll. When the experimenter proceeds in each of these single-toy units to intrude ("What shall I do?" and then, "Which is mine, which is yours?"), compete ("Whose is nicest, yours or mine?"), deprive ("And now I'll play with all of them and you watch"), and exclude (*repeating* the preceding statement after actually *acting* on it, "rubbing it in")—the very distribution of the toys (qualitatively and quantitatively) is calculated to lend itself for purposes of selective ego-demarcations.

In the last two, or so-called "all-toys units," as the name suggests, the child is given *all* these toys at once, after having had the experience of playing with them in single groups, under the above conditions of graduated frustration. Here essentially the same procedure is followed as in the single-toy units—except that the increase in quantity and qualitative diversity of toys permits an even wider range for cumulatively selective expression of frustration responses. In addition, in the *second* all-toys unit an express opportunity is provided for a "frustration fantasy"— that is, for acting out a selective play-fantasy in which the various roles for child and experimenter are determined by the child. ("Let's pretend I'll be somebody I am not and you'll be somebody you are not—who shall I be, who shall you be," etc.). Here, in addition to earlier more or less overt ego-demarcations, the child has a chance to "get even" with the experimenter in more symbolical dramatic play—or act out any other kind of play-fantasy idiosyncratically congenial to him, at the end of the frustration "trail."

In the seven interpolated "stick units," the child is further blocked and, at the same time, provided with the opportunity for utilizing the stick itself for any explicitly aggressive, destructive, or other congenial purpose. That is, not only is he confronted with the gradual and repeated "loss" of interesting or attractive toys (in the five single-toy units and in the two all-toys units) —but he is also up against the contrasting monotony of having to "play with the stick," time and again. The switch-like branch used for a stick lends itself to both aggressive and destructive activities or to any imaginative or symbolical play-fantasies the child feels like indulging in, under those circumstances.

More specifically, the following are the standard experimental instructions for this play technique.

ORDER AND DURATION OF PLAY-UNITS

1. Three Mickey Mouses (identical)
2. Stick (about 2½ feet long, ¼ inch thick)
3. Two Donald Ducks (one big, one small)
4. Stick
5. Two toy trucks (one big, one small)
6. Stick
7. Two toy telephones (one clean, one dirty)
8. Stick
9. One Popeye the Sailor
10. Stick

11. All the toys
12. Stick
13. All the toys
14. Stick

The experimenter thus has fourteen units: five single-toy units, two all-toys units, and seven stick units. The single-toy units (Nos. 1, 3, 5, 7, 9) last two minutes each; the all-toys units last three minutes each (the second may last as long as the "frustration fantasies" chosen by the child may require); the stick units (Nos. 2, 4, 6, 8, 10, 12, 14) last one minute each. The total experiment may thus take about twenty-five minutes or more.

STANDARD PROCEDURES
FOLLOWED BY EXPERIMENTER

Single-toy Units (Nos. 1, 3, 5, 7, 9)

1. Now you can play with *these.* (taking toys from satchel)
2. What shall *I* do? (after thirty seconds, if subject does not offer toys to experimenter)
3. Which is yours, which is mine? (regardless of what subject does earlier)
4. Which is nicest, yours or mine?
5. And now I'll play with *all* of them and you *watch,* all right? (Experimenter actually takes toys away from subject at one and one-half minutes.)
6. Repetition of statement under 5 above, after thirty seconds, while the experimenter is actually playing with toys—grouping them in simple order, "inspecting" them intently.
7. And *now* I'll put them away, all right? (immediately after 6)

In unit No. 9 (Popeye), since there is only *one* toy involved, the procedure is slightly modified as follows:

1. Now you can play with this.
2. What shall *I* do?
3. Whose is it, yours or mine?
4. And now I'll play with it and you watch, etc.—(All the procedures are otherwise as described under 1-7 above.)

In units Nos. 3, 5, and 7, questions 3 and 4 may be followed up and further checked through the following special leads:

3/1 Could I have *that* (toy preferred by the subject) and you have *this* (toy assigned to the experimenter)?

3/2 (If above question is answered in the negative or otherwise declined): Let's *pretend* that I can have *that* and you have this, all right?

4/1 Let's pretend *mine* is the nicest, all right? (if the subject declares *his* to be nicest)

All-toys Units (No. 11)

1. And *now* you can play with *all* the toys. (Experimenter going to satchel)

2. Shall *I* take them out or you?

3. (After thirty seconds, if the subject does not volunteer to share toys:) What shall *I* do? (If ignored by the subject, repeat at ten-second intervals, twice more.)

4. Which is yours, which is mine? (regardless of what happens under 3, above)

5. Can I have one of the Mickey Mouses? (And so on, down the line, asking, in turn, for each and every toy not offered by the subject voluntarily.)

6. And *now* I'll play with *all* of them and you watch, all right? (at two and one-half minutes—if resisted, try again at ten-second intervals—but never *force* this.)

7. Repeat above under 6, after playing from ten to thirty seconds—according to how long the subject resisted under 6.

8. And *now* I'll put them away, all right? (In case of extreme resistance here:) Shall *I* put them in or *you?*

In the second all-toys unit (No. 13), immediately before 6 above, the experimenter proceeds as follows:

5/1 You know what? Let's pretend I'll be somebody I am *not* and you'll be somebody *you* are not. Who shall *I* be, who shall *you* be? What shall *I* do, what shall *you* do?

5/2 Could *I* be so-and-so (role chosen by the subject) and *you* be so-and-so (role assigned to the experimenter)? (If it does not work:) Let's *pretend, etc.* (as above)

5/3 Which is nicest, to be so-and-so (role preferred by the

subject) or to be so-and-so (role assigned to the experimenter)?

5/4 And *now* who shall *I* be, who shall *you* be? What shall I do, what shall you do? (*following* the subject's instructions in whatever play fantasy chosen—never directing it)

Stick Units (*Nos. 2, 4, 6, 8, 10, 12, 14*)

1. And *now* you can play with the stick. (Experimenter hands it to the subject.)

2. Do you like the stick? (after fifteen seconds)

3. What are you doing, why are you doing that? Do you like to do that? (whatever the subject is doing with stick, aiming at explicit or symbolically camouflaged explanation by child)

4. *You* can play with it. (if the subject is trying to get rid of it, offering it to the experimenter)

5. *Now* we have only the stick to play with. (if the subject asks for other toys or otherwise "complains")

6. What can you do with it—what would you *like* to do with it? Why? (if the subject dawdles, is completely at a standstill or refuses to "play" with the stick any more)

7. And *now* I'll put it away, all right? (Experimenter takes it, at one minute, and suspends it.)

If the subject starts hitting at any object (including the experimenter) or starts to break the stick, it may be followed up through the following special leads:

8. Why did you do that?

9. Do you like to do that?

10. Does the stick like that?

If the subject, wittingly or unwittingly, hits the experimenter with the stick too severely (it happens very seldom), further complications may be prevented by the experimenter promptly asking: "Shall I do it to you?" (Such questions, as all others, are to be asked in a spontaneous, naïve, friendly, casual tone of voice, the experimenter exhibiting a serenely cheerful facial expression throughout.)

INSTRUCTIONS FOR EXPERIMENTER

From beginning to end, it is essential to keep the whole series of procedures on the level of serenely playing a game with the nursery school child. The initial motivation, too, is in terms of "show you some *new* toys I have—some toys you haven't seen yet."

This means that, throughout the experimental session, the experimenter acts the role of a non-punishing, none-too-serious, playful adult who, however, proceeds with the standard procedures firmly, if gently, all along.

Special care is taken not to allow the subject to engage the experimenter in tangential conversation in the first ten units. Such attempts of the subject (e.g., "What can you do with this?" "What is this?" "Where did you get it?") are turned back invariably with the gentle but firm counter-question: "What do you think?" "Guess," "What does it look like?" If the child keeps asking for additional toys, he is staved off: "*Now* we only have these to play with."

LOCATION

The experimental game is played preferably in a small room having no fixtures other than a rug covering the floor and a daybed. The latter is preferred because (if covered) it lends itself to hiding or discarding operations and, through the dark space under it, to occasional special fantasy production. There may be a few pictures on the wall, beyond the child's reach—since it is interesting to see if the subject will use these or anything else for purposes of "going out of the field."

The satchel (bag, briefcase or box) containing the toys is hung definitely out of the child's reach, on a hanger on the wall. No matter how often the subject asks to see it, the experimenter does not comply with such requests ("Let me see it, let *me* take them out," etc.) until the all-toys units (Nos. 11, 13). The experimenter puts away the toys and takes out the new ones, in proceeding from unit to unit, holding the satchel carefully beyond the child's reach—without overemphasizing this fact through clumsy, hurried, embarrassed manipulations. The experimenter maintains this mystery of "what else is in the bag" in a casual, self-assured, well-practiced manner. If the subject presses the issue too persistently or too anxiously, the experimenter gently but firmly replies: "You'll see it *later. Now* you can play with this" (whatever comes next).

In starting the play units, the experimenter puts the toys on the daybed and allows the child to manipulate or move them freely. The stick is *handed* to the child—not merely placed on the floor or daybed. The experimenter then sits down on the floor about three feet from the subject—since this facilitates his playing the role of a non-punishing, playful adult.

RECORDING

In order to obtain best results, the experimenter is in the room with the subject *alone.* The experimenter does no recording whatever, since carefully following the above instructions requires his full attention at all times.

All recording is done behind a one-way mirror or one-way screen, preferably verbatim—including the fullest possible description of all concomitant "psychomotor tensions," tone of voice, facial expression, change in posture and gait, manner of manipulation, and locomotion. Recorders, therefore, ought to be well trained or experienced in observing behavior and behavior styles—and in stenography as well.

The time is noted: not only at the very beginning and end but at the end of each unit as well. With two or more recorders, the time may be noted every thirty seconds or even more often.

In transcribing the records, it is expedient for analysis to separate the observational material in two parallel columns— one to cover verbalizations of the experimenter and the subject, the other the action patterns. Circumstances *before* and *after* playing the experimental games are noted—in what spirit did did the subject enter into the experiment, in what spirit did he continue immediately afterward (in nursery school, play yard, etc.). Any special data on extreme fluctuation in mood on the day of the experiment may be noted, in order to verify how far the context was everyday or unusual, apropos of what, etc.

Thus recorded, the structure of the experiment (through its clearly defined units) conduces to a relatively definite classifiability of otherwise potentially elusive child behavior, on a step-by-step basis, so that behavior patterns may be isolated or compared not only in terms of gross total response, "explosively," but within specific sub-contexts as well. All this makes for greater terminological ease in identifying phases or sequences of the frustration process and frustration reactions in terms of specific operations or situation types. This, in turn, ought to facilitate the *rating* of frustration reactions by two or more observers.

Clinicians or educators lacking such recording facilities may grossly summarize the main findings, immediately after testing subjects. For practical clinical or educational-diagnostic purposes, verbatim recording, while desirable, is not necessary.

Discussion and Summary of Exploratory Findings[3]

As mentioned earlier and discussed elsewhere,[4] in order to analyze and synthesize behavioral findings through this and similar blocking techniques, we found it necessary to distinguish a series of functional ego-blocking *situation-types* and, likewise, a series of *response-types*. On the basis of exploratory observations in the college nursery school and through other observations in earlier child guidance work, we came to assume that general classes of possible ego-blocking (see p. 284) essentially cover the whole range of *simple primary frustrations* (that is, other than what we may call *compound* or secondary frustrations of the "conflict of choice" sort). In all these situation-types the individual may be considered to be somehow directly blocked or kept from gratifying some particular drive—in starting, continuing, or completing a given behavior trend.

In handling such situation-types (or being handled in them) the child manifests certain modes of behavior. In contrast to what we may call *primary self-operating activities* (feeding, dressing, etc., comprising the various acts of self-help and related behavior items, as classified, for instance, in Doll's Social

---

3. This discussion is based on ninety-six experiments.
4. See pages 267-72.

Maturity Scale), we may here distinguish *secondary ego-orienting modes of conduct*—concerned with problems of specific *ego-spheres* in interpersonal relations.[5] The immediate *function* of such ego-orienting modes of conduct, accompanied by heightened self-feelings and self-ideas, is assumed to be establishing or re-establishing the form and proportion of my-ness, your-ness,

Situation-type	*Operational dynamics in Ego-blocking*	*Vector diagram*	*Vector problem*
1. Collisions	Head-on blocking (through direct attack, etc.)		Can or can't I go ahead, how?
2. Competitions	Squeeze-out blocking		Can or can't I get by (through), how?
3. Deprivations	Blocking through loss of objects (taking away)		Can or can't I go on or do without, how?
4. Separations-rejections	Blocking through loss of persons		As under 3.
5. Intrusions	Blocking through crowding or violation of privacy		Can or can't I be left alone, keep him out, how?
6. Exclusions	Shut-out blocking		Can or can't I get into, how?
7. Desertions	Expectation blocking (through-unkept promises)		As under 3 and 4.
8. Prohibitions	Fence-off blocking		As under 6.
9. Obligations	Fence-in blocking		Can or can't I get out, how?
10. Disabilities	Aspiration-blocking (performance failures)		Can or can't I get up there, how?

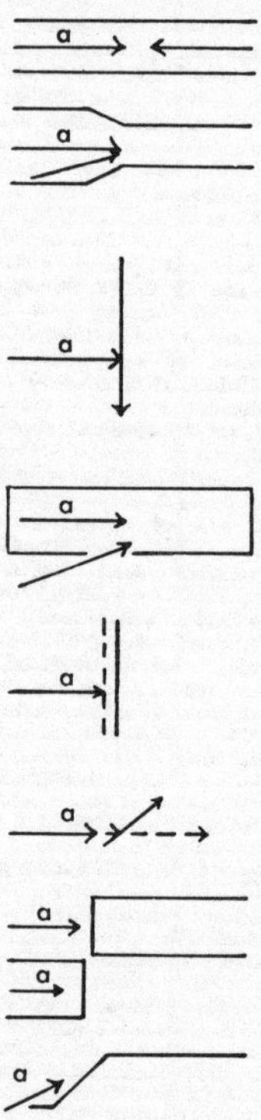

a = blocked ego-drive

Figure 26

5. See footnote 2.

our-ness, their-ness—as necessitated by the more or less unstable, because somehow ever discordant, relational balance between any two or more individuals, from early childhood on. Such functional "need" for somehow fixating relationships between what is "I" and "Not-I" is, in turn, assumed to reflect the child's quest for however ephemeral forms of *unity* and *certainty*—as problems of security and status. Whether it is a question of safely appropriating or holding onto or sharing a cathected object (toy), such ego-orienting behavior is inferred somehow to cope with the ever pressing problem of where am I, who am I (and, correspondingly, where do you stand, who are you), in line with Plant's concepts.[6] We assume it to be a broadly three-fold matter of synthesis and security for American nursery school children: what we may call (1) the problem of safe dependence, (2) the problem of safe independence or emancipatory inviolability, and (3) the problem of active ego-expansion or aggressive exploration. This *three-fold general dynamics* in shaping or defining the boundaries of *specific ego-spheres* (in maintaining, clarifying, unifying, spreading, tightening the child's immediate sphere of influence), may be assumed to lead to seemingly or actually conflicting (contradictory) ego-orientations or *ego-demarcations*, in one and the same situation or from one situation to another. According to the particular genetic sequence or proportion of admixture of these three basic goals of ego-demarcation, any given blocking situation may be selectively resolved by the child, chiefly, as now resisting unwelcome attempts at "weaning," now resisting threatening attempts against "autonomy" or "privacy," now attempting to overcome resistance to his own ego-expansive explorations and attempted conquests.

According to prevailing phases of social-emotional (including psychosexual) development reached by a given child, we assume characteristic *shifts* in such general ego-orientations or *polarization of ego-spheres*. Basic clues to particular meaning-values or "valences" may be assumed in terms of the clear-cut prevalence of the three focal goals in question, or as a matter of their ambivalent (conflicting) combinations. Thus, given chil-

---

6. James S. Plant, *Personality and the Cultural Pattern* (New York: The Commonwealth Fund, 1937).

dren's ego-organization may be chiefly concerned (1) with *shelter seeking* as a matter of dependence or anti-weaning resistance, or (2) with *castle building* as a matter of positive autonomy or privacy seeking, or (3) with *prison escaping* as a matter of acquisitive conquering, expansive ventures of exploration and self-maximation. In addition to gross age, sex, and cultural patterns of physical and social growth, temperamental trends may be assumed to tie up with such general dynamics of ego-development. Such temperamental characteristics are likely partially to determine the more or less unique manner in which maturation and socialization (the relatively common lot of all children in given cultures and families) come to shape a given child's ego-orientation or adaptive style, at any chronological age. For instance, the adaptive style or disposition of individuals may be inferentially ranged on a continuum of *active-passive adaptation*. A very extremely active-adaptor or "beaver" child may well hold on to castle building or prison escaping even in situations or stages of growth where less active-adaptors may mainly go in for shelter seeking. The reverse may apply to the extremely passive-adaptor or "chameleon" child whose ego-orientations may strikingly fluctuate under chiefly *situational* circumstances. Such temperamentally determined (and possibly "traumatically" reinforced) adaptive styles may vary from individual to individual in all gradations—just as extreme types of active and passive "styles of living" may be recognized between different zoological species (say, beavers versus chameleons).

With such broad assumptions behind them, the following general classes of ego-orienting behavior-response or *main ego-patterns* have been distinguished by us so far.

With the combined use of the two sets of working concepts (for simple blocking situation-types and ego-patterns), our ultimate aim could be *to define an individual child's style of "frustration-tolerance" in terms of characteristic sequences, intensities and ratios of his various ego-patterns, in relation to experimentally controlled varieties and sequences of simple blocking situations.*

Thus envisaged, data on frustration-profiles may be expected to throw some light on the developing personality of nursery

Continuum of Adaptive Ego-Rhythms	Main Ego-Patterns	Ego-Orienting Operations Involved
	1. ego-extending	grabbing, incorporation, possessive love, attacking, commanding-dominating, sadistic love
	2. ego-asserting	boasting-"impressing," competing, rebelling, doing-as-achieving, demanding, excluding
ACTIVITY (Assimilation preponderates)	3. ego-intruding	curiosity, peeking, intriguing-gossiping
	4. ego-disguising	"handling"-flattering, "motivating" people
	5. ego-shielding	staying put-resisting, maintaining status quo, avoiding new contacts, being secretive, hiding
	6. ego-sharing	giving generously, helping, sympathizing, exchanging
RECIPROCITY (Assimilation and accommodation near or in equilibrium)	7. ego-fusing	give-and-take (balanced masochistic-sadistic?) love relationships
	8. ego-supporting	leaning-depending, wishing for approval and recognition, seeking help or sympathy
	9. ego-yielding	obeying-conforming, submitting passively, masochistic love
PASSIVITY (Accommodation preponderates)	10. ego-recoiling	daydreaming (fantasy), narcissistic-regressive trends (thumb-sucking, masturbation, etc.)
	11. ego-retreating	fearing, running away, giving up
	12. ego-destroying	hurting-injuring, punishing oneself—up to suicide

school children, in answer to the question: *can* he take it, and *how, where, when?* Eventual charts and rating scales of ego-rhythms or ego-orienting effectiveness may be anticipated, in terms of some such behavior continua as:

(a) objectivity-egocentricity (rationality-emotionality)

(b) ascendance-submission

(c) definiteness-ambivalence

(d) directness-substitutiveness (devious)

(e) stability-volatility

(f) friendliness and empathy vs. hostility and projectiveness

(g) socio-emotional expansiveness vs. contractiveness

(h) reality-departures (Lewin's "going out of the field," neurotic postponement, retrospection, etc.)

(i) flexibility-rigidity-creative resourcefulness-narrowness

Adaptive styles thus envisaged within the specified range of the main ego-patterns, rated in reference to blocking situations of specified character on the above continua of ego-orienting effectiveness, might give verifiable clues to personality structures and eventually help reduce the now glaring hiatus between "objective-behavioristic" and "deep-level, personalistic-dynamic" concepts.

Obviously while the outlining of such assumptions is necessary for more direct consideration of the technique and the findings obtained through it, we are bound to run into all sorts of difficulties and problems in the course of actually trying to treat the research data in their light. We now propose to take the reader into the very midst of some of the problems involved.

Here is a first attempt at analytical treatment of data, in the case of Colin, aged three years, nine months.

Detailed and Summarized Analysis of Ego-Blocking Game No. 1

ANALYSIS OF EGO-SPHERE MOVEMENTS

1. Initial cathexis (in Mickey Mouse unit):
   a. First response to possessive suggestion (Which is yours, which is mine): 2-1 (2 Mickey Mouses for subject, 1 for experimenter).

b. First response to competitive suggestion (Which is nicer, yours or mine): positive egocentric (very definite, aggressive in asserting his to be nicest).

c. First response to deprivation and exclusion (Now I'll play and you watch): actively curious watching after acceptance (*What are they doing?*), followed by bold ego-asserting (*What'll I do?*).

d. First response to arbitrary termination (Now I'll put it away): acceptance (record incomplete as to details).

2. Cumulative cathexis, sequence I (progressive reactivity to recurring obligations, in stick units—from stick unit on):

a. Second unit: Vehement object-aggression: stands up on couch and slashes air with stick "making wind," with tongue moving in and out with violent gusto; then abruptly and definitely rejects stick, demanding that experimenter *Put it away, because I want you to put it away.*

b. Third unit: Immediately resumes violent object-aggression, this time via hitting couch violently, with tongue moving in and out —"spanking it"; visibly enjoying himself, looking released and saying boldly that he is spanking couch because *I like to.*

c. Fourth unit: Immediately continues violent object-aggression, successively whipping the air, hitting the couch and table—laughing, tongue moving in and out, saying *I like to;* then demanding to know why stick is given to him and firmly demanding that experimenter *Put it away, I said I want some more toys.*

d. Fifth unit: Immediately continues violent object-aggression. hitting couch, table and window, jumping up and down; bangs stick against floor and kicks it; hits experimenter, saying *I'm hitting you,* tries to pull experimenter from floor, putting stick under his arm—rejecting it and trying to force experimenter to give him other toys; looks gay, bold and firmly determined throughout.

e. Sixth unit: Proceeds immediately to object-aggression, breaks stick, climbs up and down couch, pulls up couch cover peeking under it—not paying any more attention to broken stick which he holds in hand while thus going out of field.

3. Cumulative cathexis, sequence II (progressive reactivity to recurring intrusive, possessive and competitive suggestions—What shall I do, Which is yours, which is mine, Which is nicer, yours or mine —in Donald Duck, Truck and Phone units):

a. Donald Duck unit: On intrusion commands experimenter to *Watch these,* thus excluding him; first claims both toys for himself (ignoring experimenter); under pressure gives up small one: *You have the little one,* ignores competitive suggestion, absorbed in aggressive play with big toy, knocking its head off after twisting it around, putting it back, etc.

b. Truck unit: On intrusion, assigns small toy to experimenter—

You play with the car, I want to have the big truck . . . I want the big one, declaring it to be the nicest.

   c. Phone unit: In intrusion, tells experimenter: *Just a minute(!);* takes clean phone for himself, boldly tells experimenter in competition *Yours is the dirtiest.*

4. Cumulative cathexis, sequence III (progressive reactivity to recurring deprivations-exclusions and arbitrary terminations in single-toy and all-toys units—Now I'll play and you watch, Now I'll put it away):

   a. While the first time (in Donald Duck unit) he actively and cheerfully approves of deprivation-exclusion (*All right; fine, fine*) after crawling very near to experimenter and trying to interfere with latter's play—he becomes violently resistant on all subsequent deprivations; looks visibly annoyed, says vehemently: *No, no, I want them, I want the X, give me the X*—crawling after experimenter, trying to get the toys back, repeating vehemently shouted denials, demands, and commands, hiding coveted toys behind his back in boldly open resistance; spirited locomotions and accessory body movements.

   b. Action on deprivations (after Donald Duck unit) so vehement that it shades imperceptibly over into attitude on terminations; here, however, he is less resistant and compromises by aggressively approving-commanding the experimenter: *Put them away all right* (not just passively acquiescing but actively using this part of routine, as in stick units).

5. Cumulative cathexis, sequence IV (reactivity in all-toys unit to indirect and direct intrusions: What shall I do, Can I have the, etc.):

   After completely ignoring first indirect intrusion, tells experimenter: *You run the* (small) *car,* on the second; on direct intrusions declines all other toys except two phones and Popeye-doll: *You can have one of them* (one by one); violent manipulations, locomotions—throws toys on couch, floor, under couch, coos at toy before throwing it under couch, then recovers it moving on stomach with gusto; crawls on floor, jumps across room, etc.; insists on parallel play (*Oh, you play with those toys*), clearly wanting to be rid of experimenter in undisturbed play with his toys.

6. Frustration fantasy:

   Clearly assumes relationship of superiority over experimenter; first he is "daddy" and experimenter is merely the "big brother"; he "goes to work (adult superior role), while experimenter can "go to school"; he "makes people well" (aping father's profession); then switches to being "big sand-man": *I'm the big sand-man and you're the little boy.*

7. Summary:
   a. Initial cathexis: definite, direct, ascendant in laying out ego-sphere.
   b. Cathexis sequence I: Vehement object-aggression followed by bold ego-asserting and ego-extending; continued release of hostility via lusty object-aggression in clear-cut ego-asserting manner; vehement object-aggression continued, with visible enjoyment of release as before, followed by clear-cut, bold ego-asserting; increased and expanding object-aggression, followed by bold ego-extending; increased, continued object-aggression prior to ego-intruding while actively going out of field.
   c. Cathexis sequence II: Sustained, increasing directness and ascendance in marking off ego-sphere—not only claims bigger or cleaner toy, declaring it nicest, but does not hesitate to use shutting out technique and to use of derogatory terms in characterizing experimenter's toy.
   d. Cathexis sequence III: After initial agreement to deprivation-exclusion resorts to vehement resistance on successive deprivations: strong ego-shielding mingled with bold ego-asserting; less resistant on terminations, but clings to having upper hand through actively dominating use of this routine, as of other experimental routines.
   e. Cathexis sequence IV: Tries to shut out experimenter on indirect intrusions, ignoring, commanding experimenter; shares ego-assertively and grudgingly three out of ten toys on direct intrusion; insists on parallel play to shut out experimenter; spirited manipulations, locomotions and accessory body movements, throughout.
   f. Frustration fantasy: Displays ascendant superiority toward experimenter in assuming and assigning roles in active dramatic play of domestic and quasi-domestic content.

We may attempt discussion of some of the methodological issues involved by contrasting this exploratory analysis with that of Colt, another boy of three years, eleven months.

Detailed and Summarized Analysis of Ego-Blocking Game No. 1

ANALYSIS OF EGO-SPHERE MOVEMENTS

1. Initial cathexis (in Mickey Mouse unit):
   a. First response to possessive suggestion (Which is yours, which is mine): ambivalent-submissive (first, gives experimenter one

and then another; then, while giving him a third, takes back two for himself).

b. First response to competitive suggestion (Which is nicer, yours or mine): ego-disguising (experimenter's is declared nicest, *Because I like yours better. Where's the cars?*), handling-motivating adult to demand what he wants.

c. First response to deprivation-exclusion (Now I'll play and you watch): utilizing occasion to press dependent demand, *Where's the cars*—repeated four times.

d. First response to arbitrary termination (Now I'll put it away): continuing dependent passive acceptance (*What else?*, smiling).

2. Cumulative cathexis, sequence I (progressive reactivity to recurring obligations, in stick units—from second stick unit on):

a. Second unit: Rationally-dependently, very clearly sizing up situation, asks reason for procedure. *Again? Why two times do I have to play with stick?*); admits he does not like it but turns this rejection into indirect, ego-disguising form: *No, I like a big one* (smiles), then turns this into ambivalent-submissive compromising, spontaneously: *I like a little one* (!), then tries to go from field by paying attention to outside noises, ignored by most children (*Who's there?*).

b. Third unit: Again rationally asks reason for procedure: *Why so many times?* (smiling!); tries to evade issue of liking by saying he likes stick on the road; after trying to go from field by asking irrelevant questions, tries to palm it off on experimenter: *You play with it* (diplomatic generosity); when this does not work, hits with stick at curtain rod, with dependent-sly smile fixed on experimenter.

c. Fourth unit: Repeats stereotyped-rational question (*Why do I play with the stick so many times?*), then repeats going-from-field question (irrelevant); verbalizes about breaking stick to *Make a little one;* goes from field by slyly turning off light several times (violation of adult taboo?)—not giving this up until adult attitude on this deed is verified.

d. Fifth unit: Repeats stereotyped-rational question (*Why the stick so many times*) twice; then pokes it near experimenter's eyes and proposes fantasy in which he can assume adult-superior role with stick (*Pretend I'm here and I'm Mr. Stone taking pictures and you're a little boy*).

e. Sixth unit: After taking it, looking grim, immediately reverts to fantasy assuring him superior role toward experimenter (*Now then, you're a little boy and I'm Mr. Stone . . . You look in that mirror and I do this and you go there and stand still right near the door*); then becomes adult who takes notes of children's behavior (!): *And I'll be the girl who writes down how many children are here;* after thus going from field, declines stick by offering it to experimenter (*No, you*) and, with roguish-diplomatic smile, utilizes occasion to finally articulate his real wish: *Now put it away;* asks for it again, then tries to order experimenter to put it away again, then says *It's yours,* finally coming out openly: *I don't want it any more, I'm tired to have it any more.*

3. Cumulative cathexis, sequence II (progressive reactivity to recurring intrusive, possessive and competitive suggestions—What shall I do, Which is yours, which is mine, Which is nicer, yours or mine—in Donald Duck, Truck and Phone units):

   a. Donald Duck unit: On intrusion, quickly assigns smaller toy to experimenter and anticipates-expropriates competitive question by asking it himself; then resumes ego-disguising by letting experimenter's be the nicest (*Yeah, pretend mine is the worsest!*).

   b. Truck unit: Ambivalent-submissive diplomacy followed by acting out of real wish (gives experimenter big truck, saying it is nicest, then takes it back and plays with both toys); upon intrusion now gives experimenter small toy, declares his to be the nicest, after grabbing it assertively but with a roguish-dependent smile—saying: *Changed my mind (!)*.

   c. Phone unit: Ambivalent-submissive diplomacy on intrusion followed by real assertiveness (first gives experimenter new phone, then quickly takes it back and gives him a dirty one, talking in extremely coy, throaty tone of voice); first says his is nicest but shifts and says experimenter's is the nicest, finally stops ego-disguising and declares: *I play with that one* (new one) *and you play with the worsest one,* in extremely coy voice.

4. Cumulative cathexis, sequence III (progressive reactivity to recurriung deprivations-exclusions and arbitrary terminations in single-toy units—Now I'll play and you watch, Now I'll put it away):

   a. At first, after passive acceptance of deprivation-exclusion and smilingly watching, goes out of field by starting to play with chair in room; then, after short, visibly impatient watching, coyly attempts competition (*I bet I could do that*); next, becomes visibly restless and impatient at experimenter's playing, resorting, however, only to rational indirection in attempted intrusions (*Why doesn't somebody answer? Why don't you hang up?*); next, having himself announced deprivation routine (in Popeye unit, after completely ignoring numerous attempts at intrusion), goes from field, reverting to play with chair, looking under couch; watches and accepts quite patiently the last time, though still trying to break into experimenter's play, verbally-conversationally, at least).

   b. At first, termination enables him to become distracted by noises (in Donald Duck unit); but from then on, terminations signal expectant wishes for "what else," with intermittent curiosity for what is in the bag and wish for having the bag itself, as an adult-tool; this ego-intruding really shades into ego-extending of a very indirect, devious sort in the all-toys unit where he asserts himself by anticipating experimenter's routine and utilizing it for commanding experimenter (*Get your bag down, What did you put there, What else can I play with?*).

5. Cumulative cathexis, sequence IV (reactivity in all-toys unit to indirect and direct intrusions: *What shall I do? Can I have the? etc.*):
   Even before indirect intrusions, immediately assumes coveted superior role toward experimenter (adult role), after suspiciously making sure that he got all the toys (*Is that all?*), including the stick which is a coveted power-tool of adult role (camera fantasy); *You play with all the toys, This and this* (giving experimenter all the toys except the stick!); *You sit down and I'll take them out for you, all of those things are yours and you play. Give me the stick.*

6. Frustration fantasy:
   He continues camera fantasy, earlier resorted to, in stick units; also expresses wish for having bag itself, obviously as power-tool of coveted adult-role of superiority toward experimenter; he tells experimenter to play with all the toys *While I watch*, thus reversing relationship as he envisages it (i.e., he becomes ruling adult, experimenter the helpless, inferior follower).

7. Summary:
   a. Initial cathexis: Devious ambivalent-submissive, alternately ego-disguising and ego-supporting (dependent) start in laying out ego-sphere.
   b. Cathexis sequence I: indirect, verbal ego-asserting reinforced by ego-disguising (adult handling) techniques, plus ego-intruding; continued highly indirect-ambivalent ego-asserting, with further ego-intruding and ego-disguising, mild and disguised object-aggression; continued stereotyped and indirect-verbal ego-asserting, disguising verbalized object-aggression and further ego-intruding (now used for devious ego-asserting and tentative ego-extending purposes); further stereotypy of indirect ego-asserting followed by ego-recoiling fantasying to achieve coveted ego-extending via further indirection; continued ego-recoiling with obvious ego-asserting and ego-extending purposes, followed by first overt ego-asserting, immediately alternating it with devious ego-disguising.
   c. Cathexis sequence II. Sustained, ambivalent-submissive indirectness in ego-disguising marking off of ego-sphere, with progressive crescendo in parallel, quite obvious ego-asserting.
   d. Cathexis sequence III: After initial passive acceptance of deprivations and reality departures through distractions, tries ego-disguising techniques to recover play opportunities; after initial

ego-intruding distraction, on terminations alternates between dependent (ego-supporting) and ego-intruding approaches, culminates in deviously ego-extending assumption of experimenter's role and indirectly ego-extending wish for bag itself.

e. Cathexis sequence IV: Finally unmasked ego-extending in immediately assuming adult role and reversing relationship of superiority-inferiority between subject and experimenter, with pointed use of stick (in contrast to toys assigned to experimenter).

f. Frustration fantasy: Stick used, as previously in stick units, for playing out ascendant role-reversals between experimenter and subject, in dramatic play relating to framed and unframed nursery school situations (without "referring back" to his life at home with his family).

If we compare Colt with Colin, step by step, we find the following one-to-one rank order comparisons indicated on the behavior continua discussed earlier.

Colin	*Colt*
more egocentric-emotional	more objective-rational
more ascendant	more submissive
more definite	more ambivalent
more direct	more substitutive (devious)
more volatile	more stable
more expansive	more contractive
more reality-facing	more escapist
more rigid	more flexible

Further summing up, Colin is indicated as more on the side of active-adaptor (beaver) children, with Colt more in the direction of the passive-adaptor (chameleon) end of the continuum: Colin's ego-demarcations indicate polarization of egospheres chiefly in terms of castle building (independence), while Colt seems to oscillate and veer considerably in the direction of shelter seeking (dependence). Further, in terms of total frustration tolerance in this particular situation, Colin seems definitely more released, with more clear-cut extra-punishing direction in his all-round management of hostility.

The next step would consist of scrutinizing the *clusters* of *comparative behavior ranks* in quest of possible or likely *dynamic* connections to be inferred from such frustration-profiles or comparative scores of frustration tolerance. A considerable number of such one-to-one comparisons would be needed for the purpose of distinguishing and discovering the greatest possible variety of clusters as clues to varieties of personality structure. Validation and completion of such inferential work would be in terms of behavior in other experimental situations in the nursery school and at home. With reference to the latter, the following type of outline was used. (Since then, we have worked out a shortened revision of the California Behavior Inventory of Conrad, consisting of thirty-one behavior categories.)

Teacher's Outline
for Frustration and Gratification Profile
in Unframed Nursery School Situations

COLT

I. REACTION TO FRUSTRATION
  A. Characteristic Response
    1. *When Frustrated by Objects:* Gets slightly exasperated with repeated frustration, but is apt to enjoy the falling down as much as the building up. Inclined to kick other people's buildings down when his falls. Will remove himself from situation when his feeling gets too intense, calls for adult help only as a last resort.
    2. *When Frustrated by Children:* Diplomatically argues, reasons, and generally overpowers with words until child retreats. Not much physical aggression. If reasoning doesn't work, will call in adult. Occasionally cries when frustrated too far.
    3. *When Frustrated by Adults:* Too reasonable to receive much frustration. A little sober for a minute, then off to something else. Sometimes argues a little, but does not tease.
  B. Degree of Consistency of Frustration (Ego-Blocking) Response
    Definitely consistent.
  C. Main Sources of Gloom: When Candice refuses to play with him; when he can't argue the situation his way.
    Main Sources of Anger: Shows little.
    Main Sources of Fear: Fearful of Alec's attacks, or any too vigorous aggression.

Failure and Defeat: Not being accepted in social situations by certain people on his own terms.

D. Attitude to Others When Frustrated

Rather ignores others, or becomes slightly verbally aggressive or teases them on the sly.

II. REACTION TO GRATIFICATION

A. Characteristic Response

1. *When Gratified by Objects:* Not particularly gratified by objects. Shows more pleasure, perhaps, in some muscular achievement with objects. Objects in general are much less gratifying than personal relationships.

2. *When Gratified by Children:* Immensely gratified at being allowed to be the father in playing with Candice. Shows this by his constant verbal conversation and cooperation, contributing ideas, but fixing up situation so that Candice's ideas are acceptable too. Gets gratification out of being included in any social group.

3. *When Gratified by Adults:* Seems to expect conversation, occasional assistance and rapport from adults. Sometimes a little impish and teasing when frustrated but fundamentally responds to adult reasoning.

B. Degree of Consistency in Ego-Blocking Response

Generally speaking, yes.

C. Main Sources of Joy

Mostly on the social level, being accepted and acceptable.

D. Main Sources of Success

When complimented on a good building.

E. Attitude to Others When Gratified

Not much affected by gratification. Occasionally includes the teacher, but usually not much response.

III. RESPONSE TO ROUTINES

Tolerates but not very interested in them. At his best, participates in a fairly sloppy way, with an air of getting it over with quickly; at other times tries to slide out of the situation with all kinds of verbal justifications.

IV. RESPONSE TO INNOVATIONS

Accepts them all as a matter of course, participates without much excitement. and is capable of refusing to participate if he feels like it. Has an air of being at home with innovations.

In a telescoped manner, the reader now has some rough idea of the inferential manner and direction in which short-term (limited-behavioristic) and long-term (dynamic-personalistic) treatment of data may be envisaged, on the basis of this particular play technique. It is obvious that we glossed over a good many initial and intermediate problems of interpretive inference—a cardinal issue in any research procedure.

The matter of *interpretive reliability,* much as that of *observer reliability,* seems to us an essentially simple mechanical issue. Once a group of available research investigators can systematically agree on what to call or recognize as what type of behavior response—in short, *what to become reliable about* not only statistically speaking but also in terms of dynamically meaningful criteria and clues *which can be validated* both experimentally and clinically—the matter of reliability would not seem to loom as a really serious methodological question here.

One important aspect of the problem of multi-observer and multi-interpreter reliability has to do with primary genotypic translation in *application of ego-patterns.* The ancient problem of imputing dynamic motives to essentially statically recorded "objective" behavior is involved here. While a good many behavior items, especially, though not necessarily, those accompanied by or consisting of *verbalizations,* seem at first inspection easy to classify, there are definitely more equivocal responses encountered here. Apart from looking to *total behavior contexts* (wholes) of varying size for "logico-meaningful" evidence, two points may be made here, on the basis of our own experience in observing and interpreting. First, that observers and interpreters of such data need or would be required to have at least a year of continuous intensive experience in solo and multiple observing of child behavior (both in experimental room and in nursery school). Second, that they need or would be required to have similar, simultaneous experience in discussing their primary findings weekly in post-session clinics, immediately after individual experiments, in order to learn explicitly to articulate terminological agreements and seeming or real disagreements. This may seem a both trite and somewhat tautological point—trite because it merely emphasizes the need for practice in "learning to see" here; metaphysical and tautological because it seems to assume that by greatly multiplying the number of weak crutches we can get one strong one or that by learning to talk a common observational-interpretive language (much as was the case in the personality studies conducted at the Harvard Psychological Clinic),[7] we can substitute additive "majority voting" techniques for more intrinsically valid methods of reasoning. Actually, all this is but another version of the medical emphasis on the need for extended clinical or bed-side practice in diagnostic-prognostic observation, there being no short cut in such matters.

In addition to gross application of the ego-patterns (whether a given behavior response is ego-intruding or ego-shielding, etc.) the next problem would be the matter of more refined rating and comparison, on rating scales—in trying to distinguish between more or less intensive modes of ego-asserting, ego-shielding, ego-disguising.

For such purposes, in addition to exercises in diagnostic observation in experimental post-session clinics, extended practice in using the Time-Sampling Vector-Chart[8] will likely be helpful. It is based on observations of free situations in nursery school and consists of a clock-like dial graduated into sixty peripheral units if it is a sixty-minute chart. (Thirty-minute dials, or shorter or longer dials, may be useful in given cases.) Detailed diary observations of the child's activities are plotted onto the dial, comprising all types of solitary or social behavior during standard time-sampling periods. Contacts with children are differentiated from those with adults, contacts with single children from those with groups of two or more, through the use of four concentric circles. Contacts or activities involving the use of different materials (sand, water, etc.) are distinguished, as are routine from "free periods," through the use of different colors. The direction of social contacts (whether initiated by the child or those about him) are shown through "sociometric" arrows. The sequence, duration, frequency, origin and direction of specific activity and contact types provide an initial basis for more refined diagnostic application of ego-patterns. If obtained at comparable time-sampling periods on several children, they

7. H. A. Murray, *et al.*, *Explorations in Personality* (New York: Oxford University Press, 1938).

8. In working out the chart, the helpful collaboration of the following psychology students at Sarah Lawrence College is gratefully acknowledged: Mabel Carter Darrow, Eleanor Kreusi, Elizabeth Lykes and, especially, Virginia Blodgett.

may be superimposed like so-called spot-maps in order to "read off" similarities and differences between given subjects (or in comparing a child with himself).

The general principle of *control*, while not directly applicable in using this type of play technique for total personality study,

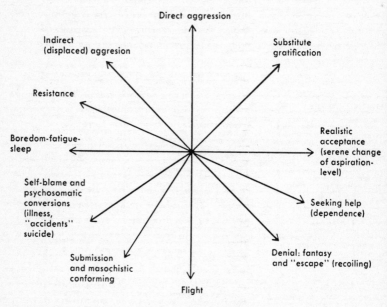

Figure 28

may conceivably be invoked in generalized (non-idiomatic-total) approaches. In studying gross individual differences in ego-demarcations and frustration tolerance, the experimental group may be gauged against a control group through elimination of the stick units in the latter, or, in yet another control group, through substitution of positively gratifying play units for stick units. The experimental and control groups may then be compared in terms of gross (average) scores of ego-demarcation and frustration tolerance in the successive toy units.

In total-idiomatic study of personality, the method of control lies in the one-to-one comparison of single rank orders and clusters of rank orders, as mentioned above. Scales of ego-rhythms and "ego-hardness" may be envisaged here in answer to the question: How far will the child go, how soon, with what repertory and sequence of techniques, with what degree of general activity, reciprocity, or passivity?

Thus, on given cathexis sequences, the type of chart depicted by Figure 27 may show ego-rhythms or movements of ego-spheres, in and out of "phases" of activity, reciprocity and passivity.

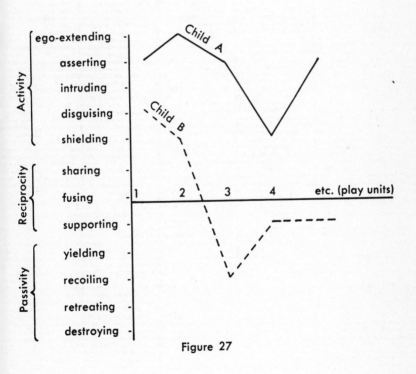

Figure 27

Evaluation of personality structure in terms of frustration-tolerance and ego-demarcation would imply a whole series of such and similar charts, with reference to the sequence and intensity ratio of ego-patterns displayed. Such sequence and intensity ratio of ego-patterns would bear some relation to the range of *universal* limiting possibilities in frustration response (in our contemporary society). The clusters of one-to-one rank orders and the separate charts of ego-rhythms may likely gain in dynamic meaning with reference to the vector chart (Figure 28).

CHAPTER 13

Blocking Technique Number 2

Aim of Technique

AS IN BLOCKING GAME NUMBER 1, our intention is to see the child somehow "under fire." Here, however, we plan to proceed somewhat differently.

In blocking game number 1 we aimed for repetitive-graduated blocking. In this second blocking game, it is not so much the repetitive part of the procedure which is emphasized. On the one hand, we wish to scrutinize the child's reactions to a still wider variety of simple primary frustrations—such as indirect and direct collisions, intrusions, competitions, exclusions, and prohibitions. On the other hand, we wish to provide an opportunity for the child to have more directly inverse authority relationship with the experimenter, in order to see how complementary his reaction is in comparison with his response in a more usual power field of the adult-child relationship. For this purpose, this game starts and continues as a "doubles" game rather than alternating in terms of "now *you* play and then *I* play with these toys." Even in those units where there is some explicit alternation of roles between the experimenter and the subject, it is not a matter of alternation in passivity but solely in play-roles as such (see Description of Techniques following). From the start, the child has a more continuous chance for having "the upper hand" or holding his own (if he so chooses to act).

Insofar as the playing is at all times in the form of a continuous, two-fold, active reciprocity between the experimenter and the subject (with neither of them in the role of one-way intruding from "without," "horning into the game" from the level of "reality"), the ego-demarcations invoked are more symbolical in that they remain throughout on the level of dramatic play fantasies. As we shall see, the nature of the experimental play fantasies is such that, from the viewpoint of sophisticated adults, such symbolical ego-demarcations do not present any special problem of "translation," with reference to the behavior continua discussed earlier (blocking game number 1 under Aim of Technique). Of course, the degree of correspondence or lack of consistency in the styles of ego-demarcation shown in the different blocking games is of further interest here.

The purpose of this play technique is, then, to verify:

1. the child's style of ego-demarcation in a further sequence of simple blocking situations, such as indirect and direct collisions, intrusions, competitions, exclusions;

2. the degree to which the child's reactions are complementary in inverse power fields of the adult-child relationship—in comparison with his responses in the more usual power fields of such relationship;

3. the degree of correspondence between the child's style of ego-demarcation shown in more continuously symbolical fields of play fantasy—in comparison with his style invoked in relatively less homogeneous fields of play fantasy.

Description of Technique

The general idea is to devise a series of play-situations in which the experimenter and child may meet, collide and otherwise interact. Each has and is represented in such interactions by dolls or trains or houses. In such experimenter-train:subject-train interactions, experimenter-doll:subject-train interactions, experimenter-doll:subject-house, or experimenter-house:subject-doll interactions, the direction of component and resultant forces is expressed chiefly or solely in terms of the movement and "control" of the symbolical ego-toys (dolls, trains, houses). There is, then, a certain amount of indirection or behavioral symbolism at play here which we assume to permit the child a rather free expression of congenial ego-drives. Through the maintenance of a field of continuous playing, the opportunity for "losing oneself" in spontaneous self-expression is likely to be of optimal proportions.

In order to provoke the child's selective-congenial responses in a more definitive manner, the experimenter's part in such interactions is standardized—so that the gross circumstances under which the child defines the situation may be held constant. Specifically, the following are the experimental instructions for this play technique.

ORDER AND DURATION OF PLAY-UNITS

1. How can I pass? (experimenter-train:subject-train interaction)

2. My doll stops your car. (experimenter-doll:subject-train interaction)

3. My doll wants to get on your train. (experimenter-doll: subject-train)

4. Who shall crash? (experimenter-train:subject-train)

5. Who gets there first? (experimenter-train:subject-train)

6. Can my doll come in your house? (experimenter-doll: subject-house)

7. Can your doll come in my house? (experimenter-house: subject-doll)

8. My house where you must not touch anything (experimenter-house:subject-doll)

9. Your house where I must not touch anything (experimenter-doll: subject-house)

The experiment thus has nine units. Each play-unit consists of three successive trials, requiring roughly from thirty to forty-five seconds, except for Nos. 6, 7, 8 and 9 which may take a little longer. Total playing time is thus roughly ten minutes or so, including preparations or "stage-setting" operations, from play-unit to play-unit. Extreme deviations in duration may be expected to reflect extremes in tempo and mood of given children.

STANDARD PROCEDURES FOLLOWED BY EXPERIMENTER

1. a. You push your car and I push my car. You come from there and I come from here. Let's meet in the middle. How can my car pass? How can I pass? (Experimenter and subject sit or kneel on the floor, facing each other. Experimenter follows subject's tempo so that, insofar as possible, "meeting" does take place in middle of track. Experimenter's further behavior is subject to subject's reaction—maintaining his original direction insofar as subject's reaction permits it.)
   b. Now let's do it once more. You come from there, etc. (Second trial as per above.)
   c. *And*—the last time. You come from there, etc. (Third trial.)
2. a. Now I come with my doll and you come with your car [train]. Let's meet in the middle. And my doll *stops* your car. What happens? What shall happen? (Experimenter's behavior starts and continues as under 1.)
   b. Repeat. Second trial.
   c. Repeat. Third trial.
3. a. Now you come with your train and my doll wants to get on your train. Can my doll get on your train? (Experimenter's doll, off the track, is waiting for subject's train to come along, at the middle of the track. Experimenter follows whatever instructions or conditions subject sets, as to where and how to put it, if permitted at all—after starting to put it in a standing position on the first of the two cars which the child now has.)
   b. and c. Second and third trials.
4. a. Now you come with your car and I come with my car. Who shall crash? What happens? What shall happen? (Block tracks are now set at right angle so that there is an "intersection point" for "crashing.")
   b. and c. Second and third trials.
5. a. Now you come from there and I come from here. Who gets there first? (Parallel tracks.)
   b. and c. Second and third trials.
6. a. Now you build a house. You build a house and (when house

is finished) my doll wants to come into your house. Can my doll come into your house? (If declined:) What happens if my doll *does* come into your house? (Experimenter does enter in either event.) My doll comes into your house. What happens? What shall happen? (Blocks earlier used for track and train serve for house building.)

   b. and c. Second and third trials.

7. a. Now *I* build a house. Now it is *my* house and your doll wants to come into my house. What shall I say? Yes or no? (Experimenter follows subject's instruction.) Now what happens? (after subject's doll enters on whatever basis) Now what shall I do? What shall happen?

   b. and c. Second and third trials.

8. a. Now I build another house. It is my house and it is a house where you must not touch anything, all right? You come with your doll and ask me if you can touch anything. (After subject does so:) What shall I say? (If subject does "touch":) But it is a house where you must not touch anything. What happens? What shall happen?

   b. and c. Second and third trials.

9. a. Now *you* build a house. (After subject does so:) It is *your* house where I must not touch anything. And I come with my doll and want to touch things, all right? (After experimenter does "touch":) Now what happens? What shall happen?

   b. and c. Second and third trials.

10. And now what shall we play—anything you want. (Opportunity for carry-over play fantasy, without experimentally set structuring.)

"Car," "train," "track," "house" are played and built with standard wooden blocks used in nursery schools. (Size and number of blocks: two long blocks for tracks, two long cars which may be coupled.) A small five-inch-tall doll is used.

INSTRUCTIONS FOR EXPERIMENTER, LOCATION, RECORDING

Instructions for blocking game number 1 hold. Blocks or doll not in use in given play-units are kept out of the subject's reach, to prevent distraction or the introduction of uncontrolled variables.[1]

---

1. See discussion concerning tangential reactions of subject, or any aggressive or destructive behavior (hitting, breaking).

Discussion and Summary of Exploratory Findings[2]

As in the case of the motivation game, due to a crowded research calendar and limited facilities we were not able to experiment extensively with the whole game technique—except for its first two units (especially since the latter comprised part of the gratification technique). However, we shall include a comparative analysis of a few cases where the complete technique has been applied, in order to indicate the possibilities for further work here.

Before doing so, we intend to give the reader an opportunity for scrutinizing with us the raw records in the case of the first unit of this game—a unit which we found of greatest diagnostic value, together with the second unit (1. How can my car pass? 2. My doll stops your car—what happens?) In this manner, more "refined" inferential treatment may be set off against the first raw research assumptions "in action": a procedure usually not detailed in "finished" research reports. Problems of diagnostic interpretation can thus be made more explicit for other investigations.

ABIGAIL

How SHALL MY CAR PASS? Abigail sat down very swiftly after coming over to the tracks. She quickly got hold of the train and proceeded to "meet me" very cheerfully, eyeing me and smiling at me the while. As we "met," she first proceeded to resolve the blocking situation into a gleefully welcome quasi-close collision. She gently and tentatively seemed to go about bumping my car, shouting cheerfully, *Ta-ta-ta* (2 or 3 times). The whole thing lasted but ten seconds or so, and Abigail looked increasingly in a more inquisitive and permissive manner at me, as if not sure whether it was all right to play at collision. The gleeful tone of her voice while shouting *Ta-ta-ta* was in striking discrepancy with the very gently-tentative intensity of her bumping my car. She quickly gave this up when I kept pressing the question of my car passing, she looked at me with an essentially compliant smile and after a moment's stalemate (just

2. This discussion is based on fifty-nine experiments.

holding her train, while glancing and smiling at me) she quickly turned her train around and proceeded to go in the opposite direction. She quickly followed up her belated turn-about by urging-informing me verbally, saying *Now your car can pass.* In the second and third trials she only shouted, *Ta-ta-ta* once and the amount of actual bumping was even less than the first time. Otherwise she did the same thing, each time telling me, *Now your car can pass.*

Abigail did not have the courage of her conviction (at least in playing with me today) to do that which she obviously would have liked to do and which she ever so meekly started out to do —that is, bumping, colliding. The discrepancy between her accompanying gestures and vocalization, on the one hand, and her overt acting out of her original wish went, I think, very well with the rest of her conduct which was in terms of good-natured and even goody-goodyish compliance with the adult. She not merely gave up the original game she wanted to play but she made doubly sure that she conformed satisfactorily with the adult wishes, by emphasizing each time "Now your car can pass," while turning her train around and thus getting completely out of the blocking person's way most obligingly.

ALEC

How SHALL MY CAR PASS? As we "met" and the problem of my "passing" arose, he started making way for my car on the track next to his train, pushing his locomotive slightly to one side, just barely and somewhat begrudgingly allowing enough room for my car to squeeze by. After acting out this initial accommodating attitude, he quickly glanced up at me with a semi-startled, semi-hesitant and quizzical expression on his face. Then while looking as if he still meant something like saying, "Go ahead, there is some room for you there," he suddenly and quite jerkily changed his stand in the matter, when my car barely passed his locomotive and was about to pass down the line along the rest of his cars. He suddenly said, *No, no, put it on the floor.* He looked at me in a startled and semi-aggressive manner, persisting in this belated resistance without, however, taking matters in his own hands, that is, without actually putting my car off the track. In the second and third trial, when we "met," he seemed to stop short in his tracks each time. To be sure, both times (that is, both the second and third times) he seemed to start out embryonically in the same manner—that is, by jerkily and ever so slightly pulling his locomotive to the side, as if to say "Go ahead, see if you can make it." In the second and third trials, however, his initial tendency to make room was definitely less intensive and seemed more like quasi-automatic, compulsive, repetitious residues of his "set" displayed in the first trial. Then as I, in each instance, chose to take this as a quasi-green light to pass, he started to resist me much more intensively as compared with the first time. In each subsequent trial (second and third), I was able to get not nearly as far down in the line of his cars. That is, he started saying, *No, put it on the floor* (the verbal formula was identical in all three trials) sooner and in a crescendo. In both the second and third trials, he merely persisted in verbal protestations, content with blocking my path by refusing to move the rest of his train—never once resorting to more overt action.

I thought the elaborate compulsive preparation which had to precede playing the game with me (coupling very long train, adjusting tracks) interesting. Then when the issue of blocking arose, he responded in a distinctly ambivalent fashion. He neither forthrightly resisted me nor did he unequivocally retreat or reciprocally compromise with me. Instead, he started to make way for me and then, in the middle of the stream as it were, he changed his mind in an abruptly negativistic manner. Again, curiously enough there was a residual repetition of the first part of his approach in the second and third trials. To be sure, the friendly-compliant part of it definitely decreased in intensity, just as the second or negativistic approach increased in degree. This miniature first part of his technique on the second and third trials, just as his crescendo in the second or resisting part, was the more striking to me because his total pattern was so distinctly ambivalent or not at all unified. In other words, I could far easier understand or expect repetition or stereotypy in instances where the child's resolution of the blocking situation was definitely in one direction, that is, either in terms of immediate retreat or consistent reciprocity of the "live-and-let-live" sort.

CALVIN

How shall my car pass? When we first met, he just looked down on his train (without apparently taking my car into his field of vision). Then, when I kept pressing the standard question, he just kept saying, *I don't know* (that is, "I don't know what to do or what am I to do?"). He said this shyly but firmly, just gazing down, without looking up at me—and it was a beautiful stalemate, both of us holding our ground without budging. On the second trial, it again looked like a stalemate at first. This time, however, when I kept pressing the question, he, for the first time, fixed his gaze directly on my car, then flashing an ever so slight shy smile, suddenly said, after a few seconds' pause: *If I pass a little to the side you can pass.* Then while I proceeded to take advantage of the opening thus provided, he continued commenting, *But not much room for you.* To be sure, there wasn't. He again flashed a very shy but more definite smile, without, however, looking up at me. There was still the gaze fixed downward but lifted as it were a few feet from the track—at the level of my mid-section (approximately). On the third trial, he repeated the pattern of the second trial, except that he more quickly resolved the problem into one of live and let live. That is, he did not start out by saying, *I don't know,* although actually without the verbalization he did stop short for a second or so, when we first met.

It seems to me that Calvin did clearly understand the issue involved right from the start, though as a possible or alternative interpretation (as to the first trial), one may think of his resistant shyness or rather shy resistance as a matter of comprehension. The first interpretation seems to be indicated, I think, in terms of his response in the second trial. Here is a little person who is quite able to meet the adult or perhaps any other blockage in an egalitarian spirit—but he can be quite resistant until he has determined exactly what is to be done. He seemed more released after he worked out his particular solution of eating the cake and having it too. His shyness, I think, is part of a fairly strongly marked off little ego—a lot of resistance can go with that shyness. I was also interested in his very superior surveying of the situation both before and after working out the formula—he is the only child of forty-five tested so far who came to remarking on there being "not much room for you." His concern for there not being much room for me is, I think, a suggestive projection of his little ego—suggesting the kind of little person who is not very sure of there being enough room for himself in various situations. He could not have such concern about life-room for himself and, projectively, for the other fellow, unless he was seriously preoccupied with such problems of ego-demarcation.

CANDICE

How SHALL MY CAR PASS? As soon as we met she glanced up at me with a very outgoing affectionate smile, pushed her train a little to the side of the track, thus making room for my car. Upon the second and third trials, she did the same, only with a little more verbal elaboration, paraphrasing her action with the encouraging affectionate remark, *You can pass now.*

Quite in keeping with the strikingly affectionate-dependent attitude she displayed toward me before ego-blocking that day and on previous occasions outdoors, Candice found such an encouraging "live-and-let-live" solution consistently the most suitable and congenial one for her. It never occurred to her to push me out of the way nor did she find it necessary to retreat. Apparently, when you can confidently lean on an adult, you don't have to be either too aggressive or too compliant.

CLAUDIA

How SHALL MY CAR PASS? As soon as we met, she went off the track at an angle of about forty-five degrees, just as Joel did. However, after she got off the track she just stayed and stood by, as it were, waiting to see that I actually did pass. She had her right index finger in the hole at the end of her train. She used both hands in removing her train from the track and kept looking and broadly smiling at me, as if saying, "See, I did it." This smile was flashed with a crescendo in subsequent trials and at the end she said: *Isn't it fun?*

While it is impossible to guess just what would have been Claudia's complete "own solution" because of the effect of watching the games played with Joel, the style of her response is suggestive just the same. Claudia was wrapped up in cheerful compliance to the exclusion of any incidental by-play or motor activity. After getting off the track completely and thus providing maximum room for me, she just sat there smugly and gleefully, as if at the end of a little task well done. Her remarking that it was "fun" suggests that when she is playing with an adult (or, to be exact, with a friendly male adult), it does not take very much for her to have a good time. It looked as if just basking

in the warmth of the immediate relationship with adults had its
own reward. Not only was this a question of a reward in its
own right but a need of remarking about it. I felt that this remarking about "fun" went well with the bubbling-over which
Claudia displayed sheerly as a function of being within the orbit
of a close relationship with an adult. That is, I don't think that
it sounded like playing up to the adult. It was as if whatever
playing up there was or is to do, was acted out in terms of the
wide-open compliance denoted by the act of removing the train,
completely out of the way, out of my path. Complying and otherwise affectionately-dependently leaning on the adult would then
seem to conduce to a state of seemingly artificial elation which
has to be verbalized—both as completion of release and communication.

COLT

How SHALL MY CAR PASS? The first time he retreated without
turning his train around. When he got to his end of the track, he
stopped, looked up at me, and pointed, *Up to here.* He did the same
thing in the second trial. On the third trial, when we met he suddenly
said, *You back up,* and clearly insisted that I was to do the same as
he did the first two times.

He lingered on after the three trials and wanted to keep on
playing. In all subsequent trials (after the first three "official"
trials), he kept saying with more and more determination, "You
back up." In the light of such insistent residue of playing the
game on his own terms (that is, that *I* have to back up and not
he), I was interested in the fact that he started out so compliantly when the question of one of us giving way first arose.
He suggests to me the kind of little ego which is accustomed to
giving way at first. That is, he cannot apparently start out with
insisting on his own terms but he is quick to rise to the occasion
and from then on it is his show. He was far more gleeful and
warm after playing the game in terms of "You back up." By contrast, he seemed ever so slightly startled in the first two trials—
when he resolved the problem into one of retreat on his part.
This contrast in feeling tone was, I thought, quite definite, even
allowing for the novelty of the stimulus.

CORINNE

How SHALL MY CAR PASS? In all three trials, Corinne pushed her train forward to meet me in the middle with rather stiff, deliberate, jerky movements. Upon meeting me in the middle, and when the question of passing arose, she very swiftly and deliberately went off the track, and while I passed, continued to push her train on the floor right next to the track until she got to my end of the field. She seemed very determined and set in her style, starting very seriously, without a smile, in fact, as if somewhat pouting.

It was very interesting that quite uniformly in all three trials, Corinne seemed much more interested in continuing in the direction in which she was moving than in making way for me. That is, in all three trials she acted out or completed that which she set out to do. She was not interested in sitting back or watching to see whether or not I passed. It was more as if she had seen that she was confronted with an immovable body or blockage, and the only thing to do was for her to go off and then continue toward her goal (my end of the track or field). She did not go back on the track after getting off in the middle but simply continued quite close to the track on the floor, thus achieving a minimum of necessary deviation, her eyes on the goal to be attained, in terms of a momentum once gained and to be maintained. She was not interested in my giving way to her reciprocally (cf. Calvin and others). Once she found my car in the middle, it was more of a one-way stumbling block to avoid quickly so as to continue in a straight, deliberate, definitely forward direction. She did not deviate from this pattern in any of the trials, looking just as determined and serious as her squat body build and general facial physiognomy might well suggest.

ERIC

How SHALL MY CAR PASS? On the first trial, he just took his hand off his train and let it stand. He looked at me, flashed a wider but still bashful smile, then looked down on his train—and just let it stand. On the second trial, he broke into a sudden big flash of a smile, and proceeded to pull his train back, without turning it around. He stopped at the far end (his end) of the track and just waited there until I came down, availing myself of the opening thus provided. He did not go off completely, however. On the third trial, he brought over, or rather picked up, a little toy iron which was lying nearby and proceeded to draw the iron over the surface of his train (the little car coupled to his locomotive). He kept "ironing" his train and paid no more attention to the pressure represented by my recurring standard questions. He did not give way to me any more.

There was, I thought, a striking resemblance in some ways between the initial reaction of Eric and Calvin. Eric, like Calvin, was willing to call it a draw or stalemate, as it were, on the first trial—except that he did not do any verbalizing about this, nor about any of his subsequent overt responses. From the first trial on, however, Eric's response was uniquely different. I was interested in his ready compliance on the second trial and, in marked contrast, in his reverting to a stalemate or definite resistance on the third. In the light of his resolution of the problem, especially in the second trial, there can be no question of his not comprehending the nature of the problem. However, his resistance to which he was quite daringly willing to revert on the third trial was very interestingly and somewhat cagily and resourcefully masked (i.e., his use of the iron while going out of the field of compliance—standing his ground, however, by staying put right on the track).

JANET

How SHALL MY CAR PASS? Janet sat down quickly with an effortless lightness, picked up what was left of Claudia's train and proceeded to call, *Meet me.* Confronted with the question of my car passing, she quickly and with determination took her train off the track, putting it at a right angle to the middle of the track as if distinctly waiting for me to pass. She smiled at me and looked somewhat impatient, as if saying "Why don't you go ahead," while I proceeded to act on her accommodating gesture, somewhat slowly at first. As soon as my car passed, she brought her train back on the track and proceeded to continue forward, as if nothing had happened. She did the same thing in practically the same style and spirit on the second and third trials, without saying a word.

It was interesting to me that Janet was able to get off and on the track with an apparent minimum of emotional effort. To be sure, she was getting out of my way in that she got completely off the track—but there was a quality of "Come on hurry up, you are holding me up" about it all. And she was very quick to resume her forward progress as if nothing had happened. She did not retreat like Claudia nor did she seem particularly friendly or subserviently compliant about it (cf. the affectionate-dependent response of either Joel or Candice). In short, it was giving way when blocked, but being quick about it and expecting the other person to be quick about it, and getting it over with, and then going on and completing a momentarily interrupted act. It was or seemed to be the accommodating attitude of a little person who knows her mind even while temporarily getting out of the way, if necessary.

JAY

How SHALL MY CAR PASS? On the first trial, he just stopped short, held his line and kept answering with a devilish smile, *I don't know* (that is, "I don't know how your car shall pass"). He touched my car without budging himself. On the second trial, he bumped my car, pushed it backward with increasingly applied motor strength. After pushing my car back a few inches (I was resisting him, applying some of my own strength) and while I kept pressing the standard question, he suddenly pulled his train to the side of the track, thus making room for me and suddenly blurted out, *Now* (that is, "Now you can go"). On the third trial, when we met in the middle, he bumped my car lustily and then held his line just a little shorter length of time than in the first trial, and then suddenly helped himself to a smaller block which lay nearby on the floor. He put the small block as a subsidiary track at the middle of the regular track, then went on the small block track with his train, and said *See?* (that is, "See, this is the way you can do it").

There was plenty of vigor in Jay's resistance when blocked in a novel situation. He not merely held his line in the first attempt, but he somewhat aggressively touched and handled my car. Then he picked up the matter of bumping as such, actually pushed mine backward (the only child to do this so far) and did not give way until after he was satisfied that I could take it. In giving way, there was none of the coy, or even feminine, one-way compliance exhibited by Patsy (who on the third trial took off her car completely and waited on the floor for me to pass when signaled). First, he let me pass by making a little room for me while he himself essentially stayed put. Then he resorted to the use of an auxiliary track. It is an open question in my mind whether he did this because (1) it was a generally crowded situation for him, or (2) because he wanted me to have more room in passing him, or (3) because he was chiefly thinking of himself in not wanting to be crowded off the track while making room for me. I should incline to the latter hypothesis as more in keeping with the total context here.

JOEL

How SHALL MY CAR PASS? As soon as we met in the middle of the track, he quickly and very alertly grasped the problem and solved it very swiftly and gracefully, by simply going off with his train at an angle of about forty-five degrees and then getting apparent enjoyment out of gliding his train on the floor. He had to be brought back to the stimulus-situation on each of the subsequent trials. He did this same thing on all three occasions, smiling, looking at my car and at me freely. Before proceeding to enjoy gliding his train on the floor, he waited in each instance for me to pass, but then it was all a matter of enjoying the motor activity involved in the gliding of his train. He was cheerful, confident, and compliant, but essentially unconcerned with the problem as such, except in terms of the incidental or collateral pleasure which he came upon while making room—plenty of room—for the adult (that is, the movement of his train, unhampered, on the floor).

I was interested in the very superior, alert grasp of the problem. He was very quickly onto the issue and handled it in an essentially free, affectionate-compliant manner. It was interesting that in each instance he first waited for me to pass after he got off the track—but then quickly and joyfully he felt free to proceed with the enjoyment of the motor game on the floor where he was not blocked. It suggests to me the functional use this kind of little ego makes of affectionate-dependence on adults. It is as if making sure of behaving well or "being nice about it" would then liberate or justify one's independent, unhampered, enjoyment of activities of one's own choosing or discovery.

JOYCE

How SHALL MY CAR PASS? On the first trial, she turned her train around and retreated completely, going off the track at her end of the field—and incidentally going completely out of the field. That was all that she was willing to play at this time. At about 10:41 she again came near my life space, pulling a very long train on the floor. Again she was not overly eager to play with me at first. Once, however, she got hold of the train on my track, she flashed a quite vivaciously angry look, accompanied by a distinctly coy half-smile (as if saying "I'll fix you"). As soon as we met in the middle of this second trial, she announced with coy antagonism, *Your car shall not pass*—then she simply lifted my car clear off the track, adding in an ominous tone of voice, *Leave it there* (this when I attempted to put my car back on the track, after Joyce was able to proceed with her train to my end of the track). Then I put it back on the track, trying to continue and complete my own "drive," somewhat secure in the knowledge that Joyce was already near her own goal at the far end of the track. However, I missed my cue here, as it were, because Joyce, not at all content with having gained her free path so very forcefully and effectively (having lifted my car off the track a little earlier), kept watching the situation from the corner of her eye and quickly came back to throw down my car with marked vehemence, announcing gleefully, devilishly, *Knock it down*. At this point she also caught a glimpse of Kene, who meanwhile proceeded to busy himself with a train and track left behind by Joyce. She dashed over and proceeded to fight with Kene over the possession of these toys. This meant that she was out of the field again. At 10:47 she came near my field again, and again was willing to accept an invitation for this, the third trial. This time when we met she simply went off the track in the middle and went way out of the field. She kept pushing the train on the floor and had to be called back for a fourth trial in view of the various irregularities of this experiment so far. This time, she simply blocked me in the middle and coyly-maliciously announced, again with the aggressive half-smile, *Don't pass*. When I proceeded to start all over again, accepting the stalemate, she objected even to that by saying, *Don't put it there*. And this was the end of my "blocking" Joyce.

In keeping with the coyly hostile mood in which Joyce entered the situation, she showed two very distinct and, as it were, alternating patterns. Either she completely retreated or went out of the field as if saying "I won't play with you," or else she was aggressively blocking and attacking me. It was very interesting, I thought, that with the four trials she gave two of each of these techniques. Apparently she can find going out of the field a very effective technique but, if pressed, she is quite willing and able to let out aggression and go about "not playing with you, the way you want to" in a far more severely drastic way. It is very much like the young, the very young, child who will either have the game on her own terms or else will stop playing; and, at the same time, if the game cannot be played on her own terms, there will be the kind of gross hostility which will result not only in refusal to give way to my car but in the complete elimination (destruction) of the car—by knocking it down, throwing it down and preventing it from regaining a foothold on the track.

KURT

How SHALL MY CAR PASS? We met without any difficulty and then he stopped short, gave me a quizzical characteristic semi-smile. After saying *Hm* two or three times, while I was pressing the question of my car passing, he suddenly seemed to understand just what there was to do about the situation and proceeded to pull his train backward—without turning it around, however. After drawing it back a little distance, he stopped as my car proceeded to go forward and to occupy the space thus freed for his use on the track, drew his train back, then stopped again. This kept up in this fashion, in dribbles as it were—I would make a little progress and stop, and so on. When he finally got to the end of his track, he didn't get off but stopped, waiting there until finally I proceeded to pull my car back to start "meeting" all over again. No sooner did the car proceed backward to its original position at my end of the track than Kurt started to follow me all the way to the far end of the track (instead of trying to meet me in the middle). Then, as I proceeded to come forward again from my end of the track, he broke into one of his real full-fledged smiles and quickly proceeded to draw back this time swiftly in one continuous sweeping movement. I stopped in the middle waiting for him to come forward to meet me there but he just kept waiting at the far end of his track, smiling at me for all he was worth, and practically inviting me to come down near his train, using those smiles plus looking down at his train and then at my car in a sense of silent invitation to the dance. When I came down, as he apparently wanted me to, to his end of the track, he beamed even more gleefully as if getting what he wanted me to do. Then, as I proceeded to go back again to start "meeting" all over again the third time, he turned this into a rhythmic motor game even more explicitly, swiftly following my car on my way back at a close distance, and then starting to go back in installments the full length of the track starting from my end, before I had a chance to get to the middle. In this fashion, he managed to make sure that I would fall in line with his evident wish to make this a game of simply swinging back and forth just for the sheer fun of it.

Kurt found this blocking game distinctly to his liking in that, and simply because, he managed to play it entirely on his own terms—as a nicely rhythmic motor game of swinging back and forth in nicely harmonized, parallel movements. It was very interesting how he was willing to give in but only in small installments both at the very beginning and again after the second trial. This could stand both for giving in this far and no further, and, whether primarily or secondarily, for a technique of either initiating or suddenly picking up a fascinating new game involving the sheer joy of motor expression per se. Once he was sure that I would take him up on this (particularly after the second trial), he was quite willing to indulge in a more trusting, confiding, sweeping manner—in that he was willing to give up the staccato, jerky, withdrawing technique in installments, only to substitute fuller and sweepier swings of parallel rhythm. His initial giving way was more of the nature of an exploratory-tentative steping aside, perhaps, and, more and more, he turned the situation into one to be played entirely on his own terms. From then on his compliance was increasingly more "managed" by him until he finally broke into an exuberant expression of real joy at having managed to convey to the experimenter this manner of playing and getting the latter to play ball accordingly.

PATSY

How SHALL MY CAR PASS? On the first trial, as we met, she bumped my car and held her line. Then she went back a few inches, stopped again and held her line again, saying, *You bumped my car.* On the second trial she bumped into my car more vigorously, then she retreated a few inches and said, *Now you bump mine.* On the third trial, after bumping my car with increased fervor, she flashed a big wide open smile, suddenly went off the track, held her train near the middle of the track and abruptly announced: *Now you can go.*

She enjoyed the bumping part of the stimulus situation more than anything else. This bumping seemed to me to be at once aggressive and a sort of bumptious, cozy, warm friendliness toward the male adult. She took the initiative in the bumping relationship but she quickly turned this into a reciprocal, affectionate, two-way contact by inviting me to bump her in return. When on the third trial, she suddenly switched from the initial bumping to letting me go, getting completely out of my way as it were, this suggested to me the manner in which an adult (especially a male adult?) may reach this ego. That is, if she can have her own way in a bumptiously affectionate manner, then she will play ball with the adult on completely and contrasting complying terms. Another way of looking at it may be this: that if you obey and take your medicine from her in a nice spirit and you keep doing this for a while, then you can be rewarded. In the latter event, Patsy may projectively use a formula of handling adults or other persons to which she herself may be accustomed at home. There was nothing strained or excessive about her emotional tone here; the crescendo of vigor with which she was doing her bumping in the progressive trials seemed to go well with the evident satisfaction she was getting from the game.

Against this intensive inspection of the first unit as such, we may now set off the comparative analysis of complete records on Alec and Betsy. We broke up the continuous records into triple segments for purposes of more effective comparison.[3]

HOW SHALL MY CAR PASS?

Alec:

Choo, choo, choo. (Moves train along the track down to experimenter's.) 1. How can I pass? *How can I pass? I knock you off the track.* (Suits words to action and knocks experimenter's train off the side of the track and then continues on down to experimenter's end of the track.) 2. Now . . . *Now.* You come from there. (Remains at what was formerly experimenter's end and experimenter goes to opposite end of the track.) How can I pass? *How can I pass?* (Repeats process of trial 1.) 3. You come from there, etc. *Choo, choo.*

---

3. Numerals 1, 2, and 3 denote first, second, and third trials respectively.

How can I pass? *How can I pass?* (Repeats identical process of trials 1 and 2.)

Betsy:

Do you remember this game? *Different doll.* (Settles down on floor as experimenter brings out ego-blocking toys.) 1. Now you push your train, etc. (Moves her train down to experimenter's in rapid, clear, sharp movements, banging into experimenter's train, and then draws it back to her end of the track as experimenter pursues after holding her train in middle for a while.) 2. Once more, etc. (Collides with experimenter's train, pulls it back to her end of track in clear concise actions.) 3. And the last time, etc. (Repeats processes of trials 1 and 2, smiling as she draws train back.)

MY DOLL STOPS YOUR TRAIN.

Alec:

1. Now I come with the doll and you come with the train, all right? *Ok. Ok. Ok. Choo . . . Choo . . . Choo.* My doll stops your train, what happens? (Stretches his kneeling position and rests on all fours.) *Now I'll stop . . . I'll stop your doll.* (sniffles) *Choo . . . Choo . . .* (pushes the doll off the side of the track) 2. My doll, etc. *No, my doll stops your doll.* What happens? *Push it off the track.* (Suits words to action.) 3. Once more, the last time, etc. (Sniffles several times.) *Push her off.* (Rather vigorous push and the doll tumbles off.)

Betsy:

1. Now I come with my doll, etc. What happens? *Killed.* (Bumps her train into doll, kneels further forward on all fours.) 2. Now my doll, etc. *She's broken.* (Raises her legs and shifts over to the other side of track after repeating process of trial 1.) 3. Now the last time, etc. *Breaks a leg!!* (Looks very pleased at last idea.) Breaks a leg? (Happy, but does nothing, just as in first two trials above.)

CAN MY DOLL GET ON YOUR TRAIN?

Alec:

1. Can my doll get on your train? You can have a double train. (Alec hooks them together.) Can my doll get on your train? *No.* Why? *Because it has too many people.* (Moves his train past experimenter's doll.) *Choo, choo, choo.* (Moves it entire length of the track.) 2. Now can my doll get on your train? *No, it has too many people again . . .*

Choo . . . Choo. B-r-r-r-r. (again passes doll by) 3. Can my doll, etc. *Yes.* (in a very short matter-of-fact answer) *Choo . . . Choo . . .* (Picks up doll and train and tosses them down.) *Because I wanted to.*

Betsy:

1. Now you come with the two trains and my doll wants to get on your train. Can my doll, etc. *Yes.* (Moves train down to doll and pauses. Experimenter puts doll on, very carefully moves train down to end of track.) 2. Now I come from here, etc. Can my doll, etc. *Yes.* (Bunny-hops after train as she moves it. As she moves train the doll falls off; laughs heartily, gurgles with delight.) 3. Now the last time. Can my doll, etc. *No . . . Ha, ha, ha . . . Yes.* (Brings train back to where doll is situated and moves train along as doll is placed on top. Holds train sideways, doll falls off, goes off into gale of laughter.)

CAN MY DOLL COME IN YOUR HOUSE?

Alec:

Now let's build a house. Shall I build a house or shall you? *I want the new things.* 1. Can my doll come in your house? *No, and when you come in, then I'll push you out, all right?* (Peeks out of one eye at experimenter.) I come in anyway? *Yes and I'll push you out.* (Experimenter moves doll toward house, Alec grabs the doll, jerks it from experimenter.) Why did you push it out?

Betsy:

You build a house and my doll wants to come into your house. *Yes but you can't.* (Very busy and engrossed in building house, twisting and turning, a great deal of motion to reach blocks and build the kind of a house that suits her.) Can my doll, etc. *No.* What happens if my doll, etc. (Experimenter puts doll in house.) *Get killed.* My doll is in your house, etc. (Tries to take doll out.)

CAN YOUR DOLL COME IN MY HOUSE?

Alec:

1. Now it will be my house, all right? And you ask me if your doll can come in. *Yes, you have to sleep.* Well, you didn't ask me. *Can I come in your house?* What shall I say? *No.* No, you cannot. *But I will.* Then what? *Now you pull it away from me.* Now I pull it away from you? Now what shall I do? *Throw it away.* (Experi-

menter does so and Alec follows the action closely.) Now let's have
a house. . . . *And I'll break it.* (Kicks his feet out and knocks over
the house. Almost exact reciprocal projection of own behavior.)

Betsy:

I'm going away. (Gets up with doll in hand, walks over to where
radiator is partially built in wall and endeavors to throw doll behind
it.) *It's my turn for the doll.* (Walks back toward the blocks.) 1. Now
you ask me if your doll can come in my house. *Can my doll come
in your house?* What must I say? *Must say?* (contemplates) Shall I
say yes or no? *You must say "Yes."* (With characteristic brisk movements puts doll in house, making doll squeak.) 2. Now let's do it
again. *Can my doll come in your house?* (Bounces doll in house.)
No. (Pays no attention to experimenter's answer, but is busy making
doll walk around house.) *She's in.* What shall I do? *She's in.* But I
said she shouldn't come in. *Then she knocks your house down.* (Wide
sweeping uncontrolled movements as she hits the doll against the
blocks and causes them to topple over, laughs heartily.)

YOUR HOUSE WHERE I MUSTN'T TOUCH ANYTHING.

Alec:

This will be a house where you mustn't touch anything, all right?
Whose house shall it be, yours or mine? *Mine.* Yours. Can I touch anything? *No, you mustn't touch and I'll take your doll.* Can I touch
anything in your house? *No, then you have to touch it.* (As experimenter does so, Alec hits his hand several times.) *Throw it away.*
(does so) Now it will be my house and you have the doll, all right?

Betsy:

Now it will be your house where I mustn't touch anything and
I'll come with my doll, etc. *Yes.* Can I touch anything? *No-o-o-o-o.*
What happens when I do? *Get . . . out . . . of there . . . I knock
your house down.* Now the last time. *I want to do it.* This is a house
. . . whose house is this, yours or mine? *Mine.* What happens if I do
touch everything?

Now what shall we play? *Something different.* You tell me. *Different toys.* Let's see what we can play with these toys. *Nothing else.*
What can we play with these toys? *I don't like them.* (Has been
slowly sliding over toward couch, puts hands up on top of couch, and
holds them there.)

MY HOUSE WHERE YOU MUSTN'T TOUCH ANYTHING.

Alec:

Now it will be my house and you have the doll, all right? *Can I touch anything?* What shall I say? *No.* No, you cannot? *I touch it with the doll then you take it away.* What? *You throw it away, now what shall I do?* I know.

Betsy:

Now this will be a house where you mustn't touch anything, all right? (Pays no attention, makes murmuring sounds to self as she creeps rapidly about floor on all fours, disappears behind chair.) 1. You come with your doll, etc. (Comes over with doll and waves it about in same uncontrolled wild motions, touching everything and incidentally knocking everything over.) You musn't touch anything. *I did touch everything.* 2. Let's do it again. (While experimenter is putting the house to rights again, Betsy sits back sticking doll's head in mouth and biting it, thus causing it to squeak.) This is a house, etc. (Makes sure she touches and knocks over every block.) 3. And the last time, etc. (Chews upon doll's head.) Let's pretend, etc. (Very violent in actions, great glee as the blocks fall on the floor as her doll does touch everything.)

WHO SHALL CRASH?

Alec:

What's that going to be? 1. A cross track. You come with your train from there and I come from here, who shall crash? *I shall.* (Brings the train down rather vigorously upon experimenter's hand after he has moved his train up to experimenter's.) 2. Now . . . *No, I'll do it in your face.* (Starts doing so on second trial, barely restrained by experimenter.) 3. That may hurt, would you like it if I did it to you? *No, let's do it again.* (Above process repeated but Alec gets even more energetic in hitting experimenter's hands.)

Betsy:

(Experimenter arranges tracks at right angles to each other. Betsy puts doll on train and moves it toward the meeting place of the two tracks; doll falls off as she rounds corner.) *Ha-ha-ha-ha.*

(hearty joyous laughter) 1. You come with your train and I come with my car. You come without the doll this time. Who shall crash? *Me.* (Deliberately tosses train off track and across room.) How? 2. Now do it again, etc. *Doll . . . Give . . . me . . . the doll, my doll.* Who shall crash? *Me.* (Moves train down to experimenter's and around corner in movements that are so fast it is hard to follow them.) 3. Now the last time, etc. *Me.* (Bumps into experimenter's train in much the same manner as trial 2.) How did you crash? What happened? *The train.* What happened? *Broke you.* Now let's do this.

WHO SHALL GET THERE FIRST?

Alec:

1. Now who shall get there first? *I shall.* (Moves his train very rapidly to the cross-section and on to the opposite end in order to beat experimenter.) 2. Once more, who shall get there first? *I shall.* (Process of trial 1 repeated.) 3. Once more, etc. (Process is again repeated.)

Betsy:

(Experimenter fixes tracks running parallel to each other.) 1. You come from there and I come from here. Who gets there first? *Me.* ("Skids" train up to end of track getting there ahead of experimenter by several seconds.) 2. Once more. Who gets there first? *Me.* (Repeats trial 1; so vigorous that train slides off end of track.) 3. Now the last time, etc. (Starts ahead of experimenter, but backs up and starts over when he is ready.) Who did get there first? *Me.* Do I ever get there first? (Shakes head, holding train close to mouth.) Shall we build a house? *Yes.* Shall I build it or shall you build it? *Me, I build everything.*

If we now look at this double performance, unit by unit, we are able to make the following comparisons. (We are not at this time translating the observed behavior trends into our usual ego language as we did in the analyses of Colin and Colt in ego-blocking game number 1. Having demonstrated there the possible manner of primary genotypic translation, we do not wish to burden the reader with unnecessary difficulties in comprehending the analysis. It requires considerable practice in using the terminology of ego-patterns and blocking situation types before a smooth understanding at a quick glance is possible.)

HOW SHALL MY CAR PASS?

Alec: Initial aggressiveness in very high gear maintained throughout.

Betsy: Embryonic aggressiveness (very tentative bumping) followed by compliance.

MY DOLL STOPS YOUR CAR.

Alec: Initial active resistance (stopping experimenter's doll) followed by high aggression (pushing it off).

Betsy: Verbal aggression (speaks of doll being killed, broken, breaking a leg), but actually overt passivity throughout. Talks aggressively but does nothing.

CAN MY DOLL GET ON YOUR TRAIN?

Alec: Two consecutive aggressive rejections, followed by acceptance. This acceptance, however, is quickly turned into high aggression in that he tosses both the train and the doll down immediately after giving doll a ride. Simply cannot go through with ambivalent kindness.

Betsy: Two consecutive acceptances—with only slightly indirect aggression on second, when doll "falls off," and she laughs with undisguised delight over it. This is followed by ambivalent rejection on the third (*No, ha ha . . . yes*). She picks up the doll but it again falls off and she laughs with hearty defiance.

CAN MY DOLL COME IN YOUR HOUSE?

Alec: Immediate highly vehement rejection, accompanied by violent aggression on "violation." He clearly prognosticates-projects what is to come (*No . . . no, and when you come in then I'll push you out . . . All right?*).

Betsy: Rejection accompanied by only verbal aggression upon "violation" (again she speaks of the violating doll "getting killed" but does nothing).

CAN YOUR DOLL COME IN MY HOUSE?

Alec: Projective insistence on exact reverse of what *he did* to experimenter (telling experimenter to say "no" to his request, and "now you pull it away from me"). This intense projective reciprocity probably stands for urgently needed and administered self-punishment.

Betsy: Insists on acceptance by experimenter. This is a matter of "rights" for her, in that she even paraphrases this unit with *It's my turn for the doll.* When experimenter supplements the acceptance with a deliberate rejection she at last becomes released enough to resort to direct, overt aggression for the first time(knocks down the house in wide-sweeping movements). This would suggest that with the doll, on the level of greater unreality (experimenter's hand is not in macrospheric contact with the blocking toys), she dares to act out that which in the earlier situations she only dared to release on the verbal plane.

YOUR HOUSE WHERE I MUSTN'T TOUCH ANYTHING.

Alec: Rejection and very clear-cut vehement aggression. Voices "touch tabu," threatens doll and acts on threat not only on the microspheric, but on the macrospheric plane, in that he hits experimenter's hands in addition to mistreating the doll.

Betsy: Rejection accompanied again by merely verbal threats. (Note that this time experimenter's hand is in macrospheric contact with blocking toys; in previous unit she acted more boldly because her relationship to experimenter was more microspheric.)

MY HOUSE WHERE YOU MUSTN'T TOUCH ANYTHING.

Alec: Insists on exact projective reversal of what he did in previous unit. He completely outlines in rather compulsive details just what shall happen, and how (experimenter is to say "No" and then, *I touch it with the doll then you take it away. You throw it away*).

Betsy: Again shows the kind of aggressiveness she didn't dare to show earlier. (Experimenter's hand is again not in macrospheric contact with the toys as it was in the previous unit.)

WHO SHALL CRASH?

Alec: High-gear aggression, with tremendous crescendo progressing from the microsphere on to the macrosphere. (*I'll do it in your face.* Hits experimenter's hands as well, etc.)

WHO SHALL GET THERE FIRST?

Alec-Betsy: Both "win." The freedom provided by parallel play here provides a levelled opportunity for ego-assertive urges, thus erasing individual differences, so to speak. There probably are individual differences, even here, but they are far more subtle to record non-mechanically, without motion-picture or sound-record apparatus.

SUMMARY

Alec: He shows quite uniformly marked need for vehement hostility release throughout. Provides for self-punishment with projective reciprocity and compulsiveness in exact reversals of hostility scenes.

Betsy: Rather consistently displays merely verbal aggression on direct collisions. Shows decidedly more released defiance on microspheric level and on a basis of taking turns.

As to *positive* educational and therapeutic applications we may consider here the record of Dusty. She was outstanding in consistently "bottling up" her hostilities during her two years in nursery school—in experimental situations as well as in general. A very gifted child, she was quite indirect and verbal, even at the peak of her "anger." At the same time, as an evidence of such "bottled up" normal needs for hostility release, she showed signs of fear-laden fantasies. In an earlier played-off ego-blocking game number 1 (immediately preceding the game recorded below), the experimenter, in the last stick unit, provided for induced catharsis (after the experimenter broke the stick it was finally possible to induce Dusty to do so). The following record shows a continued, if decreasing, trend toward "bottling up"—with only hesitant willingness to indulge in overt hostility-release.

How CAN MY CAR PASS? Dusty: *When does the boy stop it?* 1. Experimenter: First we play it this way. This is your car and you come from there and I come from here. Let's meet in the middle. How can my car pass? [Moves train fairly rapidly down to experimenter's, pauses at middle and then shifts block over to side of track and continues down to experimenter's end on a live-and-let live basis.] 2. Now once more, etc. [Repeats trial 1 in every respect. Completely silent.] 3. And the last time, etc. *Only now how can my car pass?* And how can my car pass? *No, no! Remember what you promised about my car!!* I promised? *Yes, how can my car pass?* [Pauses in middle of track as on trials 1 and 2.] How can I pass? [Moves train to side of track. Exact repetition of two previous trials.]

MY DOLL STOPS YOUR CAR: 1. This time I come with my doll. *Yes.* [Eagerly settles itself for this particular phase of ego-blocking.] Let's meet in the middle, etc. My doll stops your car, what happens?

[Contemplates problem very seriously, abruptly moves train off side of track on floor, completely getting out of the way.] 2. And again, etc. [Repeats trial 1.] 3. And the last time, etc. [Repeats trials 1 and 2.]

CAN MY DOLL GET ON YOUR TRAIN? Now do you know what we can play? I'll tell you what, you have both trains. 1. You have both of the trains and you come with your train and my doll will be waiting here. Can my doll get on your car? *Yes* . . . [Permits experimenter to put doll on train, moves train for as long as doll remains balanced on it. When doll falls off, ceases.] *And now we'll do that again* . . . 2. Can my doll get on your train? *No*. Why not? *Because it's a freight train.* 3. And once more, etc. Can my doll get on your train? *Yes* . . . [Repeats trial 1, even to stopping point.]

CAN MY DOLL COME IN YOUR HOUSE? Look. Now it will be your house. See . . . and my doll will come. That will be your house, all right? Now my doll comes. [Sits at far end of house.] 1. Can my doll come in your house? *No*. Why? *Because this is a private house.* Suppose he goes in? [Experimenter puts doll in house, Dusty leans over purposefully and firmly removes doll out onto rug.] 2. All right. Again. I'll come, etc. Can my doll come in your house? *Yes* . . . How . . . where? [Removes small block, opening door as it were.] I'll come in this way. [Experimenter puts doll in house over the side, neglecting to take advantage of the opening Dusty had provided.] 3. And the last time, etc. *No*. Why? *Because it's a private house.* [Removes doll as in trial 1.]

CAN YOUR DOLL COME IN MY HOUSE? And now it will be my house and you come with your doll, etc. [Hops over to desk and approaches house with doll in a dignified manner.] *Now* . . . *Can my doll get in your house?* 1. What shall I say? *No*. No it cannot. Why? Because I don't want your doll to come in the house. *Suppose she goes in anyway. Then what?* What do you think, what shall I do? [Puts doll on floor, raises hand as if to strike it, but pulls her punch completely and does nothing.] *Spank* . . . *Take it out* . . . [Experimenter repeats Dusty's remarks.] *Spank it* . . . You didn't spank my doll. *No*. 2. Let's do it again. *Can my doll get in your house?* What shall I say? *Yes*. Yes, you can come in. 3. And the last time, etc. *All right* . . . *Dee* . . . *Dee* . . . *Dee* . . . *Dee*. [Hops doll over to house in rhythm with improvised song.] *Can my doll get in your house?* What shall I say? *No*. No. Why? What shall I say, why? *Because it's a private house.* Because it's a private house so you can't come in. [Puts doll in house.] *Well* . . . *You can spank him this time and send him home by himself.* [Experimenter repeats Dusty's remarks.] *Yes.* Why didn't you spank my doll? *Because mine wasn't as private as yours.* I'll tell you what . . . Did you say I should spank it? *Yes* . . . *When he comes in anyway* . . . Shall I spank it or you? [Spanks doll hesitantly

330

the first time; after that takes turns slapping it with experimenter.] *There!*

Your house where i mustn't touch anything: Now this will be your house where let's pretend I can't touch anything. 1. I come with my doll. Can I touch anything in your house? *No.* Why? *Because it's full of fire . . . There's fire in here and it will pop out at you.* [Points to sides of block structure.] Well I'll touch it anyway. What happens. *He gets burned up and killed.* [Voice fades away into nothingness.] 2. All right. Once more. Can my doll touch anything in your house? *Oh no.* Why? *Because there's fire in the house and it will pop out.* [Experimenter repeats Dusty's remarks.] *Yes.* I'll come in anyway, what happens? *The doll is all burned up . . . It's killed.* 3. And the last time, etc. Can I touch anything? *Yes.* I can? How is it I can now and I couldn't before? *Well the fire's all burned out.*

My house where you mustn't touch anything: Now it will be my house and your doll comes. *Can my doll touch anything in your house?* 1. What shall I say? *No.* No, you cannot. *Why?* What shall I say, why? *Because there's fire in these things.* [Touches knobs on ends of small train blocks.] Because there's fire in those things! *Suppose I touch it anyway, then what happens?* What shall happen? *He's burned up.* Mmm . . . Let's spank him, all right? [Looks at experimenter with a fogged air of bewilderment. Experimenter spanks; Dusty does not.] 2. Let's do it again. *Yes.* You come with your doll. What do you want? *Can my doll touch anything in your house?* What shall I say? *Yes.* Yes, it can. 3. And the last time, etc. *Then we'll put these in a different shape, all right?* [motioning to blocks] Yes. *Can my doll touch anything?* What shall I say? *No.* No, you cannot. *Why?* What shall I say, why? *Because there's fire in these things.* Because there's fire in these things. That's why I don't want you to come in and touch anything. [Puts doll inside structure warily.] *Spank him.* What shall I do when he comes in? *Spank him.* Spank him, and he doesn't get burned up. Spank him. [Experimenter and Dusty take turns in striking doll.] How about spanking it a little harder? [Dusty, upon experimenter's suggestion and stimulation, increases the vigor of her blows, increases activity even more.] How about some good whacks . . . Good. How about doing it real hard? [Follows experimenter's suggestion, but only on the basis of taking turns with experimenter.] Now we'll play something else, shall we?

Who shall crash? [Experimenter places long blocks at right angles to each other.] 1. This time you come with your car from here and I come from here and who shall crash? *Me.* Who shall crash? *Me* . . . [Spans gap between blocks and moves her train over on track with experimenter's; moves it to the side and passes experimenter on a live-and-let-live basis similar to "How can my car pass?"]

Is that crashing? *Yes.* 2. All right, again. You come from there, etc. Who shall crash? *You.* I crash? [Repeats trial 1.] 3. And the last time. Who shall crash? [repeats] *Me.* [Repeats trials 1 and 2.] Is that crashing? *Yes . . . Now we'll play another . . .* What shall we play now? *I'll get the game now.* All right.

DUSTY IS ALLOWED TO SET THE PATTERN FOR THE GAME: [Puts long blocks at an angle to each other with a small block at each end.] *And now you come with your doll and ask me if I . . . if your doll can come in, and I say no because water will squirt out and it's oil and so that will kill him.* 1. I see. I come with my doll. What should I do? *You ask if your doll can come in my house.* Can my doll come in your house? *No.* Why? *Because there's water in these things . . . They will squirt out . . . And there's oil in there . . . It will kill him.* Well I don't care, my doll comes in anyway, what happens? [Pushes doll gingerly out of structure.] *Then he comes out and finds . . . And falls over.* Why did he fall over? *Because he's killed(?).* 2. All right, I'll come again, etc. *No . . . Now we'll have another game.* All right, you tell me what. [Puts long tracks flat on floor, parallel to each other.] *See, here's a station where trains come and your doll is waiting here. And that's the track and your doll will ask can he get on this train, and I'll say, "Well you can get on the next train that goes by." I say: "You can get on this train if you can't get on the next train."* I see. Can my doll, etc. *No, he has to wait for the next train.* Well, I'll get on anyway. *No, that's not the way.* That's not the way? *No . . . This is a different game. Then this train turns around and comes back.*

MY DOLL STOPS YOUR CAR (second time): I'll tell you what. 1. You come with your train . . . go ahead, and I come with my doll, and my doll stops your train. What happens? *Then the train goes over on the other track.* 1a. I'll tell you what. Now do you want to stop the train with your doll? *Yes.* All right, your doll stops my train, what happens? What did you do? *Stop the train.* Do you know what I'd do? [Experimenter knocks Dusty's doll over and whacks and collides into it with his train.] 2. Do you want to do it again? *Yes.* All right, I come with my doll, etc. *You come with your doll and stop my train.* All right, my doll, etc. [Zooms train down toward doll with great speed, but abruptly stops it a few inches away. Takes doll away from experimenter's hands, turns it around facing the train, and definitely holding back, knocks the doll off the track in installments.] How does that feel? *Horrible!* Horrible? 3. Let's do it again, etc. *I want to go back now.* How about spanking the doll once more? Who shall spank it? *Me.* [Gets in some vigorous, exhausting whacks, eyeing experimenter warily.] All right, now we can go back. *Now we can go back . . . Go back . . . Go back. . . .* [Starts to get dressed slowly.] Let's see if you can get dressed faster than when you came over. *If it doesn't . . . Don't blame. . . .* Don't blame? *No.* Who do you mean to blame? Blame whom? *Blame me.* I won't blame you. Does anybody ever blame you? *No.*

AFTER PLAYING THE GAME, upon questioning, she said that she didn't particularly like any part of the games. When, however, the experimenter asked what toys or games to get for her next time she insisted on leaving that to him. She said something to the effect that "You get them and whatever you get will be all right with me." She said this in a very cheerful and confiding manner, looking up at experimenter with a very charming facial expression.

As may be seen Dusty occasionally still protested verbally about overt hostility-release, although she subsequently acted on it with obvious gusto saying, "Horrible!" with a semi-serious facial expression and then immediately getting in some of the most vigorous, exhausting whacks directed at the blocking doll —eyeing the experimenter warily.

Later in the morning she spontaneously commented to her nursery school teacher that "I like that game where Mr. Lerner says: 'My doll stops your train.'" That is, back in the ordinary nursery school situation she was able to recognize and admit to herself and to a female parent-substitute that it felt good to let off steam. In the case of another child, the mother reported carry-over of such "release" responses to behavior at home. The mother observed the experimental procedures and gladly accepted the implications explained to her at the time.

PART IV

Observing Children
in Nursery School Situations

by EVELYN BEYER

CHAPTER 14

Introduction

IN THE EARLY DAYS of nursery school education a perusal of record files often revealed volumes of records on elimination-frequency, quality, quantity; on sleeping habits—hour retired, hour asleep, hour awake; on food intake and refusals. Such fact-finding records are limited in that, although the files may contain a three-years' record of Alison's eliminations, they contain no picture of Alison herself, and little evidence of the attendant circumstances preceding and following the check on the chart.

Insightful observation of young children places more emphasis on the "how" of behavior, and also extends the "what." When urination is charted the teachers include records of the child's general emotional state on a day of frequent urination intervals with any background of information as to what caused tension—that is, what kind of behavior accompanied the chart. Was he jittery, tense, aggressive? Or was he lethargic, pale, listless? Did he give any clues as to the source of his anxiety? A check and a notation of 10:30 after Calvin's name could not possibly tell what really occurred on that occasion: Calvin's reluctance, his statue-faced refusal, his self-consciousness, the shutting of the bathroom door. And these are the things that tell about Calvin.

Quantitative recording is a valuable short-cut method of

revealing certain basic data. However, its value is enhanced when it is supplemented by descriptive material. Even attendance records can be enlivened by adding reasons tor absence, which often reveal rich material on individual children. In looking over the attendance record of three-year-old Kene, for instance, and discovering that except for a whooping cough episode his absences were due to various and extended trips to sport shows, dog shows, aviation exhibits, etc., we learn something about the status of Kene in the eyes of his family, of their image of him, and we are able to observe more intelligently the use he makes of the nursery school world in the light of the spacious extension of his home world.

Since the nursery school is relatively unhampered by the limitations imposed by "real" schools to teach specific skills, it is a rich and profitable ground for observing personalities in the process of discovering themselves, their abilities, their limitations, their use of materials and people, their joys and woes. In the following pages I should like to present a rather sketchy picture with illustrations of some of the kinds of information about a personality, its demands and needs and ways of adjusting, which are observable in everyday nursery school situations.[1] These situations vary from the completely free spontaneous play times to the more structured routine "fact-of-life" occasions which confront even two- and three-year-olds. Naturally enough, some situations provide richer, more provocative material than others, but in all of them there are clues that reveal something important about the child.

---

1. Detailed observation of the behavior of a child during an intelligence test and a pediatric examination is presented in Volume II.

CHAPTER 15

Observing Behavior
in Nursery School

Routines

IN THE NURSERY SCHOOL at Sarah Lawrence College there was a minimum of emphasis on the routine "must" part of life. The rituals of washing and toileting and resting, of clearing up toys and partaking of the mid-morning juice were flexible and genial. As a matter of fact, we were probably much less concerned with the degree of conformity to a particular pattern than we were with the varieties of approach and feeling toward any one of these situations. If a child refused juice, no issue was made thereof. If he rinsed his hands under the running water, rather than soaping deliciously and ruminatively for twenty minutes (as Claudia did) these patterns were accepted but not dismissed, because they seem to tell us something about the individual. A minimum of conformity was expected in "putting away" situations. There was an understood rule (among the four-year-olds) that at the end of the morning's work, everyone turned in to help in putting away the play materials that had been used. We found that some children were adept in evading these chores, others definitely resisted, others were cheerfully cooperative, others ostentatiously helpful.

"Resting time," a time of teacher-imposed relaxation, was another of the "fact-of-life" situations in which we observed endless variations of response, from those who mischievously sought to disrupt the peace, to those who contentedly tucked thumb in mouth and lay curled or stretched in complete physical relaxation. The following record taken from an end-of-the-year summary of activities describes a particular rest period of a child who had been extremely retiring and depressed most of the year. The whispered conversation with the teacher who was sitting near him might appear to be a most un-rest-like procedure, and yet for Christopher it was good, and an indication of his increasing freedom.

[Christopher chose a place near Miss Beyer. Stretched out on his stomach, head raised, hands holding head, elbows on floor. Made several subdued mouth noises, snorting-snoring variety. Announced in whisper that he needed to spit. Miss Beyer suggested that he do it in toilet. Skipped out, came back, lay on back, hands stretched above head. Yawned, whispered:] *Mamma wants me to have an extra rest, except she didn't say so.* Miss Beyer: You can have one if you feel like it. [Crossed legs. Whispered conversation to Miss Beyer:] *It's spring now . . . What comes after spring—summer?* Yes. *Then what comes?* Fall. *Then comes winter.* [smiling] *Then comes spring . . . Then comes summer. It seems to me like it goes around in a circle.* [fingering circle in air] *But it doesn't really go around in a circle . . . Wallace has a watch, It's gold or silver.* [Wallace is an older brother.] *Wallace says black and white aren't colors . . . When will a minute and a half be over?* [generally relaxed throughout]

This rest of Christopher's was relatively typical. He was usually physically relaxed, occasionally made distracting noises, but was rarely as conversationally inclined. This volubility was characteristic, however, of his drive at that time in general, increased motor and social activity, attended by greater vocalization.

The following summary records of bathroom procedure will reveal some of the individual differences in attitude and approach that are observable among children in this universal situation: the cautious, surreptitious attitude contrasted with the casual, indifferent, fact-of-life attitude.

Calvin rarely goes to the bathroom and is never observed. Always goes alone, even shuts door in outside bathroom when no one is in yard. It is distinctly a private affair. He frequently peeks at others, especially when girls are in the bathroom. The last time he went to the toilet alone and locked the door from the inside.

[Colin goes to the toilet more frequently than any other child in the group. Usually announces:] *I have to tinkle.* [or jerks a thumb or his head toilet-ward and departs] [Enjoys social accompaniment. Once when urinating at the same time as Alec, announced:] *We're big men, aren't we, Alec?* [Will linger in the bathroom if other children are about—seemingly not with curiosity, but interest in people, not in toileting. Is joyfully responsive to Camille's toilet talk.]

[Camille announced that she had to go to the bathroom while we were on our pussy-willow hunt. She looked a little worried. I told her we would scoot back to school. Cappy said:] *Maybe she'll wet her pants.* [Shortly after this, Camille did. There was a somewhat apprehensive look down the legs, examining the snowsuit with Cappy. She did not seem upset—had a kind of "that's that" attitude:] *I had to do it, so I did.* [little obvious fear of consequences. When we got back to school I took her to the toilet, although she said,] *I don't need to go now.* [As she pulled down her panties she said,] *Milly makes my pants so tight, I guess she wants to choke me.*

Motor and Creative Activities

Included in the teachers' "Summaries by Activities" which were written in November and again in June, were records of general physical abilities such as running and climbing and jumping, as well as records on activities involving a lesser expenditure of physical energy, such as painting, clay work, sandbox, crayoning, etc. In all of these categories we found dramatic variations among children. In running and climbing we were interested in observing not only the mechanical use of the body, but also the purpose to which running or climbing was put, and its meaning to the child.

Colin's run is a steamy little run that never really gets there, as if the fuel content were low or the run was a scenic excursion type where you might stop at any moment to admire the view or a fossil. Little swinging through space. *Walk* is much more characteristic than his run, a jaunty, jouncy confident movement through space.

Patsy's run has a thistle quality of frisking over the ground. Buoyant, scooting, effective. Apparent pleasure in movement, same quality of drinking deeply as in high swinging motions.

Randy's run is characterized by ineffective tight movements. Shoulders tied, legs not free. Rarely runs, except to chase an aggressor. Little apparent pleasure in movement for itself.

Hal is a clumsy, inept climber. Does a certain amount of tree-climbing and ladder-tilted-against-packing-case climbing. Large lumbering movements, puffing effort.

Painting and clay offer opportunities for observation of an activity involving the use of a raw material demanding ingenuity and imagination and exploration. One child chants ecstatically, "Red shine, shine! Shine red, shining red!" as she splashes paint on in large masses, almost intoxicated by the color. Another child solemnly struggles to achieve a reproduction of something "real," and is so inhibited by his lack of skill that there is no zest in the performance. Some children enjoy the smearing—the wetness—others seem happiest when they are creating a pattern of balanced design.

[Jill took the blue brush, made an aimless line pattern. Experimental strokes.] *This is purples.* [Turned with back to painting, hands folded in front surveying Janet who was claying. Turned toward the painting, placed hands flat on paper.] *I'm finished painting.* [Took green brush, put it back, took red, began filling in space outlined in blue. Brush too full of color, red dripped, caught drip with back of hand. Covered entire paper blue, covering red space first. Paper and hands well smeared, beamed,] *I have to wash 'em.* [Picture formless. Fairly typical painting performance. Result usually shapeless, little joy in color itself, no sense of pattern or design. Amiable, casual attitude toward it.]

Clay, as a sensory substitute for mud, or as a creative material offering opportunities for making things, was used in as many ways as there were children. It was manipulated, squeezed, patted, sliced, smeared, pounded, shaped, or sometimes tasted, according to the desire and need of the child.

Alec: Give me somefing to clay with. Teacher: A flat stick? *Yeah.* [pounding mass flat with board] *Could I have anuvver piece of clay for on top?* Surely, if you need some. [Alec whammed second lump on top of first.] *Feel how soft; Miss Beyer, feel how soft.* [Continued pounding with board and fist. With tongue depressor scooped under mass, slicing pancake horizontally.] *This is going to be a piece of cake, Miss Beyer.* [Smiling. Tense pounding-face accompanying pounding with fist. Left clay to participate in height measurings with Adele and Abigail which ended in a slapping battle with Adele. Returned to clay, poked fingers in.] *Look, I can make my name in clay.* [Sliced the cake, cut piece off, pounded it on top of board. Tore it from block, pounded it on table. Picked it up, put it on board again. Stuck a rolled cylinder on top.] *Look at the smoke stack. Vis is a steamboat.* [Pushed it around with motor noises. Held it upright.] *Don't you fink it looks like a foot?* [Smiling. Scraped it off, pounded it into lump, put it away.]

[This is fairly typical of the variety of ways in which Alec uses clay, with the aggressive pounding predominating.]

Jeremy: [Took large lump of clay, rolled it slightly into pointed shape, looked very pleased.] *Look, look—my gun, my pointy gun—my bending gun, it bends!* [Laughing, eyes shining and popping. Pointed it at Alec, laughing, rolled it.] *It's a sea lion!* [Laughing, made sea lion noises and faces, nodding head.] *Waugh, waugh, waugh.* [Rolled it longer—about 18 inches long, laughed.] *Look! Look!—A long sea lion, it reaches down the stream!* [Betsy:] *It looks like a snake! Yes.* [Sliced the roll with a knife, careful cutting motions, bunched sliced pieces into ball.]

Crayoning and painting and claying are dominantly individual projects. Occasionally there are painters or clayers who may affect or be affected by a single child's enthusiasm, but the activity is primarily a matter of individual feeling and attack. Except for occasional aggressive attacks, no one is likely to poach on another's paper. In the sandbox it is different because, although a child may be absorbed in constructing a garden or just digging deep, the sandbox is a social institution, and other children may be as deeply engrossed in using the same sand for quite different pie-making purposes. Here again is a fruitful area for observing not only the specific use of the material, whether it be road building or cake making, but the sensory value of dripping and fingering, and the aggressive use as a material to be disseminated in eyes and on hair.

[Jay came running into sandbox with a tall can and a scoop.] *We need ice cream on the train.* [Hastily filled can—hurried spilling scoops—rushed out of sandbox toward train, shouting:] *Ice cream, ice cream, chocolate ice cream ten cents.* [Speed, dramatic content, purposefulness, all characteristic of Jay's energetic use of materials—sand as well as blocks or babies.]

Betsy's dominant sandbox activity is acquisition. She spends most of her time hoarding or collecting dishes and spoons, howling if hers are taken and retrieving them violently. Actual use of sand dramatic and domestic—making of cakes, all varieties. Urges adults to taste. Fills innumerable pans, sets them out neatly in rows. Little digging or manipulation for its own sake.

The Use and Meaning of Language
for Young Children

The use to which young children put language does not differ greatly from the use adults make of it. The earliest grunts and gurgles and sputtered sounds may be produced either for communicative purposes, or experimentally as play with sounds. This dual use of language never really ceases, although some individuals effectively seal the experimental faucet at an early age, or receive such constant discouragement that it dries up and ceases to flow.

The pure communication kind of language is the language that receives the greatest adult attention and response. Articulation, grammar, vocabulary—these become the emphases of grownups who want their children to speak properly.

Some children respond readily to the adult demands in this area, and find real satisfaction in conforming to the verbal expectations which are pushed at them. One physically and temperamentally retiring four-year-old child took great pleasure in his verbal precocity. "Anyhow, I know lots of hard words," he would say as a kind of justification for his lack of success in other areas. Some children quickly learn that they can use the tool of language in reverse, as it were, as a machine for bombarding the adult. Garrulity, incessant questioning, repetition of demands can be very annoying. Similarly some children have learned that to refuse to use language is an effective negative defense against the encroachments or deprivations of powerful adults. Nursery school is often the Waterloo for this particular kind of resistance, because the child finds himself among his own kind by whom he wants to be understood and with whom he wishes to communicate, so that he is forced by his own desires to acquire the tool he has rejected.

Since communication, either of one's wants or questions or pleasures or refusals, is likely to be a pedestrian affair, and since so much of language *is* communication, it is natural that most of the language of young children should become as dull as that of the adults they imitate.

If adults had sharper ears they might listen to the language of young children and learn that often it is not dull, until we deaden it. Children begin experimenting and playing with sounds before they know words. When they have learned words, they play with them. And when they begin using words to express ideas, they are likely to express them more vividly than properly, until we correct them and subdue their language with propriety. We make it as black and white and gray as our own.

The language of many young children is fresh, and often the purest kind of unself-conscious poetry. Its images are startlingly direct, probably because the children themselves are still so close to feelings and experiences. Young children have not yet become dulled by too much living with words. The inevitable short-cutting of clarity and the substitution of pedestrian smear words for bright image words has not yet become a habit.

Words can have a "please pass me the butter" function, but they can also have a "the snow looks like darning" quality, if adults will sharpen their ears and their own tongues and thoughts.

Play as a Clue to the Child's Experience and Use of the World

It is probably in situations involving the use of materials which invite dramatic play—either individual or group—that we find the richest fodder for sorting out a child's use of the world in which he finds himself. If you are four and beginning to learn about mailmen and mail, you may play out your knowledge and clarify it for yourself by being the mailman with a paper bag and some papers for pretend mail. Grocery play, fireman play, train and boat play, endless family play have an almost recital quality of "These things I know and understand." Plays of being sick, of shutting out "the animals," of "mad witches" provide dramatic opportunities for bringing into the light fearful and exciting things that may lurk among the tangled thoughts and images of some young children. Materials which invite "playing out" these fears and knowings are blocks, and housekeeping toys, lengths of cloth, motor toys, etc. Stanley was a very contained four-year-old who usually exerted his feelings of aggression toward the world with unobtrusive magic devices. In fact it was not until I had watched and listened to his play that I discovered these aggressive tendencies that he usually disguised so neatly. In the following record, I found a clue.

[Stanley works and plays pretty much in his own little world. He is now interested in playing with roads and the little trucks. Today he made a road which turned sharply and ran parallel with itself. He used the ramp blocks to make little hills up and down. The whole thing was compact and neat. He sat beside it running the trucks up and down, talking quietly to himself, very intent and interested. Occasionally with truck in hand he would shove the road into a crooked mix-up—chuckling,] *He made it that way, he wanted it to be that way.* [Then he would fix it straight. Although Nan had a road around her house and Christopher had a complicated road pattern, there was no attempt to tie these up or unify them. Stanley talked to himself almost constantly,] *I'm a clever mechanic, I guess I'm the best mechanic in this school. Yes, I guess I am, that's true. And this little tractor is a busy little thing. I guess this road will have an up but not a down thing, it could make the cars go pop right down. A wreck, it really could.* [on and on sometimes directing some of this to me—frequently just accompanying his play with the words]

Social Contacts

A great deal of loose talking and writing has been done about the social benefits of nursery school for young children and studies have been made on social contacts, usually from the point of view of direction, contacts received, contacts delivered, with insufficient emphasis on the quality of these encounters.

The variations of approach and reproach are greater than even the numbers of children in a group, because each child is experimenting with and in process of learning the devices that satisfy and express himself. The confidently aggressive child is easiest to observe and usually easiest to direct.

A large portion of Alec's social life the year he was four was spent in a struggle to achieve certain socially acceptable four-year-old amenities of behavior. Alec seemed rather suddenly aware of devices for entering upon or directing away from social intercourse. He learned to use "Can I play with you?" and "You can't play with me" effectively. He seemed eager to be accepted. This was a new stage in Alec's social career. He had become warmly attached to Jill. During juice one day, he sat lovingly beside her, gazing raptly and warmly into her face as he said, "We're friends, aren't we Jill? We're friends." This attachment was carried over to the playground where in order to be included in the Jill-Camille menage he consented to be the "baby" and was pushed around in the carriage by Jill who was the big sister.

He was concerned with the forms of agreeable social living and struggled to adapt them for his uses. One day while building with blocks he reminisced, "Remember vat day when Colt gave me a block when I needed it? And remember vat day when I gave Colin a truck he needed? Vat was a very fing to do, don't you fink, Miss Beyer?"

The development of Jay from a passive acceptor of aggressive attack to a bouncing retaliator, and his joy in the discovery of his power, is revealed somewhat in the following record.

This week Jay has emerged from a rather feebly protesting acceptor of other children's aggression to a rip-roaring puncher, hitter, and bopper in his own right. He wallops effectively—seeming to have some skill in the actual physical direction and quality of the punch, and seeming also to enjoy the experience greatly. It is interesting that it should have begun to happen almost on the day his mother had asked if he accepted snatching from other children without retaliation. She said that they felt he was a little too amenable and agreeable and didn't stand up for his own rights sufficiently. He is now definitely standing!

He still spends much time on what seems to be pure expenditure of excessive energy. He runs around the yard with stiff, almost backward bending, torso and quick running legs—beaming—*Look, kids, let's run.* He is an intermittent "daddy" in Camille's household, but not an ambitiously constructive or consistently faithful one. He tears off to do something else, usually justifying his departure in dramatic terms, *I have to go to work now—so long.* He seems to have a slap-dash relationship with nearly all the children—plays with whoever is on hand at the moment. Laurel seeks him out and the two of them have a hearty rough and tumble relationship.

Relations with Adults

The relationship of young children toward the adults in the situation is usually indicative not only of the child's own personality pattern, but also of the feeling the adults have for him. In the following record Colin's acceptance of adult dicta, which although reasonable and without ill-feeling, must have seemed very distasteful to him, illustrates my meaning.

Toward the end of the morning, Colin shuffled through Abigail's buildings, destroying them completely. This did not seem to be impetuously done—but meditatively and deliberately. I told him that I thought Abigail would feel pretty bad about it and that I thought he had better put the blocks away—as a way of helping him to remember not to bust up other people's buildings. He was very reluctant to do the job—asked me if I would help him. I said I would help and started piling. He pushed the piles down and generally obstructed the process. I had to leave and explained that pushing down blocks made me feel like not helping him. He began putting the blocks in wrong shelves, practically building within the shelf—result: tumbling out of blocks. He announced he was tired. By this time the rest of the group was having juice. Jay and Laurel volunteered to help him and did so, and soon the job was done. Colin did not seem to harbor resentment toward me for pressing the job. He stood close to me, smoothed my hair back of my ears, grinned and said: *You look funny with your hair like that.*

Included in the Summaries by Activities report on "attitudes toward adults" was the following typical record.

Corinne shows an awareness of what is expected and clear understanding of "rules," etc. along with persistent and sly aversion to accepting them, alternating with apparent whole-hearted cooperation—the latter having a distinctly moral quality. Sudden bursting into laughter after saying or doing what she believes is not acceptable —flaunting her rebellion in the teeth of the adult. Seems to rest heavily and peacefully on a few "you're not alloweds." Accepts these with apparent comfort and sense of reassurance. Rarely uses adults as referee. In general independent of them, although occasionally seems to need to have warmth and hearty relationship.

Emotional Expression

Adults have learned so well the devices that successfully mask spontaneous feeling. They know which feelings it is proper to express and which ones it is proper to suppress. Young children fortunately have not learned these disguised subtleties of adult behavior, so that in watching children we are able to observe pure and undiluted feelings of joy and woe, and anger and fear, through their hearty direct expression of these feelings.

The following records can only slightly portray the contrasting pictures of Alec's bouncing joy, and Christopher's grim despair.

[Alec bursting with *joie de vivre!* Body unable to keep up with his mouncing spirits. Began fire engine play with Jay but easily and intermittently diverted by Jay's deliberate distractions, e.g., his nonsense sounds, rhythmic gestures, interpolated into building.] *Boy gee me.* [chanted] [Announced that he was going to be a fireman until he went to Sunday School. Outdoors ate pecks of snow, said his hands were] *Cold as dead!* [Picked up large flat solid snow piece and called it his dinner! In general, sportive, joyous, scattered.]

A bitter day for Christopher. He came into the yard with his usual gloomy face—greeted no one. There was a big drive on—digging out one little corner of snow in which Nan, Stanley, Kurt, and Cappy were engaged. It was a small space and there was some congestion. Christopher began pelting Stanley with hunks of snow. Stanley and Nan received the attacks in good spirit, smashed the hunks with shovels. Christopher was very serious throughout the attacking—tried to hit Stanley's face—succeeded a few times. Stanley laughed and returned the attack with vigorous smashings of snow. After a period of this, Stanley and Nan began tossing shovels of snow toward Christopher. Christopher fled into the garage, shut the door, emerged only to attack when he had the advantage. It seemed rather certain that to Stanley and Nan it was definitely a game—they laughed and

ducked away. To Christopher it was a bitter, aggressive business—
you hit without being hit. When the attack turned on him, his face
had a worried, tense expression.

The contrasting records of how two different children express their feelings of fear is revealing; Stanley intellectual and
devious, Camille direct and clear.

[When the tree sprayers came into the yard with their truck,
and began filling their tank with water, Stanley watched obviously
interested but fearful as well. He stood back covering his nose and
his mouth with his hands, said:] *It kills doesn't it? The spray?* [I
explained that it killed bugs and insects that destroyed the trees—
that they ate leaves covered with spray, that smelling it couldn't
hurt you. He was torn between wanting to see the process and fearing the results. Toward the end he said,] *You know if I ever got to
be a sprayer man then I wouldn't mind the spray, would I?*

[After juice, while standing beside me, Camille said conversationally:] *I bet you can't tell me something that will scare me.* Teacher:
You tell me something that scares you. *I can't—cause I don't know
what scares me.* Do animals scare you? *No.* Do voices, loud scary
voices? *No. I'll tell you what scares me—real tears of crying when
big people cry.* Why? *I don't know. It just does.* Have you ever
seen any big people cry? *Only my mother when she pretends.* Does
she really? *I don't know, that's what scares me.* [all this in easy, non-
apprehensive quality]

There are many variations in spontaneously expressed aggression from those with a verbal jesting quality and a puppy-like
bopping, to those seeming to have a tense and violent intent to
destroy.

[Alec was absorbed working on "a apartment house." Jeremy
was constructing a garage and Colin was ranging about with a car,
waiting for the garage to be finished. There was a general air of business and satisfying activity, when Alec in passing Jeremy's building
said:] *Tomorrow I'm going to bring my great big saw and saw everybody's head off!* [smiling] Jeremy: *Not me.* Alec: *No, not your's.*
Colin: *Not mine.* Alec: *Calvin's?* [Calvin was on the edge of the
play.] Colin: *No, not Calvin's, he's a nice boy!* Alec: *Carla's?*
Colin: *No-o-o.* Alec: *Colt's?* Colin: *No-o-o.* Alec: *Miss Beyer?*
Colin: *No-o-o!* Alec: *Calvin?* Colin: *No, he's a nice boy. Don't saw
Calvin's up because he's my friend.* Jeremy: *I'm a nice boy.* Alec: *So
am I.* [This conversation had quite an air of jollity—no intensity—not
even verbal aggressiveness, rather a rhythmic joke quality.]

[Later in the morning Alec upset Colin's cube box which he was carrying in a dump truck.] Colin: *You know what? Next Tuesday I'm gonna chop you up and saw you up—on the neck.* [laughing] Alec: *No, you won't—I'll chop you up and saw you off in a jiffy.* Colin: *Not me! You couldn't do it so fast!* Alec: *Well, I could start anyway next Tuesday.*

Alec: A day of *Sturm und Drang*—bumptious; aggressive; lightning attack; stony-faced destruction; violence; bloodshed; rending asunder; battering; bopping; scratching, etc. Began morning with definite idea of playing train—arranged "lumber" blocks along wall. Joined by Jay. Altercation at once over some slight difference of opinion when Alec tackled Jay. They rolled in puppy-like clinches, neither one very violent. While under the pile, Jay offered in his most beguiling tones: *Alec, I have an idea!* Alec responded by removing his body and listening attentively to the idea proffered.

An unseen beginning of a battle with Calvin. It was silently waged, with Alec definitely on the victorious side, until I saw what was happening and rescued Calvin, bleeding and weeping, deep scratches close to the eye and on mouth and forehead.

Sudden forays with Colin, head boppings with boards, unable to listen to Colin's reasoning or mine. Removal from scene of conflict only method which worked—i.e., stopped the slaughter.

These are some of the things we see in looking at young children; children as spontaneously scattered as leaves, or as contained as preserves on a shelf; children fumbling to learn to use themselves and the materials they find for their use; children conforming to or resisting adult standards; children clear and confident about human relationships or puzzled and incompetent; children whose bodies are effective instruments for their development and delight, and those whose bodies are clumsy impediments; children whose imaginative powers encompass a world of constantly unfolding wonders that stimulate endless and varied activity, and those whose understanding and capacity seem limited to a thin periphery of life's experiences. The opportunity which nursery school provides for observing not only individual pieces of behavior, but sequences and development in a particular area, makes it rich hunting ground for learning something about the structure of the thing we call personality. Not just what Alec did today has significance—but what he did the day before and the day after; how his behavior seemed to be affected by his grandfather's death; what a series of new maids means to a three-year-old; the effect of a new baby in the household, or Mother's going off for a trip; the complicated process of untying or loosening an overtight mother-child knot; arrivals and departures, are they casual or intense? These are some of the everyday or specialized occasions that have value to the teacher in seeking to understand what it must feel like to be this three- or four-year-old, and which offer cues toward helping children to be their most effective selves, and which incidentally provide a backdrop against which the validity of more specialized research may be measured.

The records on Stanley Thompson include a "First Impression," which was written during the first day or first few days of school; a "Summary of the Week" during the middle of October; a recorded conversation and description of play attending block play with sketch appended; a miscellaneous note describing Stanley's reaction to the tree sprayers, which seemed significant, and added to our picture of him, and two records of "first" experiences at the carpentry bench and with fingerpaints. There is also a sample of a "Summary by Activities" record which was taken twice yearly.

Records which are more group than individual are also included; for example the record on "expeditions," and language, and the long record of dramatic play.

Stanley Thompson (Age: Four Years, Four Months)

FIRST IMPRESSION—OCTOBER 11

E. Beyer (Teacher)

Stanley is a charming little boy. He is slight, pale, with an almost gnome-like face that suddenly breaks into an expression of light. In thinking of his first day I find three words coming again and again into my description of him—silent, sitting, serious. He sat on the edge of the sandbox for about forty minutes, silently digging, stopping occasionally to watch the others. He came to the block end of the yard when invited to come for tomato juice, and willingly assisted in making the table when I asked him to help me. He drank his juice silently and beamed when he saw the book *The Little Family*, and said, "I have that book. I love it. I wonder if it has the same words." He listened quietly without commenting as I read it, and when I had finished said, "It *has* the same words." He helped put the blocks away cheerfully.

He made no gross use of his body, did not attempt to handle any big materials—wagons, wheelbarrows, or blocks, except when I asked him to help me. He didn't attempt to climb on the ladder or the tree. This may be part of first day-ness, but I have a hunch it is part of Stanley-ness.

In the playroom he experimented with different toys in a quiet way, ironed, arranged the animals in a line, handled the dolls without really playing with them, seemed to be taking in the situation, rather than using it. His mother came early so that his time was limited. She said when I met her that she thought she had better come early for the rest of this week until he gets used to it. He has just gotten over a cold.

SUMMARY OF WEEK—OCTOBER 18 TO 22

Morning Records, E. W. Brown

Stanley is a little less the moving statue than he was in the early days. From sitting for long periods inside of a packing case or on a kiddykar in a desultory fashion, he has taken to hauling ladders tied together round about the yard and arranging them tilted against a packing case, and has even climbed carefully up and down them. He has done a little experimenting on the horizontal ladder, but it has been done very cautiously.

In our expeditions on the rocks he has displayed this same cautious tendency. He runs as if he were tied together and not quite free. His contacts with children have been limited because he has never seemed to seek companions, and has had to rely on those who sought him.

He spent one delicious morning of giggling with Polly. Nora and Clyde have had little to do with him, although they have not rejected him openly. He continues to soliloquize while he plays, in a very amiable way, occasionally directing remarks toward me. He likes stories and likes to make stories. He seems to have a real interest in words. After we had made the "High Story,"[1] he asked me if we could make another one about "Big Things" and then laughed and said, "And Little Things, Tiny Things, . . . and Faraway Things." He seemed to enjoy the concepts of bigness and highness, etc.

He has a delicious sense of humor. He is still pretty tied to Doggy. (toy dog), whom he brings daily. Is now reconciled to leaving Doggy in the locker; but frequently refers to him during the

---

1. See page 355.

morning and when we set forth on an expedition he remarked that Doggy would like to go because he likes to see things. Attributes rather human characteristics to Doggy, partly joking and, I believe, partly not. He is a very likeable little boy and he seems happy.

Monday, 8:45: Comes in with an elfin, quiet air and submits readily to the exam. As the nurse questions him about his breakfast he replies in monosyllables, but with each question his smile becomes broader.

Tuesday, 8:45: Brings Doggy as usual and puts him carefully in his locker saying: "I'm not going to forget where he is. I'll put him right in my locker. . . ."

Wednesday, 8:55: Comes in rather breathless from the rain: "My face got wet and my stockings got wet even under a umbrella. . . . We were just wondering how we would get in!"

Thursday, 8:40: Saunters in with hands in pockets.

Friday, 8:50: Comes in with dramatic slow effect, holding Doggy up in the air ahead of him. The nurse says, "Good morning, Doggy," and Stanley replies, "Good morning." To the nurse's questions he gives monosyllabic assent—is quiet and cooperative. (The chauffeur continues to bring him and call for him.)

SUMMARY OF WEEK—OCTOBER 18 TO 22

Expeditions, E. Beyer (Teacher)

The older group has been off on a number of expeditions this week. First to the climbing rock (near the back door) which was high and adventuresome. Nora and Clyde enjoyed the climbing especially, experimented all over its surface. Stanley climbed up once and down once and seemed satisfied with that. We went across the meadow to the southern end of the property, and found many kinds of rocks for climbing and scrambling. Even Stanley seemed to enjoy the climbing and they all seemed to have a sense of far-awayness.

We found a sloping outdoor theatre meadow and Clyde called it, "The running place." It is a wonderful place for a long run and back.

Today (Friday) we visited the men who were seeding the ground to the south of our yard. The children were very interested, asked why they were rolling it and why they didn't water it right away. The men gave them seeds to feel of and to see and gave us a little package to plant. Clyde promised to bring his rake and hoe so we could do a good job of planting.

He watched the men painting the "No Parking" sign on the courtyard. This seemed to interest them moderately. Nora was more interested in being on the other side of the fence from the play yard and seeing the children over it.

Nora, Clyde, Stanley, and Celia went for a "hike" with me on

Thursday. We went scrambling in a southerly direction to explore rocky places. Clyde had names for all the rocks. One was his "resting rock," one was a "wrinkled rock," and one was a "mountain rock." The biggest rock was truly intoxicating to them. They scrambled up and down it, stood on top of it, seemed excited by its height. I called them to sit down on the highest part of it and said, "I feel high on a mountain—as high as the sky. How high do you feel Clyde?" He answered, "I feel as high as the sky. No, I feel as high as an airplane flying." The following "as high as" statements came tumbling out with enthusiasm. I scribbled them down. When they had finished I said, "You've made a story—a high story," and read it to them. They seemed pleased. Clyde said, "We could call it 'High, High, High!'"

HIGH, HIGH, HIGH!

CLYDE: *As high as the sky. . . . As high as an airplane flying in the sky.*
STANLEY: *A high place where the moon and the sun is.*
NORA: *As high as trees . . . as high as that tree.*
STANLEY: *As high as houses.*
CELIA: *As high as this rock.*
STANLEY: *As high as a mountain.*
CLYDE: *As high as a mountain that goes through the sky.*
TEACHER: *As high as white clouds sailing by.*
STANLEY: *As high as a skyscraper . . . as high as a tower.*
CLYDE: *As high as a giant . . . and that's high!*

PLAYGROUND NOTES—NOVEMBER 8[2]

E. Beyer (Teacher)

[Clyde entered skipping, smiling. Fooled around Nora and Stanley, annoying them by touching their building. He piled three barrels.] E. Beyer: It looks like a gas tank. Clyde: *It is.* [Began making a gas station. Block enclosure with parallel boards inside and barrels with ropes attached for tanks. Nora came to get gas, pulling car:] *I want some gas.* Clyde: *It's not ready.* Nora: *O.K. I'll go to the station to meet somebody. My grandmother's in the hospital. She has her tonsils. . . .* Clyde: *Go-wan, go-wan.* [Very bothered tone of "What's that got to do with it?"] Nora: *She's very sick.* Clyde: *O.K. O.K. Gowan.* Nora: *I have to meet her.* Clyde: *Awright, I said gowan, awright, awright, gowan!* [Nora went off, came back later.] Nora: *Could you fix my car up? I want it back next week. And before you get it fixed, put some gas in it and get the tires pumped.* Clyde: *Do*

---

2. This record illustrates Stanley's frequent participant-observer role with a group of children.

you want this fixed? [pointing to broken part] Nora: *Could you screw it on?* Clyde: *Yes.* Nora: *I have to have it back next week. And don't forget the gas.* Clyde: *O.K. I'll drive you home.* Nora: *O.K. My home's right over there. Wight here, it is wight here. Thanks a lot. And put some gas in and pump the tires.* Clyde: *Yes, I know. . . . I know.* Nora: *Hey, Mister, I have to get my grandmother.* Clyde: *You have to call me up.* Nora: *10.* Clyde: *No, it's not 10. You have to look it up in the telephone book.* Nora: *O.K. 9-2-1. I have to have my car back. I have to get my grandmother.* Clyde: *Where is she?* Nora: *Down by the hospital.* Clyde: *I'll get her.* Nora: *Do you have much work to do?* Clyde: *No, I can get her.* Nora: *Tell her to put her dress on, 'cause I have lunch ready.* Clyde: *O.K. I'll run down and get her.* Nora: *That little girl with the blue dress on—get her because I need to play with her.* Clyde: *What's your number?* Nora: *6-0.* Clyde: *6-0.* Nora: *Who's speaking?* Clyde: *The gas man. I think I can't get her.* Nora: *O.K. I'll be over.* [Nora over to garage.] *Could we have our car wight away?* [Returned from roof of house.] *Wight away, wight away . . . wight away pease madame. How much you gonna charge?* Clyde: *Fifty cents.* Nora: *I don't have much money. Only five dollars. I have fifty cents too. And I have to have the car wight away.* [In all of this Stanley followed Nora, without a word.] *We're goin' to go fishin' now.* Clyde: *You have to come and get your car.* Nora: *You have gas in it?* Clyde: *No—I'll put it in. You need your tires checked?* Nora: *Yes, we need 'em checked.* Clyde: *You don't need that one checked, or that one, or that one. You have to go home and talk over the telephone.* Nora: *4-2-1-9.* Clyde: *Hello.* Nora: *Hello. Hey wissen. I need my tires checked very bad.* Clyde: *You don't 'cause I just feeled them.* Nora: *Well, put some gas in.* Clyde: *Yes, you need some gas 'cause I looked in the tank.* Stanley: *Well, I think I'll go off fishin'.* [first remark after being a silent participator]: Nora: *Well, we need the car. Do you have to pay him?* [to Stanley] Stanley: *Uh uh.* [no] Nora: *Fifty cents. Do you need the whole thing? Is this big enough? That's fifty cents. Here's fifty cents.* [Juice intervened. Play resumed immediately.]

Nora: *Well now we better go fishing. You wanna go Clyde?* Clyde: *Yes, this is my day off.* [They went off to the sandbox and cast ropes off the edge of the box.] *I'm pretending this is a fish.* Stanley: *I'm mad, 'cause this fish is going to bite me.* Clyde: *Nora, the little kids bother me.* [in a very tolerant voice] Nora: *What?* [Clyde repeats above.] Nora: *I think we have a lotta fish. We're gonna have fish for supper. You mind if we carry these buckets, we need 'em for the fish.* Clyde: *I'm not fishin' now.* [Makes cakes in sand. Stanley and Nora go off, Nora pulling Stanley half-way and Stanley then pulling Nora to garage. Clyde running up yard.] Nora: *We want to have our car fixed.* Clyde: *You can't have it fixed.* Nora: *We have to have it fixed.* Clyde: *It's closed.* Nora: *Is it going to be closed tomorrow?* Clyde: *Yes, and the next day, and the next, and the next, and the next.* Nora: *Well, we're gonna build a gas station of our own.*

[Play ceased at this point. All joined climbing and jumping from Polly's house. At end of which Nora said:] *Clyde, you want to wive with me?* [and to Stanley:] *Stanley, you could be the garage man.* Clyde: *O.K.* [Climbed inside.] Nora: *I have to get the supper ready. There's your room.* Clyde: [Came climbing out.] *I don't like the smell.* Nora: *You want to wive with me, Stanley?* Clyde: *You don't want to when you smell her. It's your mother that smells.* Nora: *You're a bad boy.* Clyde: *You mean you're a bad boy.* Nora: *He smells.* [Stanley climbed into house. Clyde reached in between boards.] Stanley: *He reached in. Clyde is reaching in the house.* [They climbed on the roof.] E. Beyer: *How was the fish?* Nora: *We didn't eat it, we put it in the garbage can. We ate out.* E. Beyer: *Where did you eat?* Nora: *At Longchamps.* [And so ended a long play that was sustained throughout most of the morning.]

FIRST CARPENTRY BENCH EXPERIENCE—JANUARY 20

E. Beyer (Teacher)

Very eager to work at it. Announced he had a good idea to make an airplane—a China Clipper. He selected his wood and started out purposefully and with a definite idea and skill in handling tools. He needed and asked for little help. Set to work in a very businesslike way and in a relatively short time produced the completed airplane which was solidly constructed and definitely realistic in appearance. He was pleased with it and wanted to continue working at the bench.

PLAY WITH BLOCKS—JANUARY 26

E. Beyer (Teacher)

[Stanley made a fort with cannons and men—"standpatter" dolls —on top.] Stanley: *They're hiding down behind the cannons and when anyone comes along they boom them right off.* E. Beyer: *Anybody who comes along? Yes, anybody!* What if you came along? *Oh, I'm the man that works it. They pop at anybody except me. The men sleep underneath. See all those men on top—they're shooting cannons. There's a doorway just where the walk is. There's a cannon on top of one place where the walk isn't. Some sleep inside—some sleep there. They're very busy men. Some men are shooting that way. They're shooting anything—anything that comes along.*

This play was almost entirely verbal plus a slight manipulation of the "men," and was entirely without "cannon" character. There was not a single "boom"—the whole thing was conducted in a laughing, busy way—almost joking quality.

TREE SPRAYERS AND INDOOR PLAY—APRIL 6

E. Beyer (Teacher)

April 6

You know I know how houses are made 'cause I've seen how they do it. And I've even seen how they tear them down. [Stanley spent the morning building a complete road and elevated highway—bridge-like structure. He used the measuring stick:] *You know real carpenters uses these and they're even longer.* [He commented from time to time that it was "70 high" and "70 long."]

FIRST FINGERPAINTING EXPERIENCE—APRIL 25

E. Beyer (Teacher)

[Asked to have all the colors. Used right fourth finger—dipped it into the red, then used small painting strokes, black line added—definite attempt to make lines.] *You know I wish I had fingerpainting at home. . . . You know, I wonder why you just give me a stick of it. You know, I wonder why you have to have it the right way. I wonder why it has to be wet. The next time I'd like to have it dry. I think it would make pretty pictures just the same. See—you could wash it right out. Can't you? We got lots of colors, haven't we? My black is all used up.* [Made a large circle.] *With fingerpaints it always does that. Do you know why it leaves a white place between?* [Dots with fingers.] *You have to wipe it right off, don't you? I wish I had these at home. . . . This just needs to be spread around here.* [wiping off onto other hand] *Scrape it off with your nail. There, I guess that's done.*

[Stanley was his usual loquacious self. Obviously pleased with the new thing. He did not seem especially concerned with the smear element—attacked it with painting techniques as he knew them. Tremendous interest in the process, the wet paper, what caused the white lines, etc.]

SUMMARIES BY ACTIVITIES—JUNE

E. Beyer (Teacher)

M. Gay (Music Teacher)

Sandbox (May 17)

[Chose corner.] *Don't anyone come here!* [Stood outside box. Made a wall by pushing up sand.] *You know how you can make it higher . . . by pushing sand away with a shovel, that's how you do it.* [Removing sand from outside of wall, made deep moat. Kenneth backed into it, crushing wall. Stanley:] *Ooohh! He did it, he does it even if you tell him not to. You know, I don't think these shovels are much good tin, they bend so easily.* [Kenneth came nearby again. Stanley held him off.] *If he busts down my wall, he'll get the darn heck* [repeat] *. . . that means sand on his sweater. Urr, it bent again. If I had another layer of tin, I'd stick it right on. It's tin, I know. Oh, it's so delicate, it's bending when I dig. You know, I know what they can do easy—bust!* [Kenneth busted wall.] *There, now I'm going to give him the darn heck.* [Sprinkled a little sand on sweater.] *I'm mad. I'm gonna plant a tree—and I'm never gonna have a termite on it . . . not a termite on a tree!*

[Found rock, imbedded it in sand.] *That's the best idea—a good idea. You know, Jean got the darn heck, 'cause her foot pushed my wall. Now I'm gonna make a pile just for the darn heck. Here's some deep, deep, deep property, no one can get in it.* [Dug deep hole, piling sand, excavated onto rock. Stayed outside of sandbox all the time.] *I'm gonna dig down to the dirt, I think in two more shovels full I'll be at the dirt. I can feel the dirt! Did you know that the sand lies on the dirt, the sandbox is just a square. Why do you call this a sandbox, it's just a square of wood. I know a good name for it . . . a sand square!* [smiling] *You know, I could have a house and be a plumber.*

I think I need some trees to plant. I'm going to pretend it was just planted. [Planted pine cone.] *Now I'm making a pipe.* [Ran shovel handle length of sandbox.]

Whole business *very* typical!

Climbing and Running

Climbing horizontal ladder. Stepped on lower bar, right foot in, slipped, pulled body on top, slipped once; little arm pull; crawled on knees across top, slowly, lowered legs at end. Cautious climbing over edge, down by skipping rungs. Careful eye movements; cautious performance.

Very typical.

Stanley's run is as much from the shoulders as from the legs. He swings legs out from the hips in widely scattered movements. Head, especially chin, is thrust forward, arms flexed and vigorously assisting movement. He runs with much zest and many excess movements.

Language

Warm use of words and ideas. Tendency to use formulas in a repeated fashion. "That's true, that's very perfectly true!" "These pesky buttons!" "Not a drop of fun." Kind of language that is most enjoyable for adults to hear. Have a feeling that he is quite unaware of its charm. Real interest in words and what they tell.

Social Behavior with Children

Choosey about whom he will play with. Seems freer about playing with others in out-of-doors situations. Nora usually the chosen. Consistently resistant with, antagonistic to Clyde. Freer physical contacts, hitting Clyde, fighting, etc. Indoors prefers to play alone, usually seeming to resent intrusion of others.

Social Relations to Adults

Stanley is such a charming person that his appeal to adults is very real and instantaneous. His spontaneous sharing of what he is thinking about—what he has at home, what he did after school, etc.—is charming and satisfying to the adult. His jokes and delightful sense of humor, his imaginative fantasies which he shares rather than displays—makes him delightful.

Routines

Stanley manages routines in his usual deliberate manner. In and out of clothes is a slow business, but finally effective. He rarely asks for help, and then merely intimates that he wishes someone would help him or accuses the rubber of being "pesky." Putting away is a chore which he accepts because life has put it there, but he is meticulous about putting away *only* what he has used.

REST: Stanley usually chooses a "good place" to rest, usually the door-space into the tile room. He lies quietly, apparently oblivious of other children. He seems relaxed and easy, moves about a little, sometimes changing position from lying on back to side.

JUICE: Stanley's least favorite juice is tomato, which he attacks in a lackadaisical fashion. He hesitates long before sipping, then sips in tentative, reluctant swallows, no enthusiasm or relish. Nibbles cracker squirrel-like, gnawing edges. Long pauses between sips. Spilled juice, sopped it up with napkin gingerly. "You know, this is only the second time I ever spilled my juice." Finished drinking, put wet napkin in cup. This juice time was fairly typical of Stanley. Pineapple juice goes down more quickly, he likes it better. He never complains, but hints and intimates that he wishes we had pineapple rather than tomato juice. It is always a rather pokey process, he is usually the last to finish, wiping mouth with deliberation, putting cup on tray and always pushing chairs into table.

BATHROOM (May 16): [Came into bathroom. I was sitting on the windowsill, writing. Walked over to basin, pulled up sleeves.] E. Beyer: You might go to the toilet before washing. [Stanley hesitated, then:] *You don't need to be in here, you know.* I just thought I'd finish my writing. [Left.] [Stanley then urinated, neglected to flush toilet, went to basin to wash. Scrutinized hands, one hand was very dirty, came to E. Beyer.] *You know, I wonder why this hand is so dirty. I was just in the sandbox all morning long.* I guess you'll need to do lots of scrubbing. *Maybe it's from the pine cones.* [Washed in rather dainty fashion, rubbed soap on, did not fill bowl with water. Held hands under running tap. Rubbed hands with soap. Rinsed, dried with dispatch, and scooted out of bathroom.

The whole performance was one of restraint mixed with dispatch—something you did and put behind you, little zest or interest in process. *Result* the thing. This is a fairly usual kind of bathroom procedure for Stanley. M. Gay reports that when the little ones are in the bathroom, he is inclined to peek around, not so much seeking to see, but waiting for the coast to be clear.

Painting and Clay

Stanley paints in vigorous, over-all movements, little space discrimination, wide smears, colors on top of each other, accompanied by conversation relative to the painting. He imbues the most smeary results with objectivity . . . storms, airplanes, zeppelins, lightning, fires, etc.

Stanley attacks clay seriously and deliberately—tries to make "things"—candle holders, mountains, boats, airplanes, etc. He seems less free about handling it than some other materials and seems to enjoy it less.

Pool

Very interested. Paddles vigorously; drags boats on strings; chases ducks in with avidity. Spends long periods playing.

Music

Stanley is so concerned with intellectual ideas it is hard for him to respond emotionally. Only a fair ear, which makes him often uncertain in recognition of the music. Instinctive response in movement, is gingerly and uncertain. He makes up for this in experimenting with variations of movement not particularly rhythmic or interpretative in quality. However, he loves music and is original in his ideas and responsive to but not unduly influenced by group participation.

CHAPTER 16

Conclusion

Problems of Evaluation of the Methods

WHILE SOME OF THE METHODS of studying the young child described in this book are more formal than others, as, for instance, Eugene Lerner's Ego-Blocking techniques, a common point of view underlies all of them: the psychologist is his own best instrument; methods exist to stimulate his own sensitivity, to give him material to observe. No method described here can be used as a mechanical aid to be scored in a standard fashion; the observer must be alert to new experiences, and nuances of old ones, which each child may show him, and furthermore to the new meanings of old experiences. The best guarantee of a sound and accurate approach aside from the natural objectivity, experience, and training of the observer is his awareness of factors which may influence the child's expressions at different times; some of these I shall now discuss briefly.

PROBLEMS OF "RELIABILITY"

We have seen that different children play out concepts, problems, and experiences which are widely varied in scope. One child deals with specific, concrete "here and now" matters that have to do with recent experiences. In one play session with the Miniature Life Toys Lila re-enacted a weekend when there were so many visitors that the family did not know where to put them to bed. At another time, she re-enacted an occasion when the family had recently seen some friends off on a boat; her structure was a vivid portrayal of the mob of people who smother a major liner at its departure. On one occasion Betsy played out a recent squabble with her mother; another time she re-enacted the startling experience of moving.

Such re-enactments of specific experiences are sometimes colored by surprise, or excitement, at other times by sheer fun; and at still other times by fear or worry about the meaning of the experience. When a child deals with these concrete experiences we do not expect him to deal with the same experiences the next month or the next week in another play session; if he has healthily absorbed the experience enacted first, he will be thinking about something new the next time. In relation to repetition of *content,* the concept of "reliability" in the statistical sense of repeatability is not very useful. What may be more reliably checked is the directness of affective expression, or realism of play through the different sessions; but even here, during the rapid development of the preschool years many changes are to be expected. In the following paragraphs we shall indicate some of the factors bearing on the problem of obtaining "reliability coefficients" for the present methods.

Birthdays, Christmas, having company, trips to the zoo, camping or vacation trips, have all been played out by the preschool children we have worked with, in this spirit of reliving interesting, exciting experiences, with their zest and joy or wonder. In contrast to these specific, immediate experiences, we may group together the examples of play which deal with *problems belonging to a period of time,* or a *developmental phase,* and which are usually dealt with in repeated play sessions over several weeks or months. Such temporary phase problems are those connected with a mother's pregnancy (what goes on inside her?), the anticipated birth of a baby and the feelings connected with it (I know how to feed a baby and take care of it, or I'd like to get rid of it, etc.). Problems of conscience-formation

(I'm a bad girl or a good girl) have also appeared temporarily in the play sessions of children who showed a wide range of activities over a period of time.

In greater contrast to both of these *immediate-experience* and *temporary-phase* foci of play sessions are those dealing with *persistent problems,* or *persistent solutions* to problems. Children who act out problems have presented the following themes among others: big things can hurt little things; how and whom can I love; where can I move freely. Persistent solutions have included: this is the way out, this is how to be safe, I can fight back.

The fantasy problems may be further subdivided into those having to do with status, importance, or recognition of self (*ego-centered*); as compared with those having to do with wishes, fears, hates, conflicts, delights (*drive-centered*); those having to do with an effort to solve a puzzling question such as how do airplanes land on the ground, how does the washing machine wringer work, or how do so many different things manage together inside mother's stomach (*cognitive-centered*); or whom can I belong to now (*relationship-centered*). The same child at different phases from two to five may have two or more of these emphases, and the sequences vary in different children. Here again, reliability cannot be measured in terms of rigid repetitiousness of theme from one period to another; rather, such repetitiousness may indicate that the child is having difficulty in working through his current problems, or that a disturbing environmental situation continues to stimulate anxiety.

The same considerations apply to the evaluation of a broader type of persistent pattern which we have seen in the play of a number of children who deal with *self-in-space.* These children played out or made toy structures expressing a concept of their relation to their world in the following terms: I sit tight and spread into the world slowly; I have to fight for myself against all comers—the baby, my brothers, my parents; I can hold out against all the bossy ones—maids, nurses, policemen, fathers, and mothers.

Still more broadly, some children define *space-time patterns.* The following are examples of patterns made by our children: inside the house things are quiet and safe, outside things are noisy and dangerous; first the house gets organized, then we have adventure and fun; the wild dangerous ones stay outside my world, then I can be safe inside; beyond these limits (set by policemen at the four sides of the rug) I do not go, within them I am free and inventive.

Not all children do all of these things—some children present a picture of a life space which is objective; some children make a setting for their dramatic activity; some children do not make large patterns at all, but directly act out the recent experiences, temporary problems or questions, or persistent problems or solutions we have referred to. Moreover, the same child will vary in his approach from time to time, depending on the relationship to his real life space which concerns him at a given time.

OTHER FACTORS IN VARIABILITY: DEVELOPMENTAL RELATIVITY

Changes in the level of intellectual functioning with age changes, and the implications of these for emotional change are documented in the work of Gesell, Bayley, and many others who have worked with preschool children. The child's awareness of body details and sex differences in bodies is probably dependent on his capacity to discriminate details more sharply (due to genetic factors in development) and also to his increasing concern with his own body as he takes more responsibility for caring for it, and his increasing opportunities for observation as he moves around more freely, as well as the pressure of his family or other people in his world toward control. We can expect changes in play activities concerned with the body due both to developmental influences and to cultural pressures.

As the child develops new motor and perceptual skills and new levels of integrated ego-functioning, he acquires new potentialities which may stimulate a new view of himself (e.g., Colin's "I can make good things") which puts his problems in a different perspective because he can cope with them better. This sort of shift underlies some of the changes from one year to another in a child's play; during a period of increasing awareness without a sense of adequate skill, anxiety, and defenses it may increase; as skill increases, anxiety in the normally flexible child decreases.

These variations in status, feelings toward the important parts of his world, and in the effectiveness of the dominant functions at each age level affect his *ego-strength and ability to cope with the changing expectations and demands placed on him, and the changing level of anxiety arising from his conflicts about his own impulses.* The best adjusted two-year-olds go through storm and stress at four, so that a picture at one age level has limitations in predictive value for a later age level. In our own material we have seen children who were relaxed at two and at five, but quite concerned about guilty feelings at four; and this presented a different personality picture in certain respects from that preceding and following the period of peak tension.

CHANGES IN STATUS

We have observed changes due to *loss of relative status*—a feeling of being left out when the mother gets preoccupied with a new baby, and thus the need to develop an aggressiveness which was not present before (Karin), and *loss due to the impact of environmental stresses at vulnerable phases* (a tonsil operation in a two-year-old whose language is incompletely developed). In such instances a child may show decreased organization, loss of capacity for delight, loss of rapport with the experimenter, or a more generalized depression (one child painted in dark browns and blacks, played with her back to the experimenter, and represented people as separated from her and with their backs to her when her mother was pregnant) or a more active effort (Patsy played going off with her father when her father remarried and her new mother became pregnant).

Variations due to after-effects of illness will also be expressed in play through greater fatiguability, irritability, hostility, fearsomeness, or dependence.

Environmental changes or events, such as moving to a new home and leaving the old familiar place, or a death among relatives or friends, may stimulate a new awareness of the world, new anxiety about self and one's relation to the world, especially in children attached to places and people with strong ties (Betsy, Colin).

Changes in play due to shifts in the field-situation at home have been observed as well. (Claudia's increased organization in her painting and play after an indulgent "mammie" type of nurse had left and been replaced by a more organized, strict nurse was an example of this.)

These changes are emphasized here because they are important to take into account in relation to our basic assumptions about what is going on in play. If we accept the fact that the child is growing from within and is going through a sequence of important changes in his life experiences, we shall take it for granted that his play will reflect this changing quality of his experience in mood, content, and in structure.

Changes due to the immediate field-situation have been observed in the hilarity and bound a child carries over to her play on one of the first days of spring (with the freedom of not having to wear heavy snowsuits, as well as the stimulus of the change in climate), and other changes have been recorded when play is carried out in a different place, or with a new experimenter. Some of these variations have been documented by Sears and his co-workers.[1]

VARIATIONS RELATED TO THE TEST SITUATION

The same tester will find the child *responding differently to tests differently structured*: for example, children often meet the challenge of an Ego-Blocking test with an aggression which was not hinted at in the permissive Miniature Life Toy test. *Examiners of different sexes* will have different meanings to the child and personalities of different threat or security value to the child will evoke different behavior. Some of our children have have been relaxed or happy or creative with one examiner and tense or blocked with another. The *first testing session* with any one may be different from the next session when the child feels less need to prove himself. The *realism* of Miniature Life Toys

1. R. R. Sears, "Influence of Methodological Factors in Doll Play Performance," *Child Development,* XVIII (1947), 190-97.

may tap a different level from that reached by the more diffuse material of dough or cold cream, but these differences will vary from child to child, as will children's preferences for different media. Thus a child may vary from hour to hour, day to day, week to week, tester to tester, or test to test. This is one reason why a battery of tests over a period of time is the only way to get an adequate basis for evaluation of the range within which this variation occurs, the ceilings or limits which distinguish one child from another, and the predominant patterns of persistence and change.

CULTURAL RELATIVITIES

Bühler, adapting Lowenfeld's world-technique, has pointed to certain variations in "types of world" produced by children in different European countries;[2] this we expect when we realize, as we noted earlier, that the child's inner life must necessarily develop within the space-time structures and emotional relationships which he experiences. Such group differences can reflect literal representations of the child's space-time or personal world; they can be due to pressures and persistent deep-level problems, widespread in the culture group because they are rooted in interpersonal conflicts intrinsic to the structure of the culture; or they can reflect patterns characteristic of the sub-culture. (For example, the small family unit of American and Western European life may stimulate more intense oedipal rivalries and authority problems than develop in the more diffuse relationships of the larger joint family in India.)

More specifically, his play reflects changing aspects of the setting, his changing relationships in it, and the sequence of his problems in these relationships with his successive efforts at solution of them, in his own personal situation. In the United States we can expect comparable *normal variations in the situations presenting conflict; in the structures produced; in the symbolic value of specific objects; in the patterns of handling affect and impulse* (by setting limits, by measured releases, or

---

2. Charlotte Bühler, "National Differences in 'World Test' Projection Patterns," *Journal of Projective Techniques,* XVI (1952), 42-55.

climactic release, etc.); *in the orientation to space;* in *flexibility* of integrating materials from different sources, etc. Thus we noted that Puerto Rican slum children in New York day-care centers do not organize objects into formal patterns as Westchester children do, nor do they often make plots which lead to climactic release. These children are warm and friendly but fluid as water. By middle-class standards they seemed infantile. The living conditions of the Puerto Rican children are chaotic and there is often an almost total lack of consistent structure and of sustained relationships in their homes.

In other words, the subculture provides both the problems, and the usable resources for dealing with the problems. Such subculture variations include response to changed conditions; I referred to the fact that during the period of rigid pediatric and child-rearing techniques of the '30's, hostility to crib, playpen, authorities, etc., was more frequent than we find it now. Three dozen Miniature Life Toy cribs were expended between 1937 and 1944. In 1953 not one out of thirty children attacked a crib or bed. The prevalence of "how to do it" devices now appears to stimulate or support more concern with "how it works."

We must also give attention to *place variations*: children who live near airports may integrate the movement of planes into their experience in ways different from those appearing in other children. Children who live close to farms with many animals assimilate these to give images to their feelings, and are also stimulated to be aware of different problems from those pressed upon the airport children.

FAMILY RELATIVITY

Field-theory could have led us to assume that different *family atmospheres and constructions* would produce very different intensities as well as patterns of oedipal problem, and of sibling rivalry, or attitude toward the baby.

Major variables might hypothetically be: the emotional level of mother, father; the authority pattern of mother, father; the diffusion of parent-child relationships among grandparents and others; the number of other children; the emotional meaning of other children and the child's picture of family structure; and exposure to parents' sexual activities. For instance, in family X, with grandparents living in, four children, children's sleeping space well-separated from adults, the four-year-olds might not be so deeply involved in oedipal problems, as in family Y with two children and no adults to share their love aside from their parents. Differences in emotional relations with parents will be reflected in the range and character of other fantasies and themes.

Evaluation of Conflicts and Problems

Conflicts are part of growing up and probably all children in our culture have them; certainly the children in our groups played out many of the same conflicts about sibling relations and feelings for parents which we find in disturbed children who are brought to a clinic for help. When a child acts out hostile or angry feelings we cannot consider this aggressive action evidence of abnormal disturbance in itself. If he enjoys a wide range of relationships and interests and is spontaneous in his own quiet or active way, we can simply say that he is working through some of the typical problems of children in our culture, vigorously and evidently successfully. If some of the answers to these reality questions are uncertain, we look at the relation of (and balance of) such content with other themes, for example, the consequences in the play sequences themselves of the aggressive activities: Do they lead to a mounting crescendo of aggressive fantasy with no release? Do they arouse anxiety? If his play does not succeed in helping him to work through his problems, if he gets stuck and is bogged down with tension about them, if they make him disorganized, then he may need help.

Thus, the fact that we can find in normal groups the same conflicts and problems which bring children to clinics points up the need for clarifying the maneuvers used by children who work out their problems without serious interference with personality growth. As we have noted, we need, if possible, to be able to discriminate particularly between transient and sometimes exaggerated efforts in critical periods or at times of stress and the long-term or deeply ingrained attitudes which may be expressed in different behavior at different times.

We referred earlier to persistent problems which may be rooted in persisting aspects of the life space, such as lack of reliable structure in home life, or excessive restrictions which make the child preoccupied with finding a way out. We have also referred to certain persistent personality trends. These have their roots in (a) hereditary and *congenital tendencies* toward "activity," or "sensitivity," or special areas of skill, etc.; (b) *massive infantile conditioning* in terms of specific modes of zonal behavior which are generalized into lasting orientations; (c) *subsequent persistent pressure* such as chronic tension in an anxious mother; (d) *deeply stirring traumata,* or conversely persistent gratifications or *deeply integrating "blessings"* which weave a strong fabric of trust or confidence. Among the persistent tendencies would be those linked to persistent qualities of the organism, both constitutional and learned—economy of movement, level of activity, perceptual acuity, affective nuances, capacity for integration or for original responses, etc. A major problem of prediction either on the basis of real-life data or on the basis of "projective" data confronts the psychologist dealing with young children.

PROBLEMS OF INTERPRETATION

Problems of interpretation thus arise from the fact that content appearing in a given test may refer to any of the following: persistent generalized cortical-thalamic-autonomic patterns; *persistent problems* (e.g., bigger people threaten little people); *persistent solutions* (finding a way out); temporary *phase problems;* immediate *transitory experiences.* It is often impossible to judge whether a perceptual or affective response is related to deep-rooted persistent patterns or to one of the various transient aspects of experience which may be important to the preschool child. At a time when so much of life is bewildering, new or even threatening, the experience of seeing all of one's furniture quickly loaded on to a moving van may for the time being be of greater moment than the experiences of the family drama.

I have indicated that it is foolhardy to take interpretations of children's projective behavior for granted and that stereotyped interpretations of symbolic meanings, particularly, can easily be erroneous unless they are checked with evidence from a variety of sources.

Mistakes are very commonly made in interpreting inhibited behavior: Albert, at the age of two years, never cried during his first days of nursery school; his teachers considered him inhibited, restrained apparently by adult standards of self-control. He would stand quietly at the edge of the room, his chin trembling, an occasional tear rolling out of his eye without ever letting out a sound. Actually his parents had never seen him behave this way; a sensitive child rather easily upset, he had been explosive and free in his crying from early days. Calvin never played at school; diffident and remote, he watched all year from the sidelines, and observers felt that he was a child without spontaneity. The mother of another child at school reported to the contrary, that at home with his mother, Calvin was a lively, gay, spontaneous, laughing youngster.

Sometimes these contrasts between home and school behavior are due to a need for certain materials. Dona was silent and withdrawn at nursery school until music time when she became a released, gay child. Maggie was an earthy child encouraged to cruise freely in her neighborhood; competent and self-sustaining, she loved to play with clay, sand, dough, and "mixy" things at home. At school she seemed stolid, unresponsive, awkward, and insecure. Her teachers thought she must be under constant adult threat; home visits showed her independent and happy at home; evidently enjoying a kind of freedom and country life with animals that made the more organized patterns of school life strange and alien by contrast.

Home visits are not always necessary to evaluate behavior if a child gives clues through varying responses to different situations at school. Claudia sat and sucked her thumb most of the first few weeks at school; she made little use of apparatus, toys, or children. One of her first periods of expansion came when she was given the fingerpaints which she approached first in a gingerly way, then smeared over a wide area with great free-dom, almost aggressively.

Jay produced a number of absurd toy arrangements at first, but did not do so at a later date. It was quite likely that the absurd arrangements, like some of his nonsense talk, were largely an expression of embarrassment or confusion in the situation, resulting from a feeling that perhaps these little toys were sissy and not appropriate to the activities of a big boy like himself.

Cecily in her first session lined up toys in a rigid way against legs of the cot and desk in the room with a complete absence of any functional play, but in several later sessions did not re-peat this pattern or anything like it. Instead, she carried on a quiet play with the toys relevant to her fantasy, and at the end handled them not only with freedom but with some aggression. In this case, the apparent rigidity of the first pattern did not have so much meaning evidently for personality structure at its core, but was an expression of a way of adjusting to a new situation in which she felt insecure.

Among the children with whom we worked, however, there was no child who began with spontaneous handling of the toys or fluid structures subservient to fantasy who became rigid subsequently during the period of our observation.

These examples have been given to urge the point that in-hibited, constrained, rigid behavior in young children is not always really generalized or deep; usually checking with other materials in a stable atmosphere of reassurance releases the child to a point where other facets of the personality can be seen.

Similarly, assumptions about aggressive or sexual compul-sions appearing in play situations must be handled critically. When Camille smashed some small celluloid dolls with a hammer, or later "killed" all the dolls that might be considered to repre-sent mothers or maids, it could have been easy to assume violent hostility as a chief content of her emotional life. Actually, her daily casualness and rapport with her mother, her intellectual clarity about "good" and "naughty," her ability to "let out" an intense impulse in the "screaming room," her subtle handling of people, all pointed to the fact that her aggression was not "stealing the show" but reined by a clear mind and absorbed by a rich and complex personality. Alec's sex compulsion, appearing repeatedly in toy sessions, would have convinced anyone that here was a very neurotic little boy if one had not seen the long hours of happy play with other children, enjoyment of music, painting, blocks, and warm friendly relations with adults.

The fact that at three the normal child is changing, means that patterns like Alec's sex compulsions have not often become central or dominating, nor have the patterns of inhibition grown hard and crusty. Wise interpretation depends not only on recognition of the child's variability but a careful use of all the data relevant to interpretation of a single item which in itself might have different explanations.

A related question of considerable interest to the clinician and student of personality is whether it is possible to reconstruct a picture of the child's objective past situation from material of the sort produced in the Miniature Life Toys procedure. We may say at the outset that it would require a parallel objective record of the child's life and record of his projections to answer this question accurately. At this time we can point out a few pitfalls that must be remembered by anyone who makes the attempt. The major questions is how to understand biological predispositions in relation to the pressure of experience. When we know that Colin's mother was a sensitive and aesthetically appreciative person with a gift for sharing delight in plants, flowers, pictures, with her children, we infer that Colin got much of his delicate aesthetic responsiveness from her. But would he have been responsive to these things if he had not had a general low threshold for sensitiveness to aesthetic and sensuous experience? Would Kurt brought up by Colin's mother have developed Colin's range of sensory delights? Would Colin brought up by Kurt's mother have developed Kurt's preoccupation with mechanical gadgets and things to be manipulated? Observers of the two children think not. Clues to the origin of patterns which are well supported by the constitutional base of the child, as compared with those which are not, can be had in the degree of effort involved in supporting a pattern. For instance, Joyce had one strong trend toward a narcissistic pattern of satisfactions, and another toward aggressive competitiveness. The latter seemed forced and strained where the former seemed integral and deep and natural to her. Incoordinations may appear in a child who is trying to maintain a rapid family tempo against the pull of her own slower tempo; tensions, lack of deep satisfaction in the patterns, anxiety may arise from stress between the need to take on a family pattern and the need to fulfill one's own biological entelechy.

An insurmountable difficulty arises here in our attempt to disentangle constitutional bases of temperament and deep trends encouraged by infancy experience. For instance, how can we sort out the aspects of Joyce's individualistic sensory responsiveness which were based in original constitutional tendencies and those which grew from her response to early handling? We can only say that Joyce as a baby handled in the primitive fashion—passed around from one adult to another and treated to more social stimulation—*might* have been a difficult child, and that given the experiences of long periods alone in the crib a baby of different temperament *might* not have developed her patterns of receptive enjoyment.

At another level, to what extent can we reconstruct the child's nursing, elimination, and property training from the behavior and ideas he gives us in the play session? Is a strong urge to suck on a bottle an indication of past satisfaction or past deprivation? Is orderly handling of toys an indication of past training in neatness or of lack of compulsiveness to scatter things, or a "natural sense of form"?

Is a dramatic representation of spanking a clue to the mother's method of punishment and the child's actual experience, or to his feeling of guilt and need for a spanking, or a reaction to patterns of play which other children have carried on in the group?

Questions of this sort cannot be answered safely, if at all, without seeing each item in terms of its meaning and relation to the total pattern of the child's play, especially to points of anxiety, strain, inhibition, and perseveration. A spanking is not likely to be dramatized repeatedly over a long period unless the idea is sustained by inner feeling about it. Similarly, most children play with the toilet for a little while; the child who avoids it completely, or plays with it much longer than others is most likely to have had traumatic experiences with it. Even when we find good evidence for coming to conclusions about the child's *feeling*, it is seldom safe to infer what the objective experience was. One child may feel very slightly frustrated or delighted by a type of treatment which affected another child deeply. It is sounder to say "Evidently the child felt . . ." than it is to say "Evidently the mother did. . . ."

If we wish to summarize, then, the *ways of checking evidence* important to take account of before taking a hypothesis seriously, we may list (a) internal evidence from records of each session and repeated sessions or follow-up sessions planned to test hypotheses, and (b) external evidence from other test techniques and from observations at home, at school, and in other life situations. Both internal and external evidence may be used to answer four questions: (1) What does this behavior, fantasy, structure, or verbal pattern mean to the child? (2) How important is it: Is it central and persistent, or incidental and transitory? (3) Is it a clue to a major problem, or is the trend to which it points offset and held in suspension by capacities and trends which have not yet been fully observed? (4) What variations, in what contexts, does the trend show? (5) What is its role in the dynamic and changing picture of the child?

The relation between the implications of the material itself and events or experience at home or school will throw light on the personality organization of the child, the degree of strain aroused by home or school experience, and the child's method of handling it.

Appendices

The Analysis of
Miniature Life Toy Records

DURING THE FIRST seven years of my most intensive work with Miniature Life Toys, I developed a Miniature Life Toys Summary and a series of check lists for noting behavior, and evidences of organizing and motivational patterns in the child; these were built step by step, *empirically*, from the findings in the records of play sessions. The items included do not, therefore, represent an *a priori* framework, but a way of organizing data from Miniature Life Toy records. Every item refers to responses given by children in a particular area over a given period of time, and thus is culture-dependent to a high degree. They are not intended to be used mechanically, or as a substitute for clinical integration, but rather as a help to "the development of the observer as his own best instrument." The outlines would be different if they had developed out of work with children from another culture or even subculture; within themselves they reflect not only some of the assumptions rooted in the psychology of the last fifteen years, but also the characteristics of the children who were studied. Other children in other settings would show different qualities, patterns of balance and compensation of temperamental trends, different ways of expressing similar needs, as well as different needs. Just as one must learn the dialect of any subculture in order to communicate with its people, one must also learn to develop the relevant structure for analysis of personality. The outlines which follow are therefore to be regarded as suggestive only; any of them may be adapted and revised freely by the worker as he learns to know the group of children with whom he is working. It would contradict the spirit of this approach for me or anyone to freeze any of these outlines or to consider them a final or standardized method of analysis. They do not constitute a "test," but a series of aids, each of which will be useful to different workers at different stages of growth in child study.

The outlines include the following:

1. A schema for analyzing and summarizing Miniature Life Toy records.

2. Aspects for analysis in all free play with dolls, blocks, etc.

3. A student nursery school observation outline.

4. Outlines for the study of a child: cultural, family developmental status factors, interests, indices of anxiety, foci of anxiety, etc.

5. Temperament and spontaneity observations.

1. Miniature Life Toy Record Analysis

Child's Name:_____   Experimenter:_____

Address:_____   Recorder:_____

Date of Birth:_____   Date:_____Hour:_____

Reason for test:_____   Place and setup:_____

Other background (family constellation, etc.)

A. *Summary of the play session, its process, and implications:*

B. *Detailed analysis:*

Child's initial approach:

Relation to experimenter and changes in this relationship:

Meaning of session to the child:

Toys used first: Toys used most:

Toys rejected, handled abortively, looked at suspiciously, etc.:

Toys of no concern, positive or negative:

Chief activities: (E.g., 6 baby-feeding episodes, 3 fighting episodes, prolonged visiting, sequence of attack by enemy followed by retaliation, or what? If child tries to destroy limits or barriers or find a way out, what happens?)

Level of organization and structure, and relation of structuring to other behavior: (E.g., structure is a stage-setting; way of getting oriented, followed by no activity; substitute for activity, etc.? Instrumental values of the structure in the child's microcosm; functional relation of areas of freedom to contricted areas.)

Level of fantasy: (Realism vs. unrealism; symbolism quality and distance; dreaminess vs. object-oriented, or inner- vs. outer-stimulated fantasy.)

Process or sequences: (Alternating themes; repeated theme, plot or story; symphonic structure, or what? Which themes are repeated? Which ones are accompanied with anxiety, or thought-disruption? Which bring comfort and increasing integration? At which themes did child become tense, blocked, furtive, or released? What motives or feelings underly shifts of attitude or orientation in the sequences? Through what theme did the problem get resolved? What sequences or clusters are repeated?)

Level of emotional expression: (What feelings expressed openly; indirectly; muted; repressed; absent? Note delight, love, anxiety, or fear, anger, et al. *In response to what?* Prevailing tone warm, detached, or gay, sober?)

Motor behavior: (Tempo, energy, area, coordination of large-muscle behavior. Range of postures, relaxed-tense quality, jerky-smooth, etc. Changes in motor ease or tempo, when, in response to what stimulus or feeling?)

Manipulatory behavior: (Skill, strength, delicacy or clumsiness; variations when?)

Cognitive behavior: (Note observation, inspection, curiosity, comparisons, grouping or classifying; appraisals of size; comments on function, etc. Note accuracy of form use, awareness of details; problem-solving. For what purposes is cognition used? What drives influence different functions?)

Perceptual behavior: (In addition to the above, response to color, or other sensory qualities, and new-old, dirty-clean, broken, real-unreal, characteristics of the toys, or other persistent selective tendencies in perception.)

Sensory responses: (In addition to the above, responses to auditory stimuli, outside sounds; tactual stimuli such as soft textures; oral stimuli such as nursing bottle, etc. Body satisfactions. Kinaesthetic satisfactions.)

Verbal expression: (Little, moderate, constant; function of verbalizing—socially directed or autistic; tendencies to be fragmentary, or perseverative. Originality, conventionality, inventiveness, etc. Clarity, infantilisms, variations in maturity, when, etc. Emotional expression, sound effects, etc. Changes from predominant verbal pattern in response to what?)

Dramatizing and function of dramatization: (Completeness, realism, vigor, affective tone of acting out; attitudes of putting on a show vs. creating a dramatic story for oneself, etc.)

Use of space:

Toys: (Tightly or loosely arranged; small or large area; within assumed limits or going outside. Describe. Left-right, front-back locality of certain objects. Relation of placement of toys to child's body—close, distant. Use of body as part of the structure. Changes from beginning to end of hour.)

Child's own body behavior: (Moved arms from steady sitting position; shifted up and down from sitting position; gross movements from one side to another over entire room. Child's body is solely an instrument, or a source of kinaesthetic pleasure.)

Relation to experimenter: (Child faces experimenter watchfully, expecting help, socially or what? Turns his back to experimenter, ignoring, actively shutting out. Orients himself to the toys, resulting in different relation to experimenter at different times. Assumes experimenter's interest; expects help; is suspicious; or what? Changes during the session and feelings implied in these changes.)

Use of objects: (Limits himself to toys; uses everything in the room; asks for objects not present; wants to take things home. Expresses love toward teddy, soft kitty, mouse, baby, washing-machine, etc.; attacks wild animal, baby, father, mother; restores broken furniture, broken animal, broken doll, etc.)

Meaning of objects to the child: (Something easily mastered, something cut, something to make arrangements out of, or to construct, something wonderful—a fairyland, sissy things, or what.)

C. *Evidence and/or questions regarding child's feeling about:*

Self: (As little or big; needing protection or love; being dangerous, angry or wild; wanting limits or punishment; being included or isolated; identifying with whom, etc.)

Self in space: (Feels self as center; in privileged seat; or vis-à-vis others; competitors or authorities.)

Mother: (As caring for child, going away, being loved by father, preoccupied with baby, cross, affectionate, interested in clothes, busy with housework.)

Father: (As preoccupied with office, as loving mother, as decisive controller.)

Baby: (As cute, wanting to be fed, sleeping, needing to be tucked in, a nuisance, a thread, competitor, or what?)

Siblings: (As companions, as allies or partners in fight, as preferred by mother.)

Home inside: (Passive, graceful, safe, argumentative, neat, busy, sociable, etc.)

Home outside: (Noisy, conflicted, adventuresome, etc.)

Town: (E.g., policeman is to protect, limit, or control traffic, or punish, or what?)

Animals: (Duplicate family life, or fight, attack, engage in sex activities, go on adventures, or what?)

Other: (E.g., soldiers punish wild animals, battle the enemy, etc.)

D. *Comparison of record with child's life situation and behavior: evidence of home events congruent with or opposed to Miniature Life Toy productions.*

In Miniature Life Toys:	*At Home:*
Mother spanks.	Mother doesn't spank.
Child breaks things.	Child over-conforms.
Father plays with child.	Father dead, away much, or
Crib loaded with food,	divorced.
dirty things, babies.	Mother pregnant.
Baby thrown into corner.	Baby sleeps in Mother's room.

What inferences are suggested by difference and similarities between the life situation and the fantasy?

Note child's concern with recent events, temporary phase problems, persistent problems, persistent solutions.

Role of fantasy in the child's relation to his situation: (Uses fantasy to absorb the past, rehearse the future, compensate for the present, extend the present, or what?)

E. *Summary of strengths:*

F. *Problem Areas and the child's ways of handling them:*

G. *Comments, questions, predictions, recommendations:*

2. Analysis of Children's Creative Products, Play, and Work

A. *What evidences are there for concern with any of the following motives or needs:*

Achievement: (Tallest, longest, etc.; work, workmen, tools, derricks, construction.)

Acquisition: (Of things, friends, prestige, quality such as nicest, most expensive, etc.)

Activity: (Planes, cars, trains, things that go; body activity.)

Adventure: (Boat, plane, dog show, ocean, etc.)

Aesthetic interest: (Making something pretty, nice; balancing or organizing by colors, etc.)

Aggression: (Expressed verbally, physically to objects or people: rough, dumping, throwing, twisting, breaking; direct, completed: hitting, scratching, throwing, soiling, shooting, destroying, aborted, or interrupted gesture of attack; indirect and in fantasy, using aggressive symbols only; alligator, fire engine, locomotive, etc.

Anal: (Toileting, piling, blocked movement; dirt, clay, mud as substitutes; bedwetting, soiling, messing, constipation, or what?)

Anger: (Verbal, emotional, disruptive, etc.)

Anxiety: (Emotional, aborted behavior, inhibited movement, small area, tight organization, anxious facial expression, querulous voice, avoidance of certain objects; hesitancy, withdrawal; dolls—passive roles only, special concern with broken ones; repetitive themes, rigid structures; motor expression: trembling, jerky, nervous movements; tics; somatic: flushing, blushing, growing pale, pupil dilation, damp hands, etc.; physical symptoms: enuresis, loss of appetite, headache, vomiting, etc.; can't concentrate, disorganized, scattered; blocked insight or difficulty with attention and memory. Activity: blocked exploration, social response, verbalization, creative work, etc.)

Authority: (Coercion by, competition with, compliance: excessively careful and uncalled for putting-away, extreme clinging to suggested limits, constant lack of free movement; deference; inhibited movement or action; organization without function; monotone; preoccupation with fences, tracks, persons, cages, platforms, rigid lines, squares. Use of train, policemen, tracks, fences.)

Autonomy: (Independence of action, thought, self-care, judgments, values, choices.)

Competition: (In size, speed, importance, etc.)

Constraint: (By limits set by policeman or parent; barriers, fences, etc.)

Coping: (By limiting, selecting from the situation; shutting out grownups; soliciting help from grownups; evading, denying; balancing gratifications and frustrations; alternating tension and non-tension areas.)

Creating: (Making things; constructing houses, garages, stores, stations, airports.)

Delight: (In sensory, social, or what situations; expressed by activity, emotional expression, etc.)

Dependence: (Need for care, infantile satisfaction, love: nursing bottle, baby play.)

Depression: (Disappointment, melancholy, sadness, in what situations?)

Dominance: (Of adults, babies, older, younger, or same age children, animals, or whom?)

Excitement-wish: (How desired—rides, trips, animal chase, battle, fire, etc.; for action, noise, ideas, making something happen, or what?)

Family dependence: (Tree, house, grouped beds or chairs.)

Fantasy and legendary figures: (Santa Claus, good fairy, witch, Donald Duck, etc.)

Fear: (Of aggressive animals or birds of prey; person—father, mother, nurse, older sibling, doctor, policeman; object—locomotive, fire-whistle, water, etc.; experience or event—shampoo, spanking, departure of parents; fantasy-object—bogey-man, Santa Claus, etc.)

Food: (Desire or resistance; pleasure; choices; preparation of, in kitchen, etc.; eating retreats; parties; treats; rewards; pressures.)

Freedom from constraint: (Of crib, playpen, fence, prison.)

Frustration: (By adult, child, baby, animal, object, or what?)

Genital interest: (Size, activity, changes in penis; masturbatory impulses, etc.)

Gift desire: (Santa Claus, birthday party, coming-home presents, etc. What, from whom? When?)

Gratification: (Getting wish satisfied, reward, praise, love, food, clothes, toys, or what? With what result?)

Hate: (Antagonism, rejection, expressed how, to whom, when?)

Help to others: (Support, encouragement, consolation, protection. Who is helped, how?)

Help wish: (Desire for support, protection, etc.)

Injury-experience: (Warding off, prevention, restoration; of what?)

Jealousy: (Expressed how, to whom?)

Loss: (Deprivation, separation, isolation; from whom? Isolating, separating structures.)

Love problems: (Excessive fondling of fur dog, sitting on lap of experimenter or fondling experimenter; kissing; oral preoccupation; asking "do you like me," etc.; tucking in, cuddling, etc.)

Love wish: (Verbal, tactual, etc.)

Manipulation: (Exploring, experimenting; taking apart, putting together.)

Mastery: (Of broken object by fixing; of falling by giving a secure base, or support; of aggressive threat by attack, etc.)

Nature: (Birds, animals, moon, stars, plants, as objects of delight or satisfaction.)

New experience: (For what?)

Passivity: (People lying down, sleeping only; sitting; maintaining receptive positions.)

Perfection: (Correctness; fitting, completeness, form clarity, etc.)

Possession: (Of parent, playmate, pet, or what?)

Punishment: (Of whom, how, by whom, for what, with what result?)

Rejection: (Of what or whom by whom?)

Religious interest: (God, heaven, etc.)

Resistance: (To whom, why, etc.)

Safety devices: (Productive structures, house, bomb shelters, protective figure—father, policeman, watchdog, etc.)

Sensory experience desire: (Color, shiny surfaces, light, texture, etc.)

Sex: (Curiosity, exploration, experience, conflict; toileting, clothes, inspection; concerned with pregnancy, birth, adult sex behavior, or what?)

Togetherness: (Companionship, with whom, or what, when. Go places together, sleep together, eat, play, etc.)

B. *Form values:* (Aside from reality-demand of structure created)

Large: (Freedom, assertion, ambition, competitiveness, or what?)

Small: (Inferiority, constraint, or what?)

Open-loose: (Freedom; casualness; or if extreme, scattered; fear of constraint; or vague perception.)

Tight-closed: (Inhibited, defensive, need for protection, acceptance of limits; or realistic of actual tight structures in child's environment; or identification with adult orientation as with carpenter-father.)

Straight lines: (Control, accepting authority, or simplest organization for young child to use? Vertical: masculine, assertive; horizontal: passive.)

Squares, oblongs: (Masculine, or, if compulsive or rigid, over-dependent on authority.)

Circles, curves: (Feminine, dependent, pliant, or free like airplane flight.)

Balance-inbalance: (Degree of integration, dynamic motive, or what?)

Rhythmic-jerky: (Degree of tension, ease of impulse-flow.)

Body-image patterns: (Compactness, airiness, slenderness, fatness, etc.)

Use of form: (Functional as vehicle for ideas; design; defense; compulsive; repetitious? Used with people or not: are they active or passive? Is child inhibited or released by structure, organization, form? Is child blocked or stimulated by amorphous materials and lack of structure?)

Summary of functions of form: (Protection, achievement, creative expression, etc.)

C. Content: (Possible meanings or uses of certain objects)

People
  Adults only: (Authority symbols: police, parents, maids, doctor, or who? Aggression symbols: police, firemen, soldiers, doctor, father, mother, brother, or who? Protection symbols: mother, Red Cross nurse, policeman, grandmother, or who?)

  Children: (Own or opposite sex; own age, older, younger; sibling role; baby as companions, competitors, aggressors, defenders, dependents, something to love?)

  Adults and children: (Protective, threatening: big-little, companionable, instructing, disciplining.)

Babies: (Cute, naughty or rebellious objects of care or affection; rivals; or what?)

Animals

With people or alone: (If alone, as symbols of people?)

Aggressive: (Lion, tiger, rhino, snake, crocodile, bull, or what?)

Other wild animals, used how: (Expressing freedom, impulsiveness, wildness, sex, unstructured energy, or what?)

Love-objects: (Cat, dog, lamb, rabbit, etc.)

Objects

Without animals or people, or with?

Freedom-need: (Water-play.)

Protection-symbols: (House, bomb shelter, fence, wall, farm-yard, barn, etc.)

Adventure-symbol: (Boat, airplane, train, fire-engine, horse, cowboy, Indian, etc.)

Authority symbol: (Train, tracks.)

Constraint symbol: (Fence, crib, playpen, cage, prison, wall.)

Aggression symbol: (Fire-engine, locomotive, racer, or what?)

Release symbol: (Light, switches, knobs.)

Achievement and work: (Derricks, loading and dump trucks.)

Activity or locomotion: (Cars, trolleys, busses, trains.)

Family symbol: (Tree, grouped chairs or beds.)

Togetherness need: (Combinations, close arrangements.)

Loneliness symbol: (Landscape devoid of people—lonely house, lonely road, isolated objects.)

Dependence or need for love, or infancy-regression: (Nursing bottle, baby play, etc.)

Other aspects of choices—how are the following used? Are the differences ignored?

new—old	crude—rough
broken—whole	delicate—fine
parts—wholes	colored—colorless
small—large	plastic—rigid
soft—hard	mobile—immobile
solid—fragile	

3. Observation in Nursery School by Students
or Teachers: Summary

1. What is this child like: describe the qualities that single him out from other children:

2. What makes him   a) happiest   b) unhappiest?
    How does he express these feelings?

3. What are the points at which he is growing?
    What are the points at which he seems blocked or stopped?

4. What are his chief interest, satisfaction, or response areas in the school situation?
    Motor: (Passive; active—bike, climb jungle gym, run, jump, etc.)
    Creative: (Crayons, paint, fingerpaint, clay, blocks, music, other.)
    Verbal: (In what settings, to what ends?)
    Social: (Enjoys what relationship with adults? Enjoys what relationships with children? One or two vs. group; older, younger, same age; same sex, opposite sex? Activity contexts, typical roles, typical roles and relationships.)

5. Authority feelings and behavior.
    Response to routines: (Likes, resists, or what?)
    Response to free play: (Released, at a loss, or what?)
    Response to control from one adult: (In what situations, what kind of control, result for child.)

6. Fear, anxiety, or insecurity: (When, how shown, how coped with.)

7. Aggression: (When, how, followed by what feeling and behavior.)

8. What feelings does he stimulate in other adults, and children?
    What do you like best about him?
    What do you like least, or dislike most?

9. What does nursery school mean to him?

4. Outlines for Study of a Child

A. *Cultural factors in child development.*

Family   *Comments* (Mixture, conflict, mobility.)
    Color:
    Religion:
    Nationality background:
    Class:
    Occupational group:
    Income:
    (Add data on school, neighborhood if possible, and especially relation of the above to the predominant patterns in the immediate neighborhood as they affect the family's acceptance, status, and prestige.)

Influence of any or each of the above on
    Family tension-level:
    Food and feeding patterns:
    Cleanliness and elimination patterns:
    Clothing: (Emphasis on style, neatness, casualness, etc.)
    Property taboos: (On objects, rooms or areas of house, etc.)
    Forms of punishment: (Physical, removal from adult, removal of toy or treat, etc.)
    Expression of love: (Verbal, physical, etc.; note warmth, openness.)
    Expression of hostility: (Direct and indirect methods.)
    Emphasis on: (Language; problem-solving; creative work; manners; self-defense and aggression; friendliness, sociability; sympathy, care of others; self-respect, pride; competition.)

Other cultural factors:

Comments on child's responses to the above:

B. *Atmosphere surrounding the child.*

Home: (Describe character and feeling. Space—cluttered, neat; crowded, roomy; availability to child. Color—cheerful, gloomy; stimulating, restful. Organization, convenience, etc. Freedom-constraint level: Child is free to do what? Constrained from what? Furnishings—eating, sleeping, playing arrangements and their meaning to the child.)

Mother: (Describe kind of person she is. Mutual pattern of satisfaction and frustration between mother and child.)

Father: (Describe kind of person he is. Mutual pattern of satisfaction and frustration between father and child.)

Roles and emotional contributions of mother and father to each other:

Siblings: (Describe what they are like and their relation to subject.)

Other people: (Maids, relatives, children's friends, etc.—list and describe them and their relation to the child.)

Qualities of interpersonal relationships:

Home life: (Empty or full, bustle or peaceful, comforting or stern, stoical, gay or wooden; other dominant characteristics.)

Vacation pattern:

Previous movings:

Outstanding characteristics of this home atmosphere as it influences child: (How well do he and the home "fit"? What problems do they create for each other? Child's response to the above; how does he deal with home demands?)

C. Developmental Experience

1. Planned, waited for, surprise; meanings of the baby to the parents:

2. Pregnancy: (Physical and psychological character.)

3. Birth: (Duration, anaesthesia, instruments, or other factors affecting neonatal response.)

4. Hospital experience: (Separation from, time with mother.)

5. Home care began when: by whom: kind of person:

6. Feeding routine: (Kind of schedule, emotional context, satisfaction or difficulties for the child, areas of rigidity and of flexibility.)

7. Sleep routine: (Kind of schedule, emotional context, satisfaction or difficulties for the child.)

8. Training: (Kind of schedule, emotional tone, child's response.)

9. Play: (With whom, what kind, how much and when? Child's favorite sorts of play experience.)

10. Range of contacts with adults:

11. Surroundings: (Alone, with others how much? Confined where, for what time periods?)

12. Stimulation: (Rocking, singing, romping, music, toys, trips, visitors, other. Response to each kind of stimulation.)

13. Separations from parents and response:

14. Illnesses, accidents, etc.:

15. Other important experiences:

D. Child's status in group

Far below av. lowest 20%	below	Av.:	above	far above av. highest 20%

Looks:

Energy:

Height:

Weight:

Health:

C.A.:

M.A.:

I.Q.:

Athletic skill:

Manipulative skill:

Creativity: (Arts, shop, music, drama, stories.)

Sensory response: (Visual, auditory, tactual, kinaesthetic, oral.)

Intellectual skills: (Perceptual clarity, memory, problem-solving, comprehension, time, space, number concepts, imagination.)

Social relations: (Seeking, sought [popularity], skills, leadership, problems.)

Feelings about his status in different areas:

Ways of using and compensating for strengths and weaknesses:

E. *Interest areas*

1. Oral: (Food, nursing bottle, tasting, voluble language, kissing.)

2. Contact: (Patting, rubbing, fur animals; physical contact with experimenter; tucking in; etc.; release play with water, clay, dough, finger paint, fur, wool.)

3. Visual: (Color, form, design; watching, observing, noticing details, sizes.)

4. Auditory: (Music, sounds, vocalizing for tones, rhythm.)

5. Manipulation and construction: (Blocks, cars, etc.; houses, garages, stations, stores.)

6. Activity: (Vehicles, trucks, cars; climbing, leaping, jumping.)

7. Anal: (Toileting; play with excrement, or substitutes such as clay balls, mud, etc.; blocked movement.)

8. Sex: (Sex differences; ways of toileting; clothes; body inspection; sex activity.)

9. Aggressive activity: (Scissors, hammer, saw, guns, fire.)

10. Social: (Companions, babies, adults; animal pets or companions; dolls.)

11. Authority and barriers: (Fathers, mothers, police, soldiers, fences, tracks, enclosures, pens, cribs.)

12. Other:

F. Anxiety

Anxiety focused on:

1. Sudden or strong stimuli: (Noise, lights, sparkling toys.)

2. New situations: (People, places, demands.)

3. Body-violation: mouth open, clothes off, manipulations, toileting, knee hammer.

4. Loss of orientation: (Falling, dark.)

5. Loss of autonomy or freedom: (Confinement, authority-pressure, being coerced, dominated.)

6. Loss of limits: (Unstructured situation, messy materials, Rorschach.)

7. Loss of protection: (Mother's departure, etc.)

8. Threats of punishment, deprivation, failure:

9. Loss of adequacy: (Old or broken toys.)

10. Loss of love: (Sibling competition, etc.)

11. Demands for achievement: (Intelligence test, puzzles, or what.)

12. Demands for activity: (Singing, dancing, climbing, or what.)

13. Demands for conformity: (Eating, sleeping, eliminating.)

14. Pain:

15. Other:

Ways of handling anxiety:

1. Asking for help:

2. Retreat:

3. Defensive attack:

4. Constructive effort:

5. Other:

Indices of anxiety:

1. Face anxious, tense, withdrawn:

2. Voice querulous, flat; inability to talk; lack of spontaneous expression of joy, fear, anger, warmth:

3. Autonomic responses: (Flush, paling, damp hands, perspiration, stuffy nose—if no infection is present.)

4. Coordination jerky, tense, constrained:

5. Movement limited, tight, hesitant, aborted; restless, scattered, disorganized, repetitive, compulsively perseverative:

6. Nail-biting, thumb-sucking:

7. Avoidance of certain objects, retreat or withdrawal patterns:

8. Passive behavior, macrocosmic and microcosmic:

9. Broken dolls, objects are of special concern:

10. Extreme clinging to limits:

11. Rigid, arbitrary, non-functional, tight organization:

12. Hesitancy to use toys or compulsive use of all toys:

13. Lack of fantasy:

14. Tics, blinking:

15. Insomnia, nausea, diarrhea, constipation, chronic respiratory difficulties, etc.:

16. Extreme vigilance, alertness, sensitivity to stimulus:

17. Patterns of variation in these in different stress situations:

5. Temperament and Spontaneity Observations

Procedure:
1. Fill out this page first.
2. Rate the child on the scale from 1 to 7 on the traits on the following pages; consider 4 the *average* or mid-point.
3. Make any additions or corrections you wish on page 1 in pencil of another color.

The most unique and characteristic quality or qualities of this child:

_____

_____

_____

He (she) is most released $\frac{by:}{when:}$

_____

_____

_____

He (she) is made anxious (or $\frac{\text{(cautious)}}{\text{inhibited)}}$ $\frac{by:}{when:}$

_____

_____

_____

He (she) handles this anxiety (tension, stress or uncertainty) by:

_____

_____

_____

TEMPERAMENT AND SPONTANEITY SCALE

#	Trait		1	2	3	4	5	6	7		?	Markedly Variable
1.	Tempo or speed	Always quick, mosquito-like.								Slow, heavy.		
2.	Energy level	Little motor energy. Never does things energetically or vigorously.								Outstandingly vigorous, energetic.		
3.	Area of movement	"Covers a lot of ground," "all over the place."								Sticks to one spot or small area.		
4.	Degree of focus in response to environment, objects, experiences	Vague, amorphous.								Unusually definite, clear.		
5.	Response to objects	Very absorbed in objects and materials.								Not much interest in objects and materials.		
6.	Conventionality, originality	Relies on conventional patterns.								Extremely original, always sees things in a fresh light, expresses things in his own way.		
7.	Awareness of details	Notices details, builds with attention to details; likes little things.								Does not see details, small things.		
8.	Form	Very aware of form. Creative work always shows definite form, play follows definite organization unusual for age.								Form is always secondary to feelings, sensations, ideas or fantasy.		
9.	Color response vs. use	Enjoys color for its own sake, paints with pleasure in color—comments on colors.								Avoids bright colors, due to fear or indifference. Avoids definite colors.		

TEMPERAMENT AND SPONTANEITY SCALE (Continued)

#	Trait		1	2	3	4	5	6	7		?	Markedly Variable
10.	Receptiveness to impressions.	Thick-skinned, not easily impressed by new experiences.								Extremely "sensitive," impressionable, feels new experiences deeply.		
11.	Dreaminess-activity	An outstandingly dreamy child, lost in reverie for long periods.								Rarely stops to day-dream.		
12.	"Introversion-Extroversion	Imposes own ideas on external reality. Ideas always his own.								Takes his cue from what is going on; imitative.		
13.	Self-enjoyment	Derives satisfaction from own body—own movements, tactual sensations, own appearance, chiefly.								Unself-conscious; without consciousness about own body, clothing, voice, etc.		
14.	Tactual	Tactual satisfactions outstanding—the feel of hair, velvet, mud, rough, furry objects is always fascinating.								Indifferent to or uninterested in tactual experiences.		
15.	Oral—food, thumb	Many oral satisfactions or a few take precedence over other areas of satisfaction. E.g., food is most satisfying.								Not interested in food, thumb-sucking, etc.		
16.	Auditory—tones, melodies	Unusually aware of and responsive to sounds, the wind, tones of voice, music.								Sounds do not give pleasure but are responded to purely as language and events.		
17.	Auditory—emotional quality	Quickly sensitive to emotional nuances in music, tones of voice, reflects them in facial expression, movement, etc.								Ignores, doesn't hear changes in mood of music, tones of voice etc.		
18.	Response to people	Not much interest in people.								Always interested in people if there are any around.		

TEMPERAMENT AND SPONTANEITY SCALE (Continued)

#	Trait		1	2	3	4	5	6	7		?	Markedly Variable
19.	Verbal Interest	Plays with words, invents new ones, enjoys them for their own sake.								Words are purely instrumental, of no value except to express needs or wants.		
20.	Dramatic	Has "lots of imagination," play with toys or children always has dramatic content.								"Pedestrian"—dramatic use of materials practically never present. Matter of fact.		
21.	Directness of expression of feeling	Aggressiveness, hits; love, hugs—*straight out.*								Never expresses feelings directly; covers feelings with objective or polite front, or impish, coy, muted, masked expression.		
22.	*Rigidity* of expressive patterns: posture, gesture, voice	"Tight," "constrained," "rigid," "flat voice."								"Free," "flexible," labile, fluid, expressive patterns of voice, face, body.		
23.	Ease of being upset	Easily traumatizable; experiences that would not disturb other children are a shock.								High thresholds; "nothing" disturbs him.		
24.	Directness of adjustive reaction to difficulties	Solves problem directly.								Indirect solutions are characteristic. Fantasy, fears, body preoccupation, projection, compensations.		
25.	Autonomic Reactivity: flushing; bright, watery eyes; clammy hands; enuresis	Frequently one or more of them under strain.								Never shows "autonomic" reactions.		
26.	Warmth— detachment	Easy to feel close to, warm, resonant.								Cool or detached, not resonant, warm. No "glow."		

TEMPERAMENT AND SPONTANEITY SCALE (Continued)

#	Trait		1	2	3	4	5	6	7		?	Markedly Variable
27.	Perseveration—lability of interest	Marked perseveration of interests, activities, attitudes, relationships; "stubborn," "persistent."								Labile, fluid, shifting. "Can't tell what he'll do from one day to the next."		
28.	Consistency—variability in emotional mood	Extremely variable; gay at times, moody at other times.								Extremely stable feelings—every day is like yesterday.		
29.	Response to new experiences	Spontaneous surprise, delight, awe, amazement.								Blasé; never is surprised or delighted by fresh experience.		
30.	Somberness—gaiety	"Poker-face" melancholy, sad.								Gay, lilting, merry jolly, lusty, exuberant.		
31.	Compulsiveness—flexibility	"Must do some things even though inappropriate."								Not at all compulsive—flexible response to stimulus.		
32.	Quality of coordination: small-muscle	Fumbling, disjointed, wobbling, stumbling, poky, clumsy, "stammery actions."								Smooth easy coordination, perfectly adapted to each task.		
33.	Manipulatory (Hands)	Enjoys "small-muscle" activities; relies on them constantly.								Never settles down to small-muscle activities if large boisterous activities are available.		
34.	Large-muscle activity	Athletic; uses large apparatus; likes to move, run, climb, etc.								Not athletic, little use of large apparatus. Little leg activity.		
35.	Large-muscle coordination	Smooth, efficient, etc.								Poor motor coordination.		

Comments on dynamic relationship between traits rated above:
(Narrow vs. wide range of intake or expression; enjoys which areas most; uses which areas for comfort or defense? Which areas are stimulated, which discouraged, at home? Which areas contribute to strengths and security? Which areas threaten his poise or balance?)

Miniature Life Toys

RECOMMENDED LIST FOR DIAGNOSTIC PLAY SESSIONS IN U.S. URBAN AND SUBURBAN AREAS

Housekeeping Group:

DOLLS:

Half a dozen women dolls, in different sorts of clothes, for "house" wear, "going to town" wear, "dress up" wear; one or two nude ones

Half a dozen men dolls, in work, sport, business clothes, and nude

Four or more girl dolls of different sizes, in play, school and dress clothes

Four or more boy dolls of different sizes, in play, school and dress clothes

Half a dozen baby dolls of different sizes, nude and in creepers or nighties with buntings, baby blankets, etc.

Grandpa and grandma with grey hair and glasses

Dolls in maid, doctor, nurse costumes

House, dog, cat, mouse

FURNITURE:

Sofa, 3 or 4 living room chairs, radio-TV, piano, lamp

Dining table and chairs, chest

Kitchen stove, sink, refrigerator, stool, washing machine, ironing board

Bathroom tub, bowl, toilet, hamper

Four adult beds, chests, dresser with mirror, bedroom chairs

Several children's beds

Bassinet

Bathinette

Toilet chair

Perambulator

Crib

Playpen

Bottles with nipples

Town Toys:

Cars: 1 or 2 sedans, 1 taxi, 1 racer, 1 or 2 buses, 1 school bus

Trucks: moving van, garbage truck, general utility truck

Trains: 2 engines, cabooses, coal cars, with 7 or 8 train cars in different colors

Fire-engine with ladders

Planes: 2 to 4 planes of different sizes

Boats: motor boat, rowboat, ferry

People: 4 or more policemen, 4 or more firemen, 1 Santa Claus, men, ladies, children in shopping, strolling attitudes

Miscellaneous: park benches, trees, etc.; church, stores, hospital

Farm Toys and Animals:

Horses: 6 to 8 horses (rubber, metal or plastic) of different sizes

Cows: 6 to 8 cows of different sizes (calf to adult); 1 bull

Sheep: 4 to 6 sheep, small and adult size

Pigs: 4 to 6 pigs, small and adult size

1 goat

Furry mice, squirrels, cats, dogs, rabbits

Equipment: adjustable plastic fence pieces

Farmer

Cowboys

Wild Animals:

1 or 2 monkeys

1 or 2 giraffes

1 elephant

1 hippopotamus

1 rhinoceros

1 bear

2 tigers

2 lions

1 alligator

5 snakes of different sizes

1 turtle

Soldiers and War Toys:

10 to 20 soldiers with different equipment and in different attitudes, one or two of whom are broken

Navy men, marines, etc.

2 to 4 separate guns of appropriate size

Indians in war clothes

20 pieces of Lincoln logs in small, medium and long sizes for forts or other defense arrangements

Summary of Painting Scores

THE AVERAGE DISTRIBUTION of form-elements in the particular group studied is as follows:

Relation to Format	I (2-3 yrs.)		II (3-4 yrs.)		III (4-5 yrs.)	
Ma	4	18%	5	23%	3	11%
Ma Di	8	13%	4	18%	4	16%
Di Ma	8	42%	4	20%	4	31%
Di	5	25%	5	26%	5	24%
Ng	●		½	3%	1	1%
E	0		2	10%	1	1%

Size of Form-Elements						
l	13	63%	10	49%	4	23%
lm	3	14%	5-6	28%	6	27%
m	0		0		1	
lms	4	18%	4	19%	7	36%
ms		2%				
ls	0	2%	0-4	2%	2	10%

Movement-Element	I (2-3 yrs.)		II (3-4 yrs.)		III (4-5 yrs.)	
sm	21	105%	26	133%	28	140%
Vivid Details	0	3%	0	3%	1+	16%
		3%		3%	1±	15%
Curves	8+	42%	4+	20%	6+	33%
	2±	9%	2±	10%	3±	12%
	1∓	4%	2∓	10%	1∓	6%
Edges	½+	3%	1+	7%	1+	6%
	½±	3%	½±	1%	1±	4%
	0∓		0∓	2%	1∓	4%

Differentiated Rhythm						
	1+	1%	1+	6%	2-5+	12%
	±	2%	1±	6%	2±	10%
	∓	1%	1-5∓	7%	1±	5%

Rigid Uniform Rhythm 0

Distribution of of Form-Elements	I (2-3 yrs.)		II (3-4 yrs.)		III (4-5 yrs.)	
w	2	8%	0	1%	½	3%
v	10	52%	6	32%	10	49%
c	7	38%	5	22%	4-5	19%
n	0		1	4%	1	4%
r	½	3%	5	19%	2-5	13%
E↑E↓	1	4%	1	4%	½	2%
Balance	10+	50%	8+	37%	8+	40%
	6±	29%	3±	13%	5±	22%
	2∓	8%	1∓	3%	1∓	4%
	1—	5%	5—	18%	½—	2%
Symmetry	0+	1%	0+		1+	4%
	0±		2±	10%	1±	3%
	0∓		0∓		0∓	2%

Organization of Form	I (2-3 yrs.)		II (3-4 yrs.)		III (4-5 yrs.)	
U	2	10%	5	24%	6	27%
up	4	20%	6	29%	6	28%
cn	1		1-2		1	
cl	0		1-2		1	
sc	0		1		2	
sep	0		0		5	
r	0		7		11	

Organization of Content	I (2-3 yrs.)		II (3-4 yrs.)		III (4-5 yrs.)	
it	0			1%		5%
ip	0			15%		11%

Color Selection						
yellow	6	30%	15	74%	13	64%
red	13	65%	16	80%	15	75%
blue	13	64%	15	74%	14	68%
green	5	23%	7	36%	12	60%
brown	1		2		2	

Analysis

When I analyzed the frequency of form-elements at different age levels by using all the paintings made by the children at the age of two in Group I, those made by the three-year-olds in Group II, and those made by the four-year-olds in Group III,

I found a definite change in the second age group on several attitudes. For instance, the percentage of pictures in which the children painted completely to the margin (Ma) increased from age groups I to II, but decreased again in III. The number of pictures in which the children maintained *distance from the margin* (Di) for the most part, but went to the margin in one or two places (Di Ma), decreased sharply in II and increased again in III. In Group II a factor appeared which was almost negligible in I and III, namely, emphasis of margin by framing (E). In II there was also a marked decrease of curves, vivid distribution, and balance, and an increase of rigid distribution and rigid uniform rhythm and balance—as against Groups I and III. In all three age groups there were pictures in which the child both kept his distance and touched the margin in several places within the same picture. For the rest, the children were about evenly divided between those who painted completely to the margin and those who kept a strict distance from the margin throughout the whole picture.

In regard to *size of form-elements,* there was a great tendency in the first age group to use only large form-elements, which decreased markedly from I to II and from II to III. A greater variety and a more flexible use. of different sizes within one picture (lms) developed increasingly. A degree of interest for contrasts between large and small form-elements within one picture, without using medium sizes, developed in III. In all three age groups there were no pictures with small form-elements only.

Vivid details in line were not present at all in the first year, extremely rare in II (3%), and began to occur occasionally, and only among the most advanced children, in III. The same was true of *differentiated rhythm.*

Curves were used to a high degree in Group I, appearing, on the average, in one out of two pictures. As I mentioned above, they decreased markedly in II and increased again in III.

Forms with sharp *edges* were rather infrequent in age group I, but increased very slightly in II and III. Round forms were prevalent in I. A good form-color relation (F-C+)[1] developed gradually in III (though the percentage was small). A bad form-

---

1. Neither form-color relation nor the tendency to smear, discussed below, are listed in the scoring summary.

color relation (F-C—) was even less frequent. One cannot say that in Group I there was an unfavorable relation between form and color, but rather that no relation existed at all.

In regard to *distribution,* only a small percentage of pictures showed a very wide distribution, the highest being 8% in Group I. Center distribution was rather favored in I, but decreased in II and III. The larger number of pictures showed a vivid distribution. Rigid distribution was evident in very few pictures only, the highest number occurring in II, as already mentioned. In III this item decreased again, but was still higher than in I. A certain amount of rigidity and stereotypy seemed to be necessary for the normal process of learning order and organization.

Therefore there was also a percentage of *symmetry* and *rigid uniform rhythm* in III, but it was extremely small. On the whole, we can say that in this group a tendency to symmetry was extremely rare, and even then no child ever produced a completely symmetrical arrangement. In the matter of symmetry the group illustrated a tendency similar to that in other groups observed at the same age levels: namely, that in the age range between four and five (III) every second child will, on the average, show one out of fourteen pictures which has a tendency to symmetry. This tendency was much rarer in the age range between three and four (II), and did not occur at all between two and three (I).

In all three age groups the variety of color was greater than the variety of size of form-elements, the variety of *forms* being the least. But all three—variety of color, of form-elements, and of forms—increased from I to II and from II to III. Red and blue were used equally in a high percentage of pictures, yellow and green somewhat less. On the average, no specific preferences or avoidances were shown. The selection of brown and black cannot be evaluated with certainty in this particular experimental setup because they were not consistently available. The frequency distribution in these colors corresponded to the usual observations of other groups, but one cannot be sure that this was not a coincidence.

The capacity to *organize a unit* of the whole picture (U) or a unit (or units) in part (or parts) of the picture (up) increased in II and still more in III. This was also the case with the *secondary movement elements* (SM). A tendency to make clearly separated forms (sep) developed in III.

No incidental or interpretative (ip) or intentional (it) representation of realistic forms occurred in I. In II about 15% of the pictures showed representation of forms which were interpreted realistically; half of them were realistically drawn, but in only 1% of the cases was the use of realistic forms intentional. In III the interpretations decreased somewhat, but the intentional use of really seen objects and the successful realistic representation of them increased.

A comparison of these scoring averages of the whole group with the scoring summaries of each child showed the following deviations and conformities.

Alec painted an extremely high percentage of pictures on which he kept a distance from the margin (Di). Jeremy painted an extremely high percentage of pictures with rigid distribution in II. Camille showed the same characteristic in III. A lack of positive balance, or negative balance only, was apparent in the paintings of Alec and Jeremy in I and II, and also of Alec in III.

The highest number of differentiated rhythms was shown by Camille and Carla, both in II. Joyce in III painted a relatively high number of pictures with rigid uniform rhythm. An extremely low variety of form was shown by Jeremy in I and II.

On the whole, the children in this group preferred to paint both lines and spots from I on, which I have found to be the case in other groups. However, there was a tendency in the group to use spots more often than lines; for instance, more spots than lines were shown by Joyce, Carla, and Camille in II, and by Colin, Jay and Stanley in III. However, Candice, in III, used more lines than spots. Alec and Jeremy in I used mainly spots and no lines.

A preference or tendency to make contours around forms was also very rare, and is shown in this group only by Stanley and Camille in III.

In the age range from three to four Carla and Alec used

more brown than the other children of this group. If we could assume that brown was available with the same regularity for all children, even if not as often as the other colors, it would seem that these two children used it relatively more often than the other children. Both Carla and Alec present anal problems.

Leadership Games—
Plans of Procedure

Potential Leadership Game

I. PLAYING HOUSE
  A. Initial selection and assignment of roles
    1. Now everybody sit down here and I'll tell you what we can all play together.
    2. We're going to play house.
    3. Who do you want to be?
    4. Playing game.
    5. What shall I be?
  B. Reassignment of roles
    1. Now everybody play you're somebody else. Everybody change.
    2. Who do you want to be?
    3. Playing game.
    4. What shall I be?
II. PLAYING STORE
  A. Shifting of frame of reference and assignment of roles
    1. All right, now we're all through playing house.
    2. Everybody sit down and I'll tell you what we're going to play now.
    3. We're going to play store.

4. Who wants to be what?
5. Playing game.
6. What shall I be?
   B. Reassignment of roles
      1. Now everybody play you're somebody else. Everybody change.
      2. Who do you want to be?
      3. Playing game.
      4. What shall I be?
III. PLAYING A NEW GAME
     Now we can play something else . . . whatever you want. What shall we play?

Imposed Leadership Game

   I. FIRST CHILD AS LEADER
      A. Introduction: Now everybody sit down and I'll tell you what we're going to play.
      B. Instructions: We're going to play a game where each one has a turn to tell everyone else what to do.
      C. Invitation: Now who wants to be first?
      D. Selection of leader: All right, it's ———'s turn. (selecting first volunteer)
      E. Free play. (Approximately 5 minutes of free play follow under the leader, with adult support if necessary.)
  II. SECOND CHILD AS LEADER
      A. Introduction: Everybody sit down again and I'll put all the toys back on the table.
      B. Instructions: Now it's somebody else's turn to tell everyone else what to do.
      C. Invitation: Who's it going to be this time?
      D. Selection of leader: All right, it's ———'s turn.
      E. Free play.
 III. THIRD CHILD AS LEADER
      A. Introduction: Everybody sit down again and I'll put all the toys back on the table.
      B. Instructions: Now it's somebody else's turn to tell everyone else what to do.
      C. Selection of leader: All right, it's ———'s turn.
      D. Free play.
 IV. PLAYING TOGETHER—FIRST CHILD AS LEADER[1]

---

1. Sections IV to VI are only used when the play of sections I to III has been largely solitary or parallel play.

    A. Introduction: Everybody sit down again and I'll put all the toys back on the table.

    B. Instructions: Now I want you to think of a game everyone can play together.

    C. Invitation: Who's it going to be this time?

    D. Selection of leader: All right, it's ———'s turn.

    E. Free play: (Approximately 5 minutes of free play follow, during which time adult reminds leader that he is "thinking of a game we can all play together.")

V. PLAYING TOGETHER—SECOND CHILD AS LEADER

    A. Introduction: Everybody sit down again and I'll put all the toys back on the table.

    B. Instructions: Now I want you to think of a game everyone can play together.

    C. Invitation: Who's it going to be this time?

    D. Selection of leader: All right, it's ———'s turn.

    E. Free Play.

VI. PLAYING TOGETHER—THIRD CHILD AS LEADER

    A. Introduction: Everybody sit down again and I'll put all the toys back on the table.

    B. Instructions: Now I want you to think of a game everyone can play together.

    C. Selection of leader: All right, it's ———'s turn.

    D. Free play.

Index

The Children